THE SILENCE OF OUR FRIENDS

THE SILENCE OF OUR FRIENDS

WRITTEN BY
MARK LONG &
JIM DEMONAKOS

ART BY
NATE POWELL

INTRODUCTION BY
JOHN JENNINGS

:01 First Second

SQUARE FISH

NEW YORK

TO

JOHN V. LONG

SQUARE FISH

An imprint of Macmillan Publishing Group, LLC
175 Fifth Avenue, New York, NY 10010
fiercereads.com

Square Fish and the Square Fish logo are trademarks of Macmillan and are used
by Roaring Brook Press under license from Macmillan.

Our books may be purchased in bulk for promotional, educational, or business
use. Please contact your local bookseller or the Macmillan Corporate and
Premium Sales Department at (800) 221-7945 ext. 5442 or by e-mail at
MacmillanSpecialMarkets@macmillan.com.

Library of Congress Cataloging-in-Publication Data is available.
ISBN 978-1-250-16498-8 (Square Fish paperback)

Originally published in the United States by First Second/Roaring Brook Press
First Square Fish edition, 2018
Book designed by Colleen AF Venable
Art production assistance by Erin Tobey
Square Fish logo designed by Filomena Tuosto

10 9 8 7 6 5 4 3 2 1

AR: 2.7

Introduction

"The past is never dead. It's not even past."

—William Faulkner

The Faulkner quote I chose as an epigraph for this introduction used to confuse me when I was much younger. The forty-six-year-old Southern black man I've become understands the meaning down to his bones. You see, one needs to have lived a bit to see the wisdom in Faulkner's words. You need to have felt the world truly turn beneath your feet to understand what my fellow Mississippian was getting at. Unresolved things come back around. America's past haunts the present, and that phantom circles around in the angry veins that feed this country's heart and soul. The past is *not* dead.

As I write these words, the most powerful man in the world taunts the storm-ridden survivors of a hurricane that hit Puerto Rico. Right now, young, disenfranchised black men and women are in the streets in St. Louis. As I write this, *one of* the worst mass shootings on American soil has just happened and black football players are being called traitors for taking the knee during the National Anthem in protest of police brutality. As I write this, our nation is still reeling from an overt Neo-Nazi march that resulted in the violent death of a young woman who left this world marching for Justice. Heather Heyer *is* our friend, an ally in the constant struggle for freedom. I write these words for her.

When I first read *The Silence of Our Friends*, I was so moved by the story that I immediately figured out a way to teach it in one of my classes. I wanted my students to experience each line, each mark, and each word. Mark Long and Jim Demonakos's story is compelling, eloquently realized, and painfully poetic. Nate Powell, one of my favorite people and artists, used his wonderful gifts as a storyteller to realize, via comics, a little-known chapter in one of the most memorable eras in our country's history.

As we look back and commemorate the fiftieth anniversary of Dr. Martin Luther King Jr.'s assassination, we have to understand how much a book like this is still needed today. It's not a book about our history. It's a graphic treatise on our possible future. It's important that we use the lessons learned in this wonderful testimony of solidarity to shield us against the dark days that *must* come. They must come in order for us to fully appreciate what it means to be alive and free in America. They must come in order for us to galvanize ourselves against the coming storms that already rumble in the distance. It's always darkest before the dawn, they say, and Dr. King's dream hasn't come true—not yet. That mountaintop is still out there somewhere, waiting patiently (as mountains do) for us to climb. Mark, Nate, and Jim *understand* this. They are our friends. They are *not* silent. I write these words for them.

The Silence of Our Friends is a glorious example of what can be realized when master creators put their hearts and talents to telling the truth, especially when the truth hurts. It is an example of the power of the form and magic of the graphic image. As American comic book consumers, we are so used to seeing muscle-bound heroes and heroines fighting in our flag's colors to keep us "free." Mark, Nate, and Jim use each stark panel to strip away the mythologies of America and show us the darkness and the hope that dwell in the core of our beliefs. There is much work to do to get to the America that we *all* deserve. Some of us may not see it, as Dr. King knew that he wouldn't. Some of us will not be there in that number, as Medgar Evers sadly won't be. Some of us will be taken out by our commitments because, as James Baldwin stated, "To be committed is to be in danger."

It takes a lot of that commitment and strength to make a story like *The Silence of Our Friends*. The story changes you and gets into your spirit with every panel. Mark, Nate, and Jim are every person in this story. They had to feel all of these myriad narratives. All of the pain and frustration and all of the triumph and love is affixed in their hearts with each panel and each page. I commend them on the weight that they had to carry to reify this necessary history. I am honored to put these words together for the reprinting of this beautiful and poignant slice of our collective experience. It reminds us that we rise and we fall together, that we are much stronger as a nation when we are arm in arm. It's a graphic road map to the beginning of a long journey to a distant mountaintop not quite of this earth but a beautiful figment of a black Southern preacher's dream. His name was Martin. He is our friend. He can *never* be silenced. I write these words for him. I write these words for *us*.

For Heather.

John Jennings
Dreamer, Fighter, Black Unicorn
October 12, 2017
Downtown Riverside, California

HOUSTON, TEXAS 1968

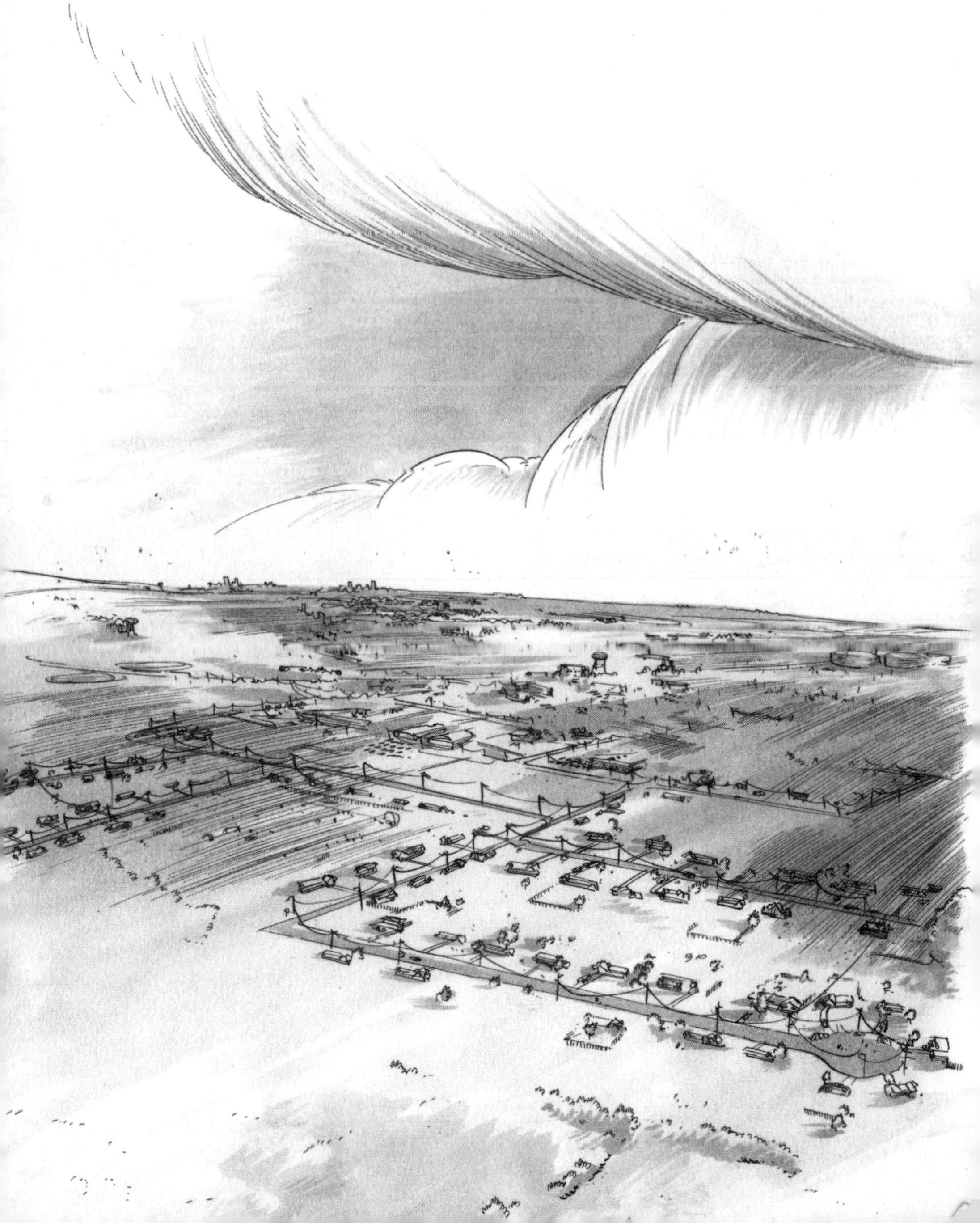

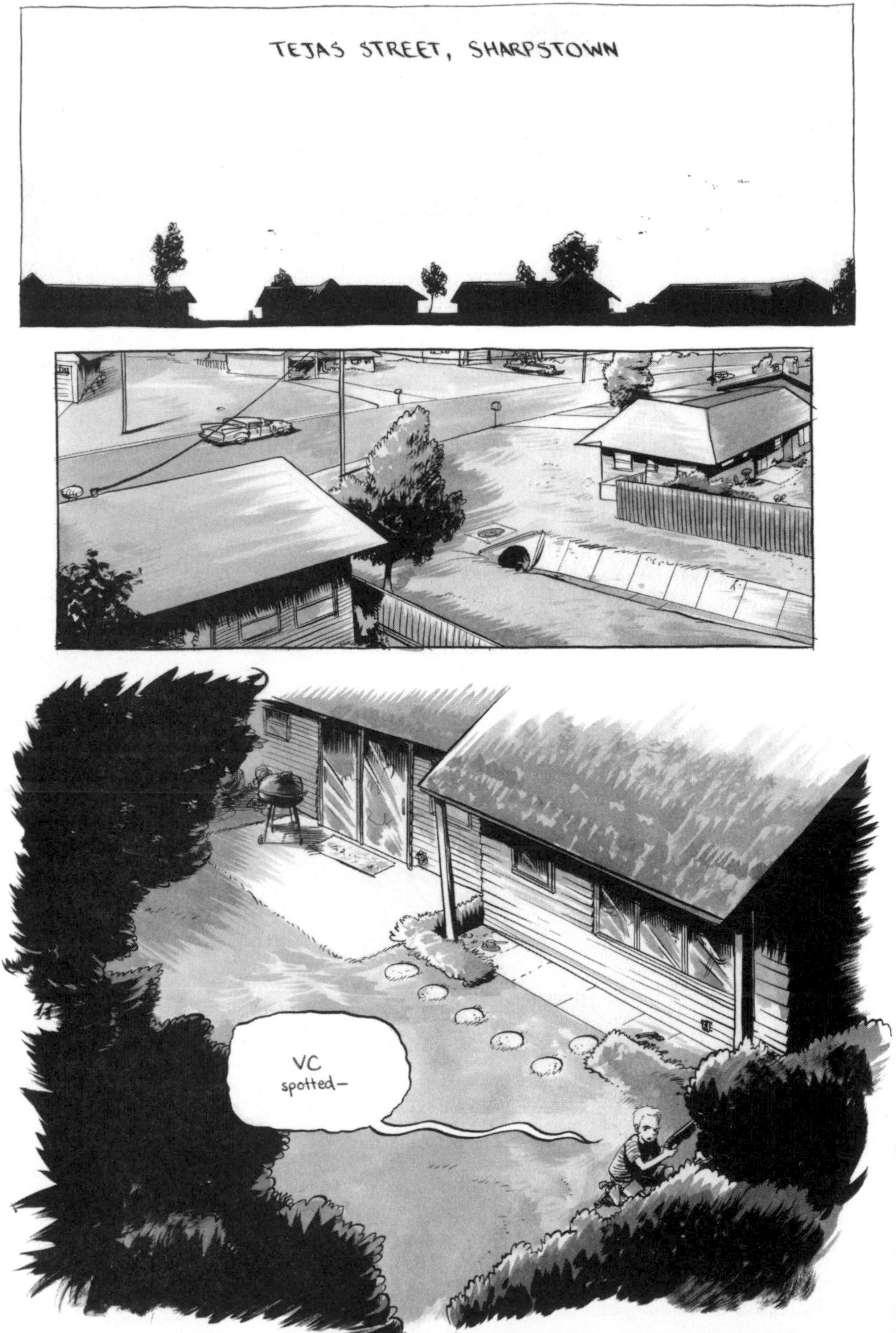
TEJAS STREET, SHARPSTOWN
VC spotted—

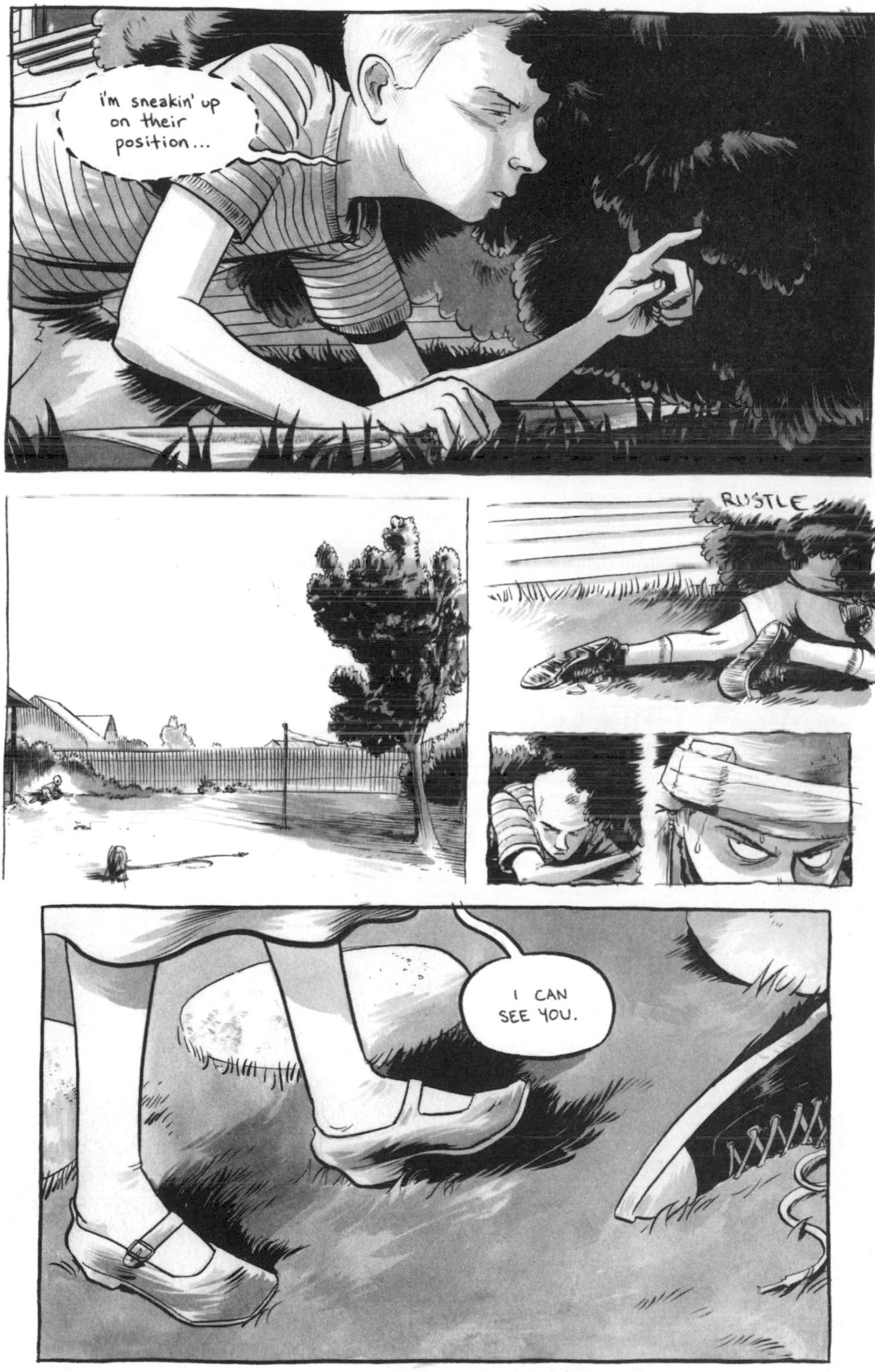
i'm sneakin' up on their position...
RUSTLE
I CAN SEE YOU.

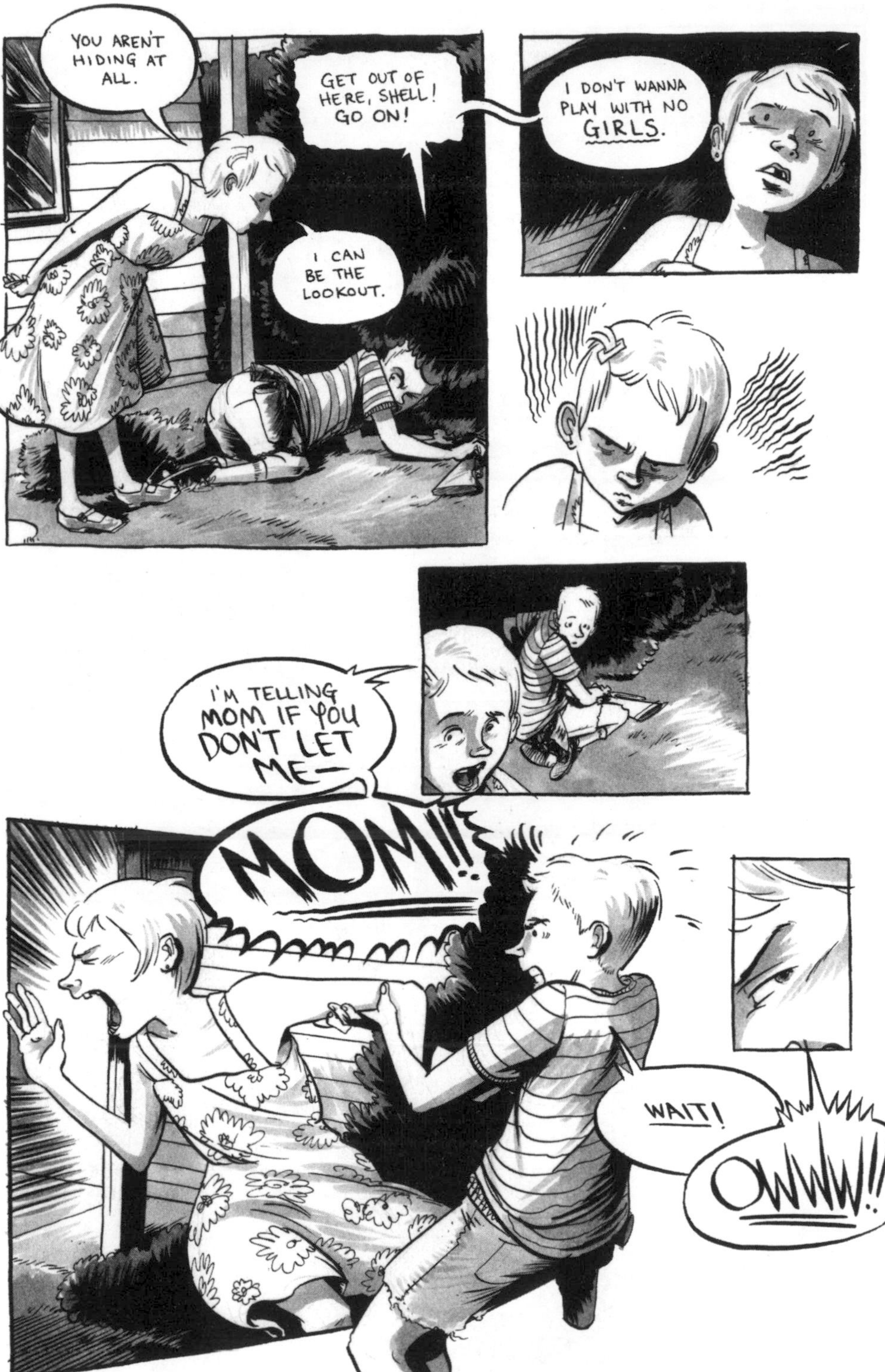
YOU AREN'T HIDING AT ALL.
GET OUT OF HERE, SHELL! GO ON!
I CAN BE THE LOOKOUT.
I DON'T WANNA PLAY WITH NO GIRLS.
I'M TELLING MOM IF YOU DON'T LET ME—
MOM!!
WAIT!
OWWW!!

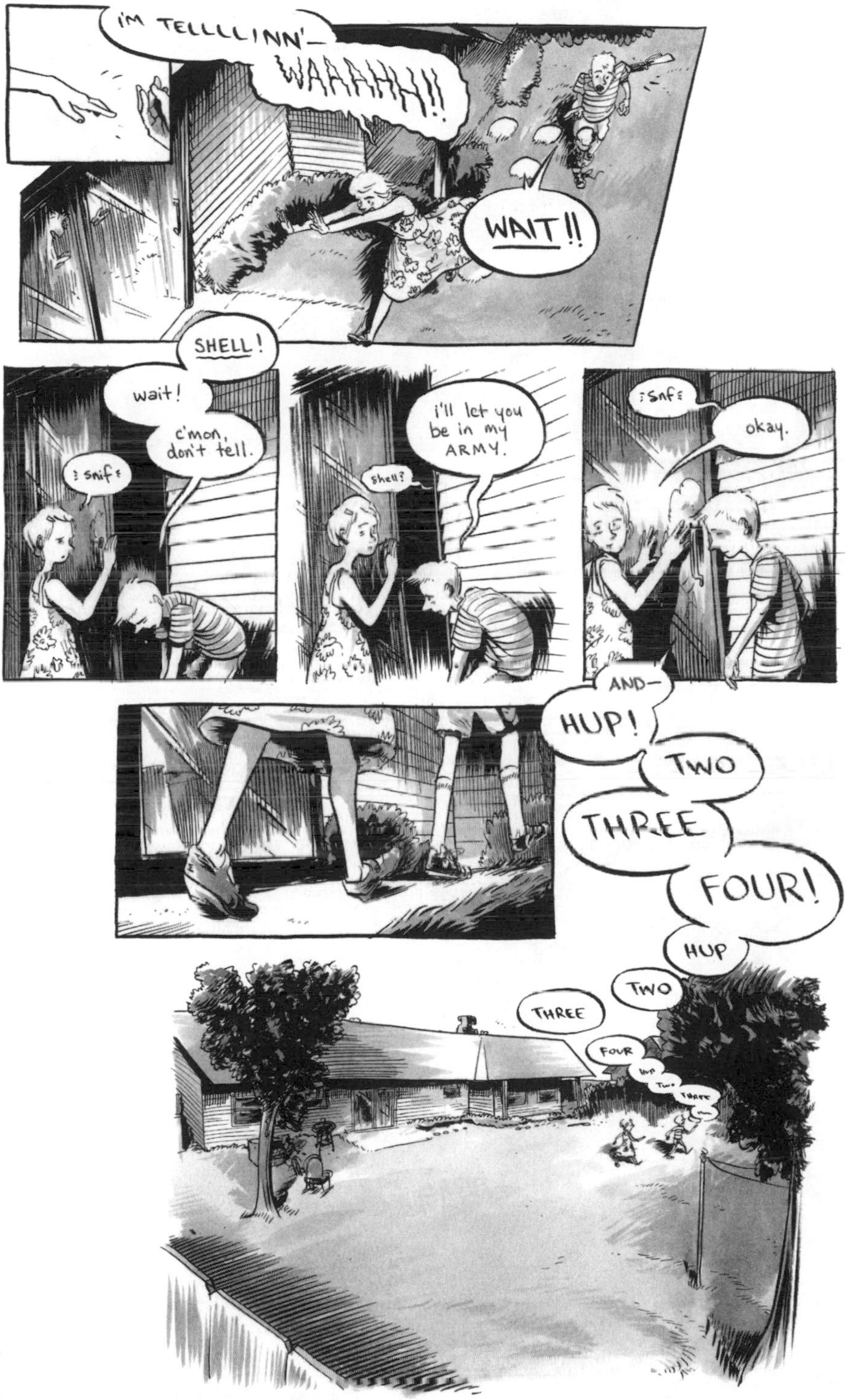
I'M TELLLLINN'—
WAAAHHH!!
WAIT!!
SHELL!
wait!
c'mon, don't tell.
snif
shell?
i'll let you be in my ARMY.
Snf
okay.
AND—
HUP!
TWO
THREE
FOUR!
HUP
TWO
THREE
FOUR
HUP
TWO
THREE

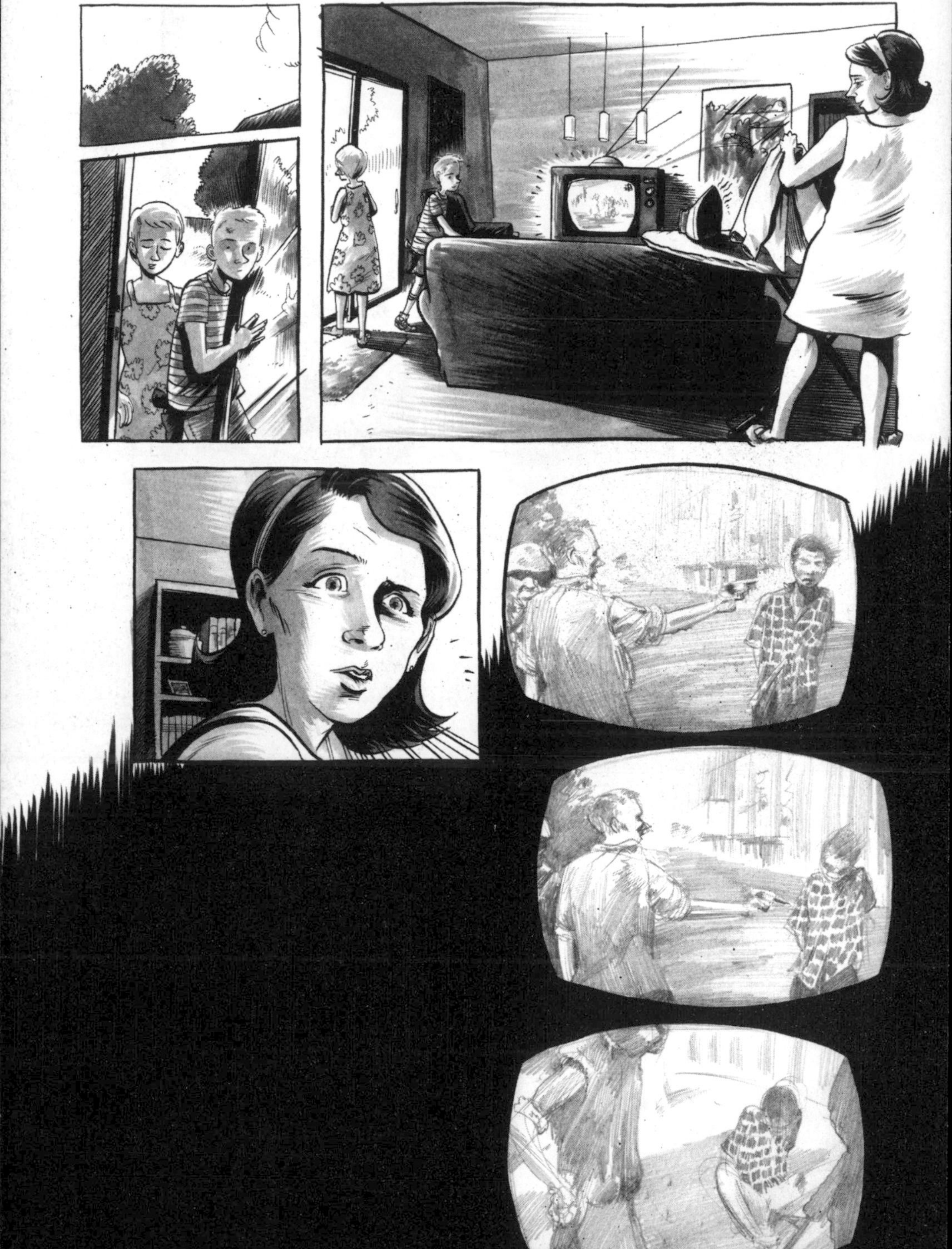

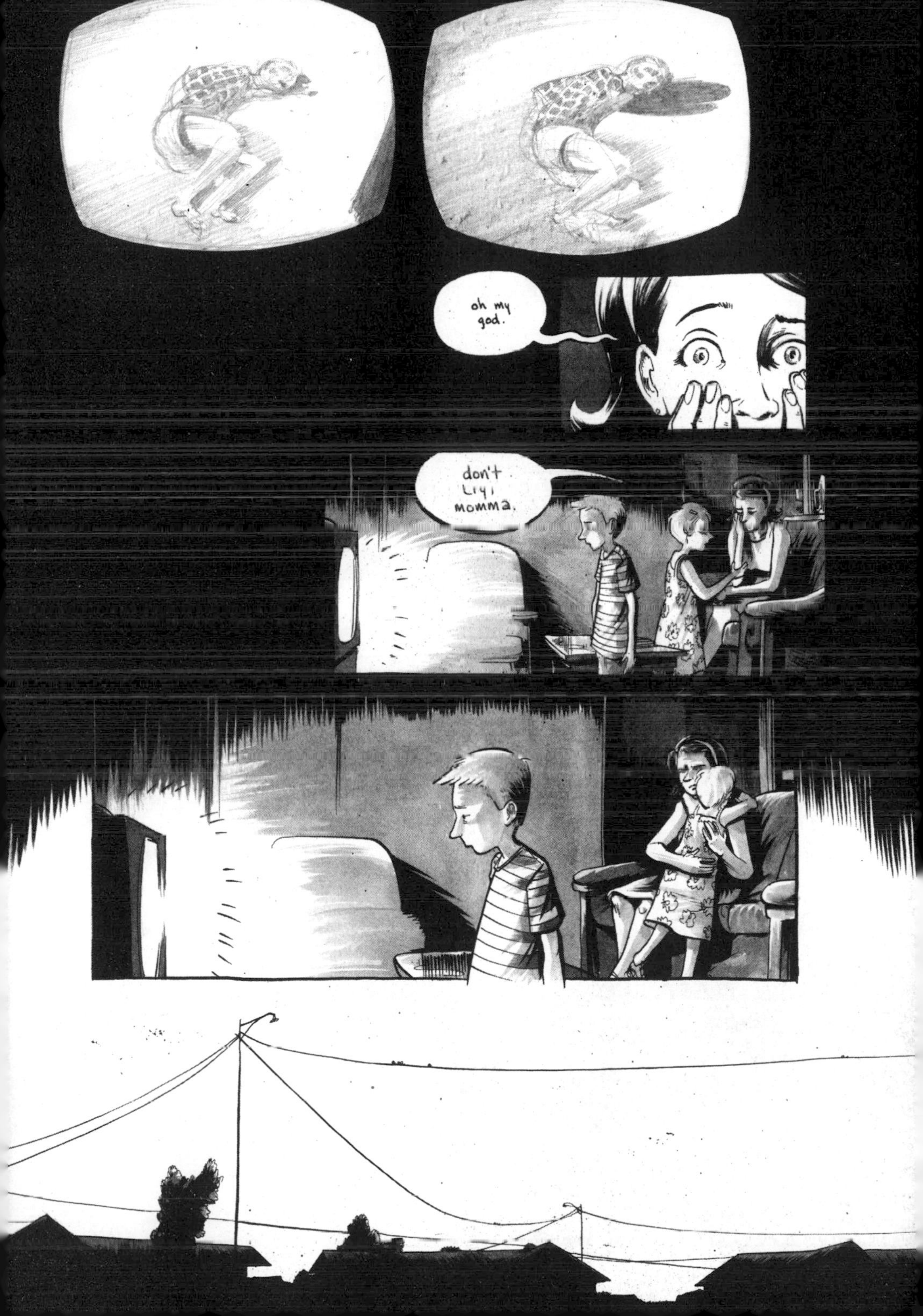
oh my god.
don't momma.

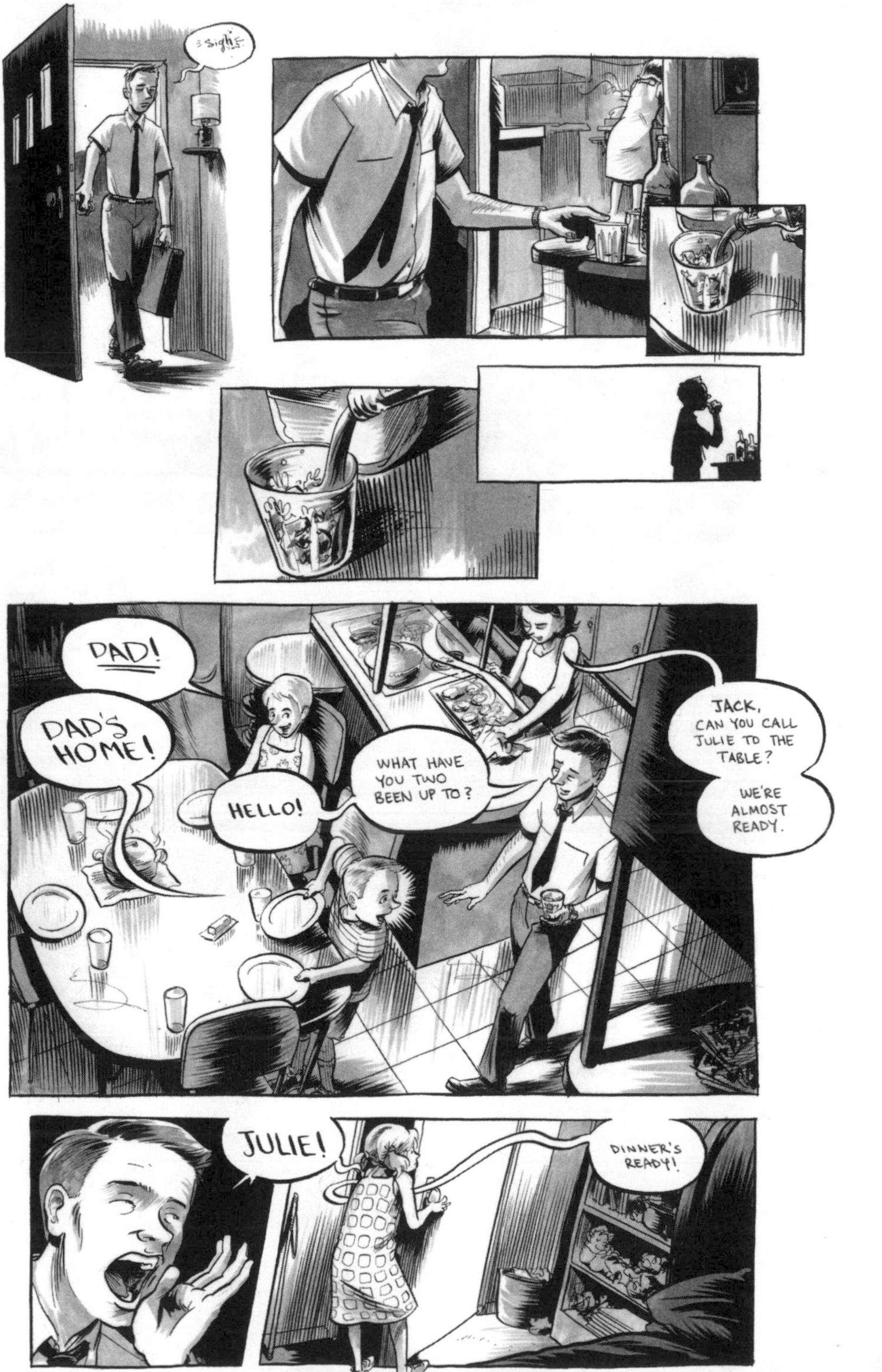
sigh
DAD!
DAD'S HOME!
HELLO!
WHAT HAVE YOU TWO BEEN UP TO?
JACK, CAN YOU CALL JULIE TO THE TABLE?
WE'RE ALMOST READY.
JULIE!
DINNER'S READY!

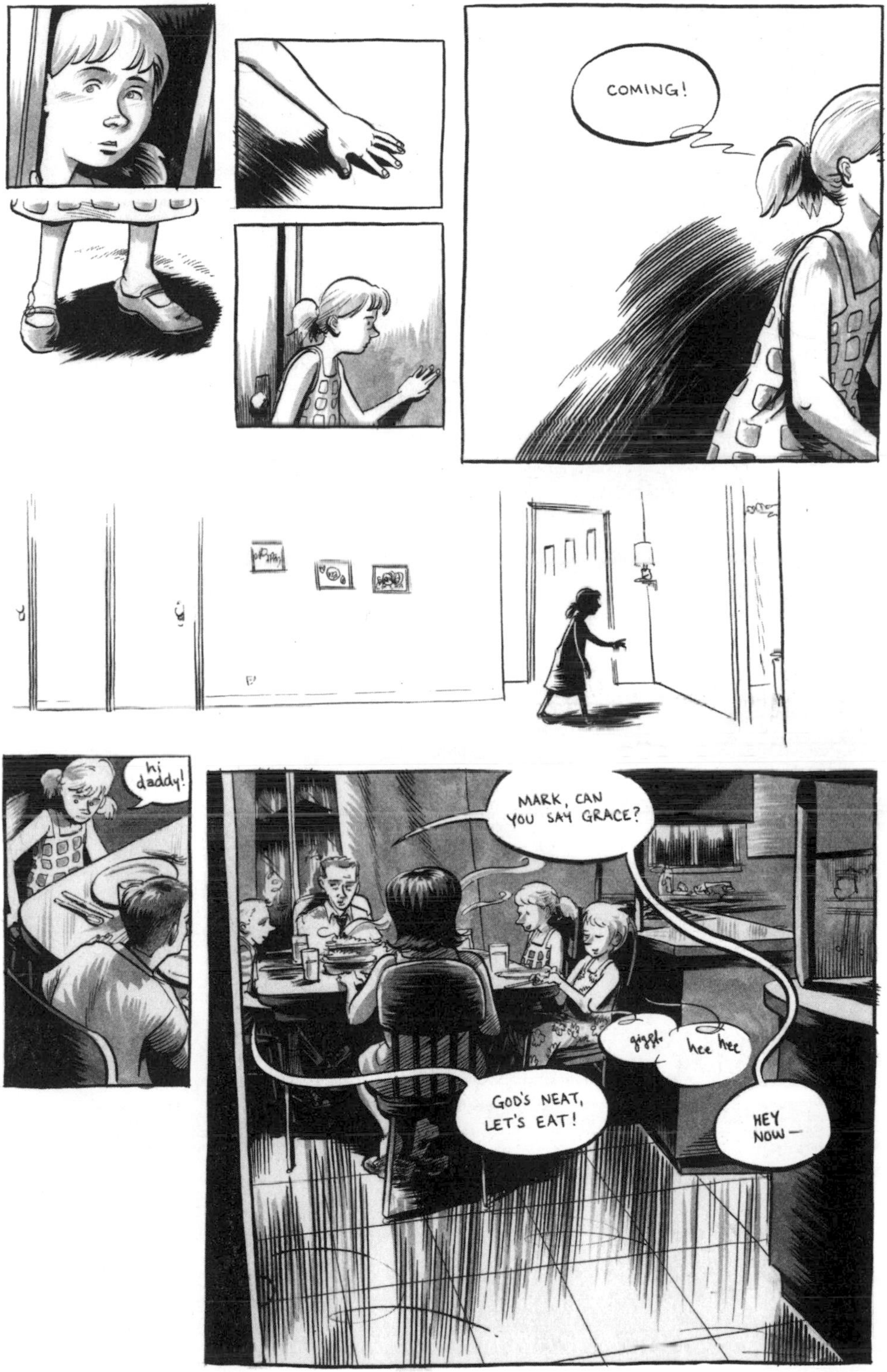
COMING!
hi daddy!
MARK, CAN YOU SAY GRACE?
giggle
hee hee
GOD'S NEAT, LET'S EAT!
HEY NOW—

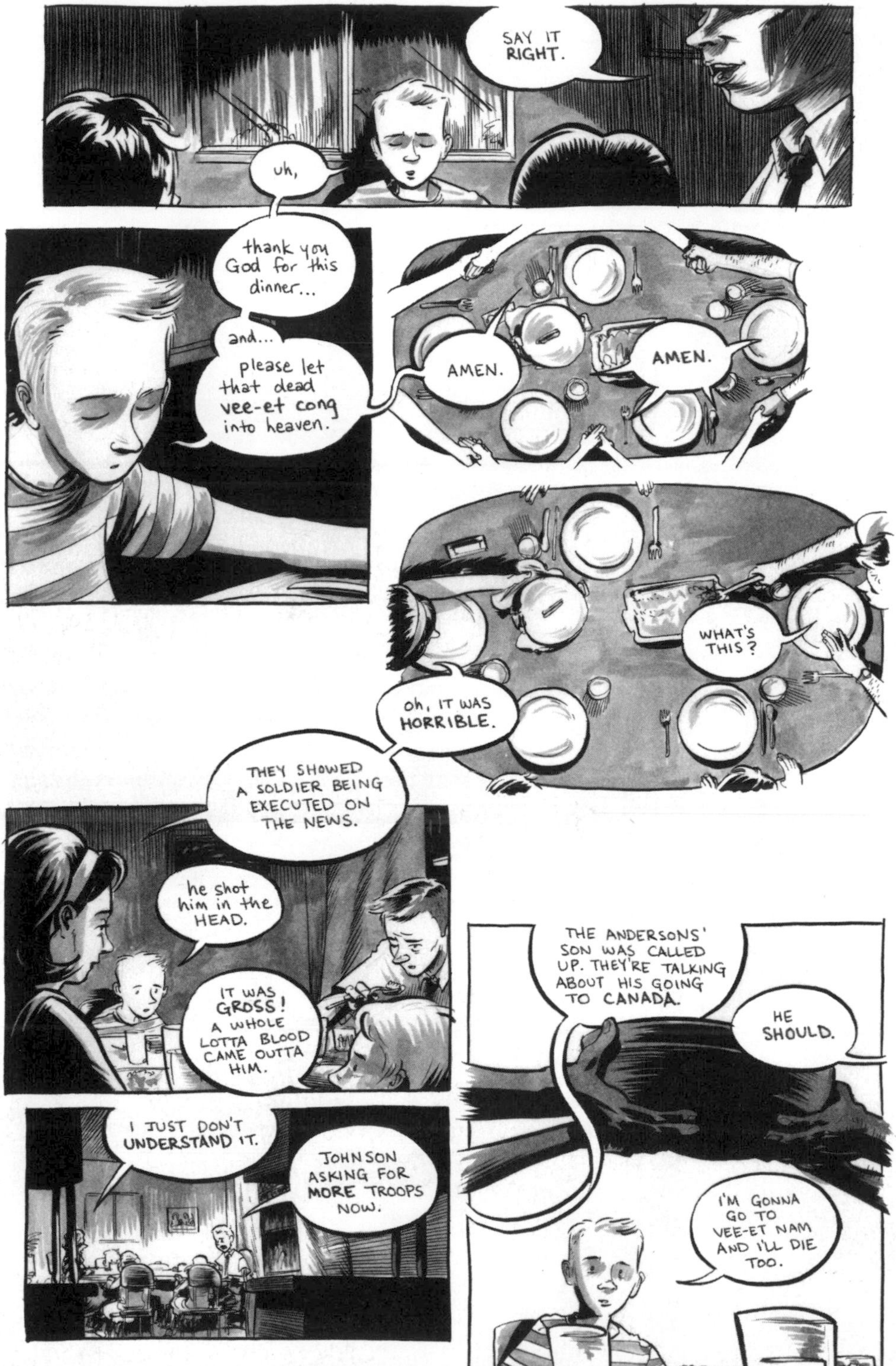

SAY IT RIGHT.
uh,
thank you God for this dinner...
and...
please let that dead vee-et cong into heaven.
AMEN.
AMEN.
WHAT'S THIS?
oh, IT WAS HORRIBLE.
THEY SHOWED A SOLDIER BEING EXECUTED ON THE NEWS.
he shot him in the HEAD.
IT WAS GROSS! A WHOLE LOTTA BLOOD CAME OUTTA HIM.
I JUST DON'T UNDERSTAND IT.
JOHNSON ASKING FOR MORE TROOPS NOW.
THE ANDERSONS' SON WAS CALLED UP. THEY'RE TALKING ABOUT HIS GOING TO CANADA.
HE SHOULD.
I'M GONNA GO TO VEE-ET NAM AND I'LL DIE TOO.

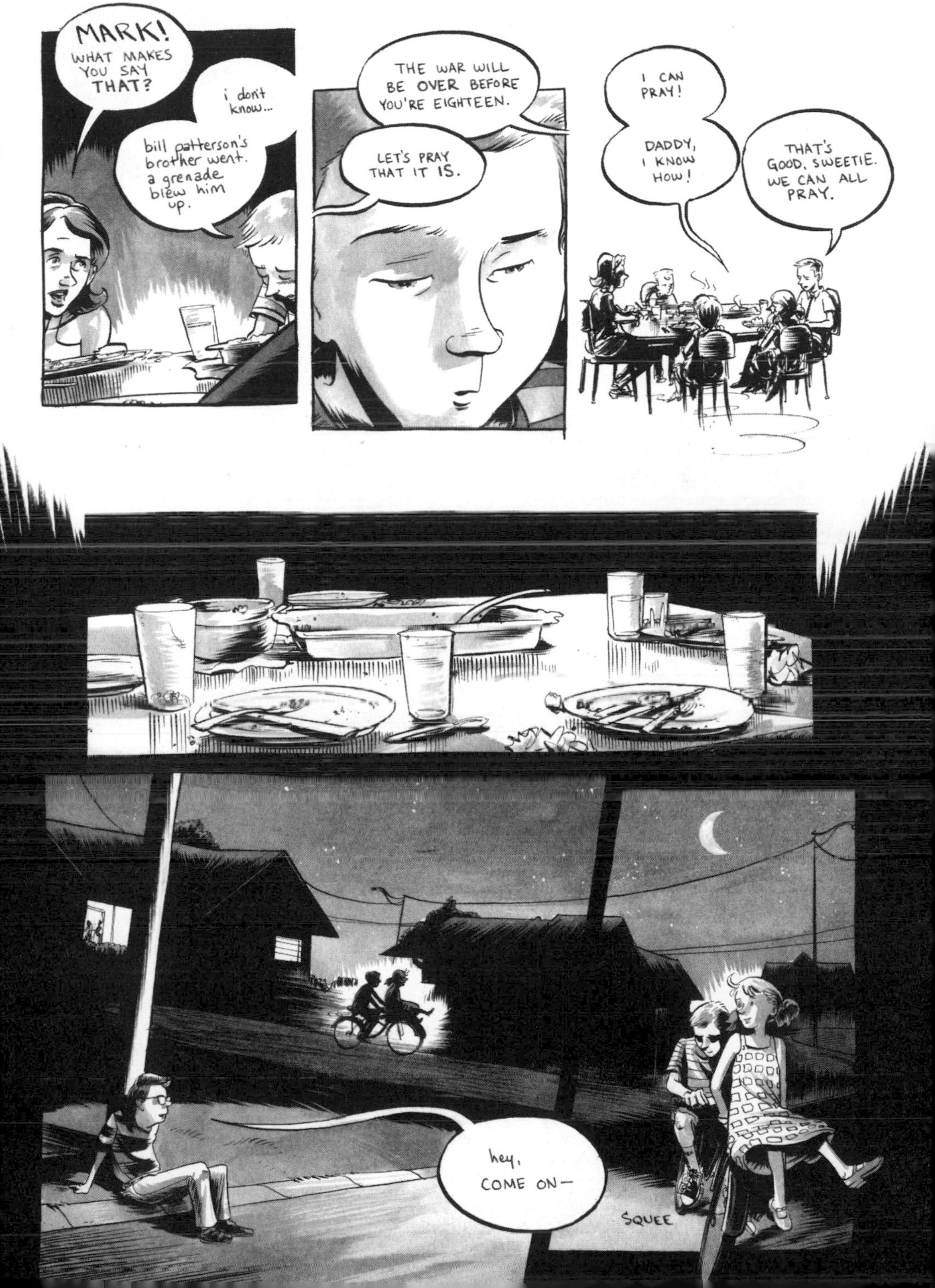
MARK! WHAT MAKES YOU SAY THAT?
i don't know...
bill patterson's brother went. a grenade blew him up.
THE WAR WILL BE OVER BEFORE YOU'RE EIGHTEEN.
LET'S PRAY THAT IT IS.
I CAN PRAY!
DADDY, I KNOW HOW!
THAT'S GOOD, SWEETIE. WE CAN ALL PRAY.
hey, COME ON—
SQUEE

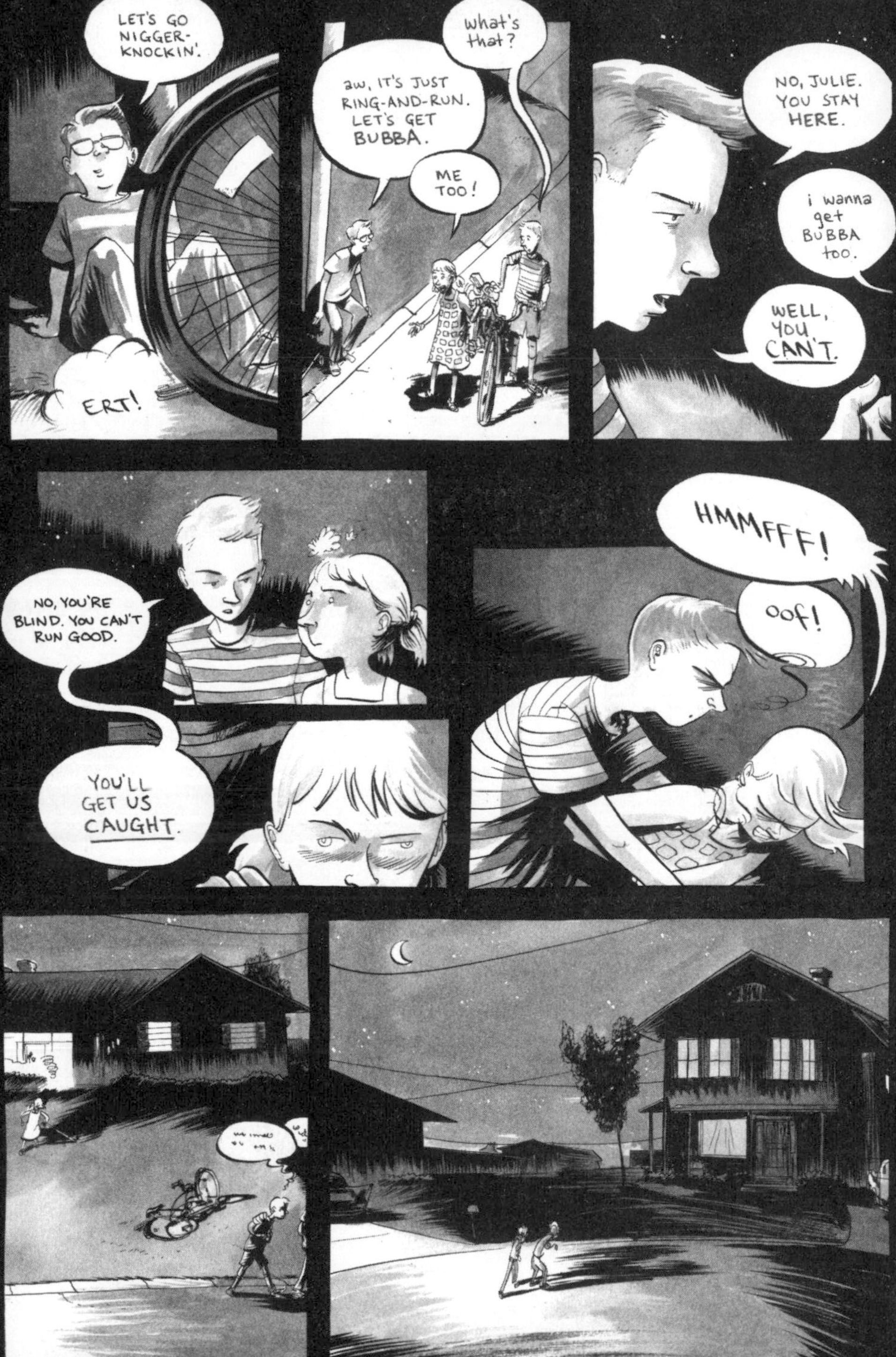
LET'S GO NIGGER-KNOCKIN'.
ERT!
what's that?
aw, IT'S JUST RING-AND-RUN. LET'S GET BUBBA.
ME TOO!
NO, JULIE. YOU STAY HERE.
i wanna get BUBBA too.
WELL, YOU CAN'T.
NO, YOU'RE BLIND. YOU CAN'T RUN GOOD.
YOU'LL GET US CAUGHT.
HMMFFF!
oof!

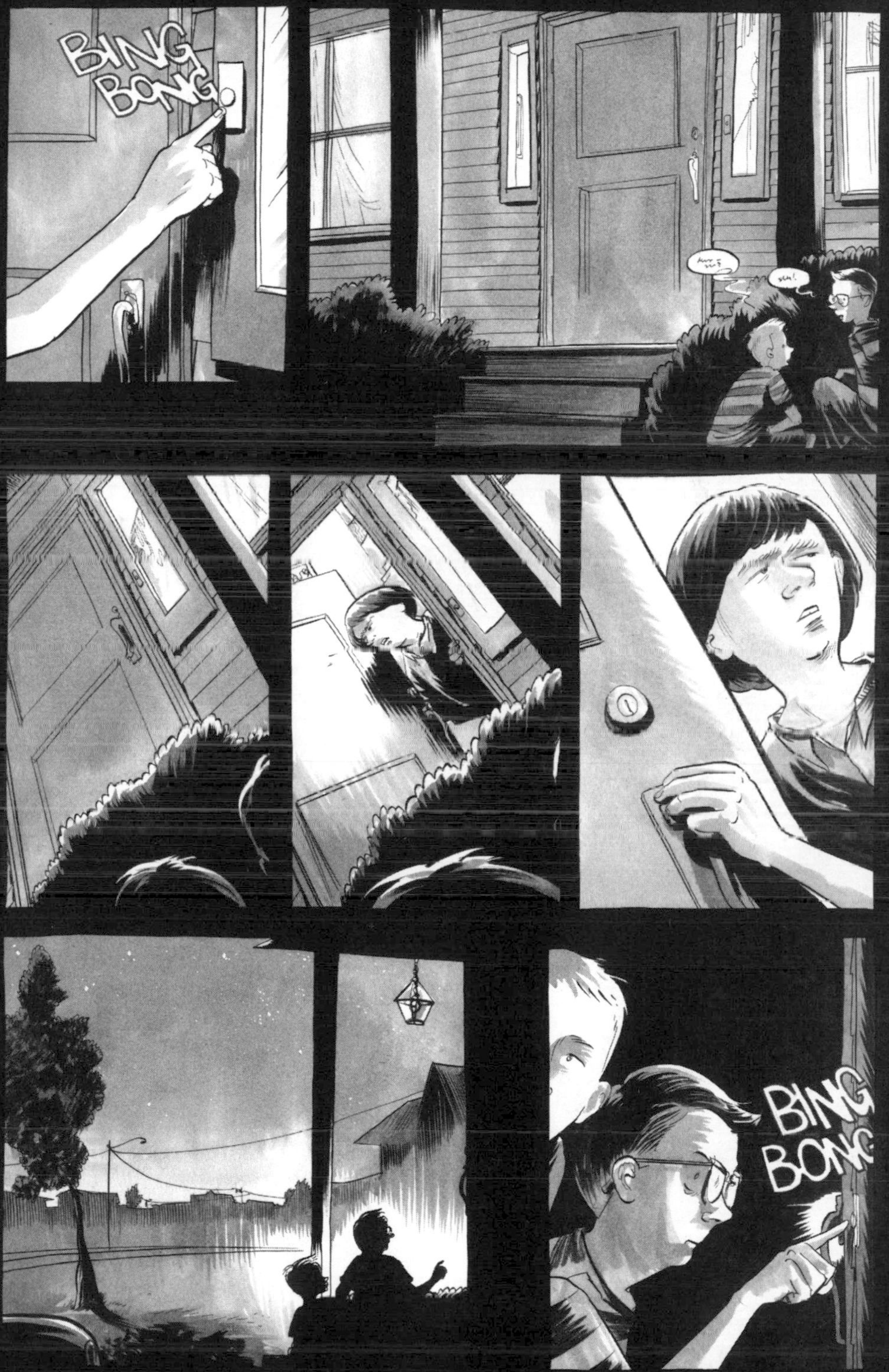
BING BONG
BING BONG

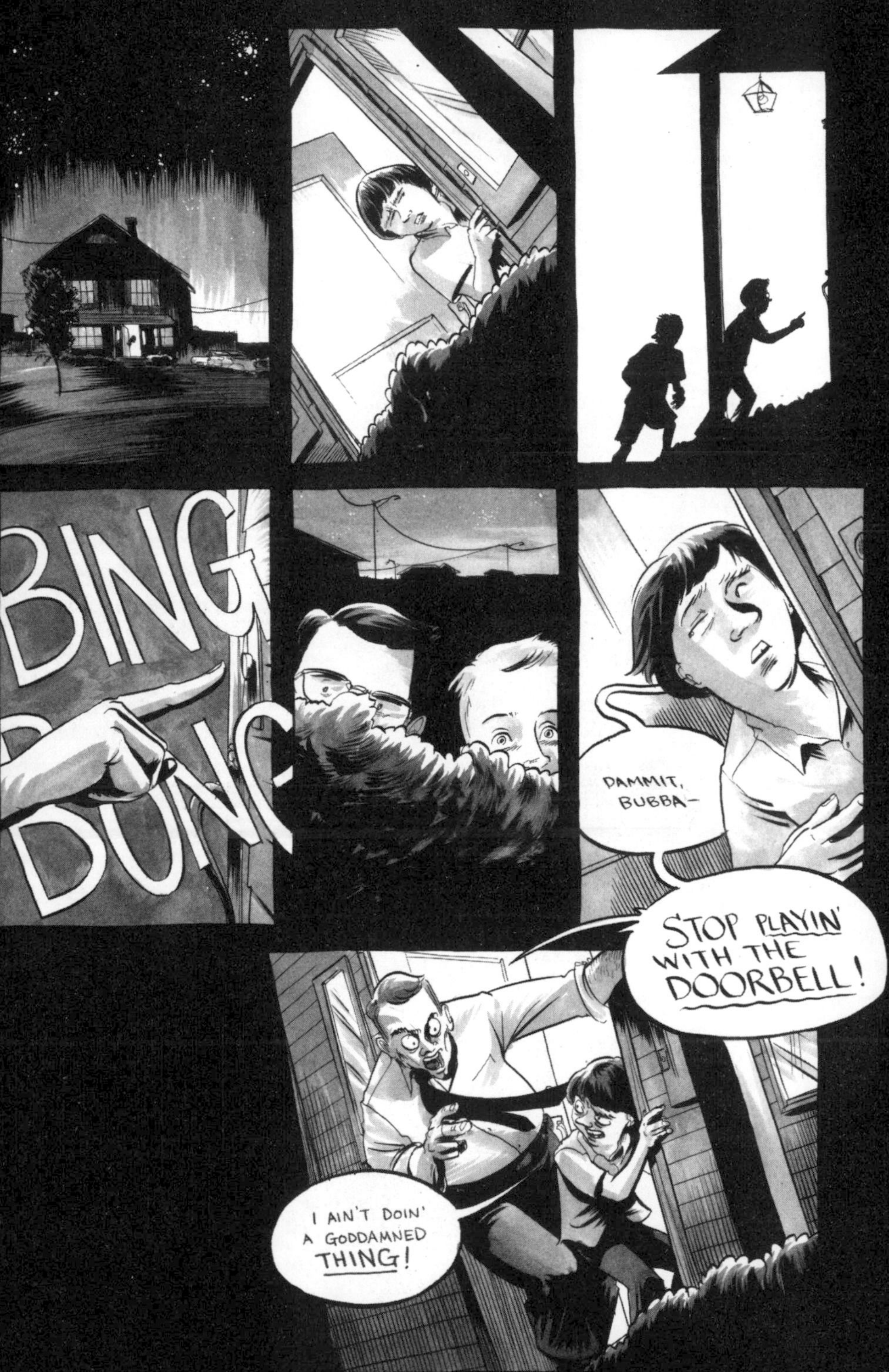
BING
BONG
DAMMIT, BUBBA-
STOP PLAYIN' WITH THE DOORBELL!
I AIN'T DOIN' A GODDAMNED THING!

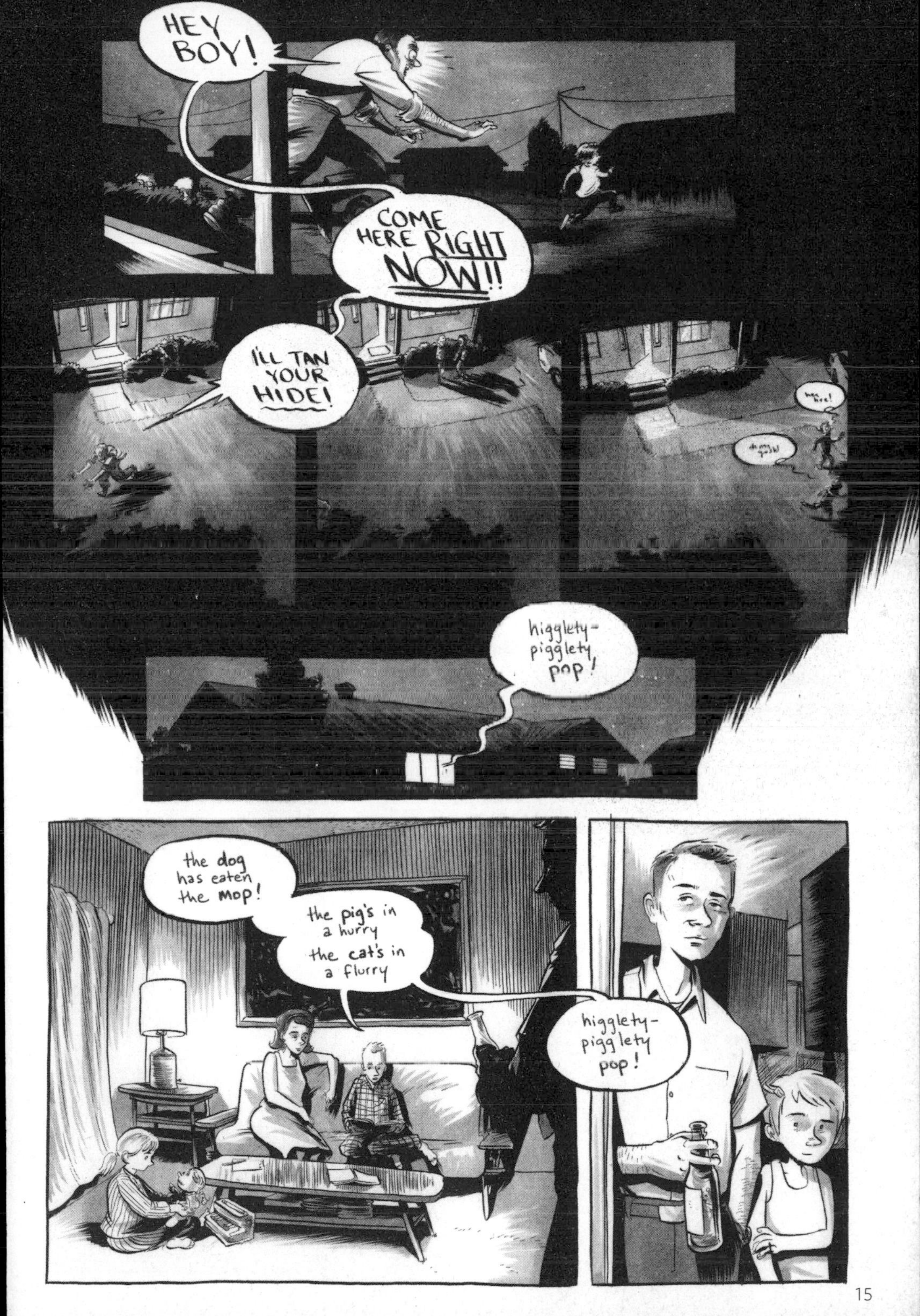

HEY BOY!
COME HERE RIGHT NOW!!
I'LL TAN YOUR HIDE!
higglety-pigglety pop!
the dog has eaten the mop!
the pig's in a hurry the cat's in a flurry
higglety-pigglety pop!

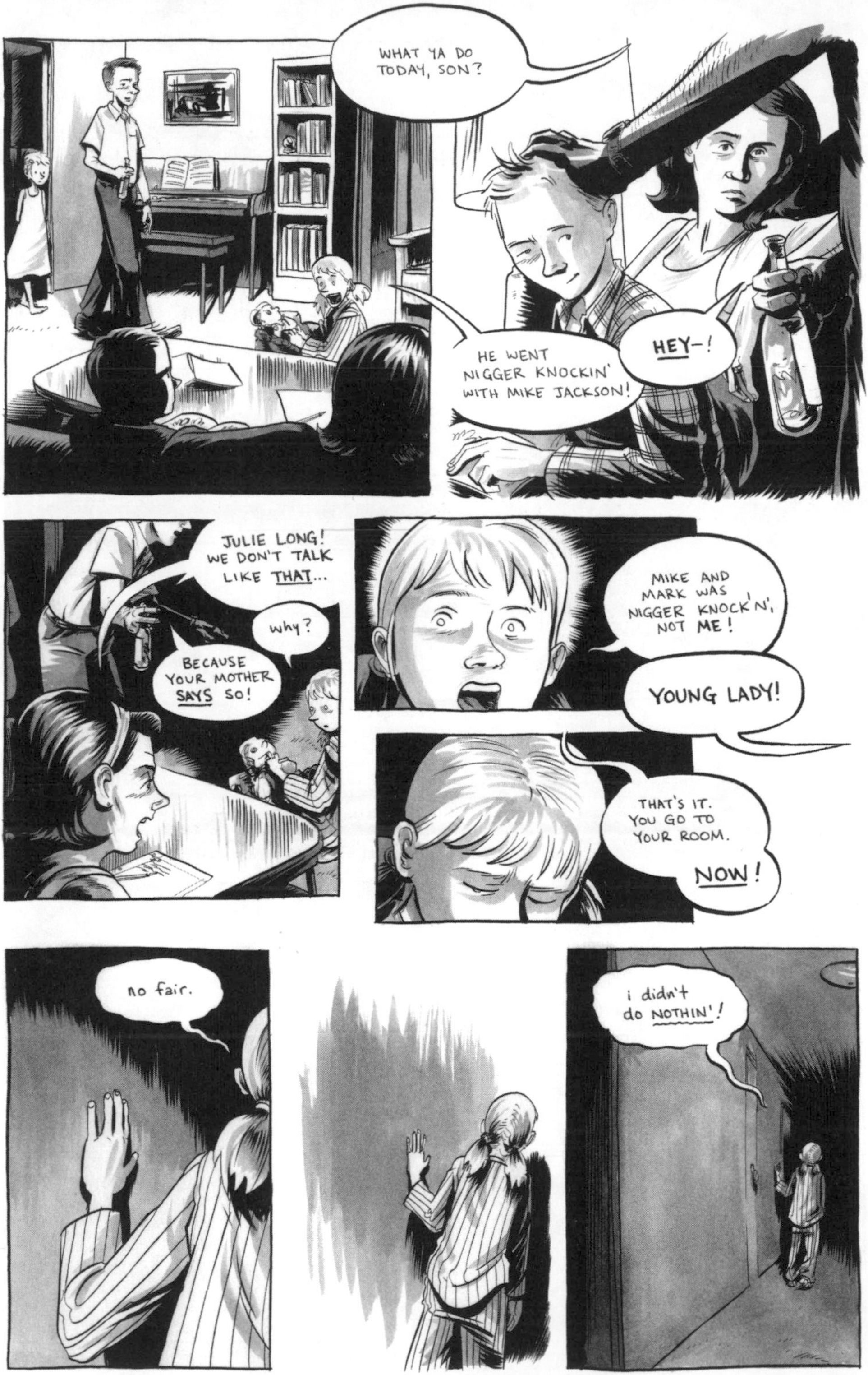
WHAT YA DO TODAY, SON?
HE WENT NIGGER KNOCKIN' WITH MIKE JACKSON!
HEY–!
JULIE LONG! WE DON'T TALK LIKE THAT...
why?
BECAUSE YOUR MOTHER SAYS SO!
MIKE AND MARK WAS NIGGER KNOCK'N', NOT ME!
YOUNG LADY!
THAT'S IT. YOU GO TO YOUR ROOM.
NOW!
no fair.
i didn't do NOTHIN'!

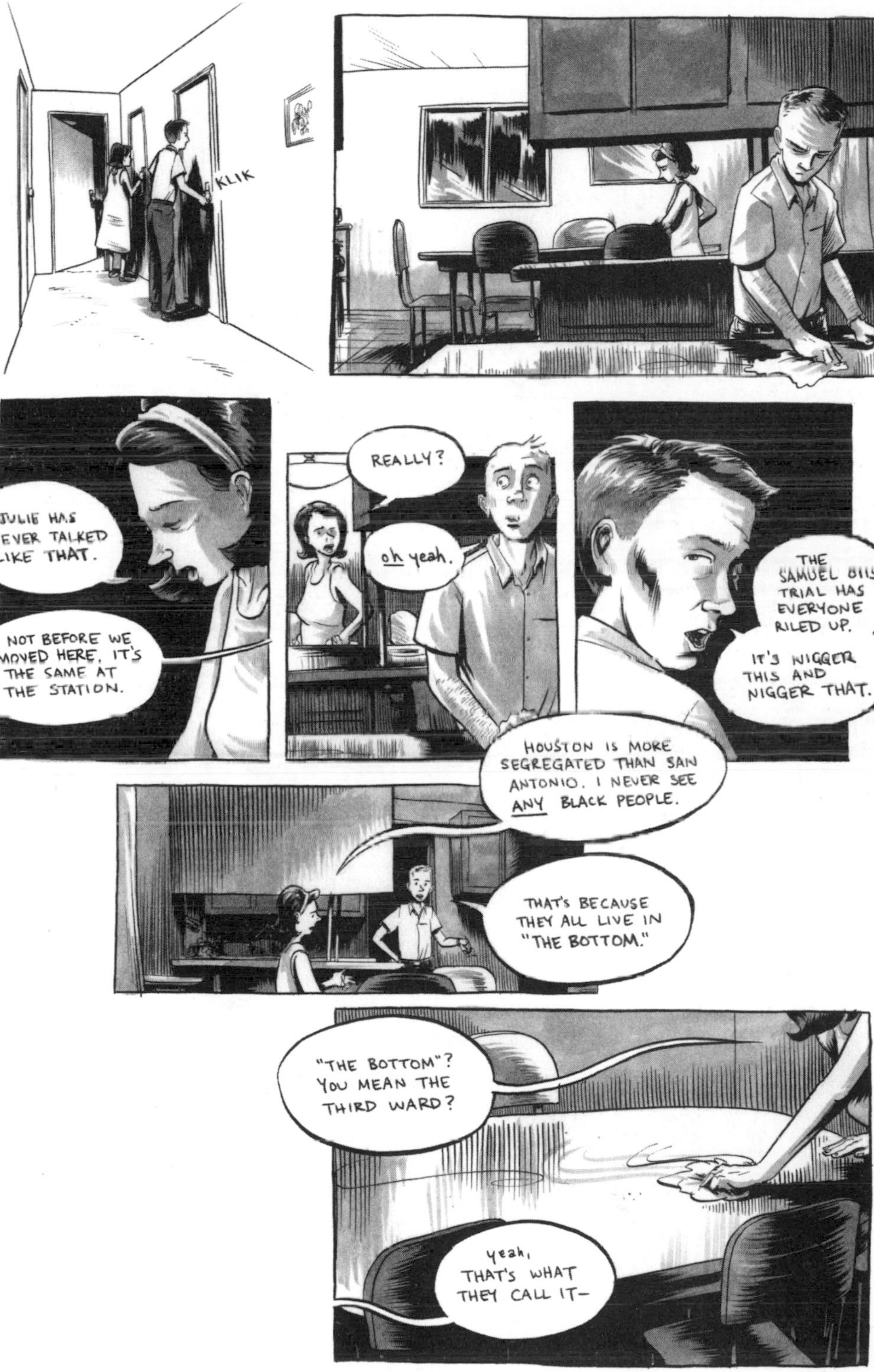
KLIK
JULIE HAS NEVER TALKED LIKE THAT.
NOT BEFORE WE MOVED HERE. IT'S THE SAME AT THE STATION.
REALLY?
oh yeah.
THE SAMUEL OTIS TRIAL HAS EVERYONE RILED UP.
IT'S NIGGER THIS AND NIGGER THAT.
HOUSTON IS MORE SEGREGATED THAN SAN ANTONIO. I NEVER SEE ANY BLACK PEOPLE.
THAT'S BECAUSE THEY ALL LIVE IN "THE BOTTOM."
"THE BOTTOM"? YOU MEAN THE THIRD WARD?
yeah, THAT'S WHAT THEY CALL IT–

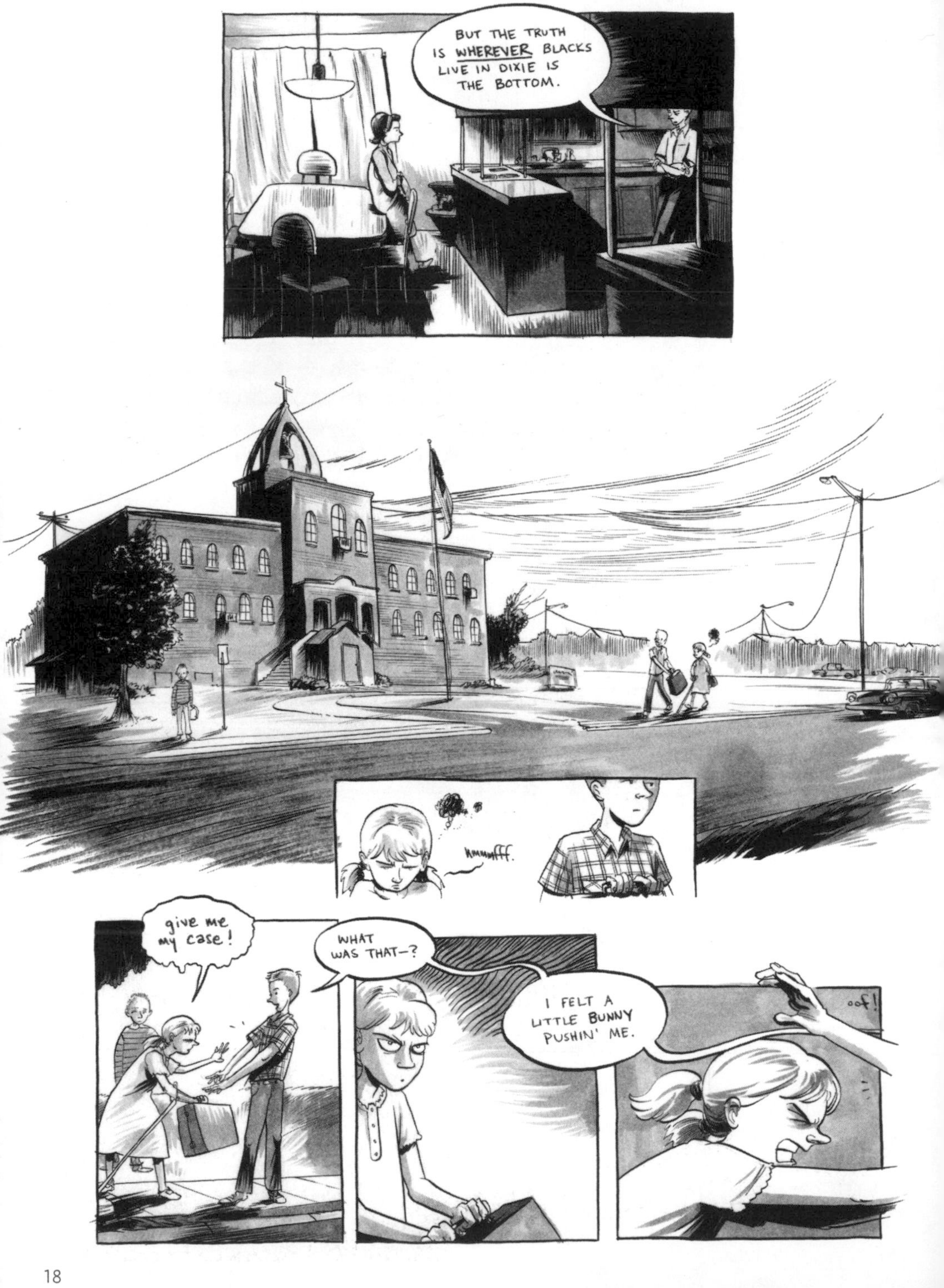
BUT THE TRUTH IS WHEREVER BLACKS LIVE IN DIXIE IS THE BOTTOM.
hmmmfff.
give me my case!
WHAT WAS THAT–?
I FELT A LITTLE BUNNY PUSHIN' ME.
oof!

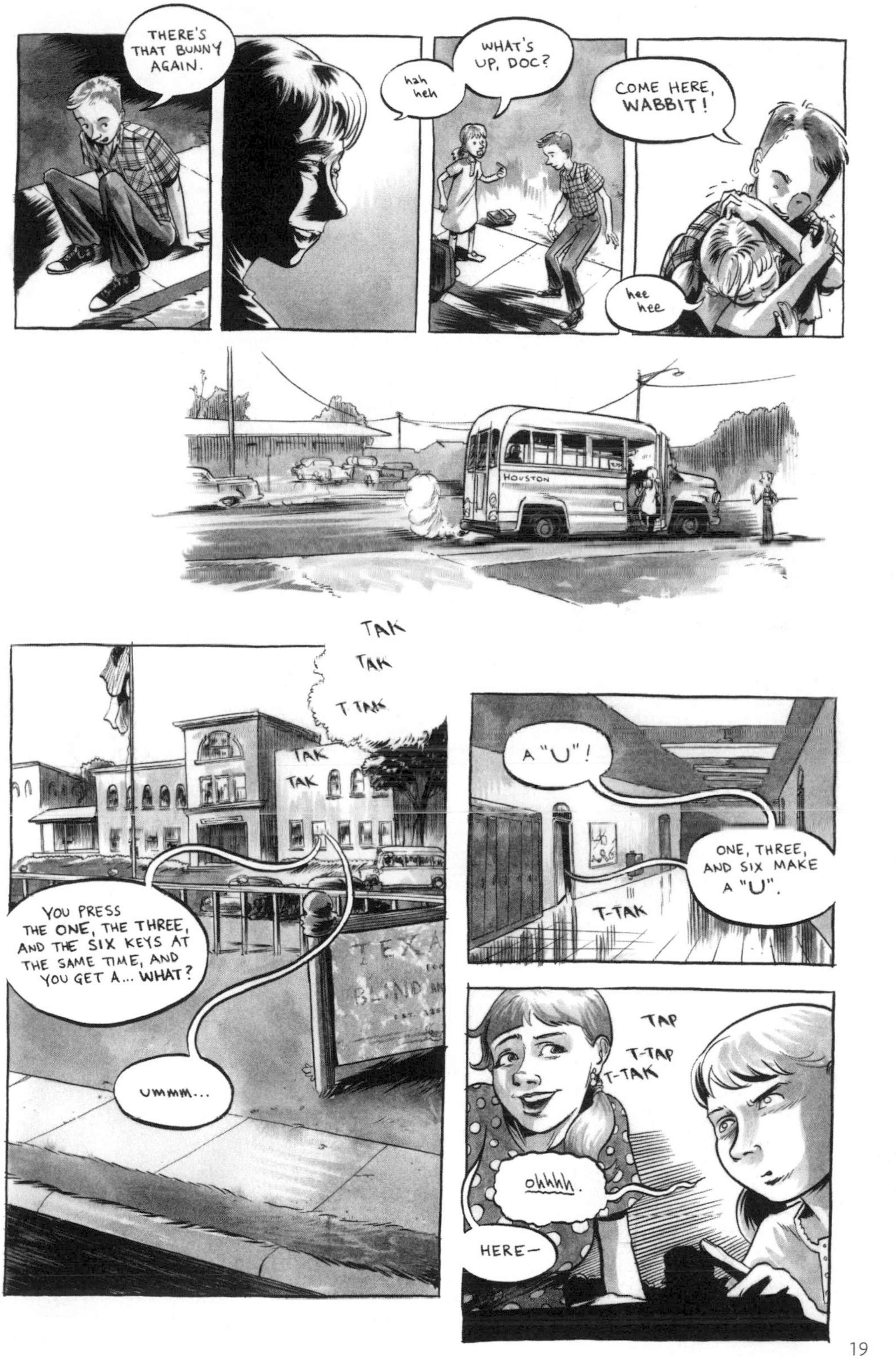
THERE'S THAT BUNNY AGAIN.
hah heh
WHAT'S UP, DOC?
COME HERE, WABBIT!
hee hee
HOUSTON
TAK
TAK
T-TAK
TAK
TAK
YOU PRESS THE ONE, THE THREE, AND THE SIX KEYS AT THE SAME TIME, AND YOU GET A... WHAT?
UMMM...
A "U"!
ONE, THREE, AND SIX MAKE A "U".
T-TAK
TAP
T-TAP
T-TAK
ohhhh.
HERE—

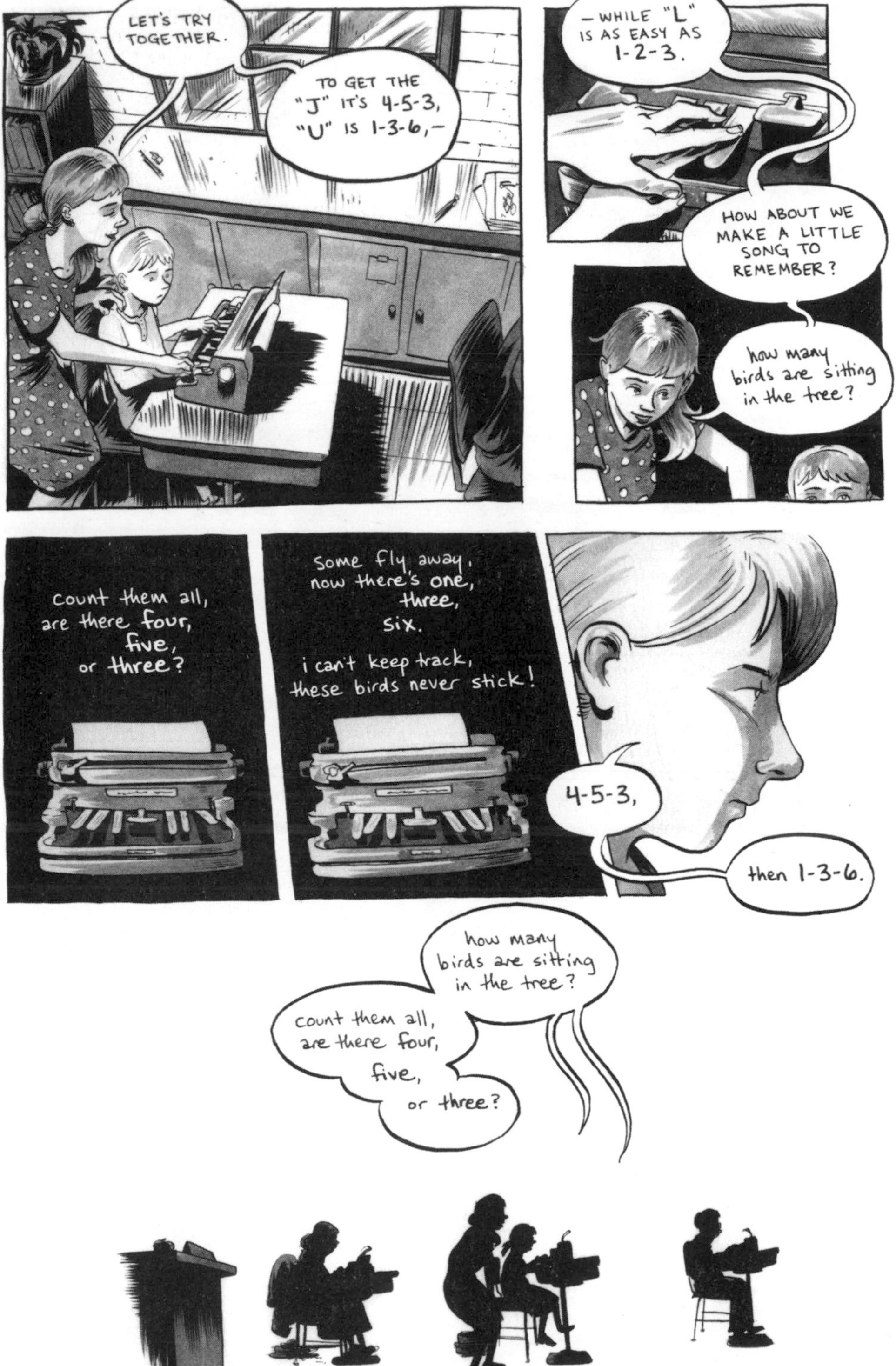
LET'S TRY TOGETHER.
TO GET THE "J" IT'S 4-5-3, "U" IS 1-3-6,—
—WHILE "L" IS AS EASY AS 1-2-3.
HOW ABOUT WE MAKE A LITTLE SONG TO REMEMBER?
how many birds are sitting in the tree?
count them all, are there four, five, or three?
Some fly away, now there's one, three, six.
i can't keep track, these birds never stick!
4-5-3,
then 1-3-6.
how many birds are sitting in the tree?
count them all, are there four, five, or three?

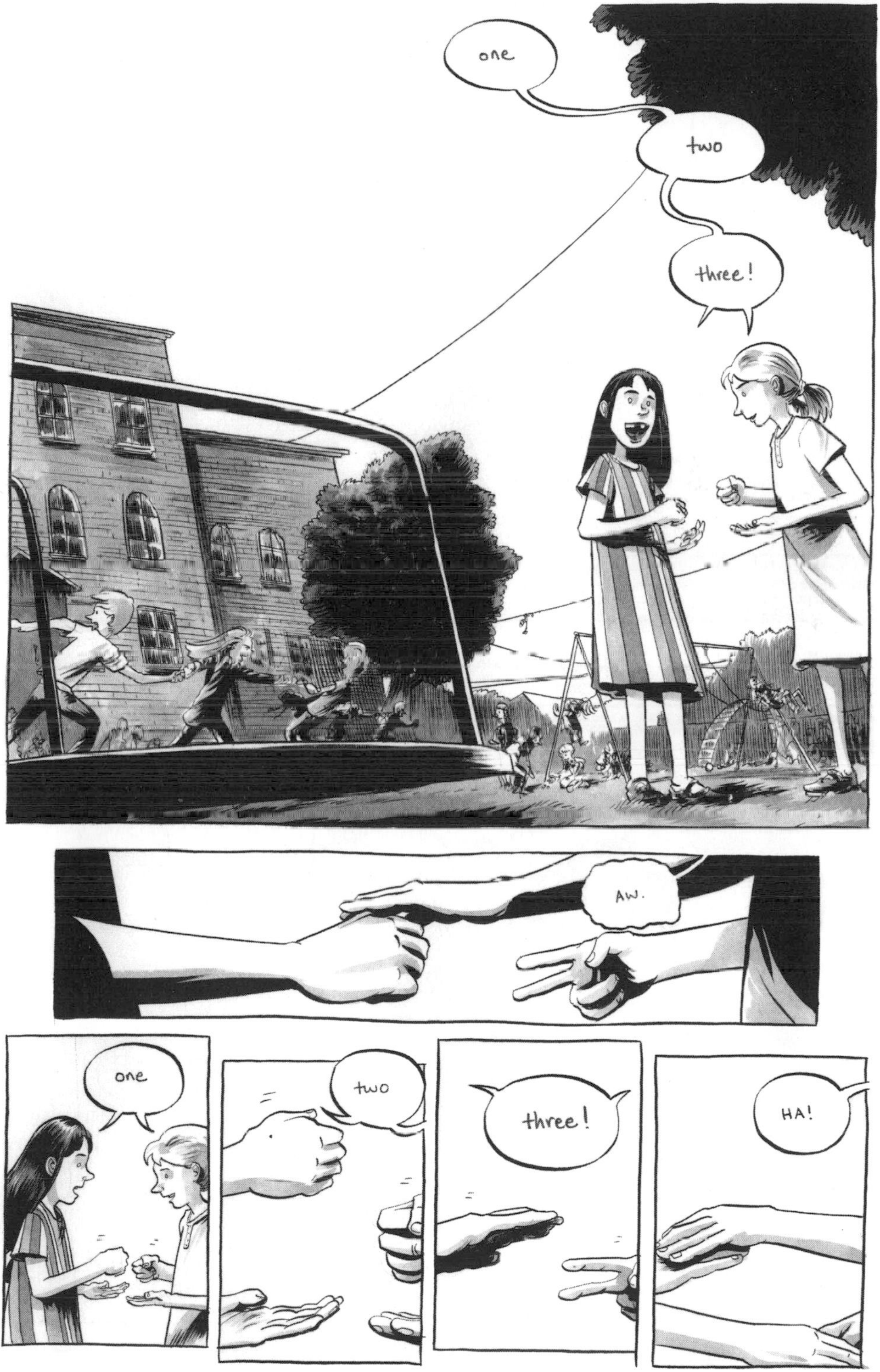
one
two
three!
AW.
one
two
three!
HA!

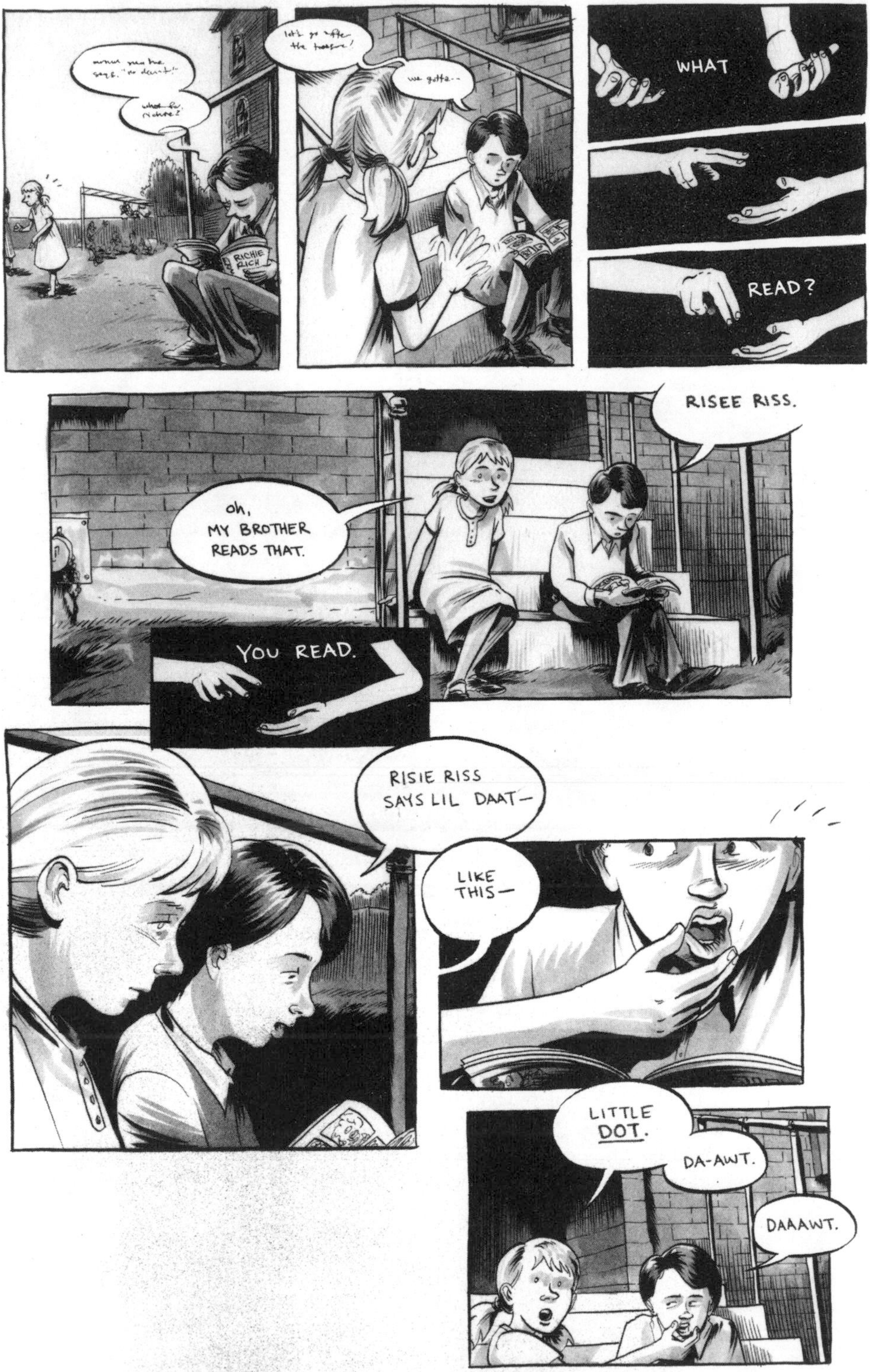
RICHIE RICH
WHAT
READ?
RISEE RISS.
oh, MY BROTHER READS THAT.
YOU READ.
RISIE RISS SAYS LIL DAAT—
LIKE THIS—
LITTLE DOT.
DA-AWT.
DAAAWT.

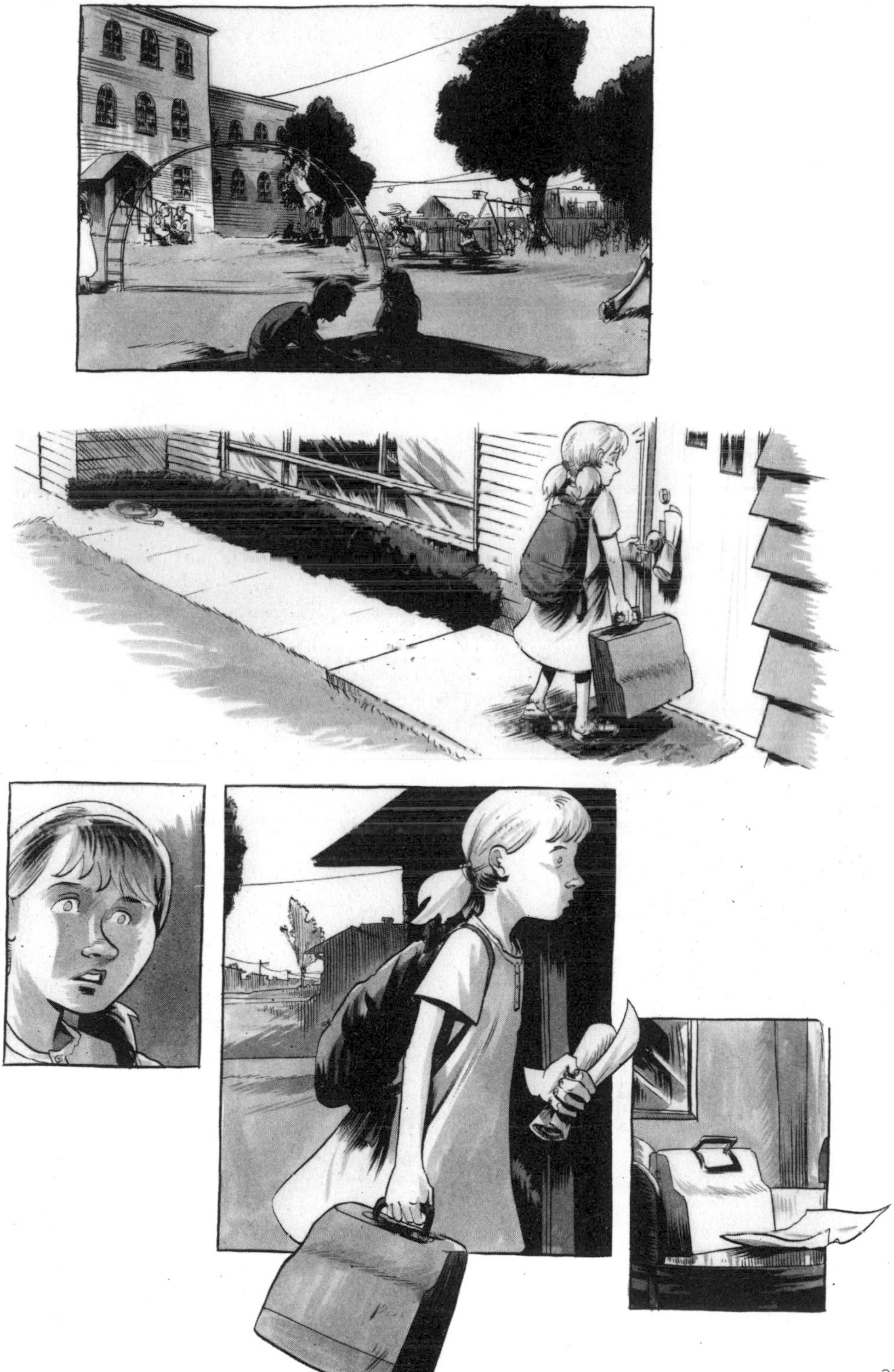

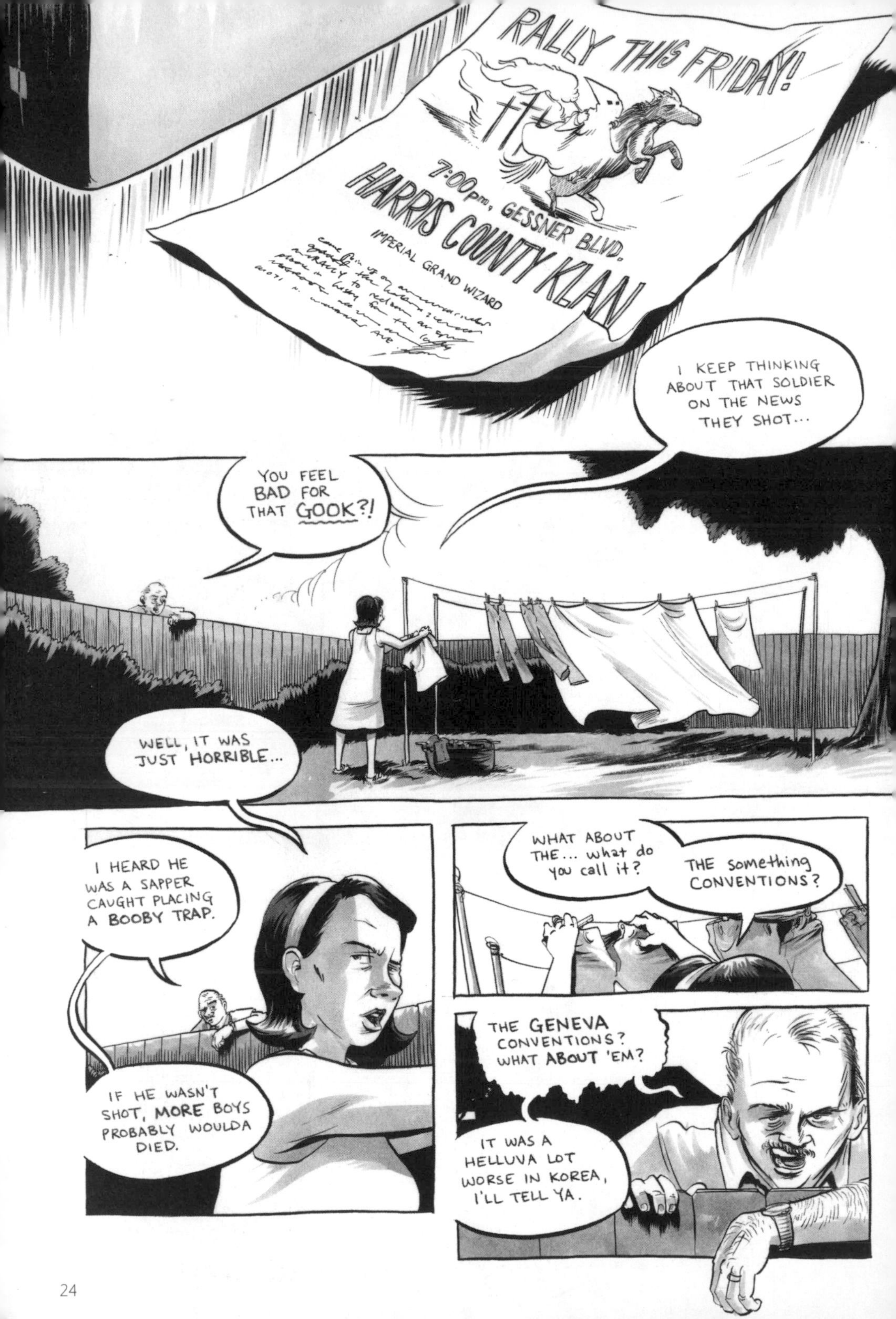
RALLY THIS FRIDAY!
7:00pm, GESSNER BLVD.
HARRIS COUNTY KLAN
IMPERIAL GRAND WIZARD
I KEEP THINKING ABOUT THAT SOLDIER ON THE NEWS THEY SHOT...
YOU FEEL BAD FOR THAT GOOK?!
WELL, IT WAS JUST HORRIBLE...
I HEARD HE WAS A SAPPER CAUGHT PLACING A BOOBY TRAP.
IF HE WASN'T SHOT, MORE BOYS PROBABLY WOULDA DIED.
WHAT ABOUT THE... what do you call it?
THE something CONVENTIONS?
THE GENEVA CONVENTIONS? WHAT ABOUT 'EM?
IT WAS A HELLUVA LOT WORSE IN KOREA, I'LL TELL YA.

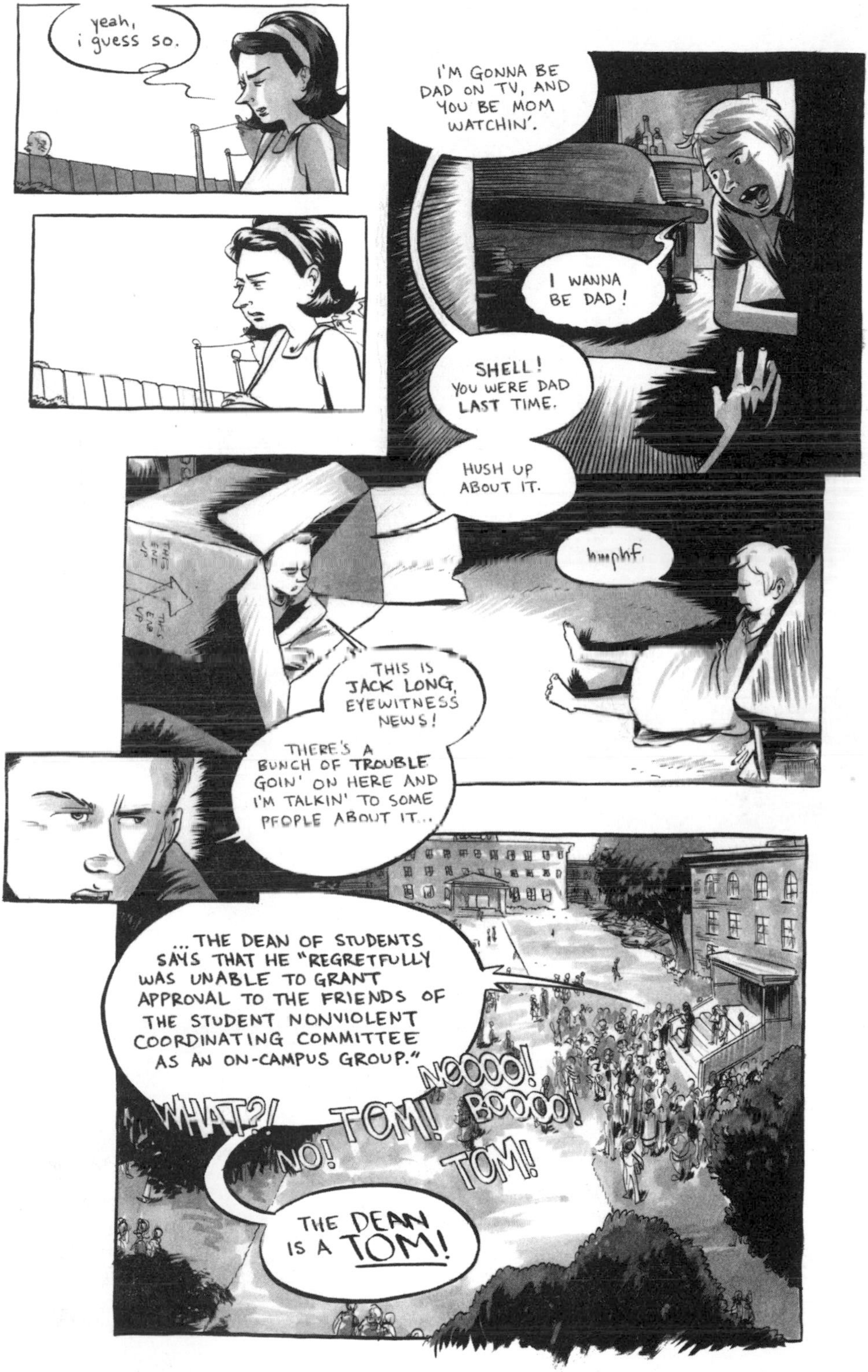
yeah, i guess so.
I'M GONNA BE DAD ON TV, AND YOU BE MOM WATCHIN'.
I WANNA BE DAD!
SHELL! YOU WERE DAD LAST TIME.
HUSH UP ABOUT IT.
hmphf
THIS IS JACK LONG, EYEWITNESS NEWS!
THERE'S A BUNCH OF TROUBLE GOIN' ON HERE AND I'M TALKIN' TO SOME PEOPLE ABOUT IT...
...THE DEAN OF STUDENTS SAYS THAT HE "REGRETFULLY WAS UNABLE TO GRANT APPROVAL TO THE FRIENDS OF THE STUDENT NONVIOLENT COORDINATING COMMITTEE AS AN ON-CAMPUS GROUP."
WHAT?!
NOOOO!
TOM!
BOOOO!
NO!
TOM!
THE DEAN IS A TOM!

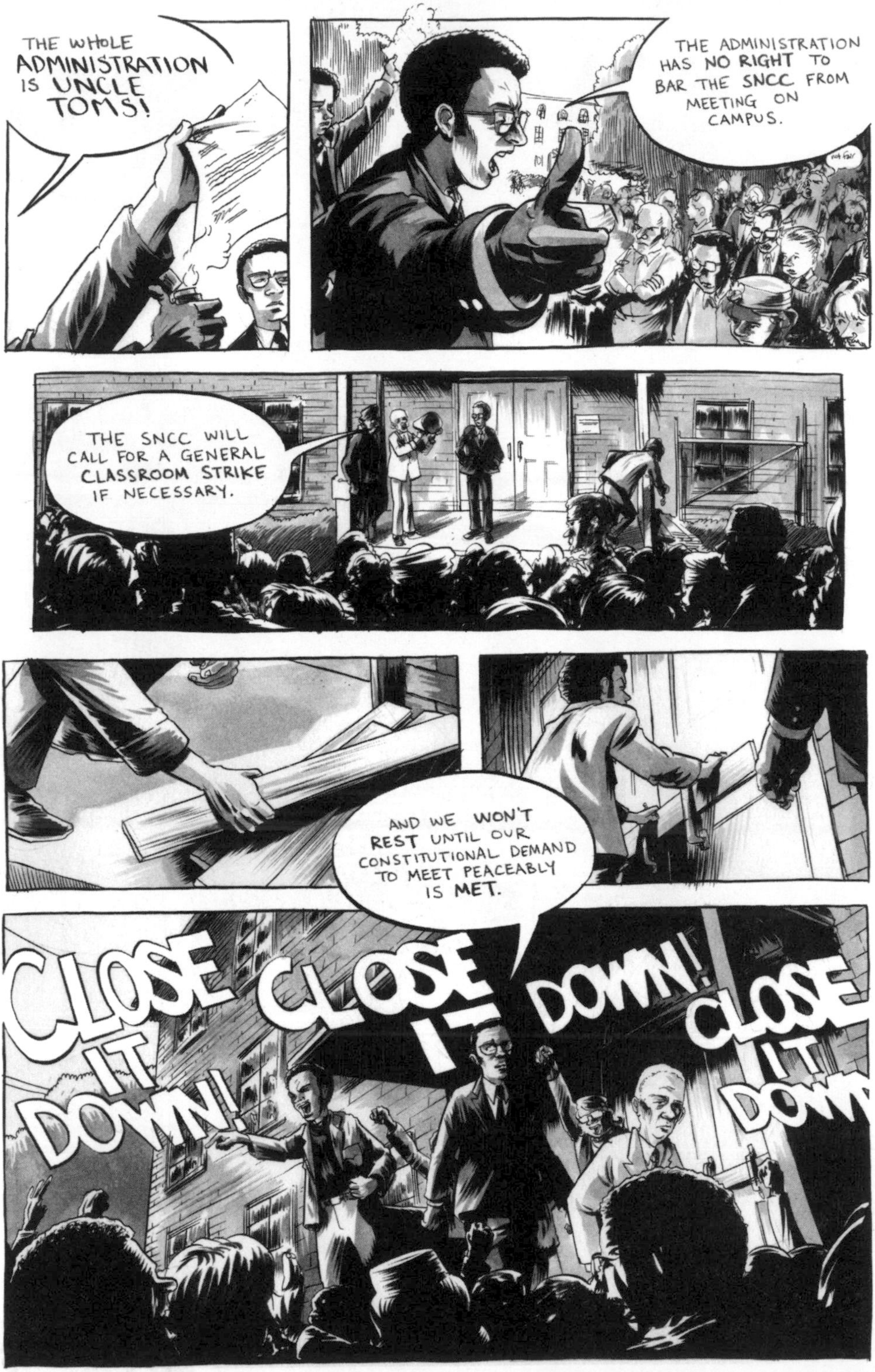
THE WHOLE ADMINISTRATION IS UNCLE TOMS!
THE ADMINISTRATION HAS NO RIGHT TO BAR THE SNCC FROM MEETING ON CAMPUS.
THE SNCC WILL CALL FOR A GENERAL CLASSROOM STRIKE IF NECESSARY.
AND WE WON'T REST UNTIL OUR CONSTITUTIONAL DEMAND TO MEET PEACEABLY IS MET.
CLOSE IT DOWN!
CLOSE IT DOWN!
CLOSE IT

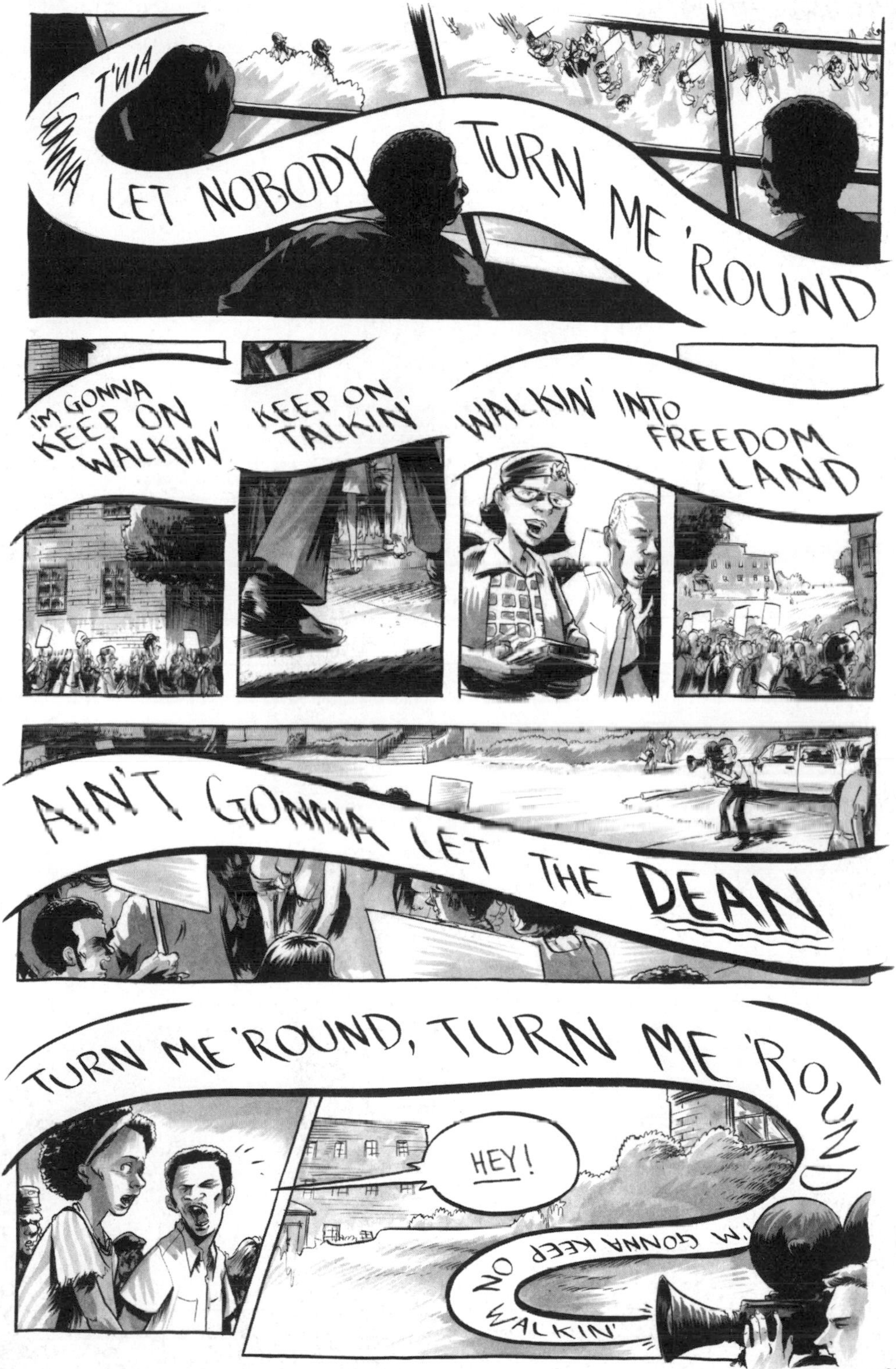

AIN'T GONNA LET NOBODY TURN ME 'ROUND
I'M GONNA KEEP ON WALKIN'
KEEP ON TALKIN'
WALKIN' INTO FREEDOM LAND
AIN'T GONNA LET THE DEAN
TURN ME 'ROUND, TURN ME 'ROUND
HEY!
I'M GONNA KEEP ON WALKIN'

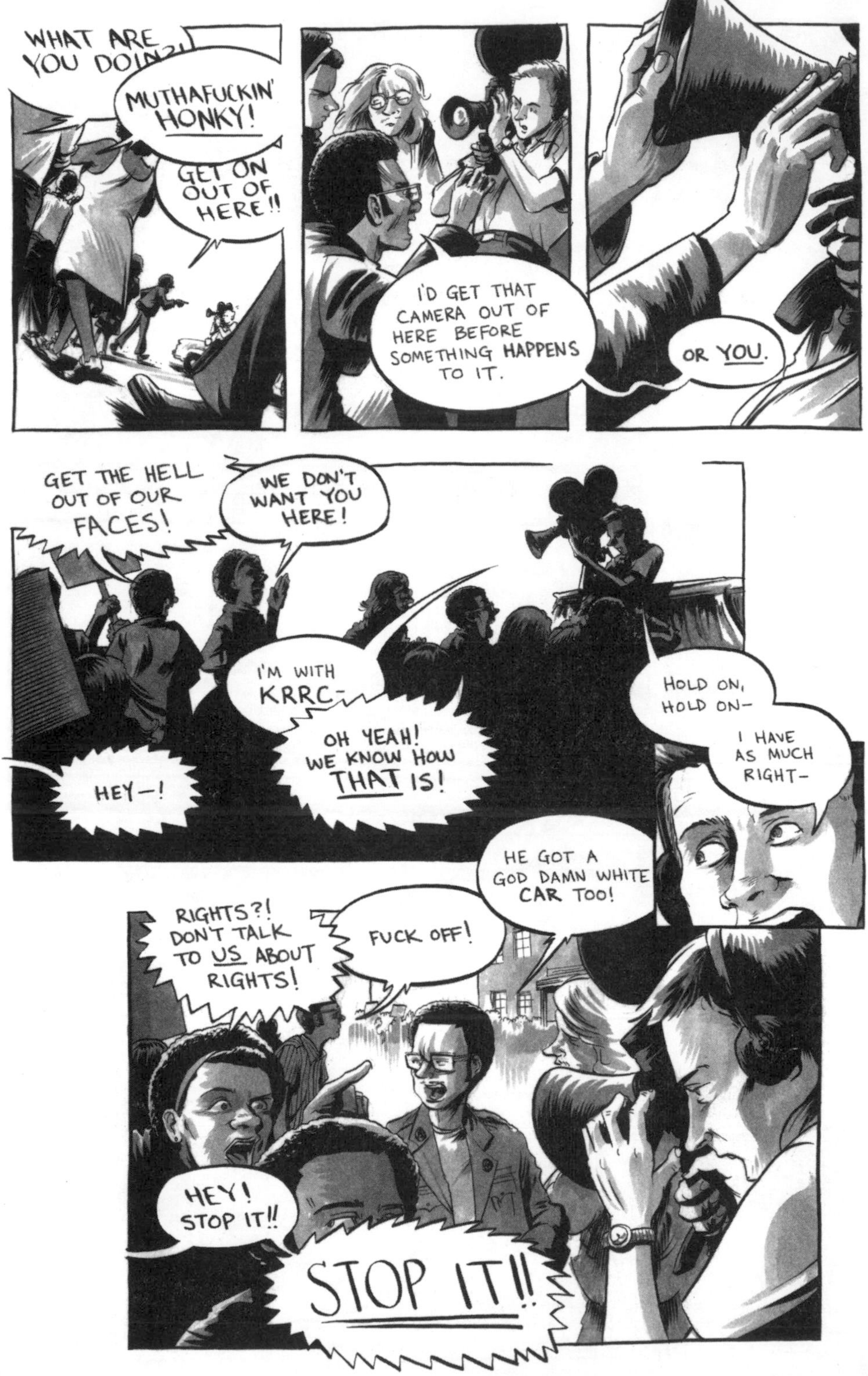
WHAT ARE YOU DOIN'?!
MUTHAFUCKIN' HONKY!
GET ON OUT OF HERE!!
I'D GET THAT CAMERA OUT OF HERE BEFORE SOMETHING HAPPENS TO IT.
OR YOU.
GET THE HELL OUT OF OUR FACES!
WE DON'T WANT YOU HERE!
I'M WITH KRRC-
OH YEAH! WE KNOW HOW THAT IS!
HEY-!
HOLD ON, HOLD ON-
I HAVE AS MUCH RIGHT-
HE GOT A GOD DAMN WHITE CAR TOO!
RIGHTS?! DON'T TALK TO US ABOUT RIGHTS!
FUCK OFF!
HEY! STOP IT!!
STOP IT!!

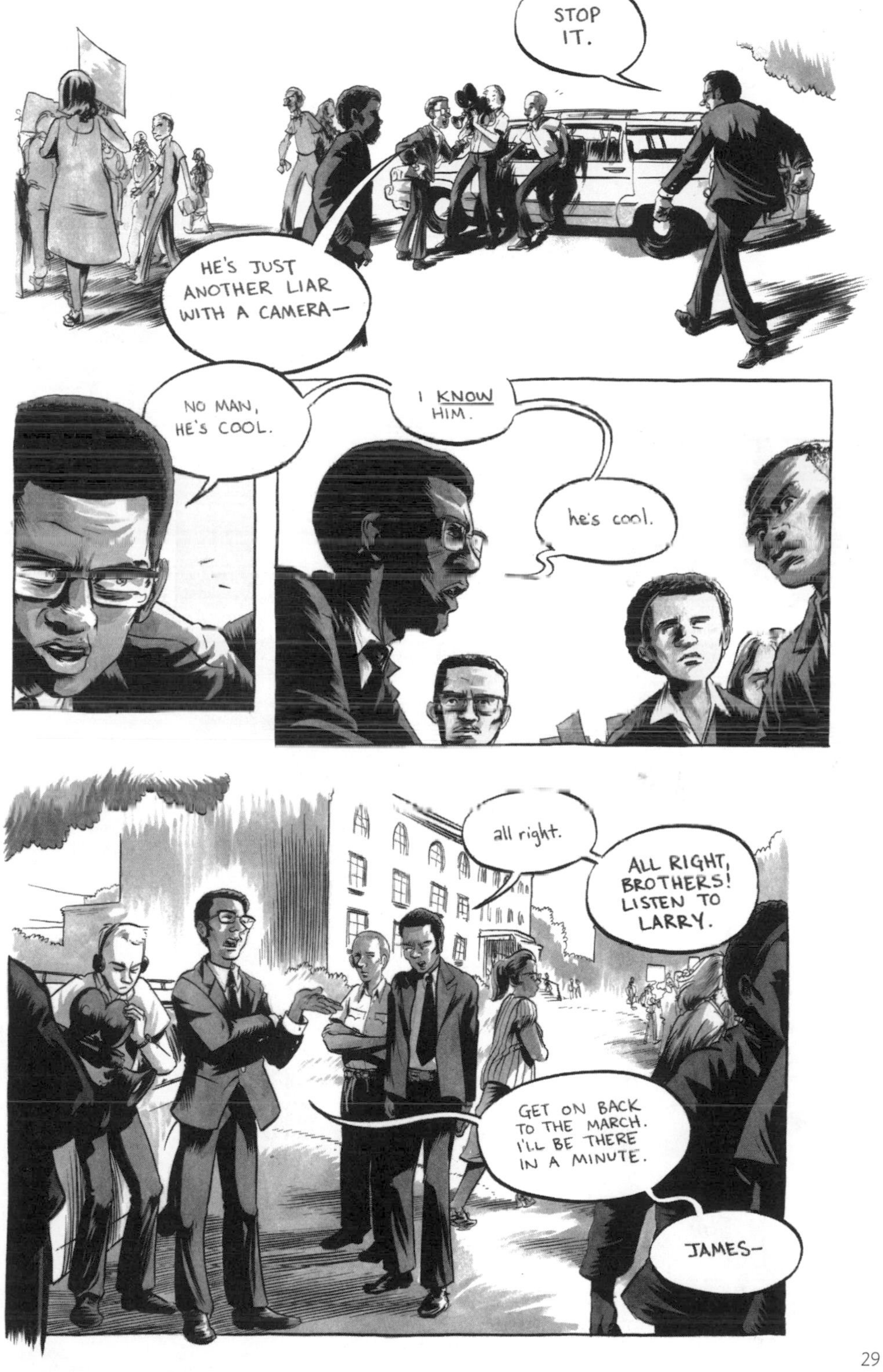
STOP IT.
HE'S JUST ANOTHER LIAR WITH A CAMERA—
NO MAN, HE'S COOL.
I KNOW HIM.
he's cool.
all right.
ALL RIGHT, BROTHERS! LISTEN TO LARRY.
GET ON BACK TO THE MARCH. I'LL BE THERE IN A MINUTE.
JAMES—

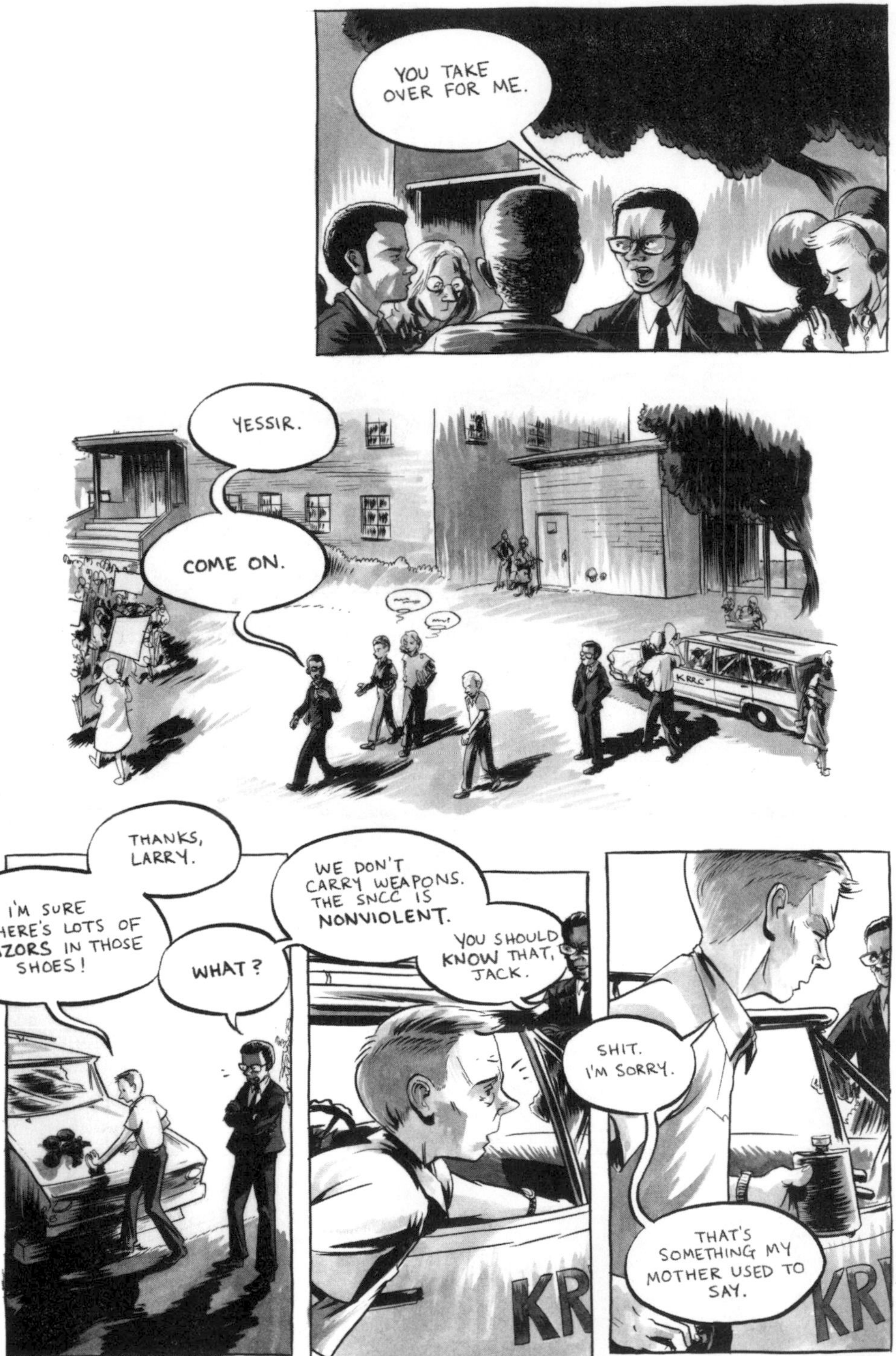
YOU TAKE OVER FOR ME.
YESSIR.
COME ON.
THANKS, LARRY.
I'M SURE THERE'S LOTS OF **RAZORS** IN THOSE SHOES!
WHAT?
WE DON'T CARRY WEAPONS. THE SNCC IS **NONVIOLENT**.
YOU SHOULD **KNOW** THAT, JACK.
SHIT. I'M SORRY.
THAT'S SOMETHING MY MOTHER USED TO SAY.

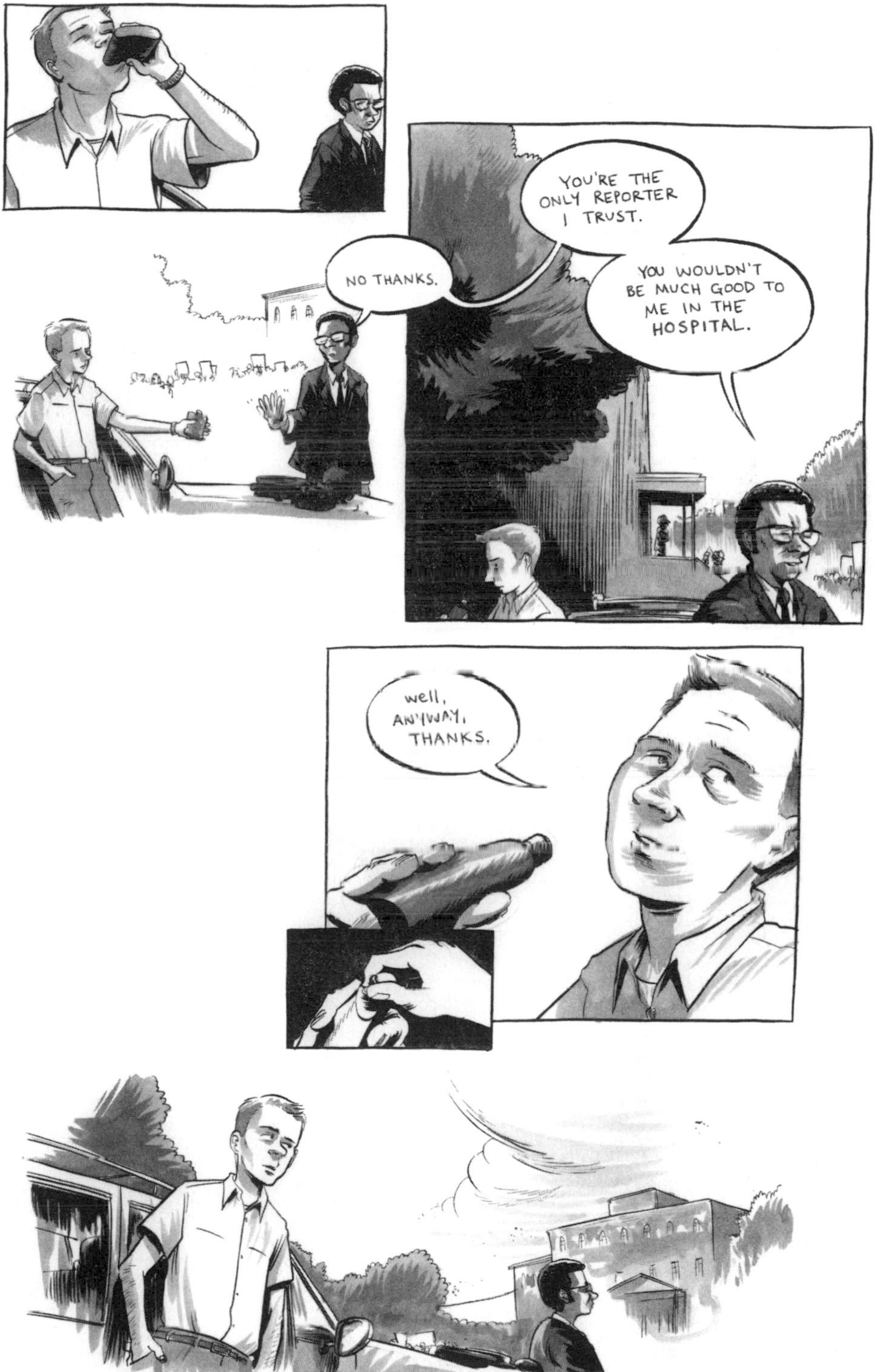
NO THANKS.
YOU'RE THE ONLY REPORTER I TRUST.
YOU WOULDN'T BE MUCH GOOD TO ME IN THE HOSPITAL.
well, ANYWAY, THANKS.

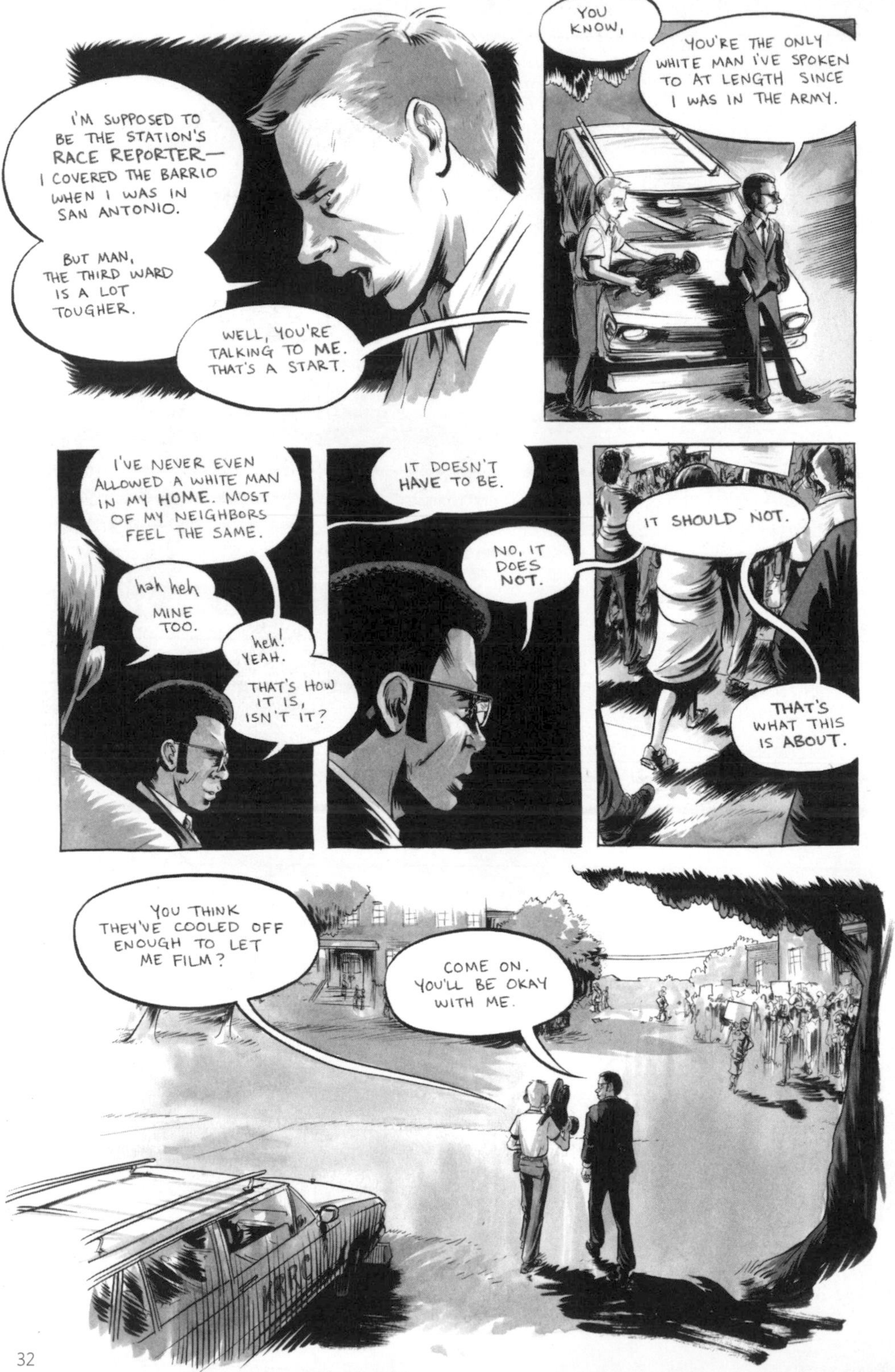
I'M SUPPOSED TO BE THE STATION'S RACE REPORTER— I COVERED THE BARRIO WHEN I WAS IN SAN ANTONIO.
BUT MAN, THE THIRD WARD IS A LOT TOUGHER.
WELL, YOU'RE TALKING TO ME. THAT'S A START.
YOU KNOW,
YOU'RE THE ONLY WHITE MAN I'VE SPOKEN TO AT LENGTH SINCE I WAS IN THE ARMY.
I'VE NEVER EVEN ALLOWED A WHITE MAN IN MY HOME. MOST OF MY NEIGHBORS FEEL THE SAME.
hah heh
MINE TOO.
heh! YEAH.
THAT'S HOW IT IS, ISN'T IT?
IT DOESN'T HAVE TO BE.
NO, IT DOES NOT.
IT SHOULD NOT.
THAT'S WHAT THIS IS ABOUT.
YOU THINK THEY'VE COOLED OFF ENOUGH TO LET ME FILM?
COME ON. YOU'LL BE OKAY WITH ME.
KRRC

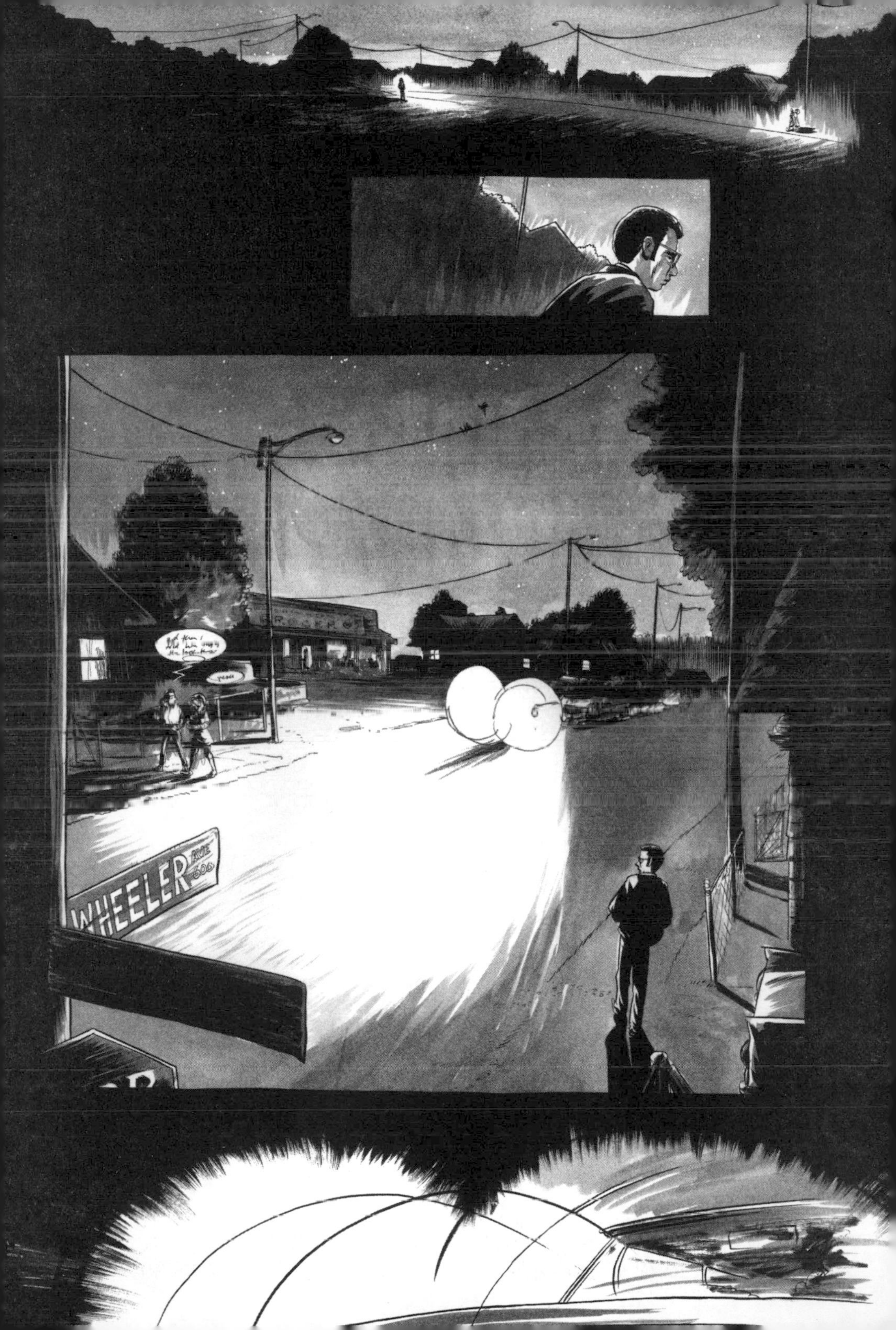

WHEELER AVE 606

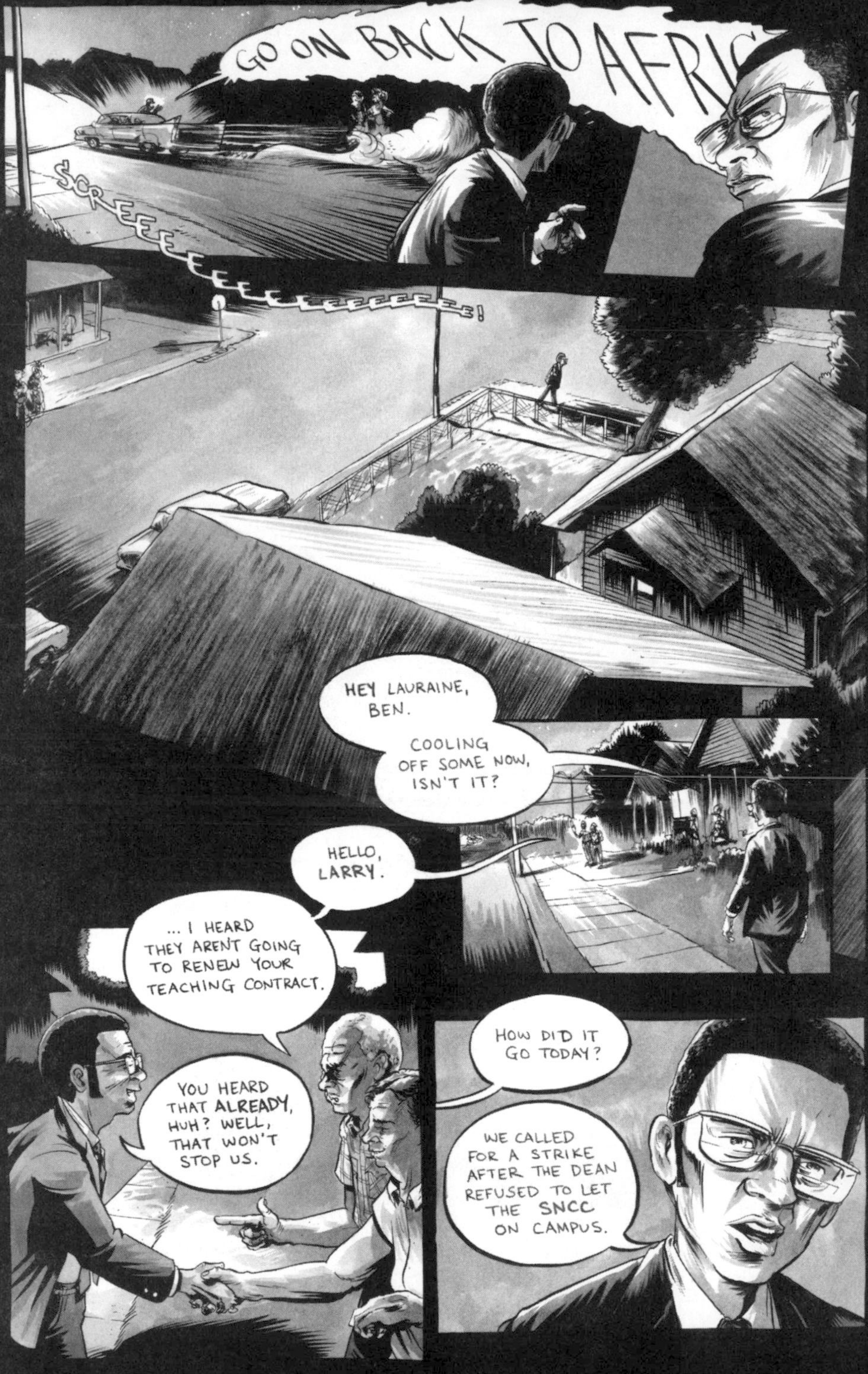
GO ON BACK TO AFRIC
SCREEEEEEEEEEEEEEEEEE!
HEY LAURAINE, BEN.
COOLING OFF SOME NOW, ISN'T IT?
HELLO, LARRY.
... I HEARD THEY AREN'T GOING TO RENEW YOUR TEACHING CONTRACT.
YOU HEARD THAT ALREADY, HUH? WELL, THAT WON'T STOP US.
HOW DID IT GO TODAY?
WE CALLED FOR A STRIKE AFTER THE DEAN REFUSED TO LET THE SNCC ON CAMPUS.

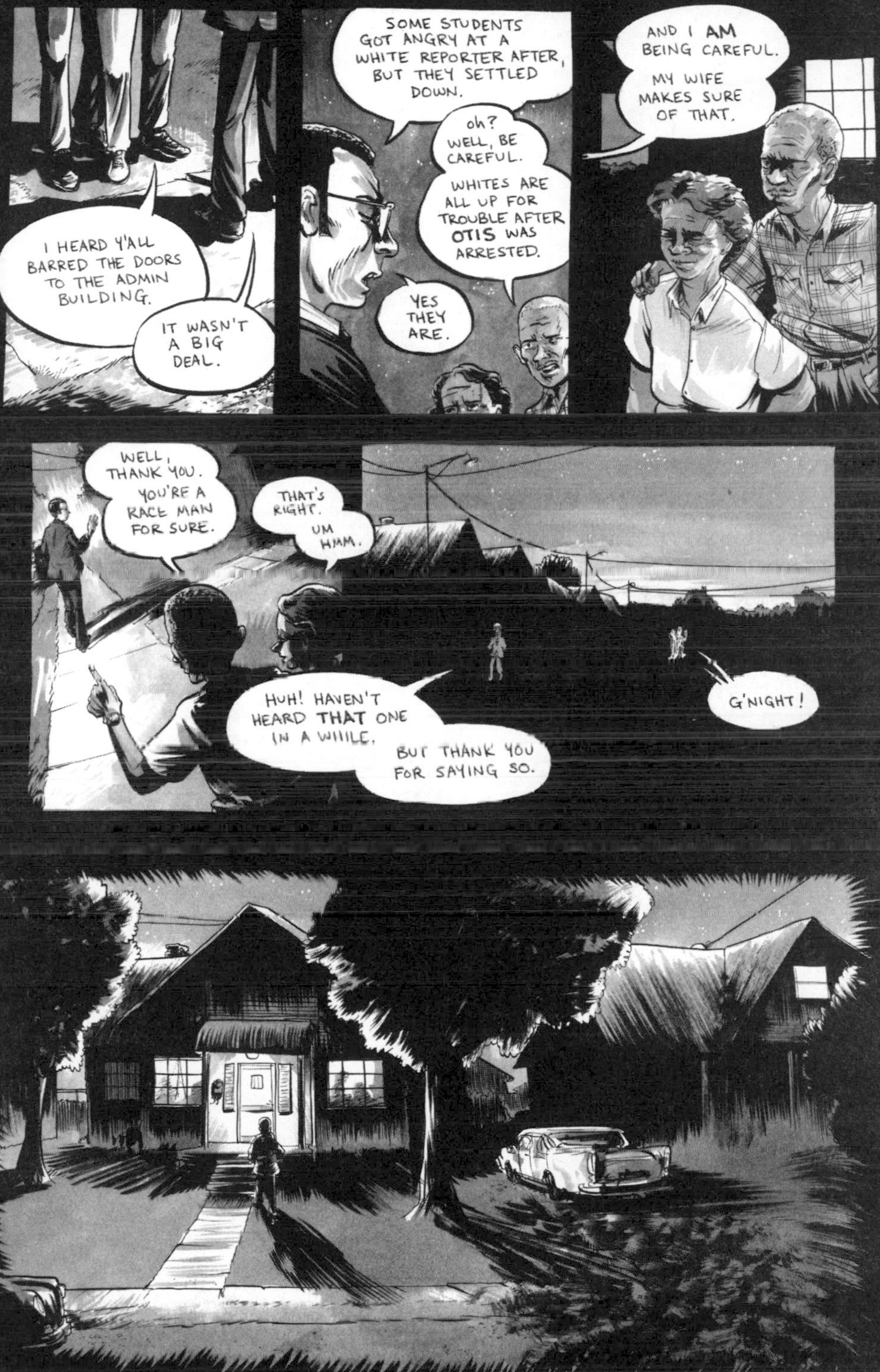
I HEARD Y'ALL BARRED THE DOORS TO THE ADMIN BUILDING.
IT WASN'T A BIG DEAL.
SOME STUDENTS GOT ANGRY AT A WHITE REPORTER AFTER, BUT THEY SETTLED DOWN.
oh? WELL, BE CAREFUL.
WHITES ARE ALL UP FOR TROUBLE AFTER OTIS WAS ARRESTED.
YES THEY ARE.
AND I AM BEING CAREFUL.
MY WIFE MAKES SURE OF THAT.
WELL, THANK YOU.
YOU'RE A RACE MAN FOR SURE.
THAT'S RIGHT.
UM HMM.
HUH! HAVEN'T HEARD THAT ONE IN A WHILE.
BUT THANK YOU FOR SAYING SO.
G'NIGHT!

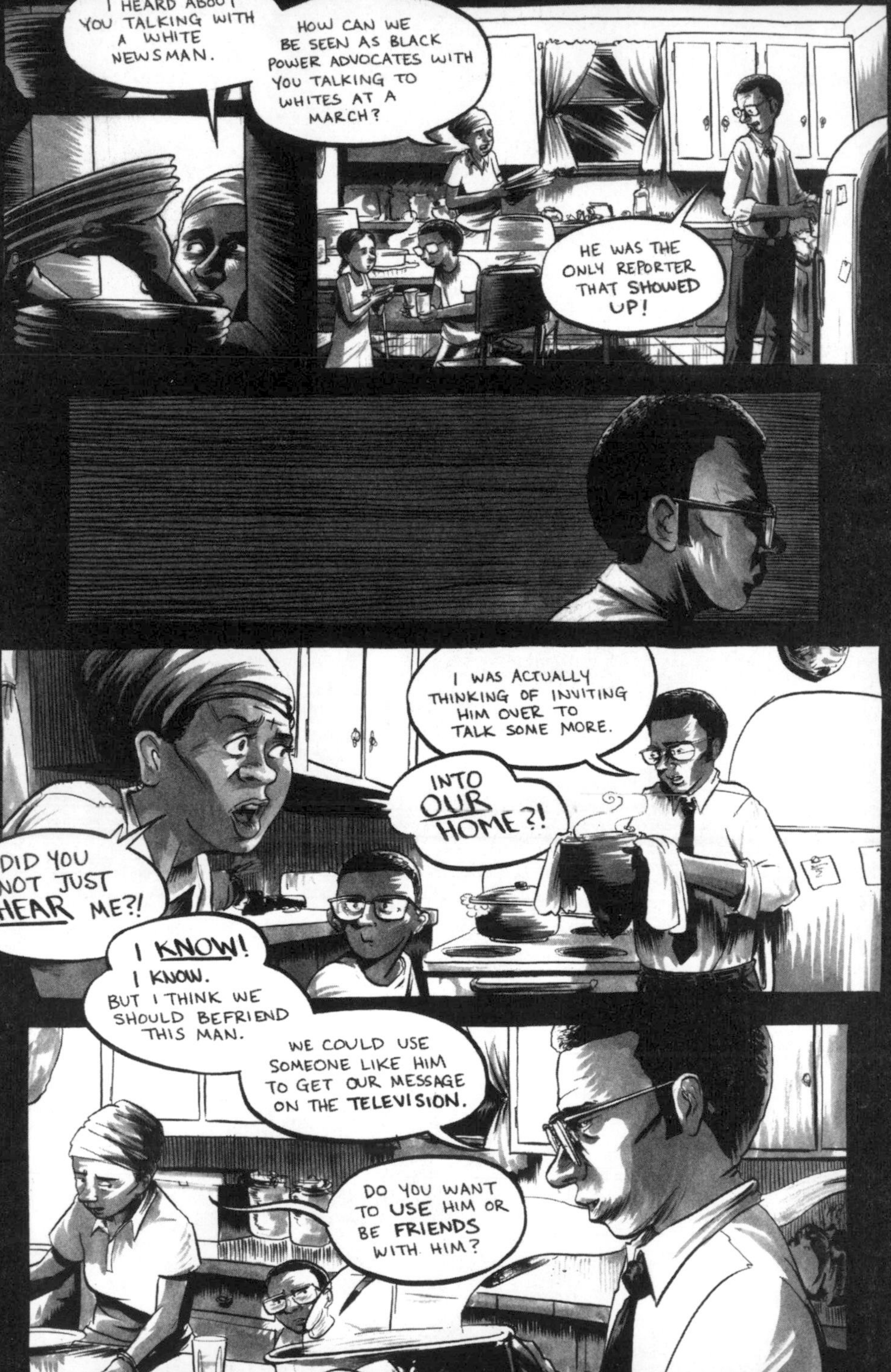
I HEARD ABOUT YOU TALKING WITH A WHITE NEWSMAN.
HOW CAN WE BE SEEN AS BLACK POWER ADVOCATES WITH YOU TALKING TO WHITES AT A MARCH?
HE WAS THE ONLY REPORTER THAT SHOWED UP!
I WAS ACTUALLY THINKING OF INVITING HIM OVER TO TALK SOME MORE.
INTO OUR HOME?!
DID YOU NOT JUST HEAR ME?!
I KNOW! I KNOW. BUT I THINK WE SHOULD BEFRIEND THIS MAN.
WE COULD USE SOMEONE LIKE HIM TO GET OUR MESSAGE ON THE TELEVISION.
DO YOU WANT TO USE HIM OR BE FRIENDS WITH HIM?

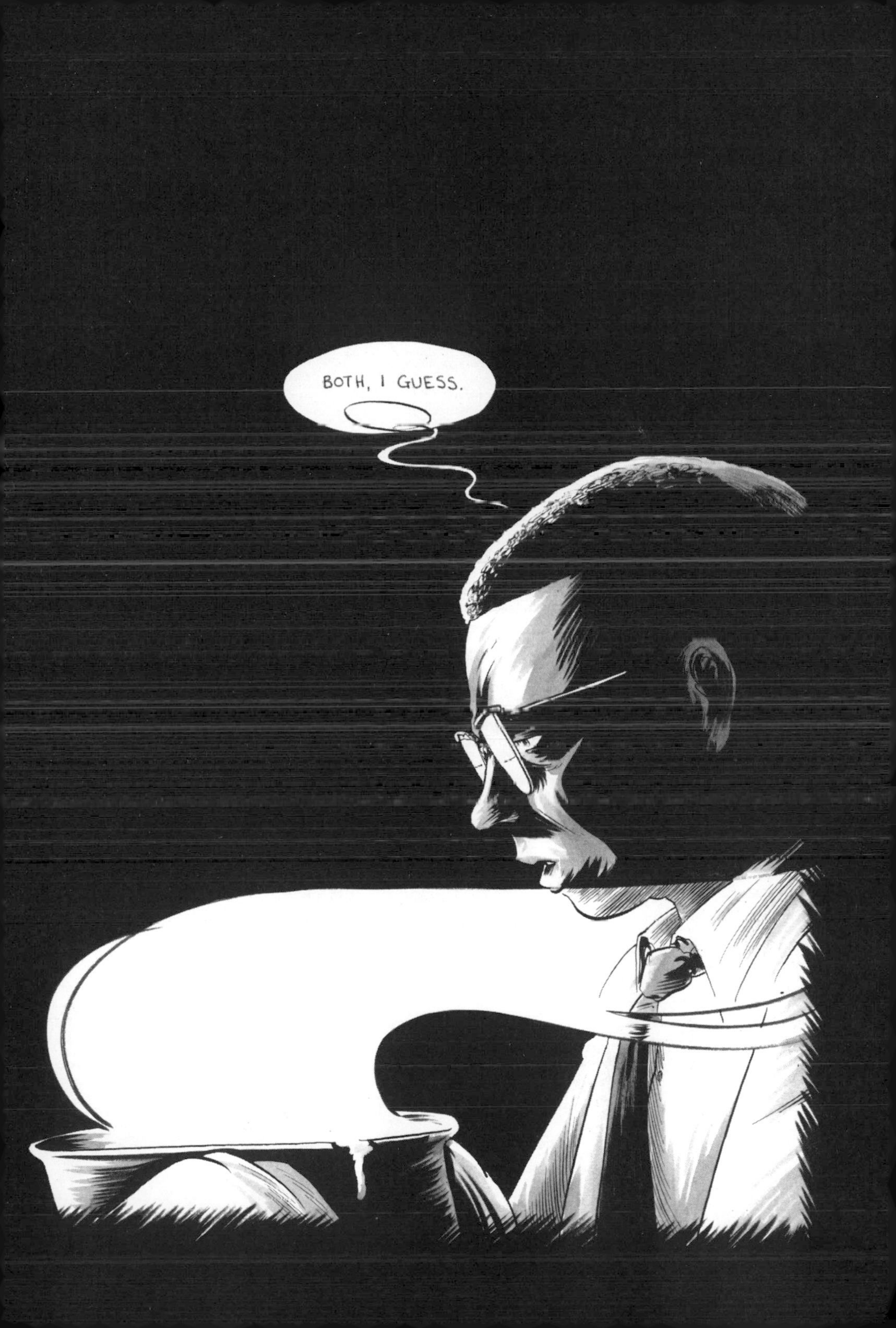
BOTH, I GUESS.

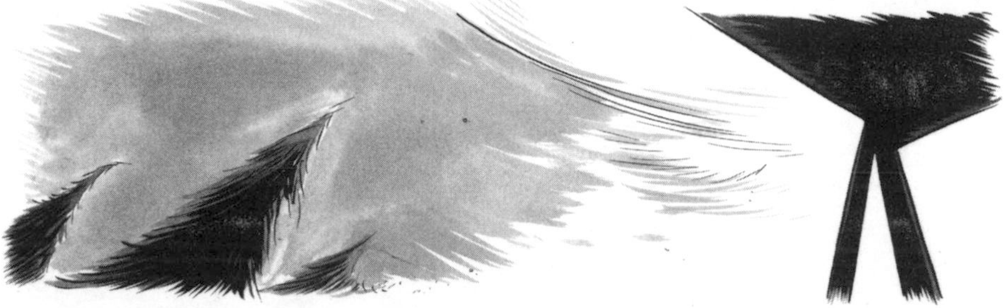

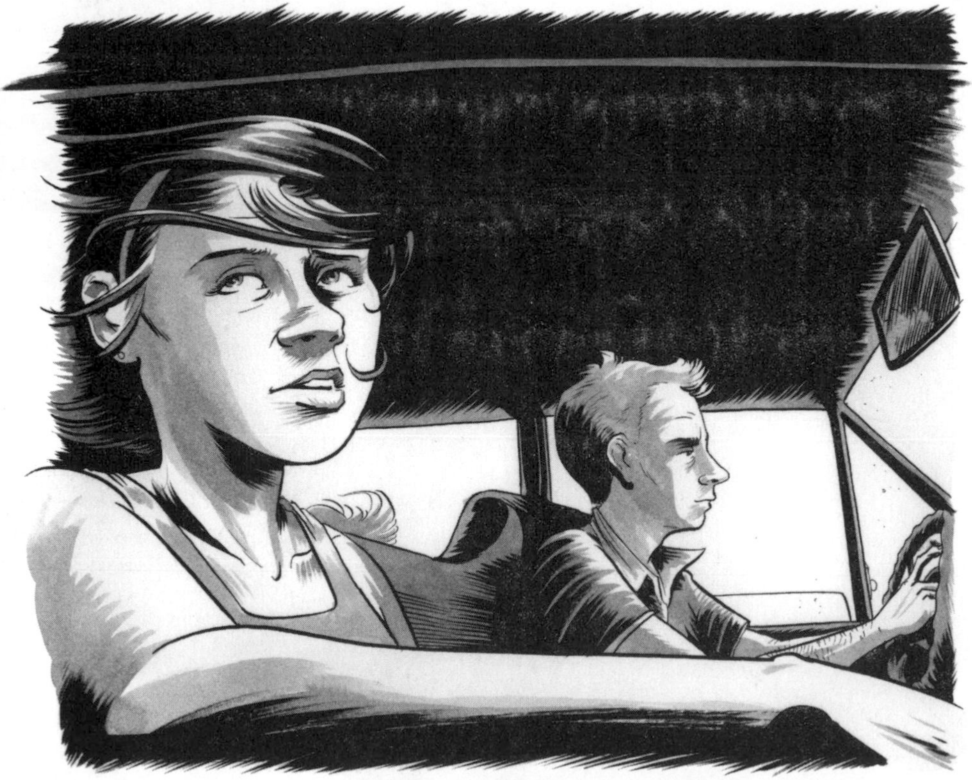

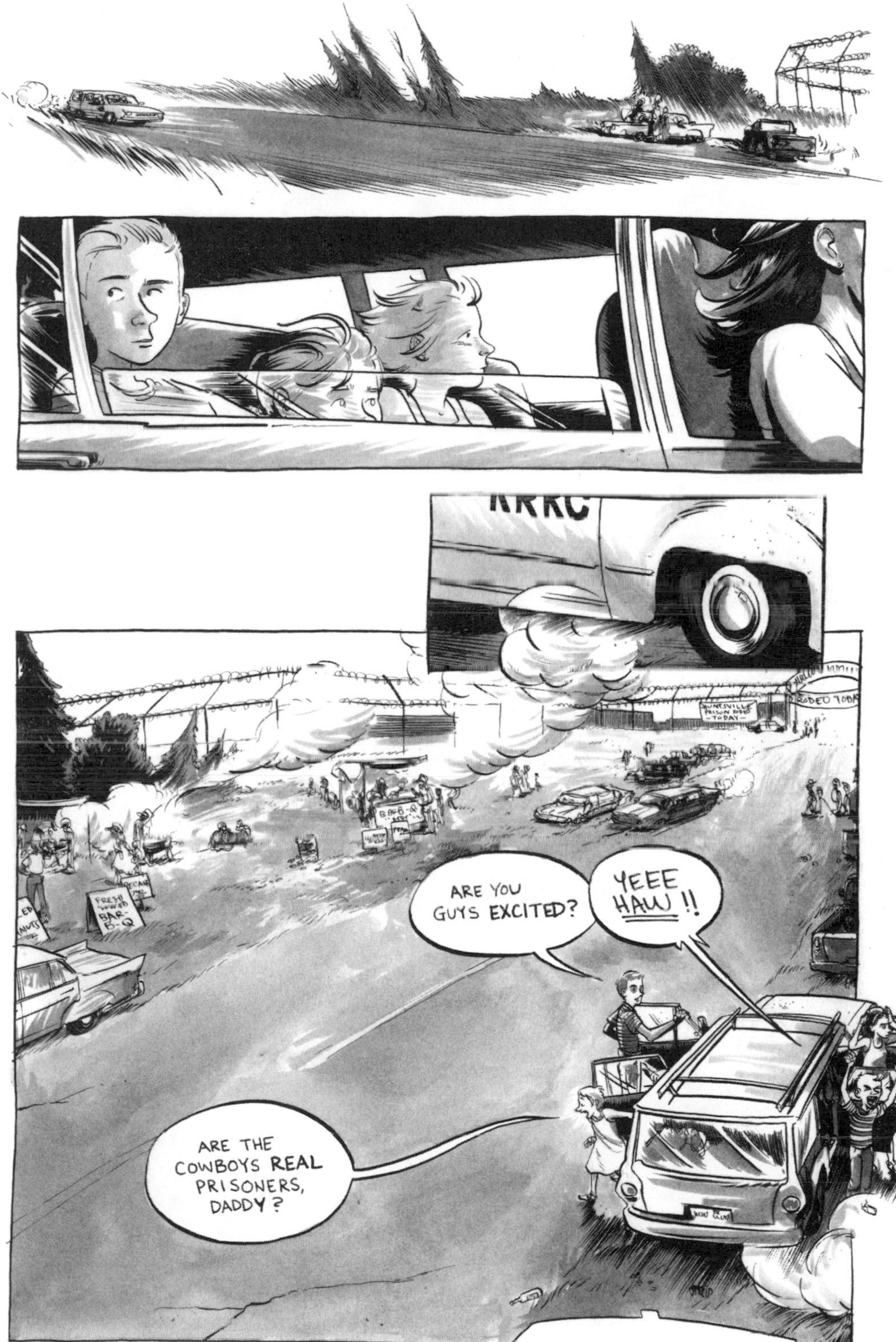

HUNTSVILLE PRISON RODEO -TODAY-
RODEO TODA
BAR-B-Q
BAR-B-Q
ARE YOU GUYS EXCITED?
YEEE HAW !!
ARE THE COWBOYS REAL PRISONERS, DADDY?

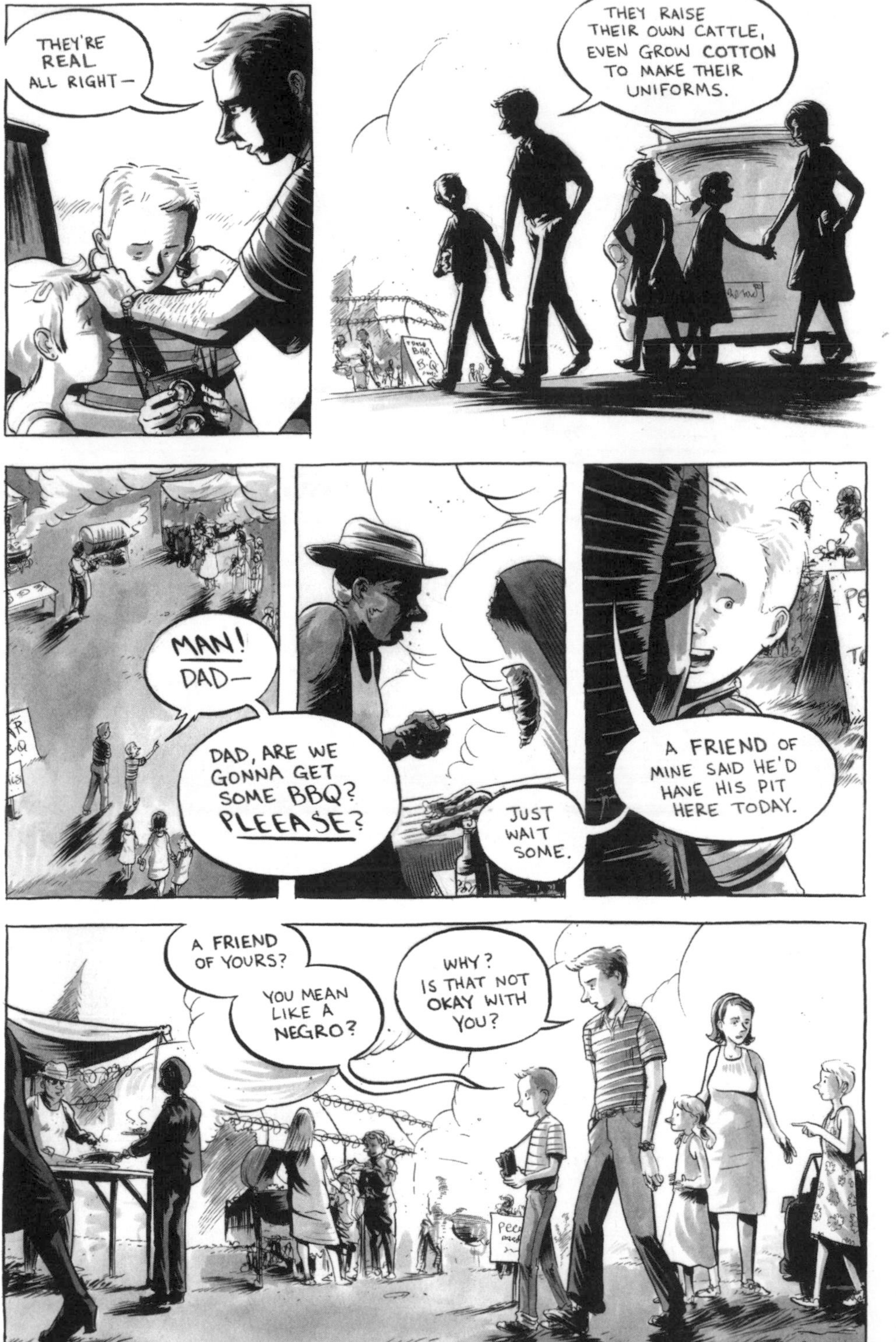
THEY'RE REAL ALL RIGHT—
THEY RAISE THEIR OWN CATTLE, EVEN GROW COTTON TO MAKE THEIR UNIFORMS.
MAN! DAD—
DAD, ARE WE GONNA GET SOME BBQ? PLEEASE?
JUST WAIT SOME.
A FRIEND OF MINE SAID HE'D HAVE HIS PIT HERE TODAY.
A FRIEND OF YOURS?
YOU MEAN LIKE A NEGRO?
WHY? IS THAT NOT OKAY WITH YOU?

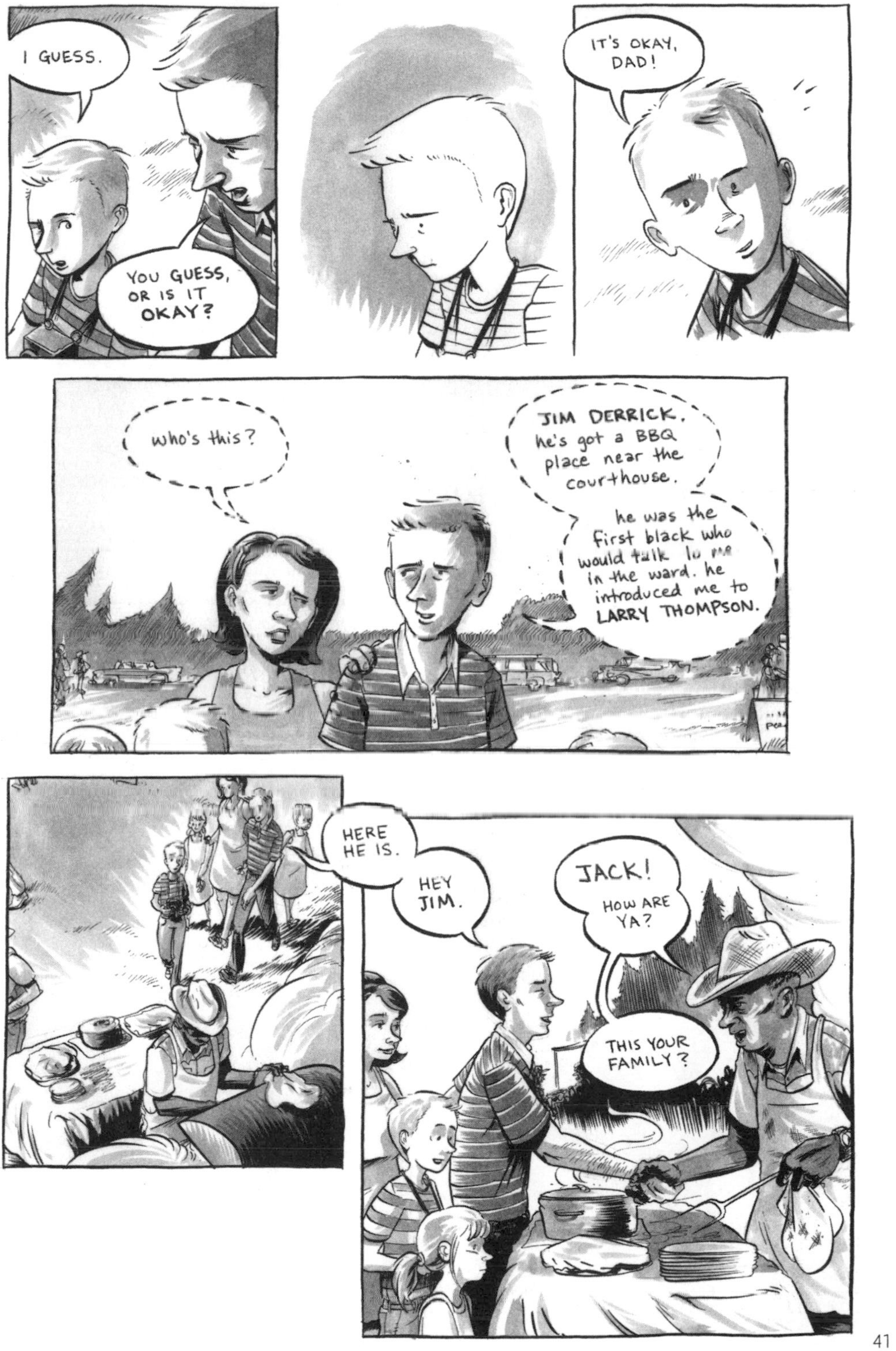
I GUESS.
YOU GUESS, OR IS IT OKAY?
IT'S OKAY, DAD!
who's this?
JIM DERRICK. he's got a BBQ place near the courthouse.
he was the first black who would talk to me in the ward. he introduced me to LARRY THOMPSON.
HERE HE IS.
HEY JIM.
JACK! HOW ARE YA?
THIS YOUR FAMILY?

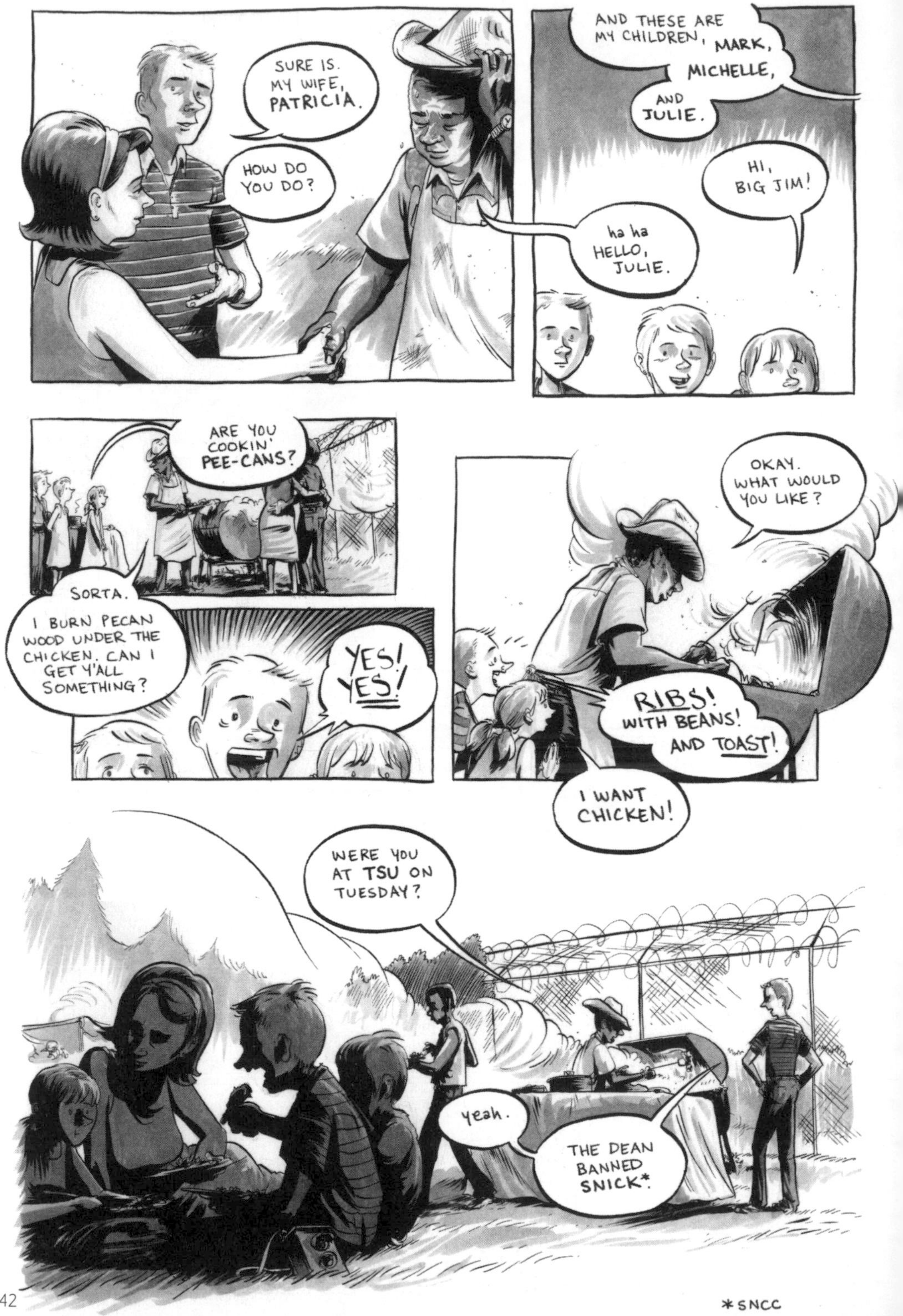
SURE IS. MY WIFE, PATRICIA.
HOW DO YOU DO?
AND THESE ARE MY CHILDREN, MARK,
MICHELLE,
AND JULIE.
HI, BIG JIM!
ha ha HELLO, JULIE.
ARE YOU COOKIN' PEE-CANS?
SORTA.
I BURN PECAN WOOD UNDER THE CHICKEN. CAN I GET Y'ALL SOMETHING?
YES! YES!
OKAY. WHAT WOULD YOU LIKE?
RIBS! WITH BEANS! AND TOAST!
I WANT CHICKEN!
WERE YOU AT TSU ON TUESDAY?
yeah.
THE DEAN BANNED SNICK*.

*SNCC

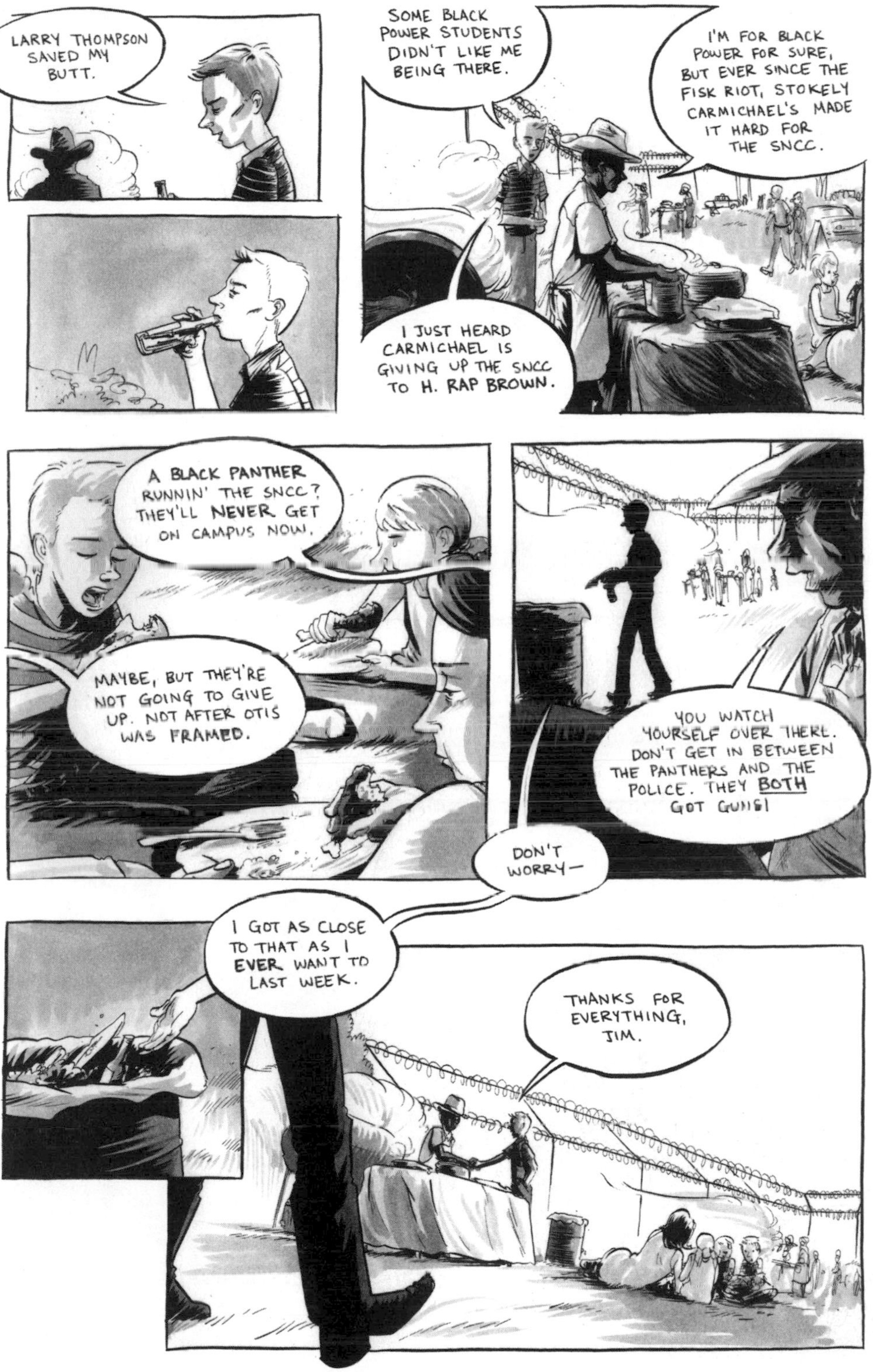
LARRY THOMPSON SAVED MY BUTT.
SOME BLACK POWER STUDENTS DIDN'T LIKE ME BEING THERE.
I'M FOR BLACK POWER FOR SURE, BUT EVER SINCE THE FISK RIOT, STOKELY CARMICHAEL'S MADE IT HARD FOR THE SNCC.
I JUST HEARD CARMICHAEL IS GIVING UP THE SNCC TO H. RAP BROWN.
A BLACK PANTHER RUNNIN' THE SNCC? THEY'LL NEVER GET ON CAMPUS NOW.
MAYBE, BUT THEY'RE NOT GOING TO GIVE UP. NOT AFTER OTIS WAS FRAMED.
YOU WATCH YOURSELF OVER THERE. DON'T GET IN BETWEEN THE PANTHERS AND THE POLICE. THEY BOTH GOT GUNS!
DON'T WORRY—
I GOT AS CLOSE TO THAT AS I EVER WANT TO LAST WEEK.
THANKS FOR EVERYTHING, JIM.

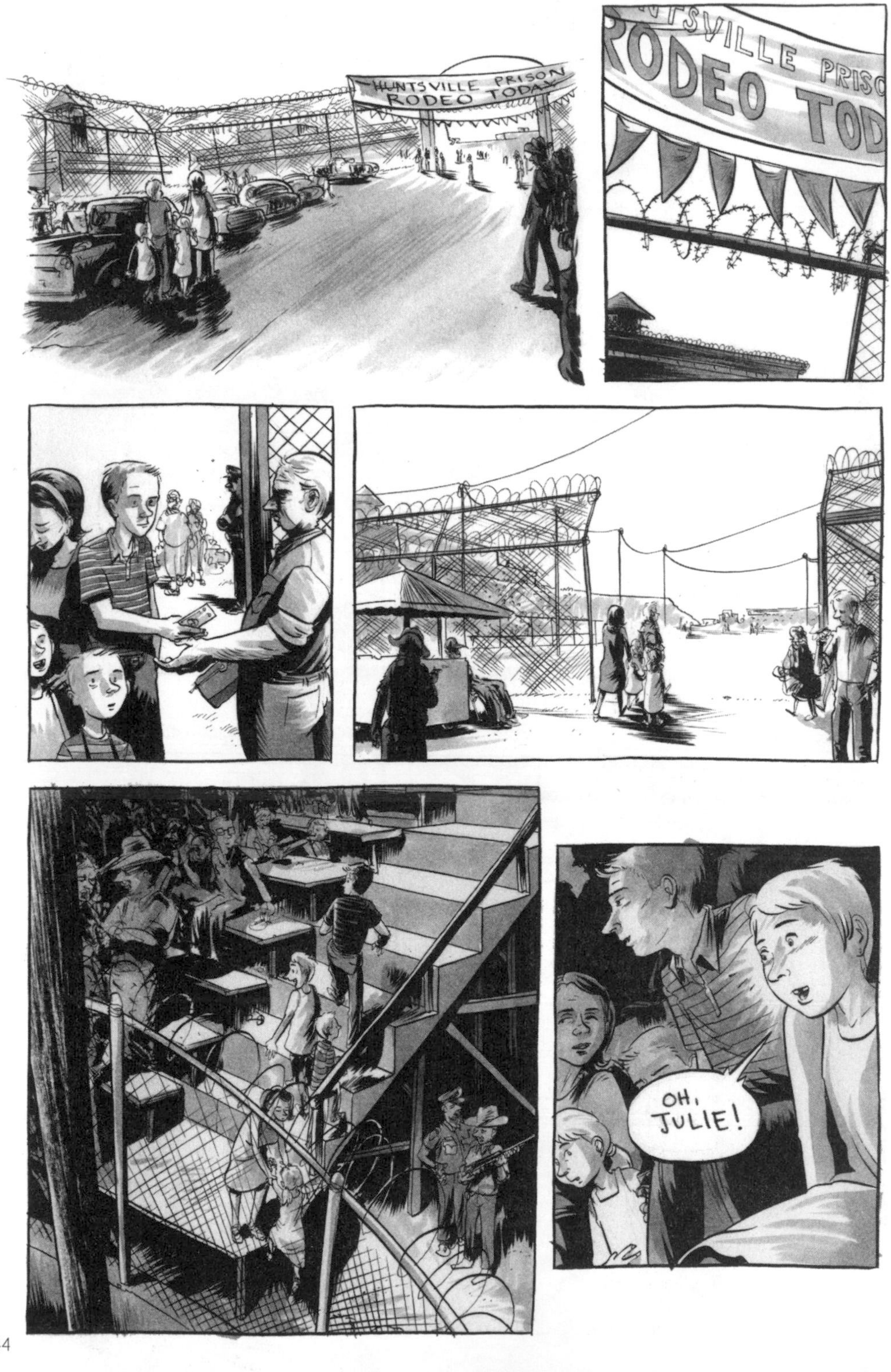
HUNTSVILLE PRISON
RODEO TODAY
OH, JULIE!

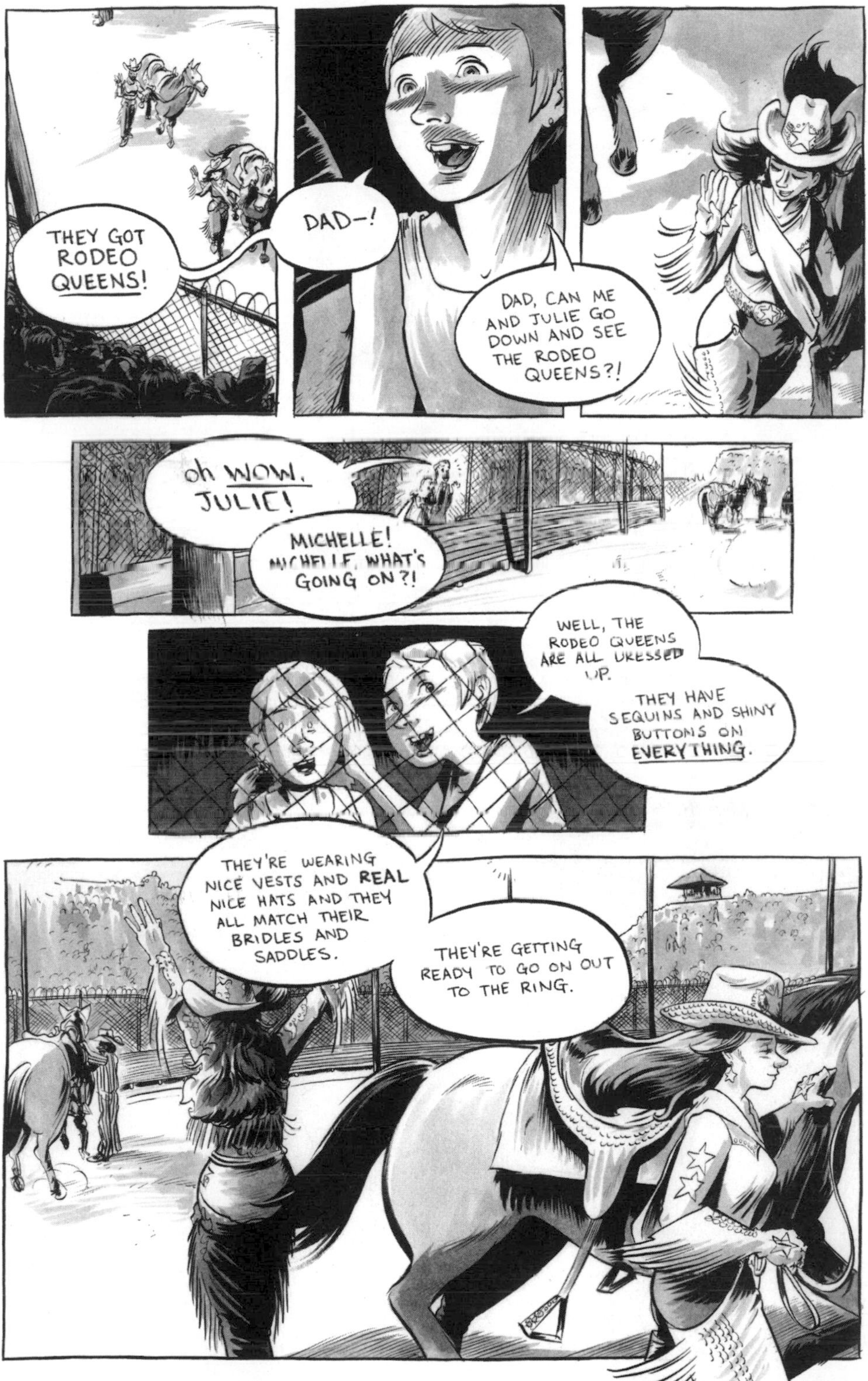
THEY GOT RODEO QUEENS!
DAD—!
DAD, CAN ME AND JULIE GO DOWN AND SEE THE RODEO QUEENS?!
oh WOW. JULIE!
MICHELLE! MICHELLE, WHAT'S GOING ON?!
WELL, THE RODEO QUEENS ARE ALL DRESSED UP.
THEY HAVE SEQUINS AND SHINY BUTTONS ON EVERYTHING.
THEY'RE WEARING NICE VESTS AND REAL NICE HATS AND THEY ALL MATCH THEIR BRIDLES AND SADDLES.
THEY'RE GETTING READY TO GO ON OUT TO THE RING.

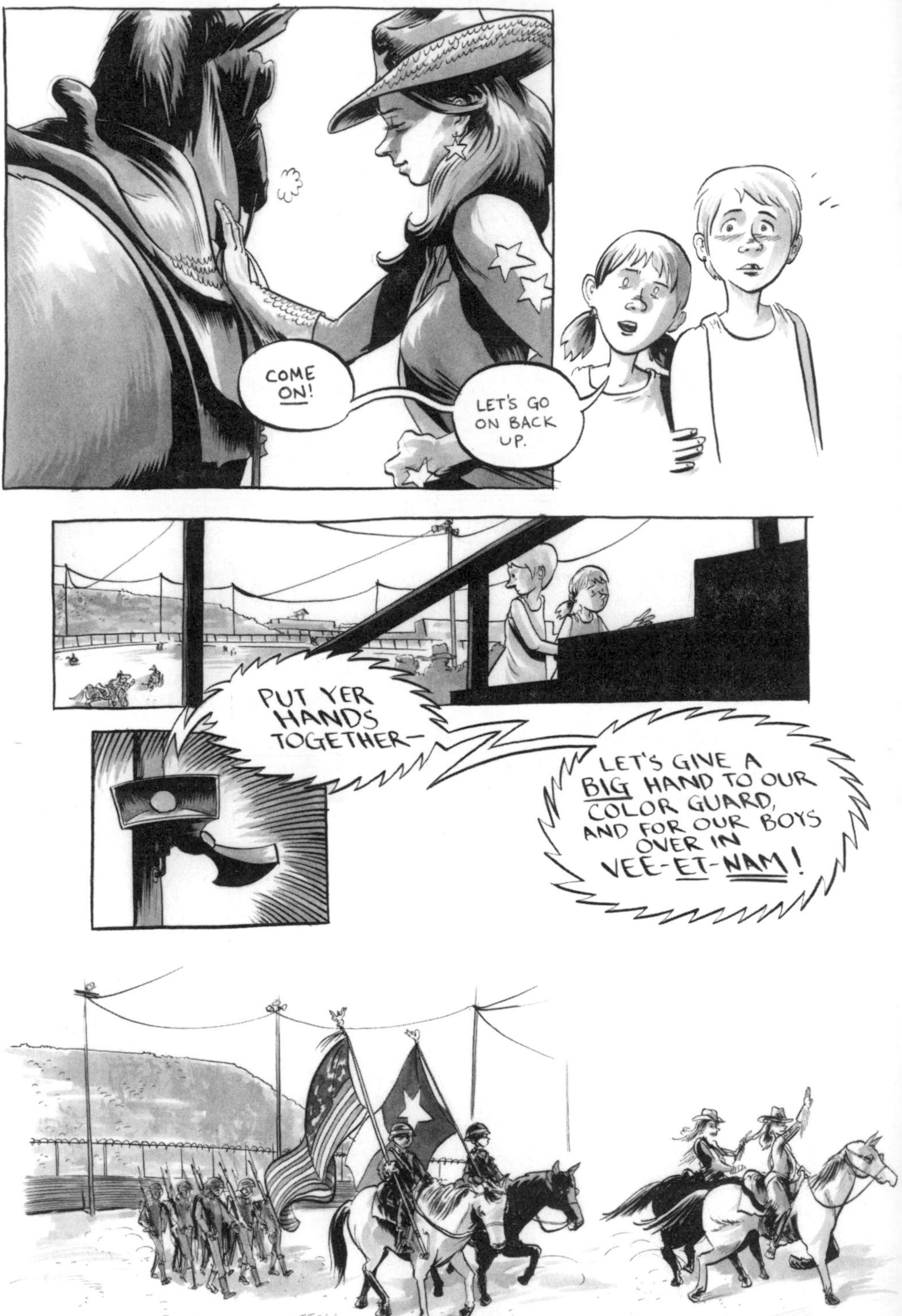
COME ON!
LET'S GO ON BACK UP.
PUT YER HANDS TOGETHER—
LET'S GIVE A BIG HAND TO OUR COLOR GUARD, AND FOR OUR BOYS OVER IN VEE-ET-NAM!

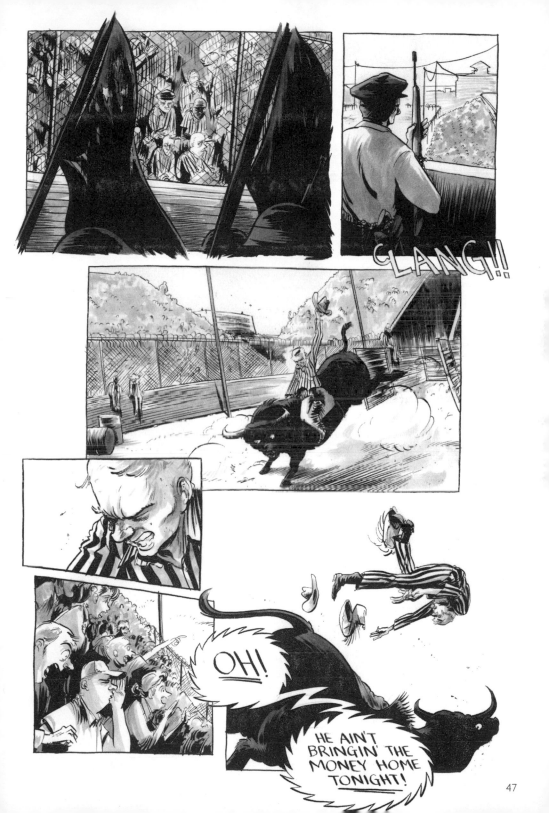

CLANG!!

OH!!

HE AIN'T BRINGIN' THE MONEY HOME TONIGHT!

47

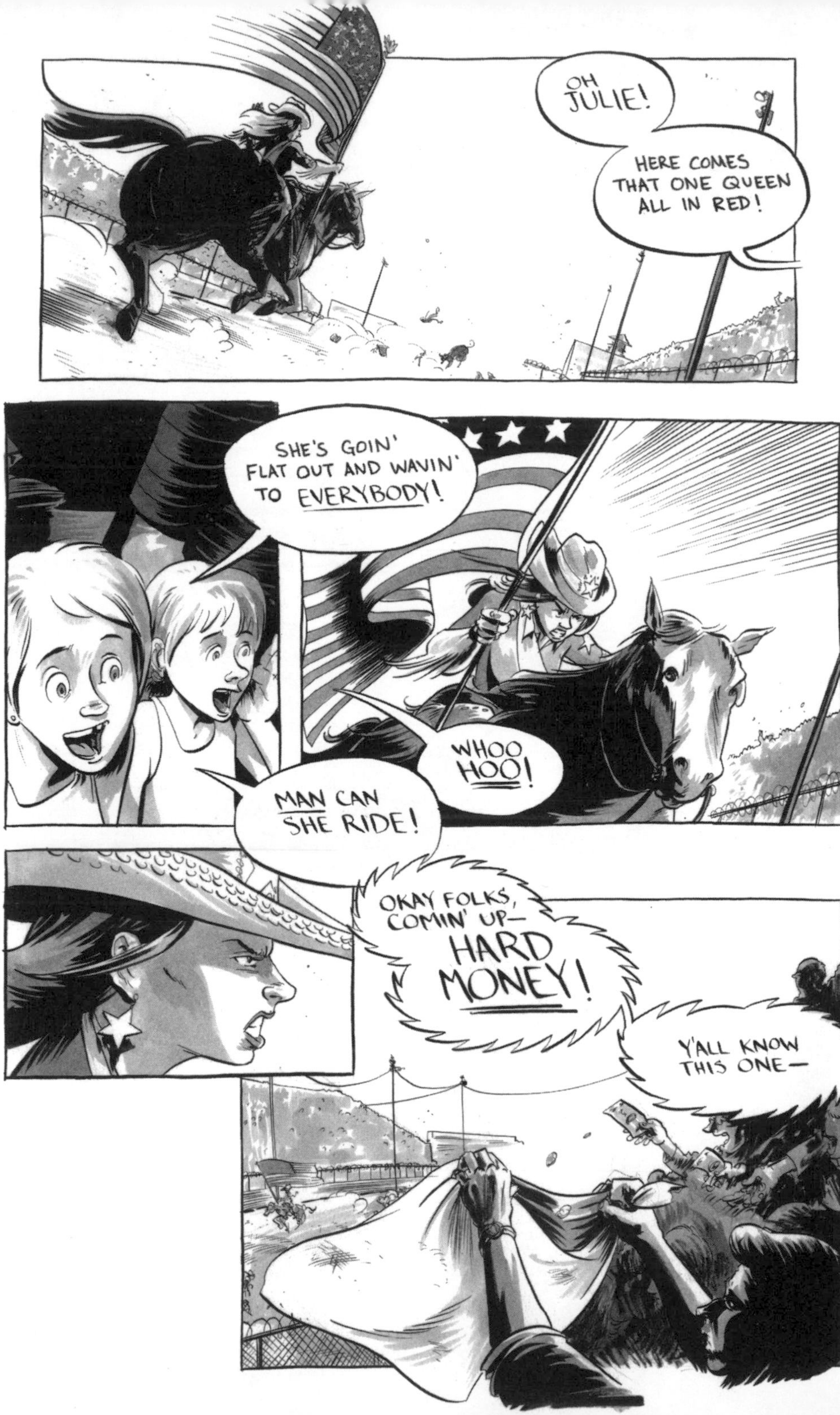
OH JULIE!
HERE COMES THAT ONE QUEEN ALL IN RED!
SHE'S GOIN' FLAT OUT AND WAVIN' TO EVERYBODY!
WHOO HOO!
MAN CAN SHE RIDE!
OKAY FOLKS, COMIN' UP— HARD MONEY!
Y'ALL KNOW THIS ONE—

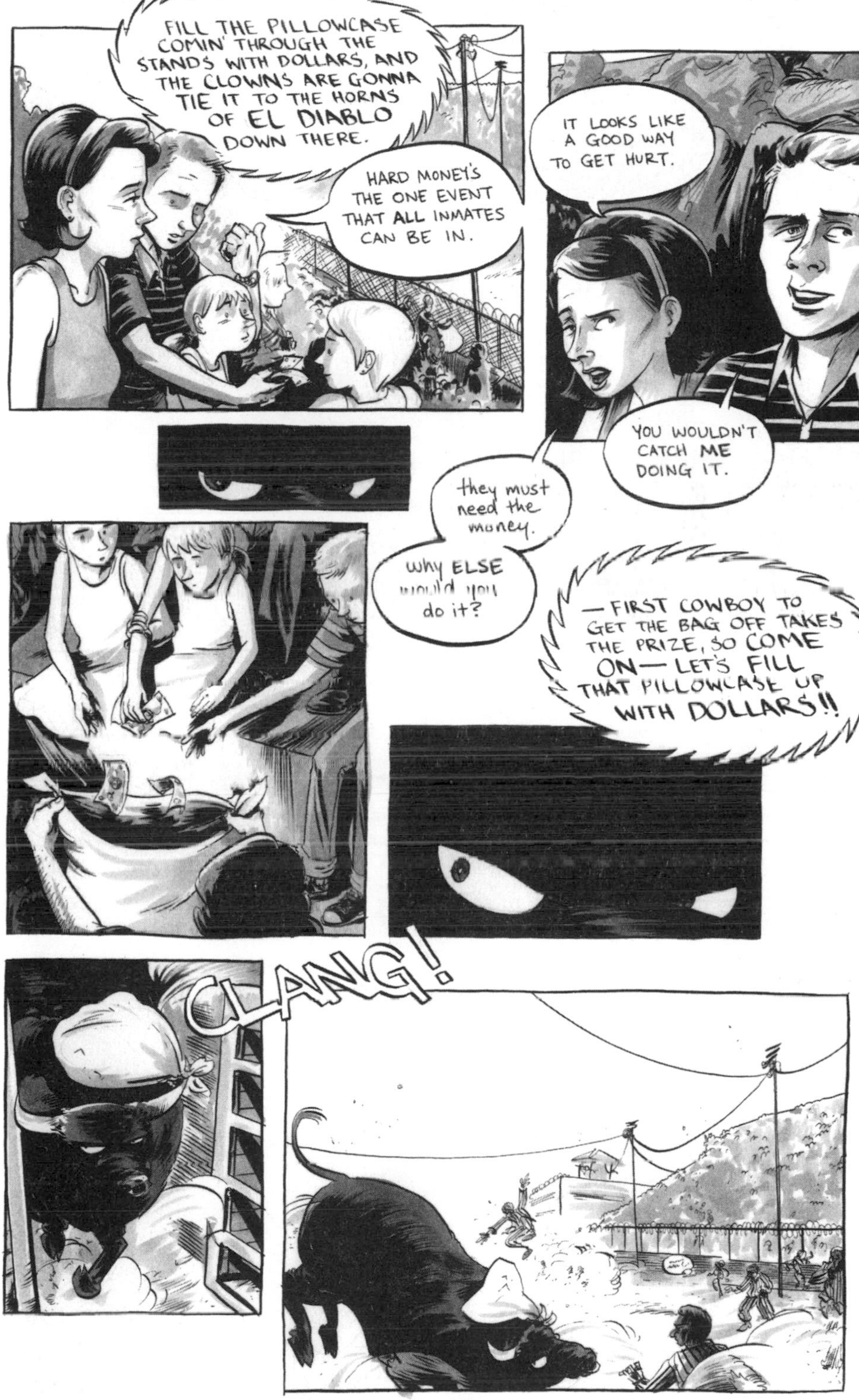
FILL THE PILLOWCASE COMIN' THROUGH THE STANDS WITH DOLLARS, AND THE CLOWNS ARE GONNA TIE IT TO THE HORNS OF EL DIABLO DOWN THERE.
HARD MONEY'S THE ONE EVENT THAT ALL INMATES CAN BE IN.
IT LOOKS LIKE A GOOD WAY TO GET HURT.
YOU WOULDN'T CATCH ME DOING IT.
they must need the money.
why ELSE would you do it?
—FIRST COWBOY TO GET THE BAG OFF TAKES THE PRIZE, SO COME ON— LET'S FILL THAT PILLOWCASE UP WITH DOLLARS!!
CLANG!

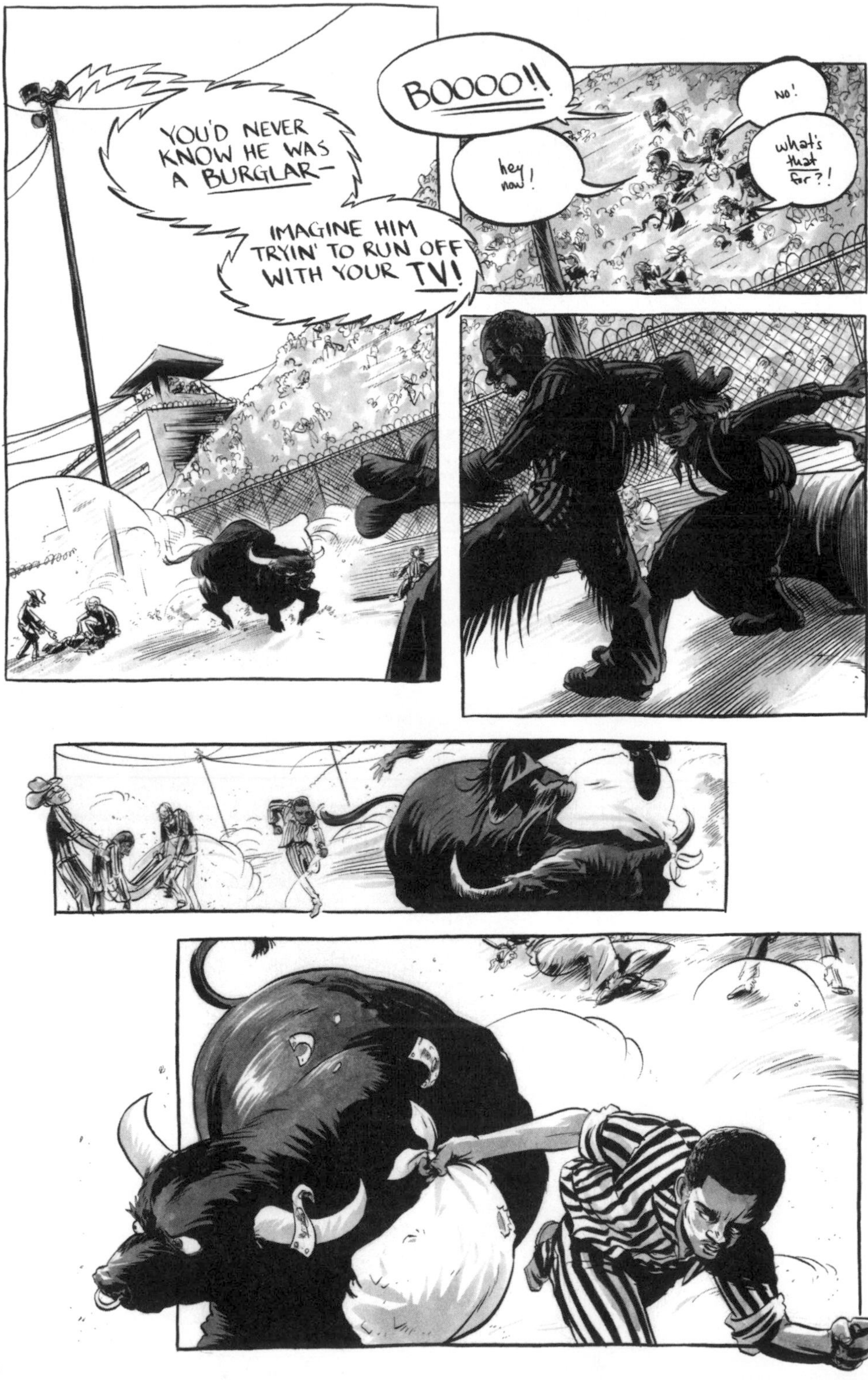
YOU'D NEVER KNOW HE WAS A BURGLAR—
IMAGINE HIM TRYIN' TO RUN OFF WITH YOUR TV!
BOOOO!!
hey now!
No!
what's that for?!

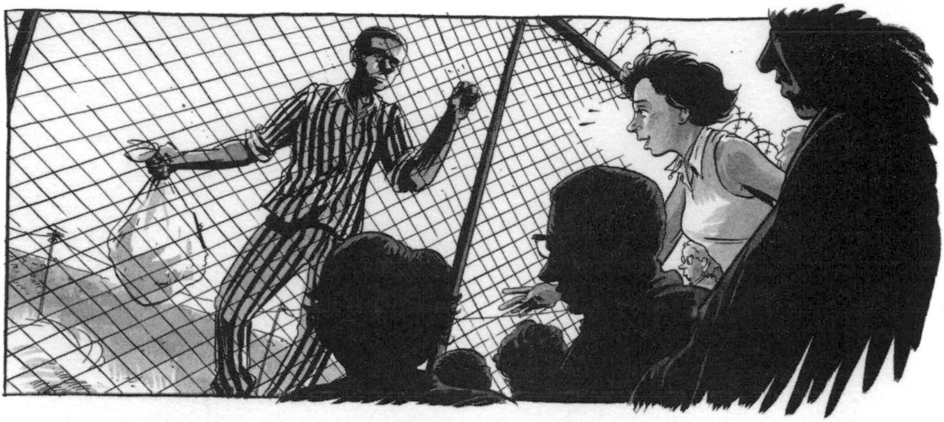

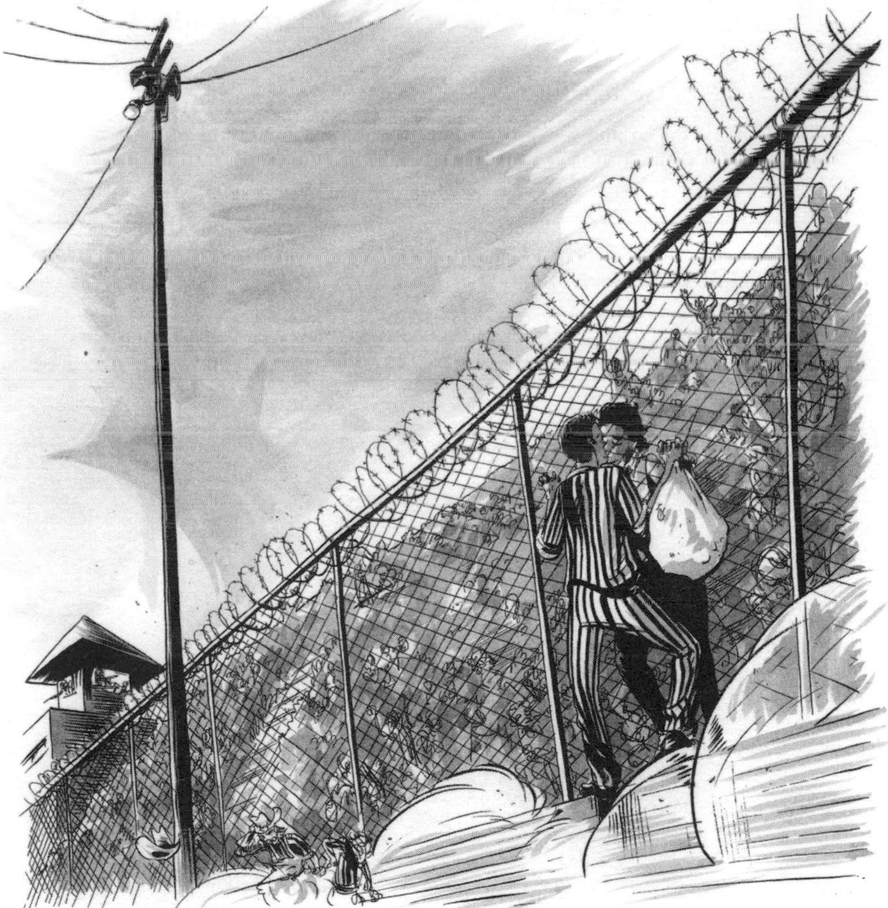

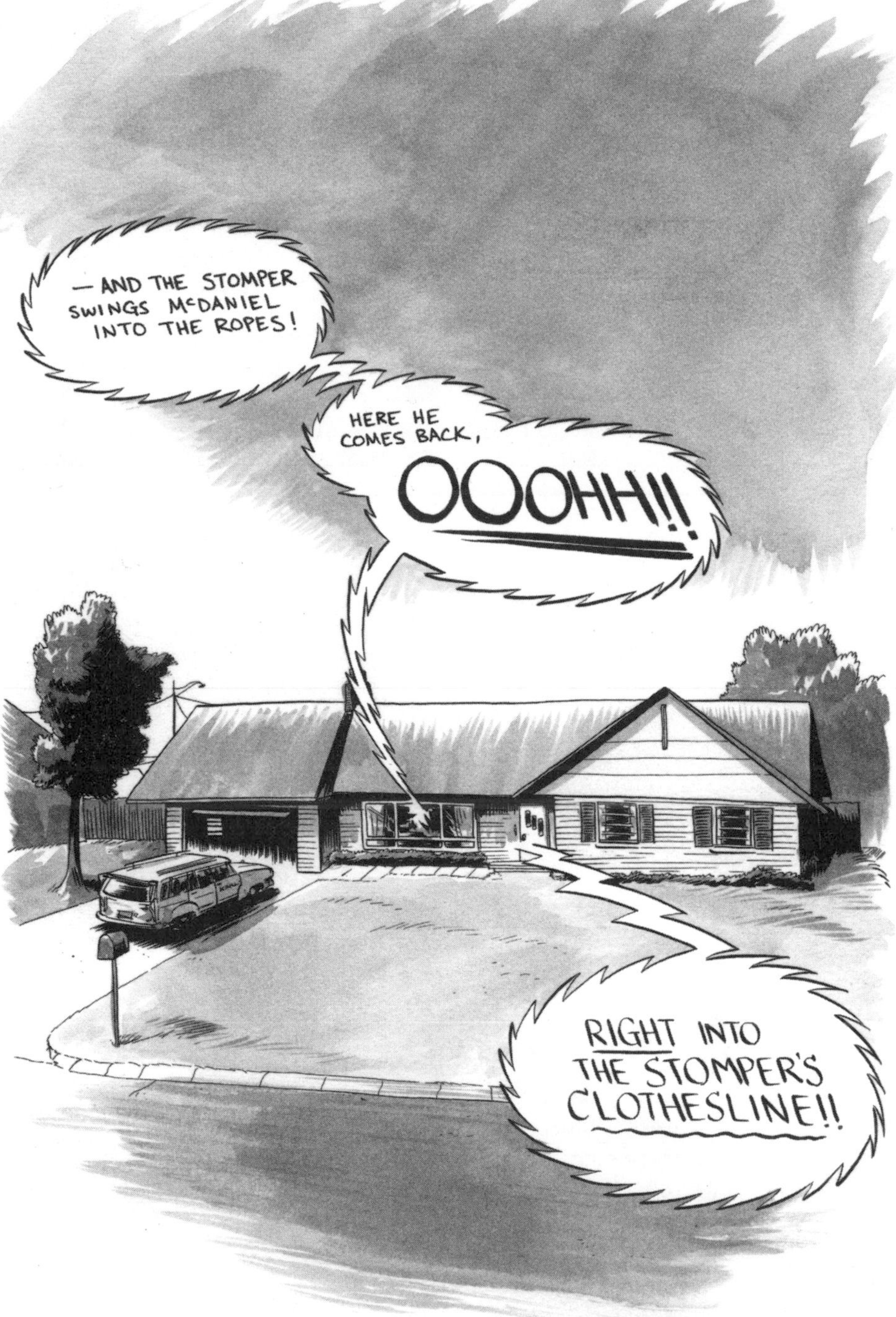
—AND THE STOMPER SWINGS McDANIEL INTO THE ROPES!
HERE HE COMES BACK, OOOHH!!
RIGHT INTO THE STOMPER'S CLOTHESLINE!!

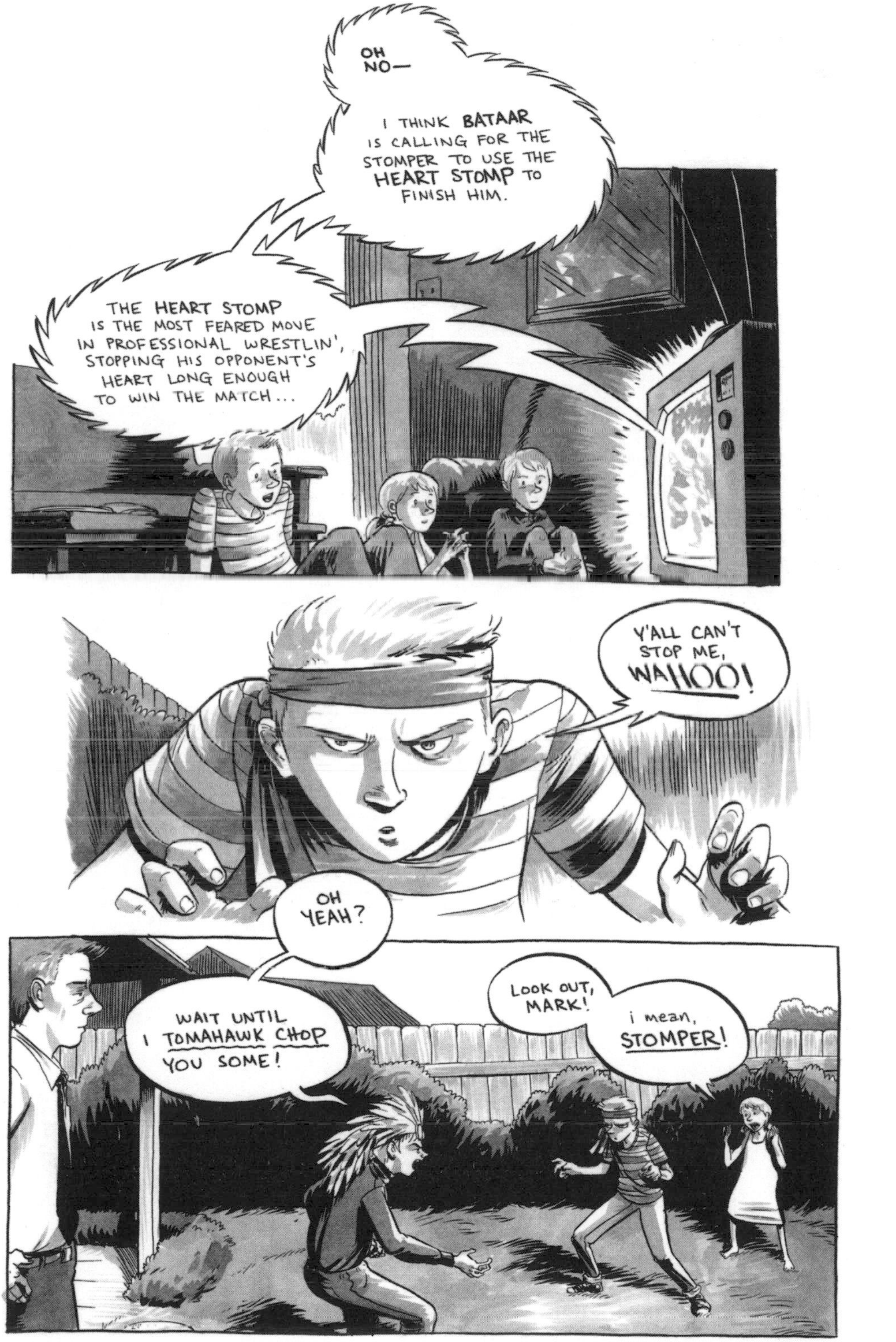
OH NO—
I THINK BATAAR IS CALLING FOR THE STOMPER TO USE THE HEART STOMP TO FINISH HIM.
THE HEART STOMP IS THE MOST FEARED MOVE IN PROFESSIONAL WRESTLIN', STOPPING HIS OPPONENT'S HEART LONG ENOUGH TO WIN THE MATCH...
Y'ALL CAN'T STOP ME, WAHOO!
OH YEAH?
WAIT UNTIL I TOMAHAWK CHOP YOU SOME!
LOOK OUT, MARK!
i mean, STOMPER!

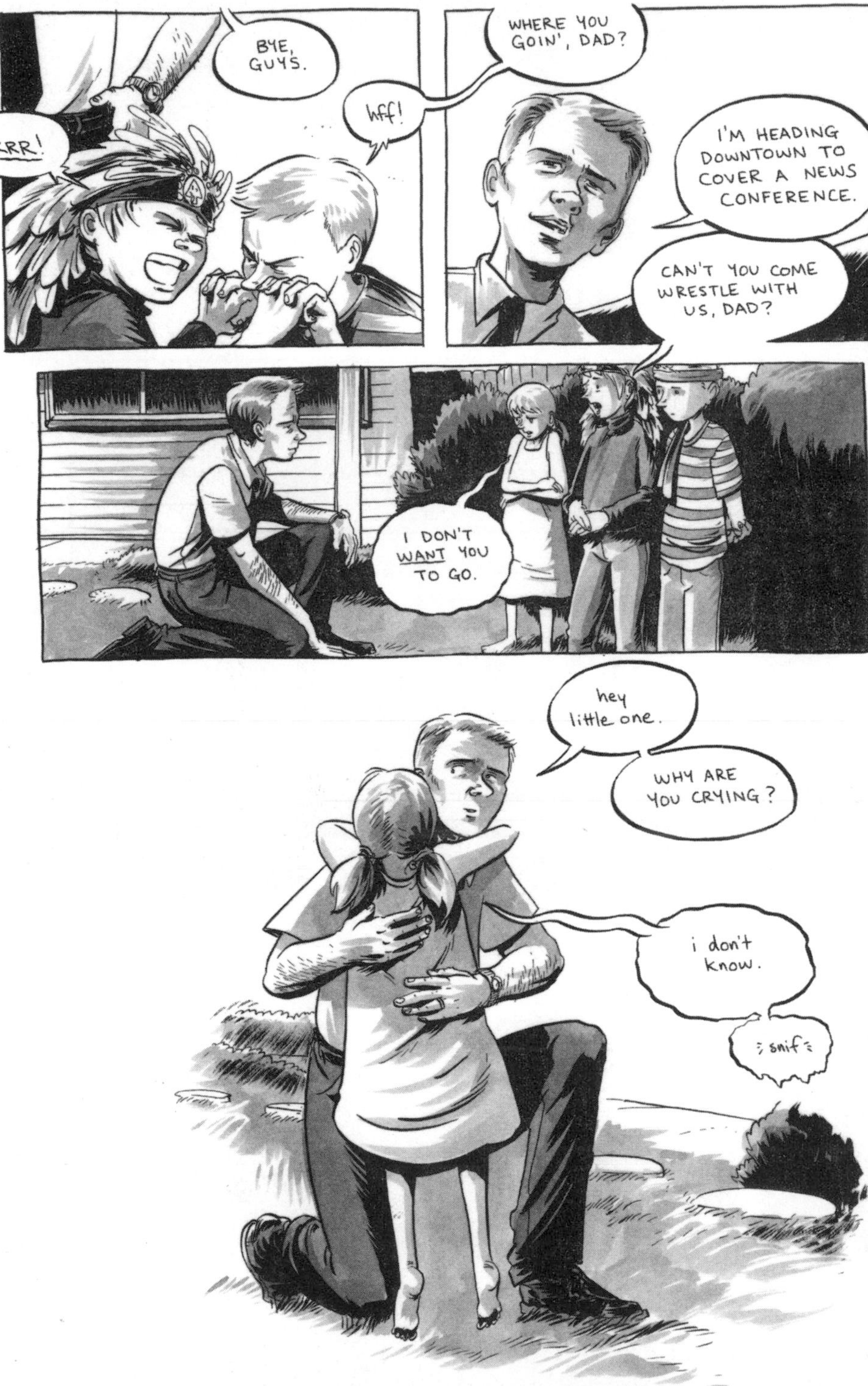
BYE, GUYS.
RRR!
hff!
WHERE YOU GOIN', DAD?
I'M HEADING DOWNTOWN TO COVER A NEWS CONFERENCE.
CAN'T YOU COME WRESTLE WITH US, DAD?
I DON'T WANT YOU TO GO.
hey little one.
WHY ARE YOU CRYING?
i don't know.
snif

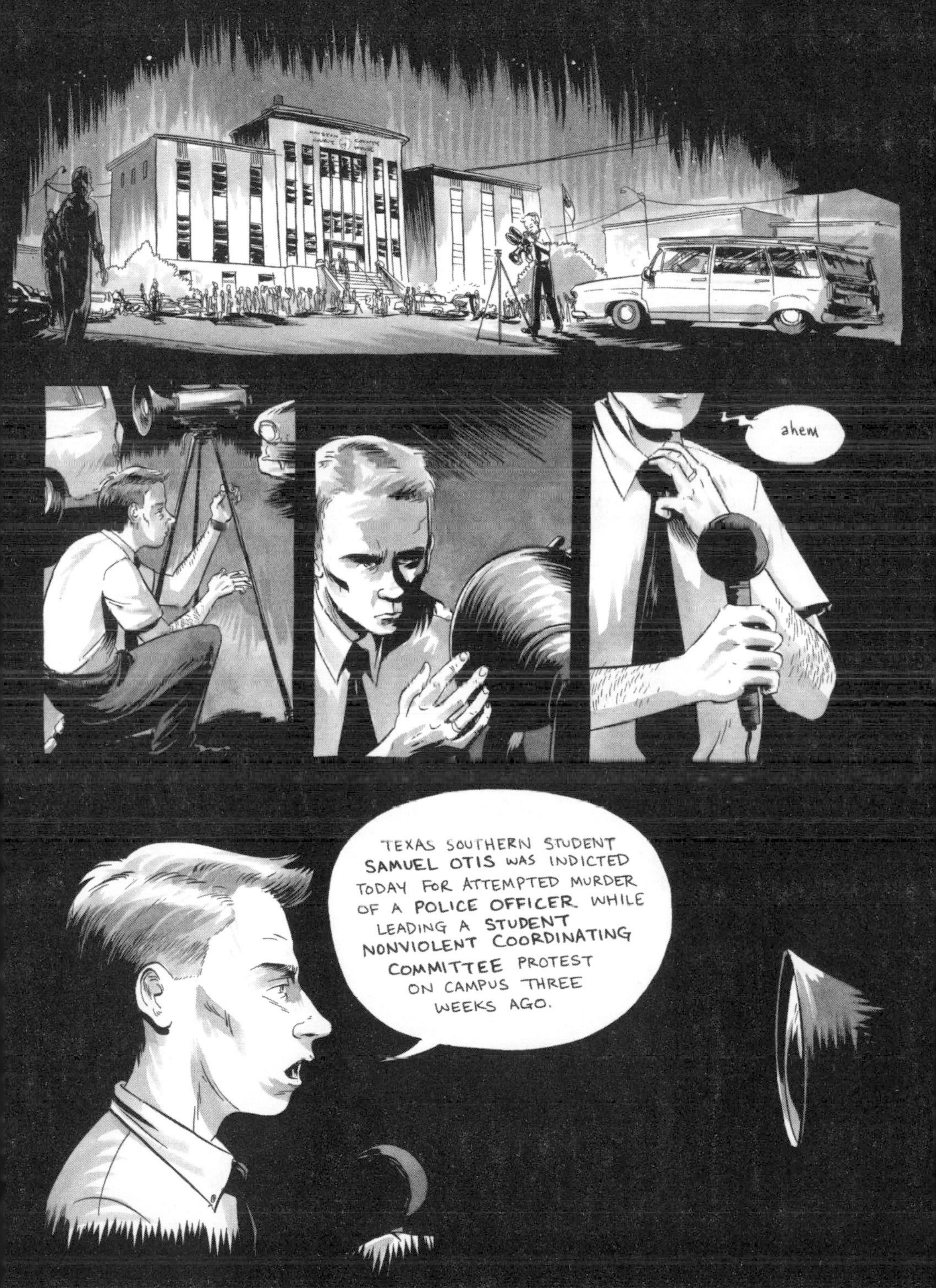
ahem
TEXAS SOUTHERN STUDENT SAMUEL OTIS WAS INDICTED TODAY FOR ATTEMPTED MURDER OF A POLICE OFFICER WHILE LEADING A STUDENT NONVIOLENT COORDINATING COMMITTEE PROTEST ON CAMPUS THREE WEEKS AGO.

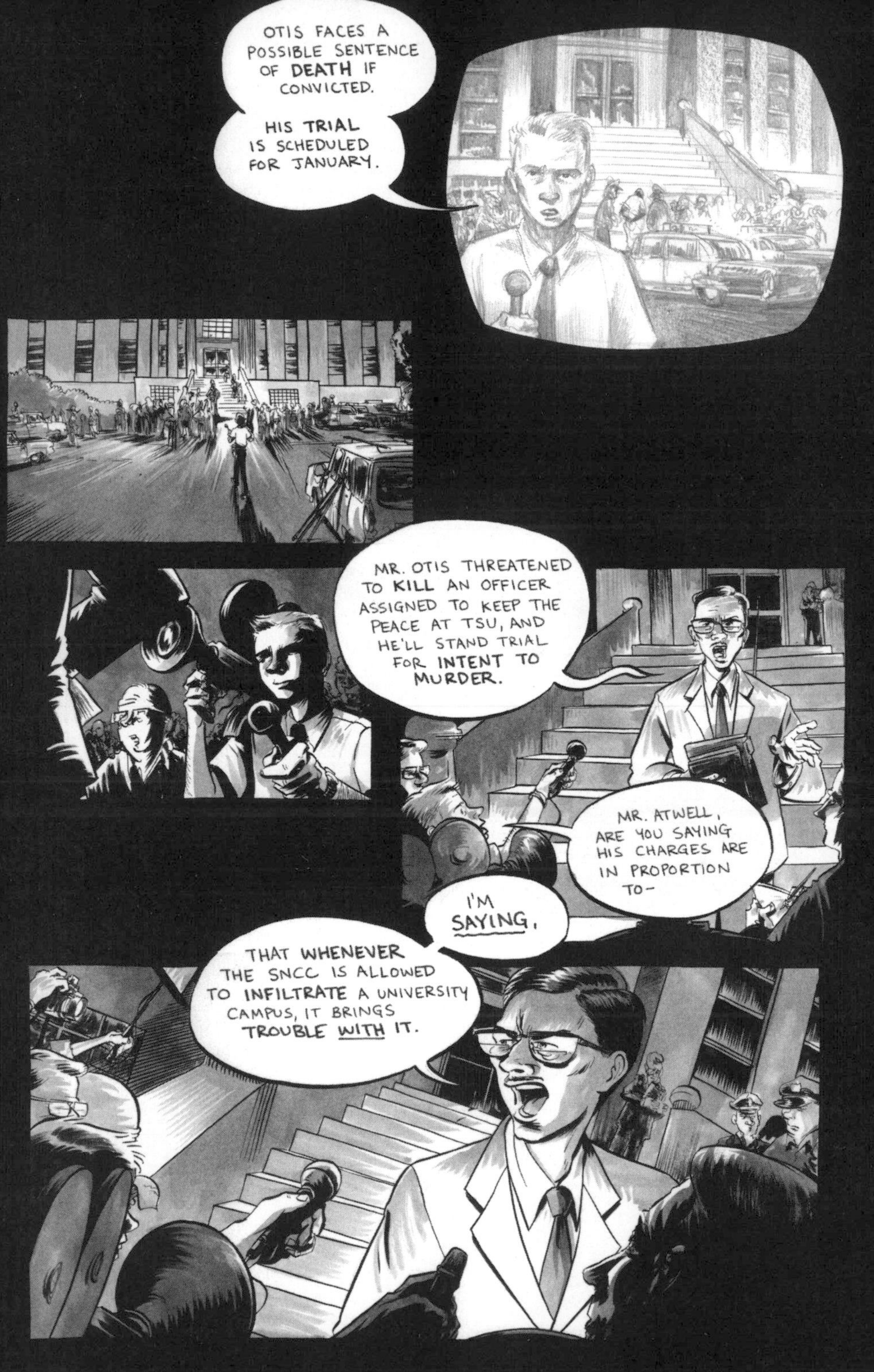
OTIS FACES A POSSIBLE SENTENCE OF DEATH IF CONVICTED.
HIS TRIAL IS SCHEDULED FOR JANUARY.
MR. OTIS THREATENED TO KILL AN OFFICER ASSIGNED TO KEEP THE PEACE AT TSU, AND HE'LL STAND TRIAL FOR INTENT TO MURDER.
MR. ATWELL, ARE YOU SAYING HIS CHARGES ARE IN PROPORTION TO-
I'M SAYING,
THAT WHENEVER THE SNCC IS ALLOWED TO INFILTRATE A UNIVERSITY CAMPUS, IT BRINGS TROUBLE WITH IT.

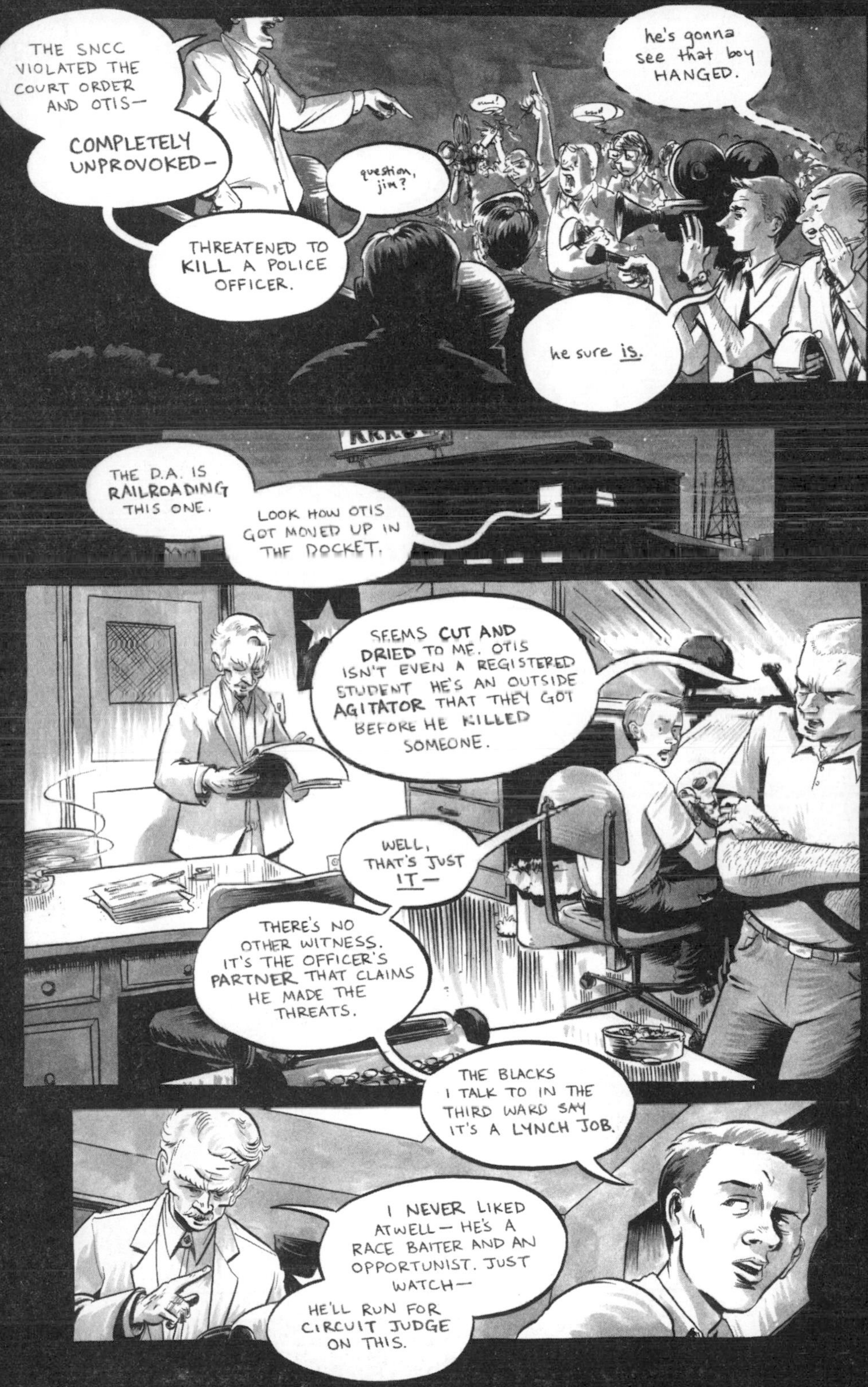
THE SNCC VIOLATED THE COURT ORDER AND OTIS—
COMPLETELY UNPROVOKED—
THREATENED TO KILL A POLICE OFFICER.
question, jim?
he's gonna see that boy HANGED.
he sure is.
THE D.A. IS RAILROADING THIS ONE.
LOOK HOW OTIS GOT MOVED UP IN THE DOCKET.
SEEMS CUT AND DRIED TO ME. OTIS ISN'T EVEN A REGISTERED STUDENT. HE'S AN OUTSIDE AGITATOR THAT THEY GOT BEFORE HE KILLED SOMEONE.
WELL, THAT'S JUST IT—
THERE'S NO OTHER WITNESS. IT'S THE OFFICER'S PARTNER THAT CLAIMS HE MADE THE THREATS.
THE BLACKS I TALK TO IN THE THIRD WARD SAY IT'S A LYNCH JOB.
I NEVER LIKED ATWELL— HE'S A RACE BAITER AND AN OPPORTUNIST. JUST WATCH—
HE'LL RUN FOR CIRCUIT JUDGE ON THIS.

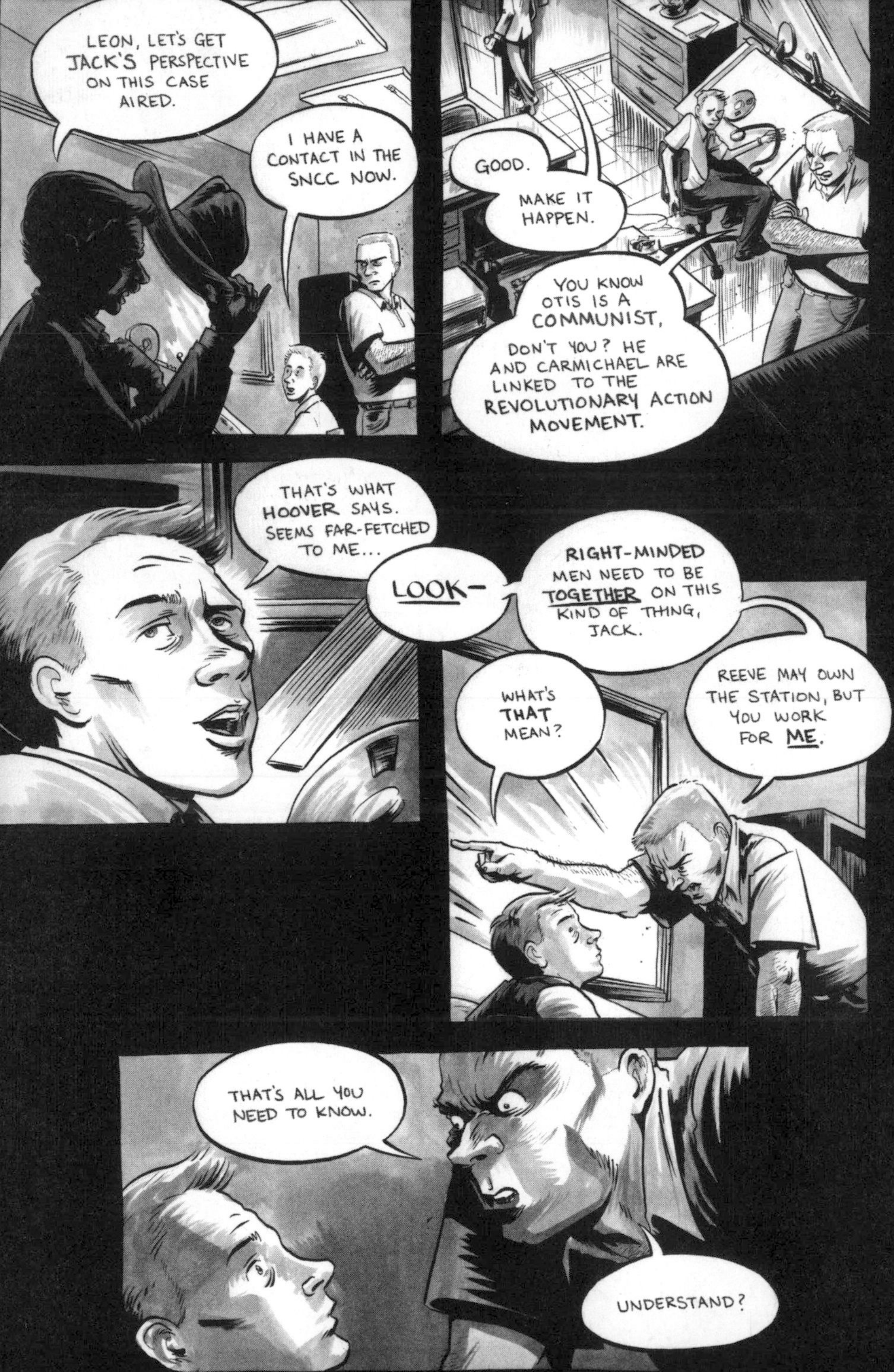

LEON, LET'S GET JACK'S PERSPECTIVE ON THIS CASE AIRED.
I HAVE A CONTACT IN THE SNCC NOW.
GOOD.
MAKE IT HAPPEN.
YOU KNOW OTIS IS A COMMUNIST,
DON'T YOU? HE AND CARMICHAEL ARE LINKED TO THE REVOLUTIONARY ACTION MOVEMENT.
THAT'S WHAT HOOVER SAYS. SEEMS FAR-FETCHED TO ME...
LOOK-
RIGHT-MINDED MEN NEED TO BE TOGETHER ON THIS KIND OF THING, JACK.
WHAT'S THAT MEAN?
REEVE MAY OWN THE STATION, BUT YOU WORK FOR ME.
THAT'S ALL YOU NEED TO KNOW.
UNDERSTAND?

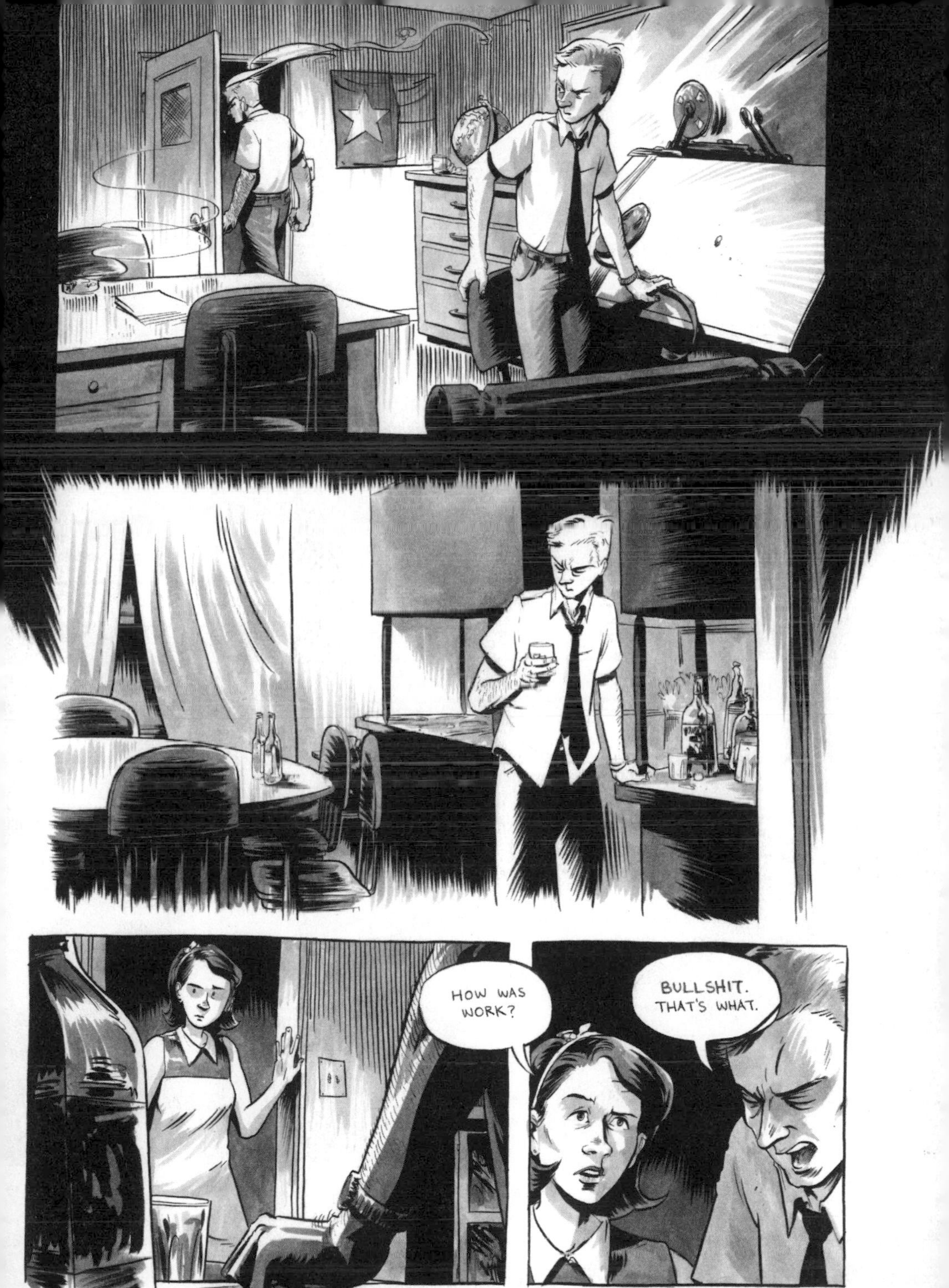
HOW WAS WORK?
BULLSHIT. THAT'S WHAT.

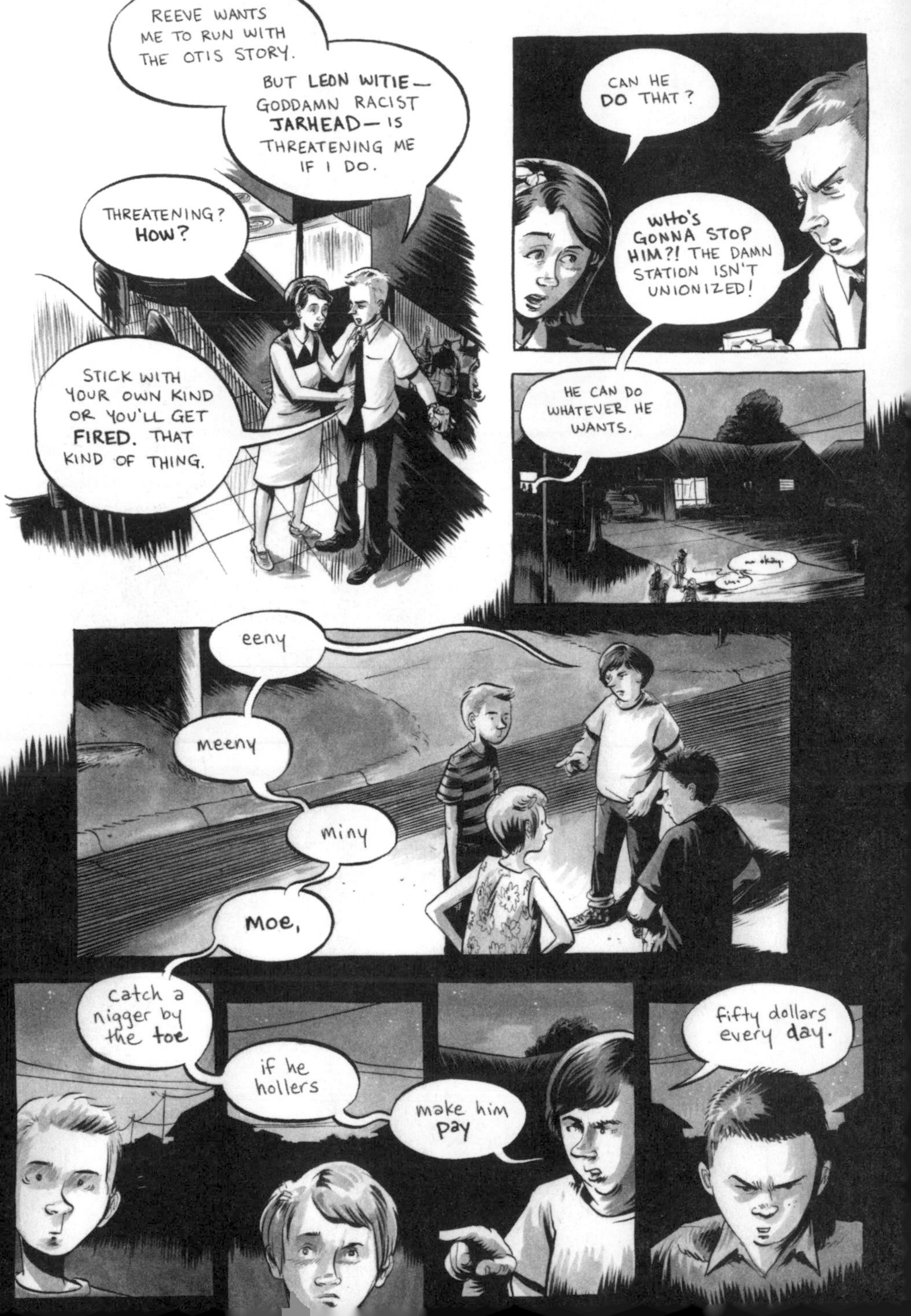
REEVE WANTS ME TO RUN WITH THE OTIS STORY.
BUT LEON WITIE— GODDAMN RACIST JARHEAD— IS THREATENING ME IF I DO.
THREATENING? HOW?
STICK WITH YOUR OWN KIND OR YOU'LL GET FIRED. THAT KIND OF THING.
CAN HE DO THAT?
WHO'S GONNA STOP HIM?! THE DAMN STATION ISN'T UNIONIZED!
HE CAN DO WHATEVER HE WANTS.
eeny
meeny
miny
Moe,
catch a nigger by the toe
if he hollers
make him pay
fifty dollars every day.

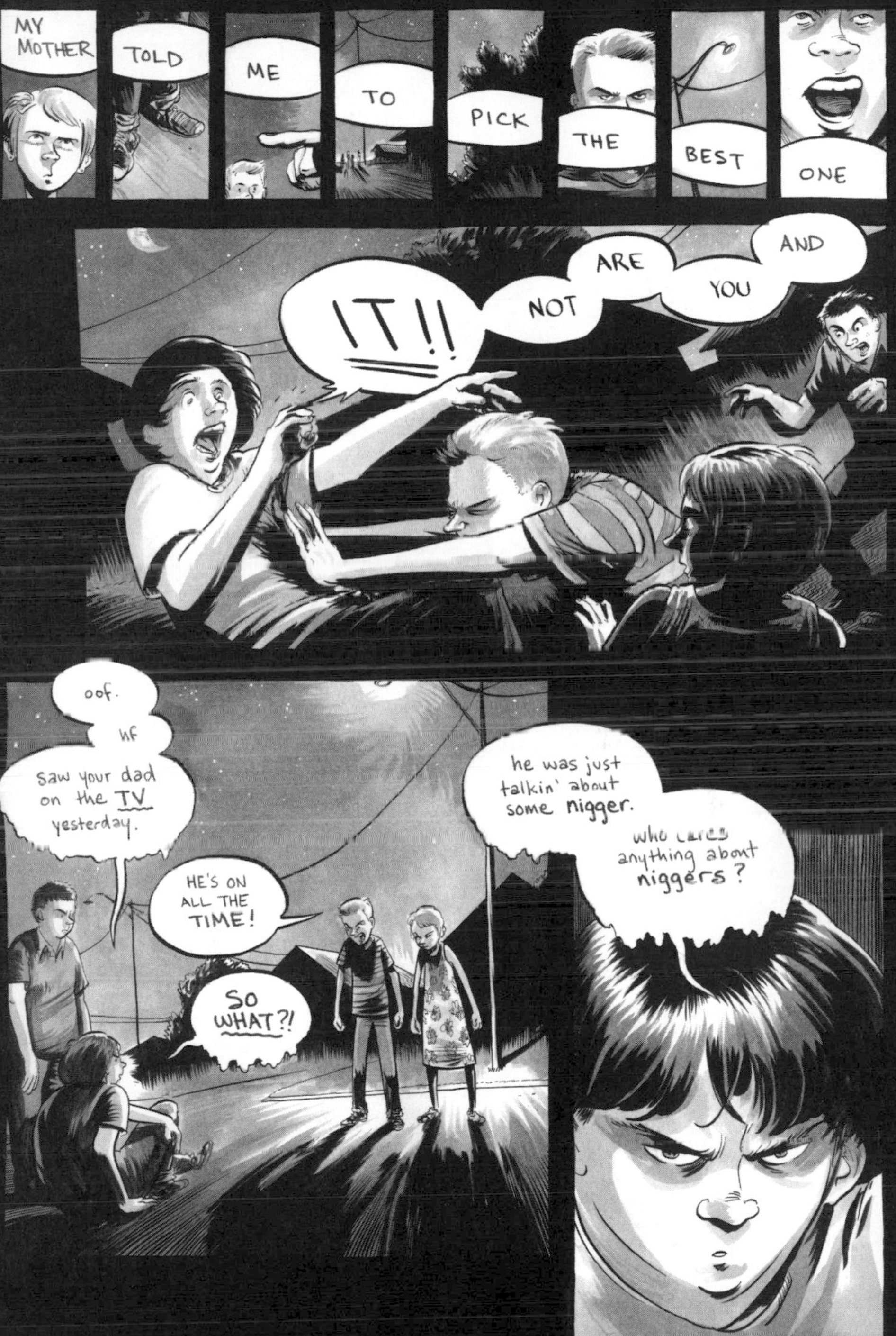

MY MOTHER
TOLD
ME
TO
PICK
THE
BEST
ONE
AND
YOU
ARE
NOT
IT!!
oof.
hf
saw your dad on the TV yesterday.
HE'S ON ALL THE TIME!
SO WHAT?!
he was just talkin' about some nigger.
who cares anything about niggers?

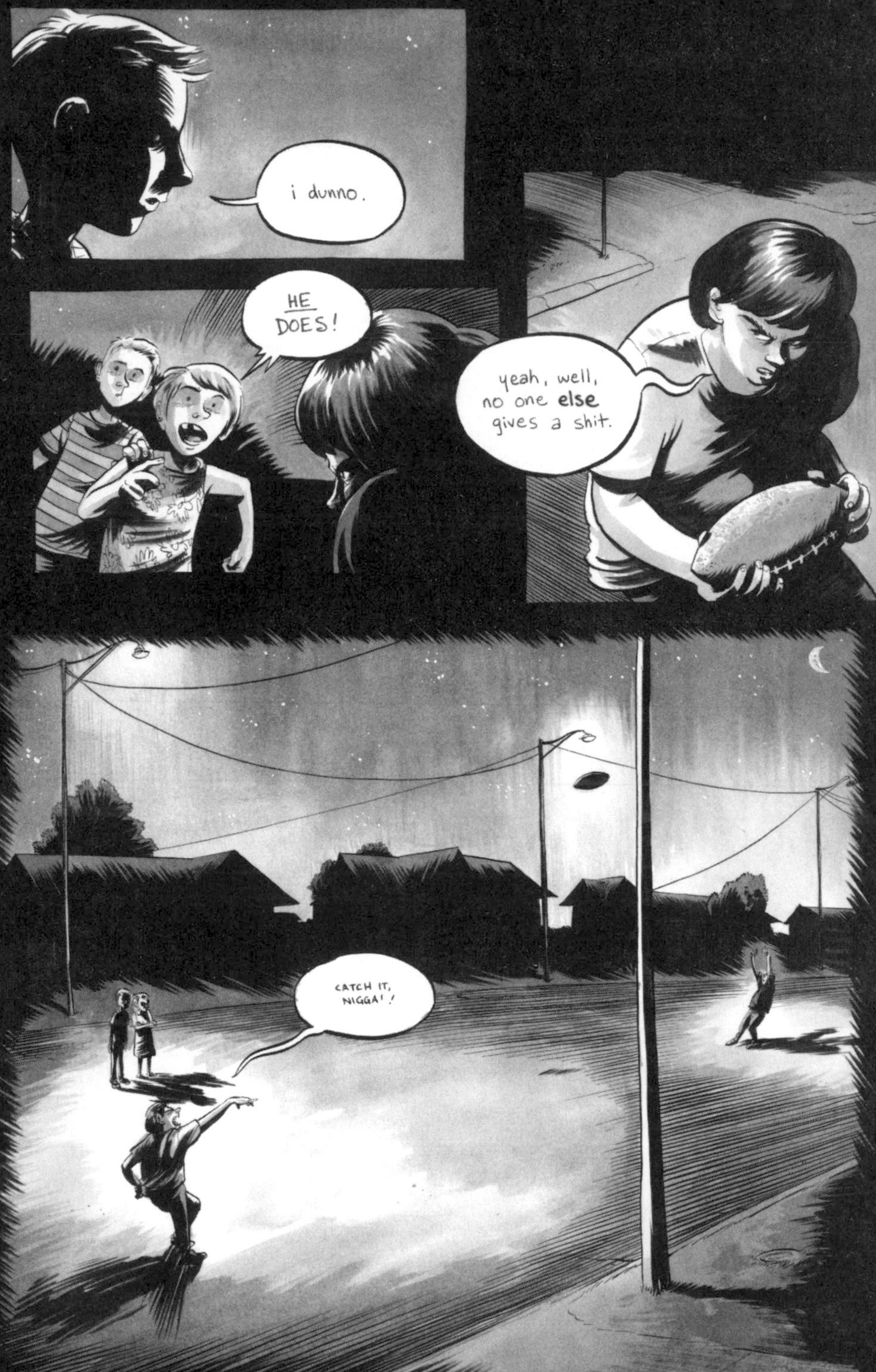
i dunno.
HE DOES!
yeah, well, no one **else** gives a shit.
CATCH IT, NIGGA!

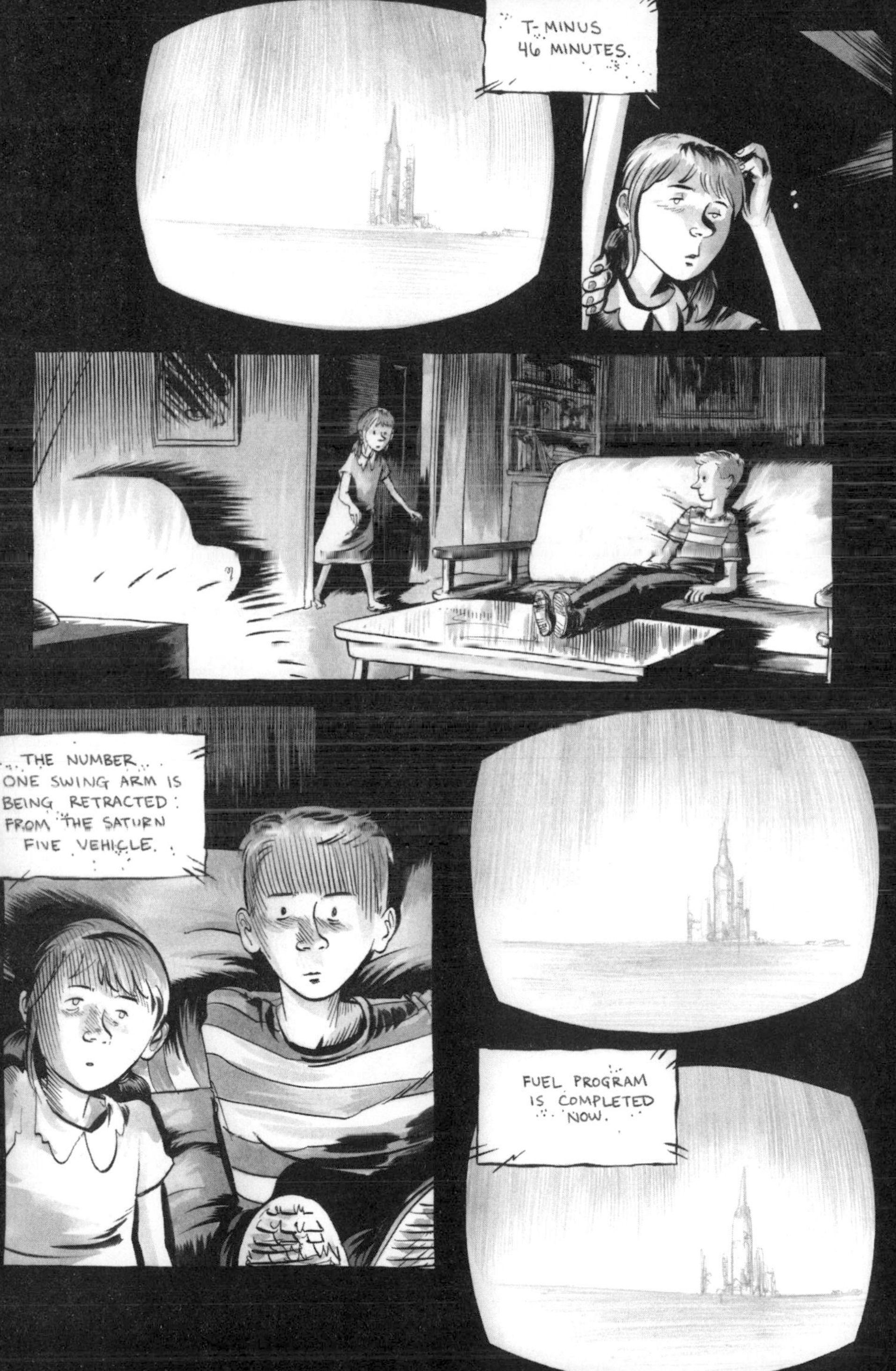
T-MINUS 46 MINUTES.
THE NUMBER ONE SWING ARM IS BEING RETRACTED FROM THE SATURN FIVE VEHICLE.
FUEL PROGRAM IS COMPLETED NOW.

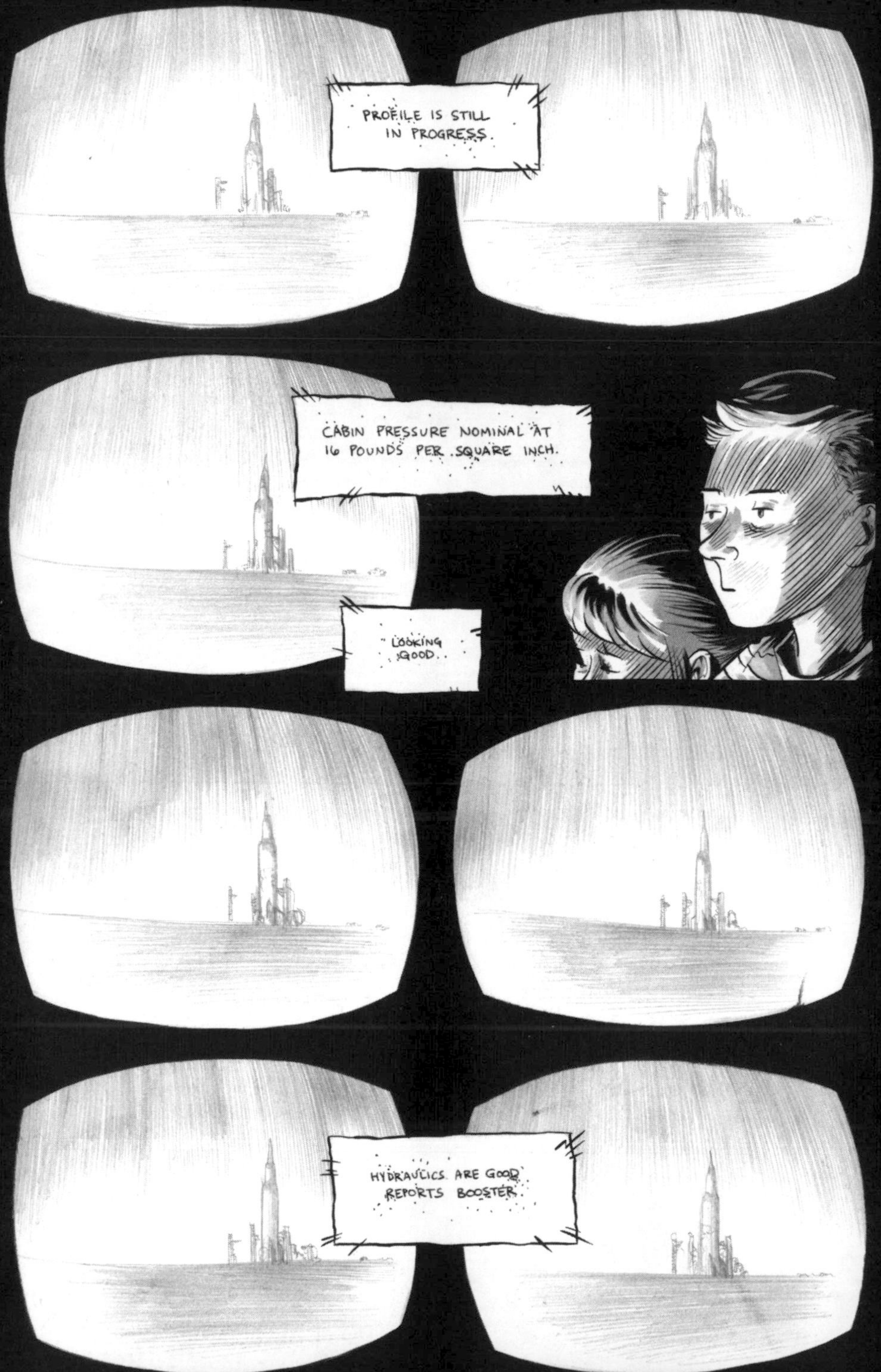
PROFILE IS STILL IN PROGRESS.
CABIN PRESSURE NOMINAL AT 16 POUNDS PER SQUARE INCH.
LOOKING GOOD.
HYDRAULICS ARE GOOD REPORTS BOOSTER.

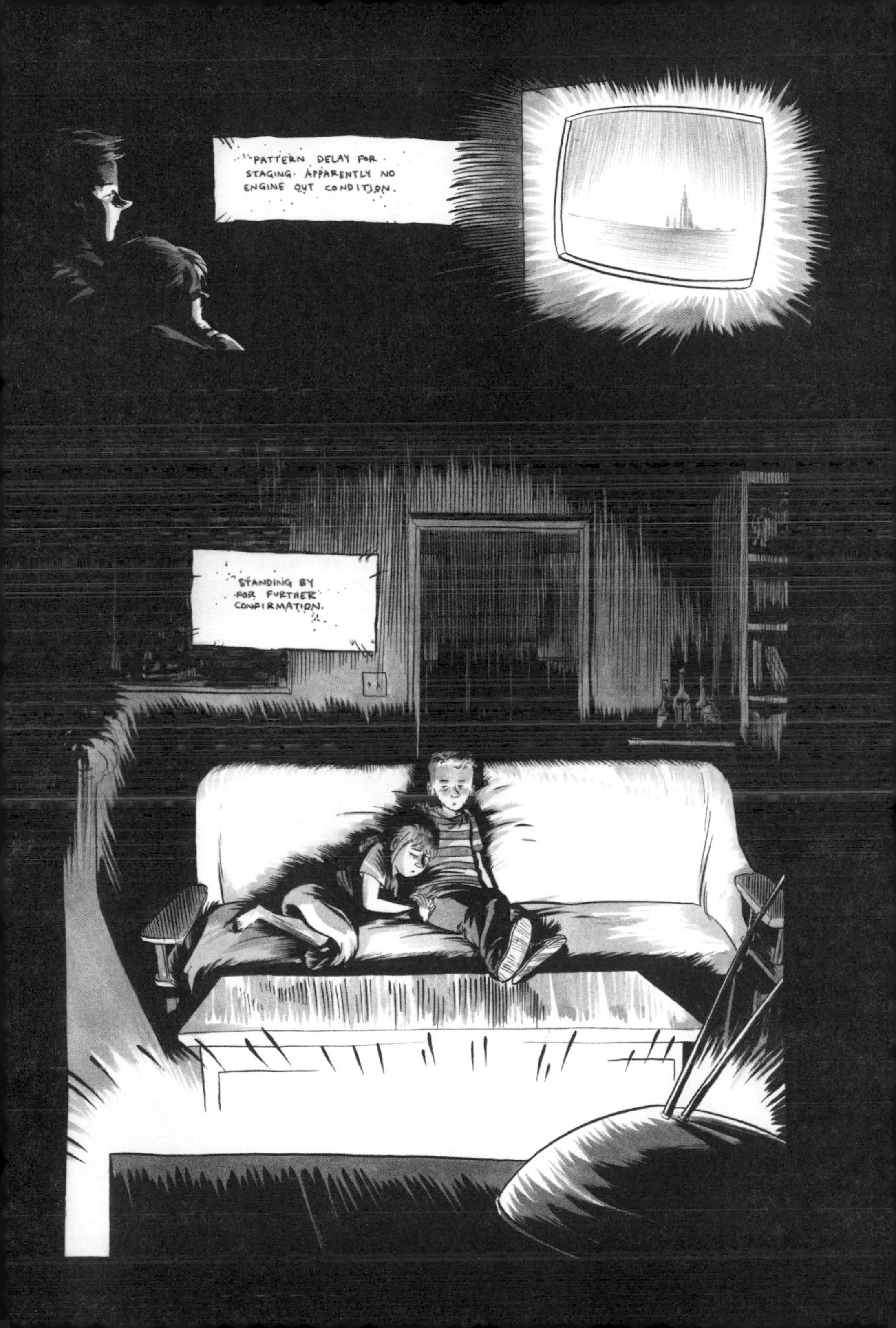
...PATTERN DELAY FOR STAGING. APPARENTLY NO ENGINE OUT CONDITION.
STANDING BY FOR FURTHER CONFIRMATION.

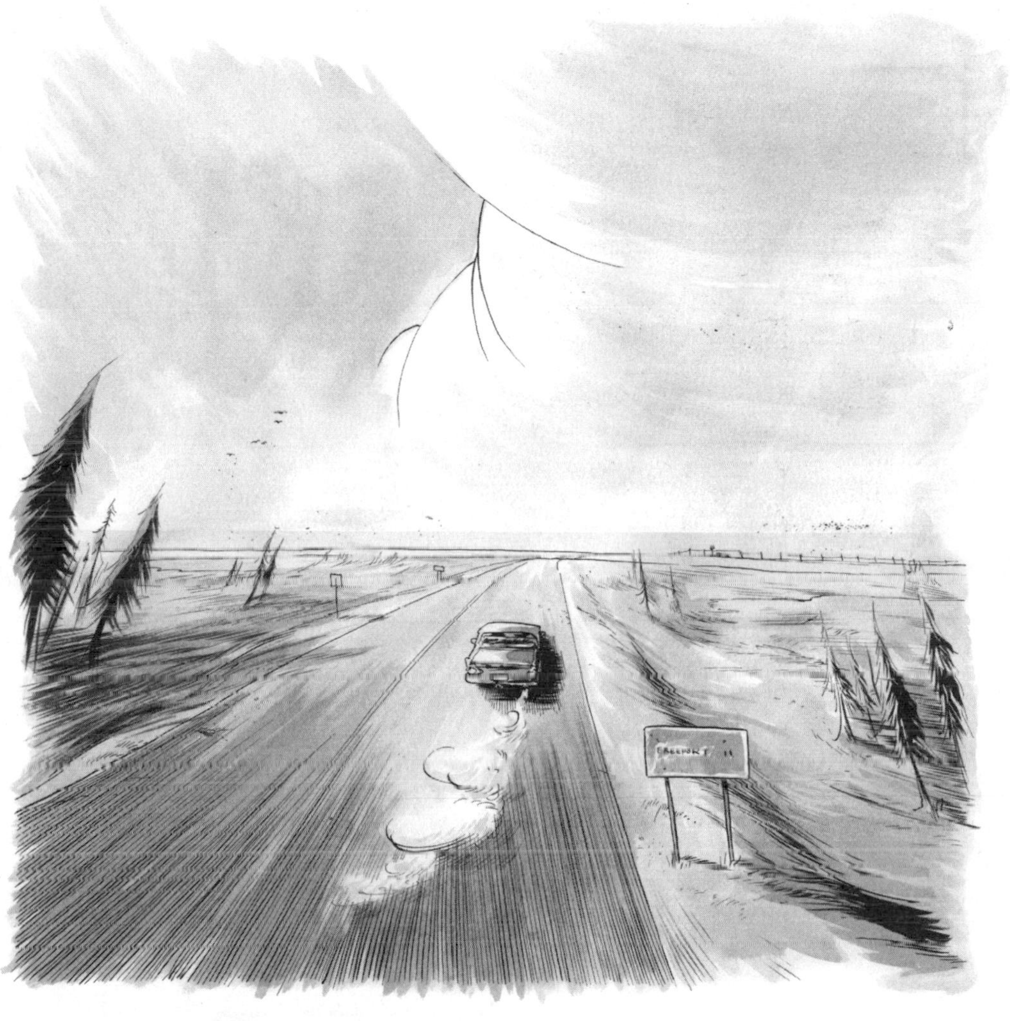

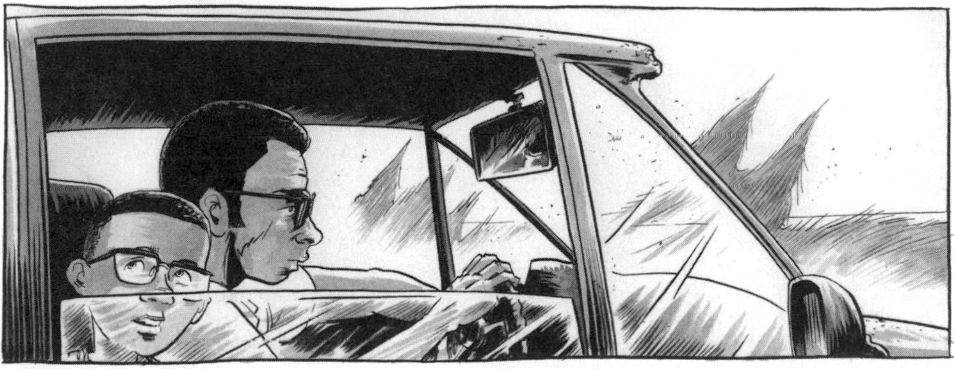

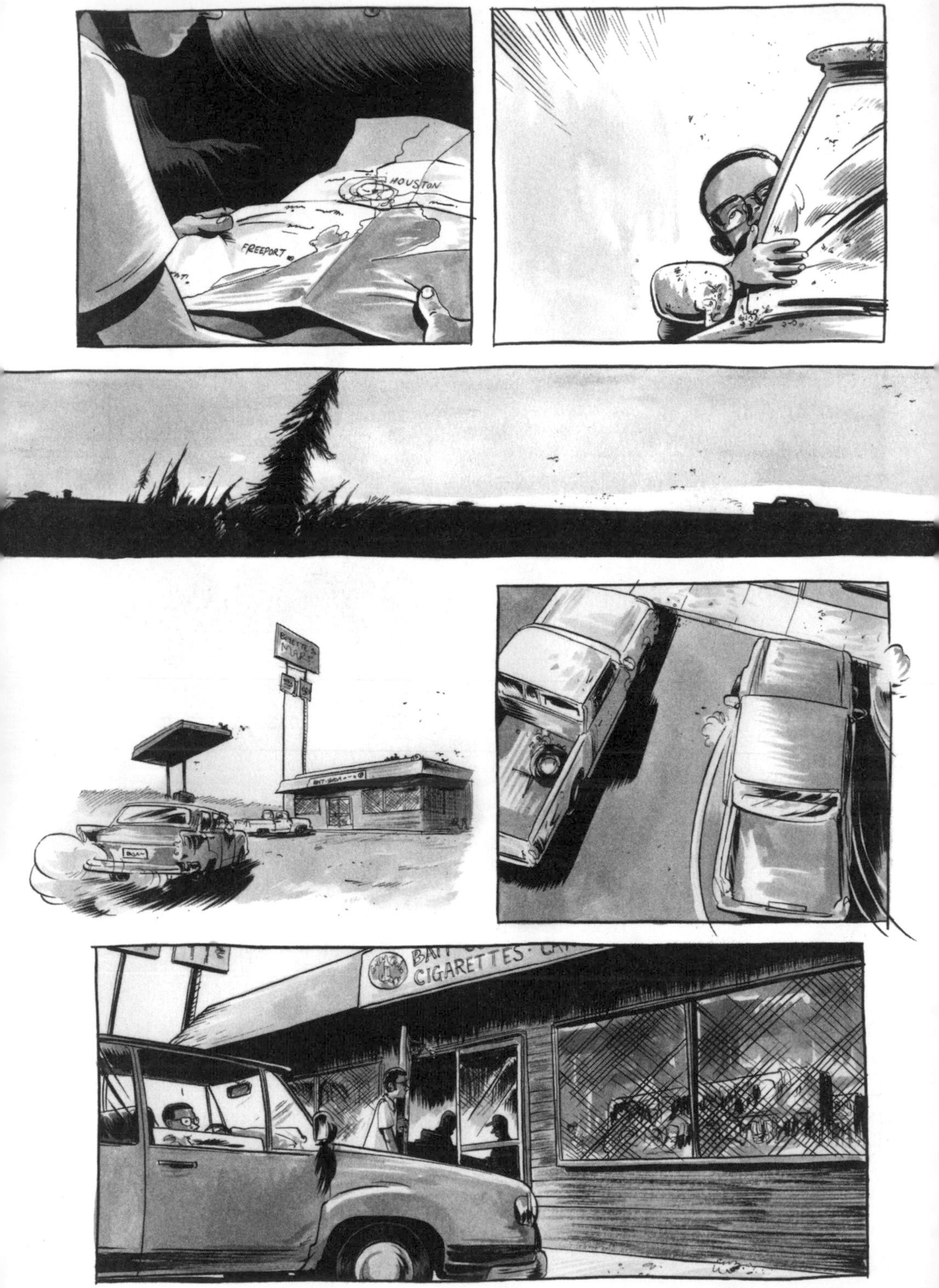
HOUSTON
FREEPORT
CIGARETTES

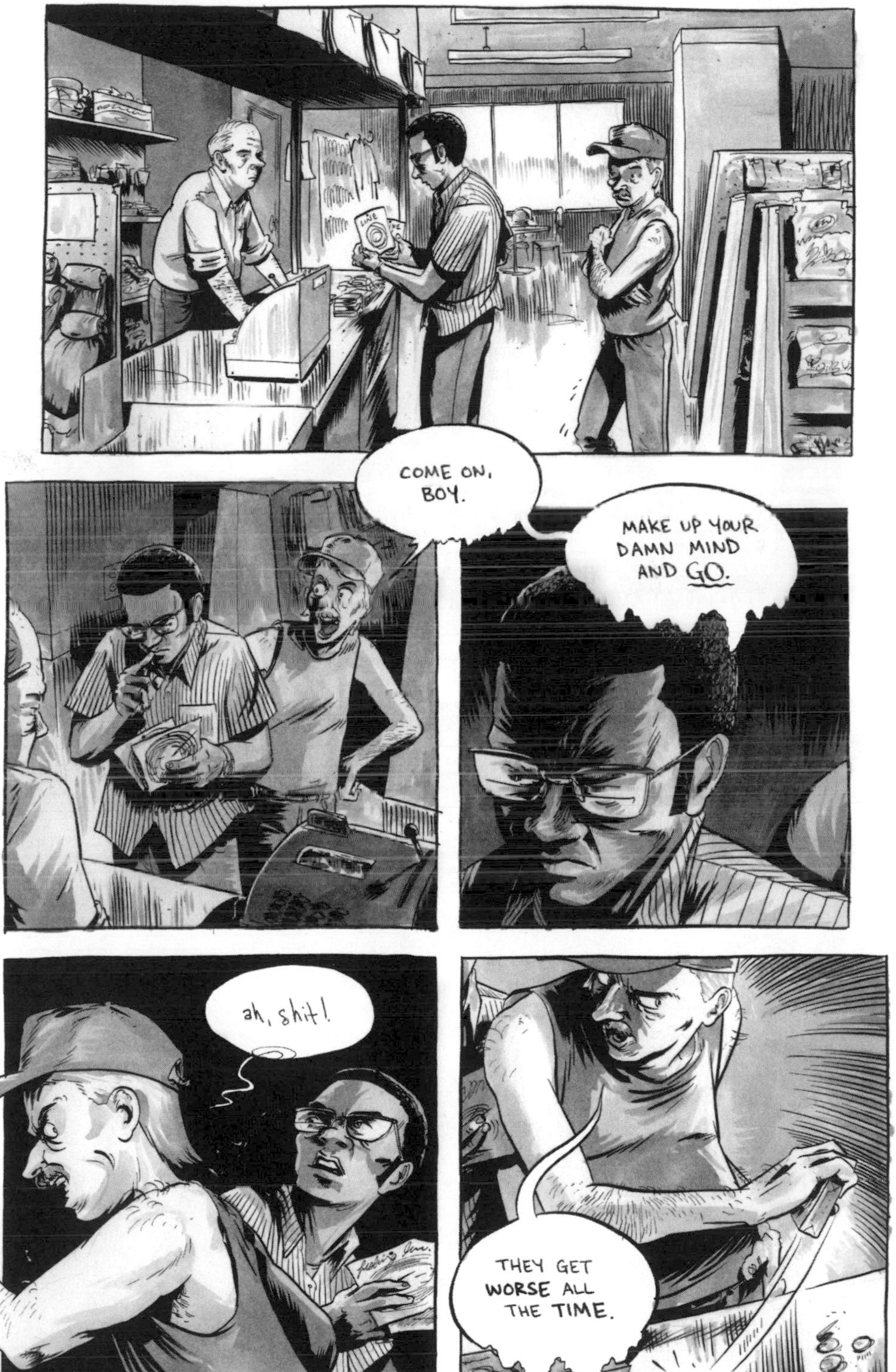
COME ON, BOY.
MAKE UP YOUR DAMN MIND AND GO.
ah, shit!
THEY GET WORSE ALL THE TIME.

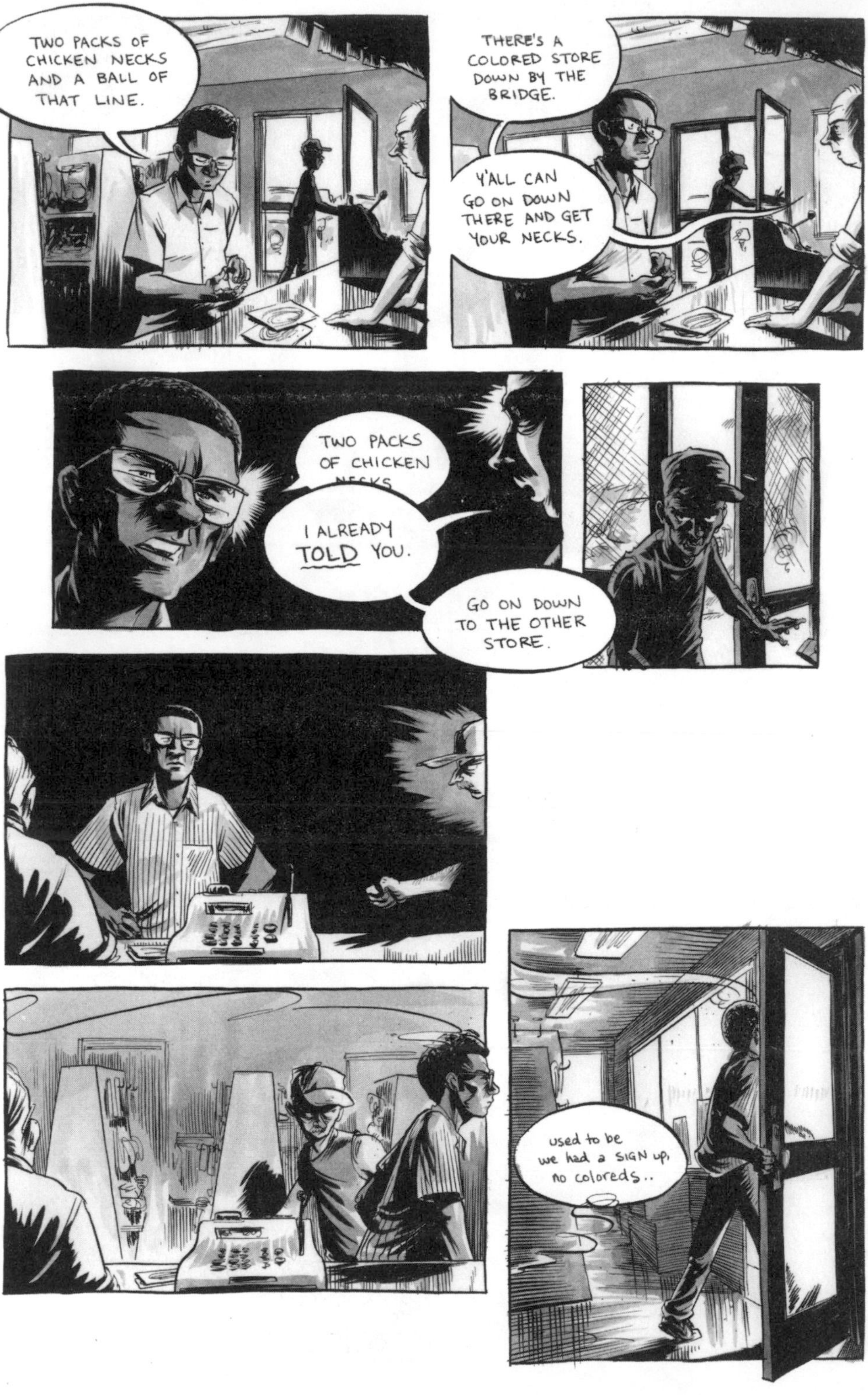

TWO PACKS OF CHICKEN NECKS AND A BALL OF THAT LINE.
THERE'S A COLORED STORE DOWN BY THE BRIDGE.
Y'ALL CAN GO ON DOWN THERE AND GET YOUR NECKS.
TWO PACKS OF CHICKEN NECKS
I ALREADY TOLD YOU.
GO ON DOWN TO THE OTHER STORE.
used to be we had a SIGN up, no coloreds..

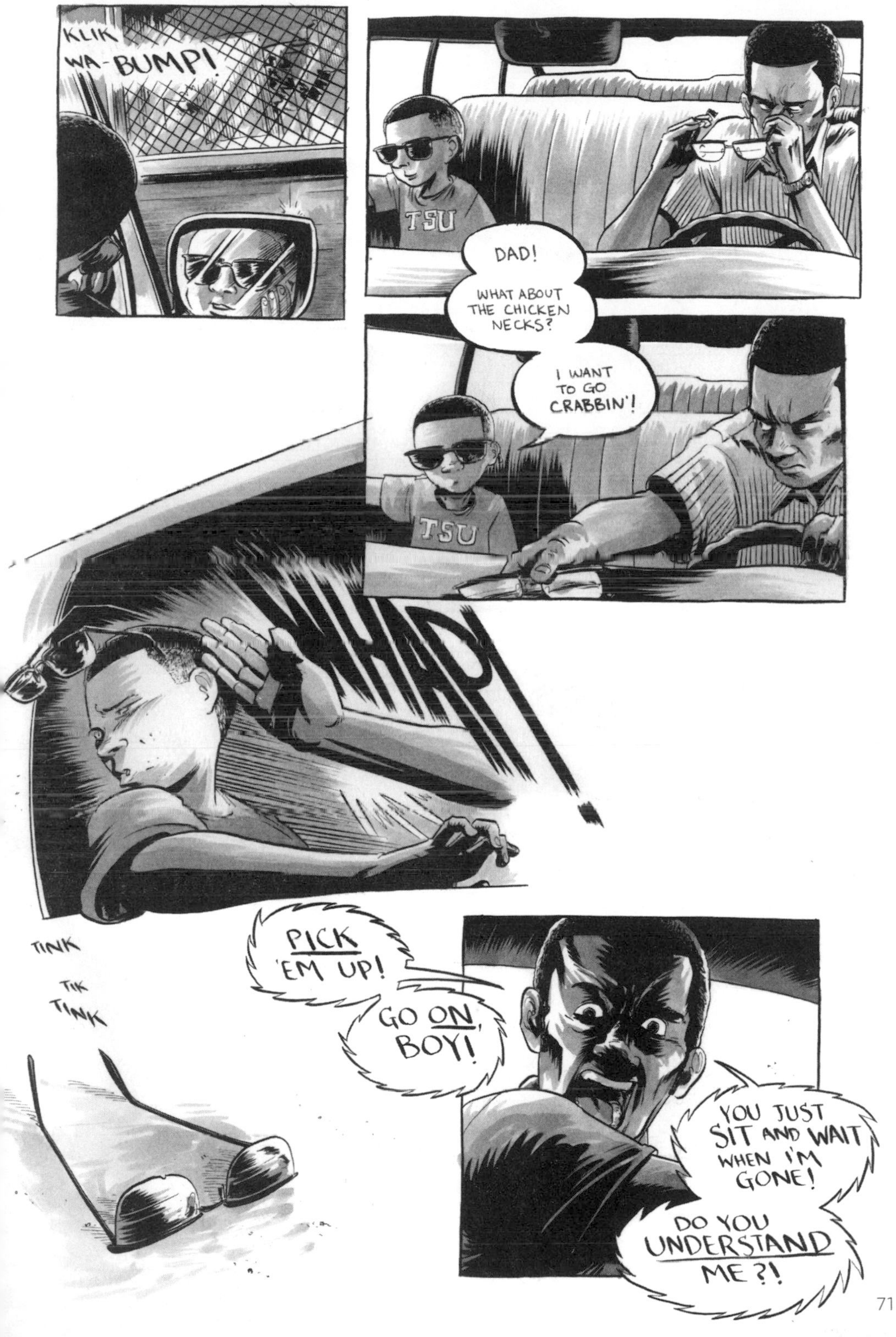
KLIK
WA-BUMP!
TSU
DAD!
WHAT ABOUT THE CHICKEN NECKS?
I WANT TO GO CRABBIN'!
TSU
WHAP!
TINK
TIK
TINK
PICK 'EM UP!
GO ON, BOY!
YOU JUST SIT AND WAIT WHEN I'M GONE!
DO YOU UNDERSTAND ME?!

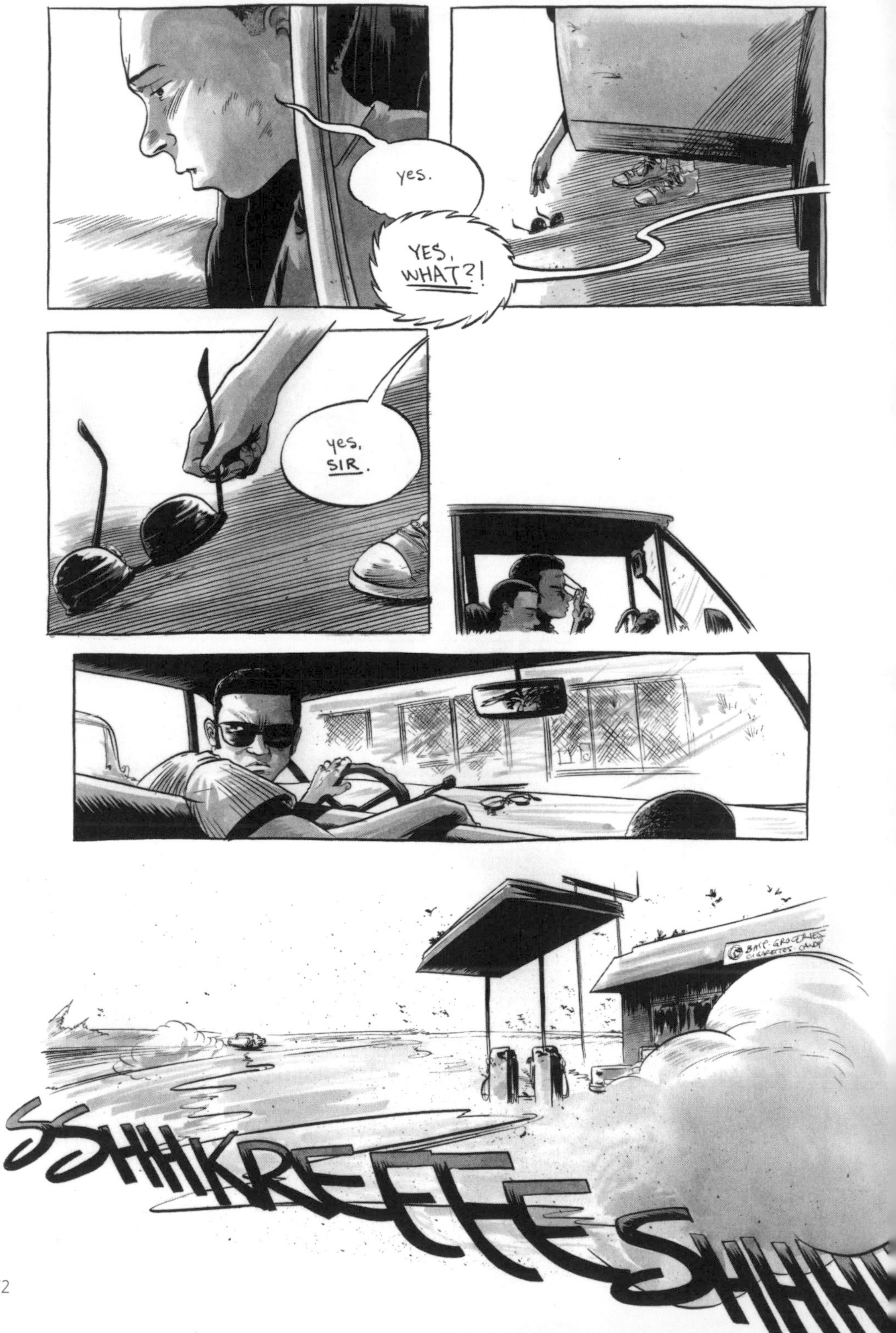
yes.
YES, WHAT?!
yes, SIR.
SSHHKREEEESHHH

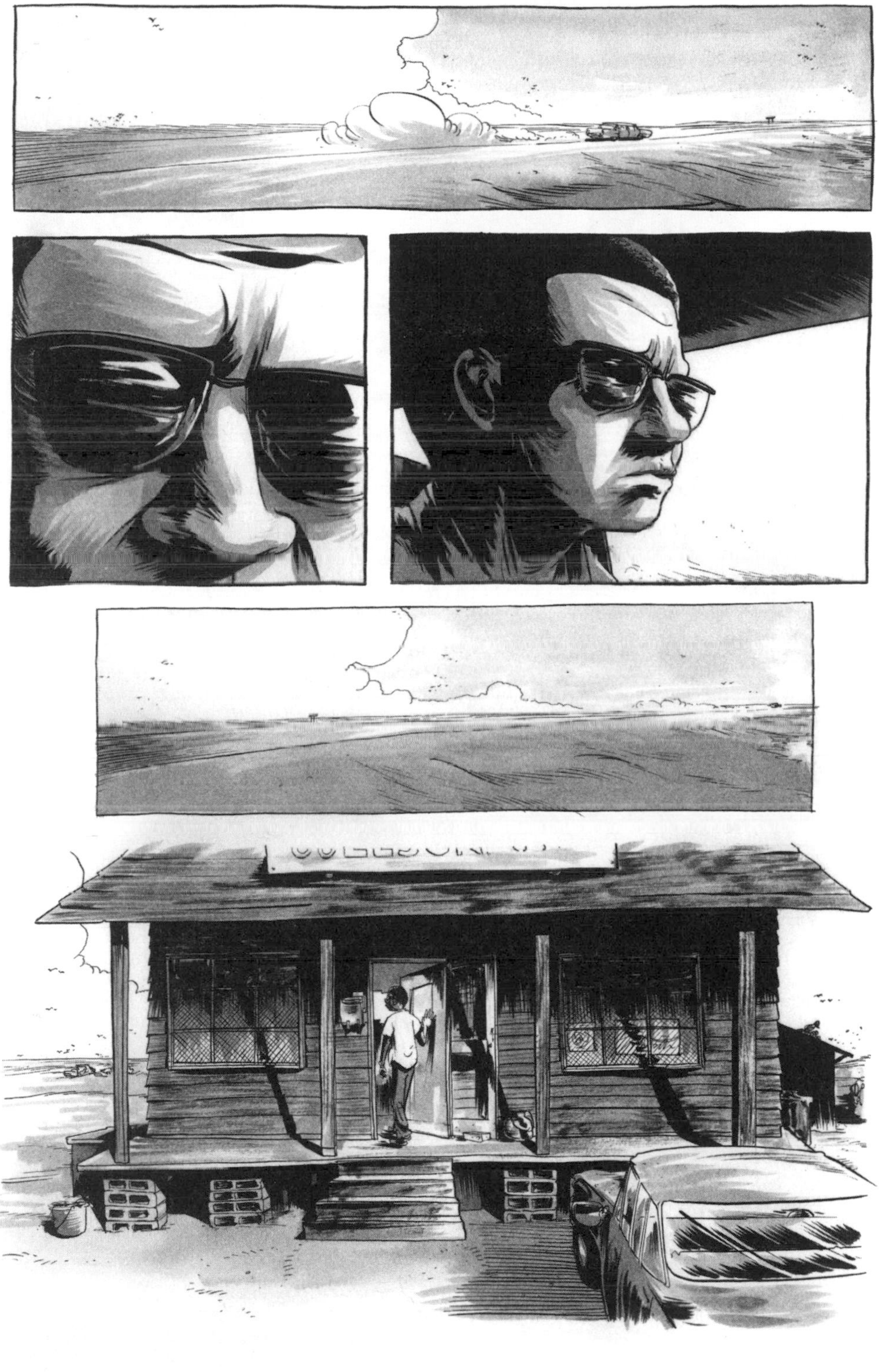

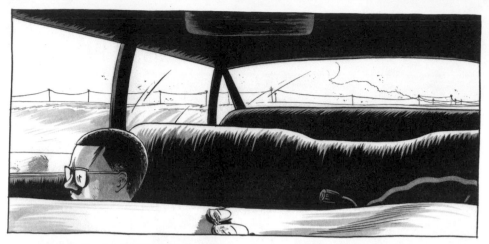

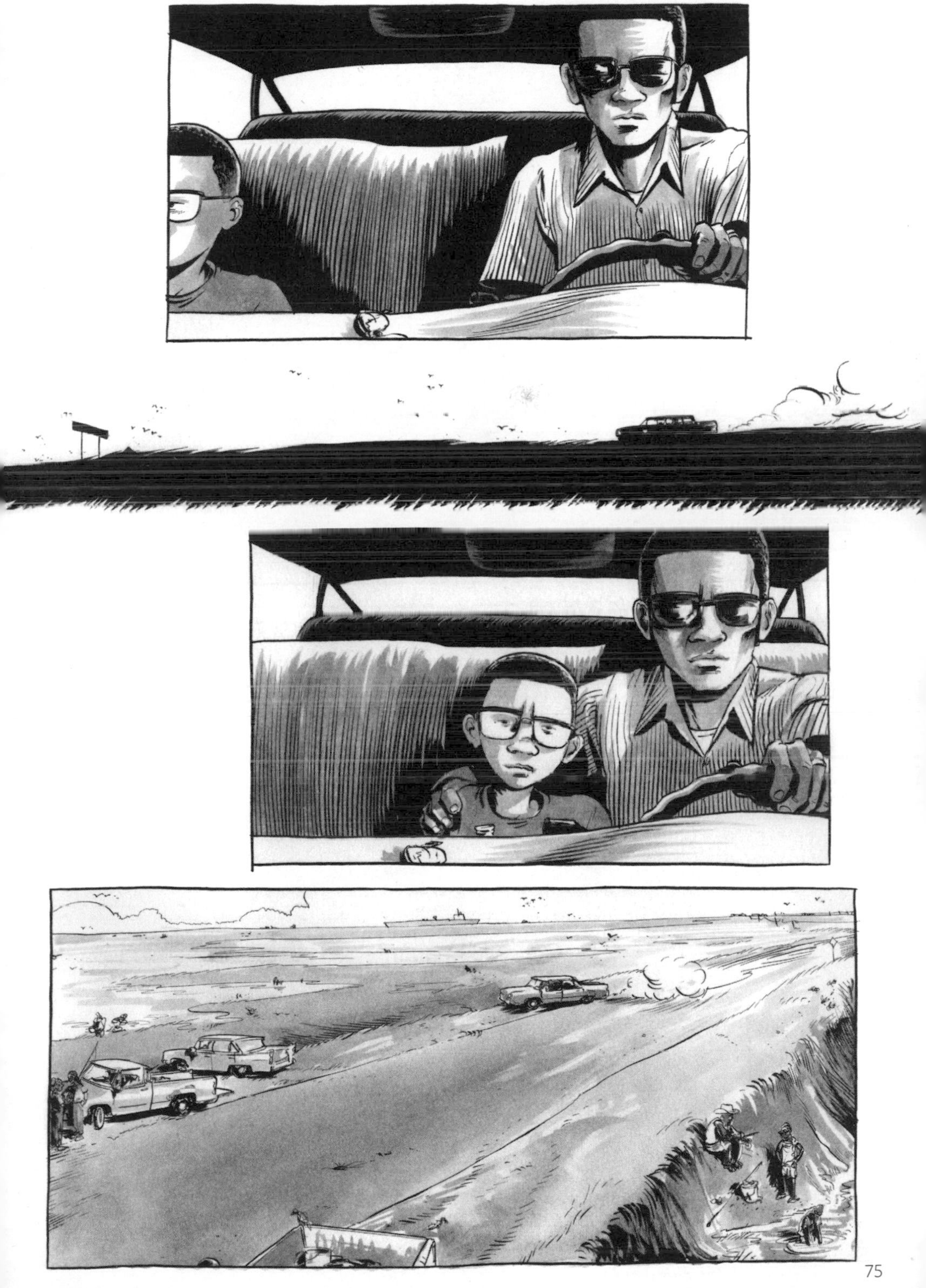

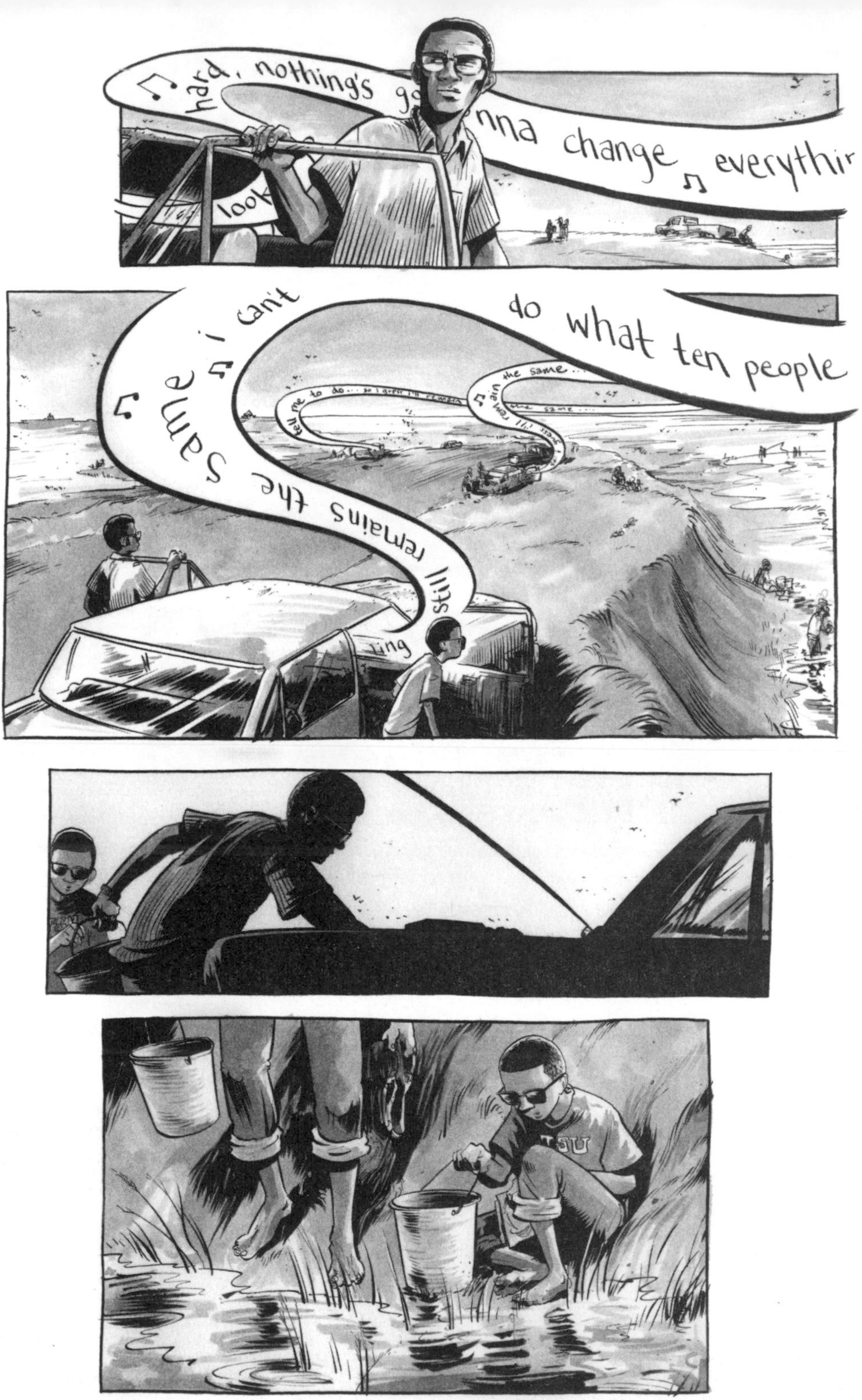

♫ hard, nothing's go nna change ♫ everythir
look
ring still remains the same ♫ i can't do what ten people

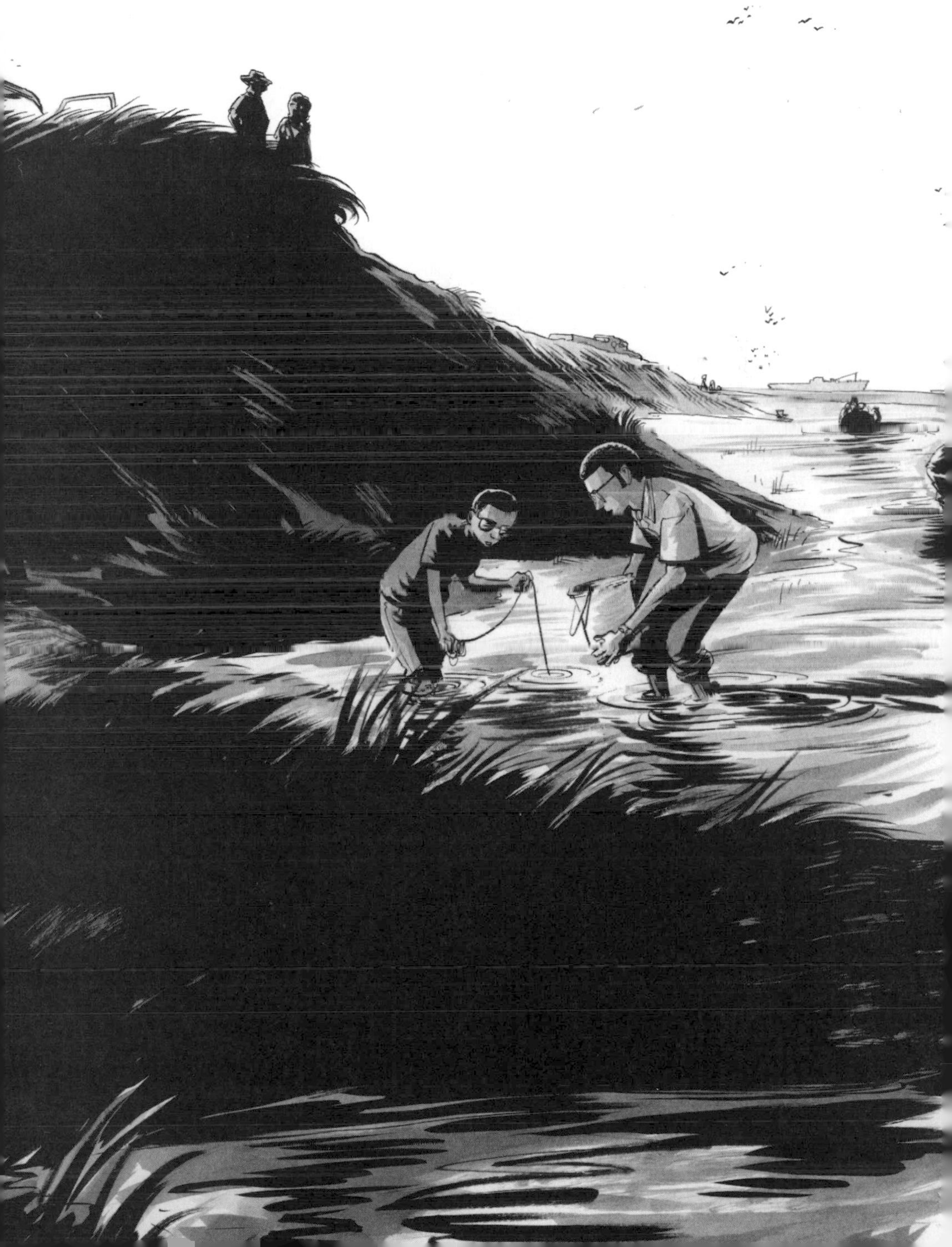

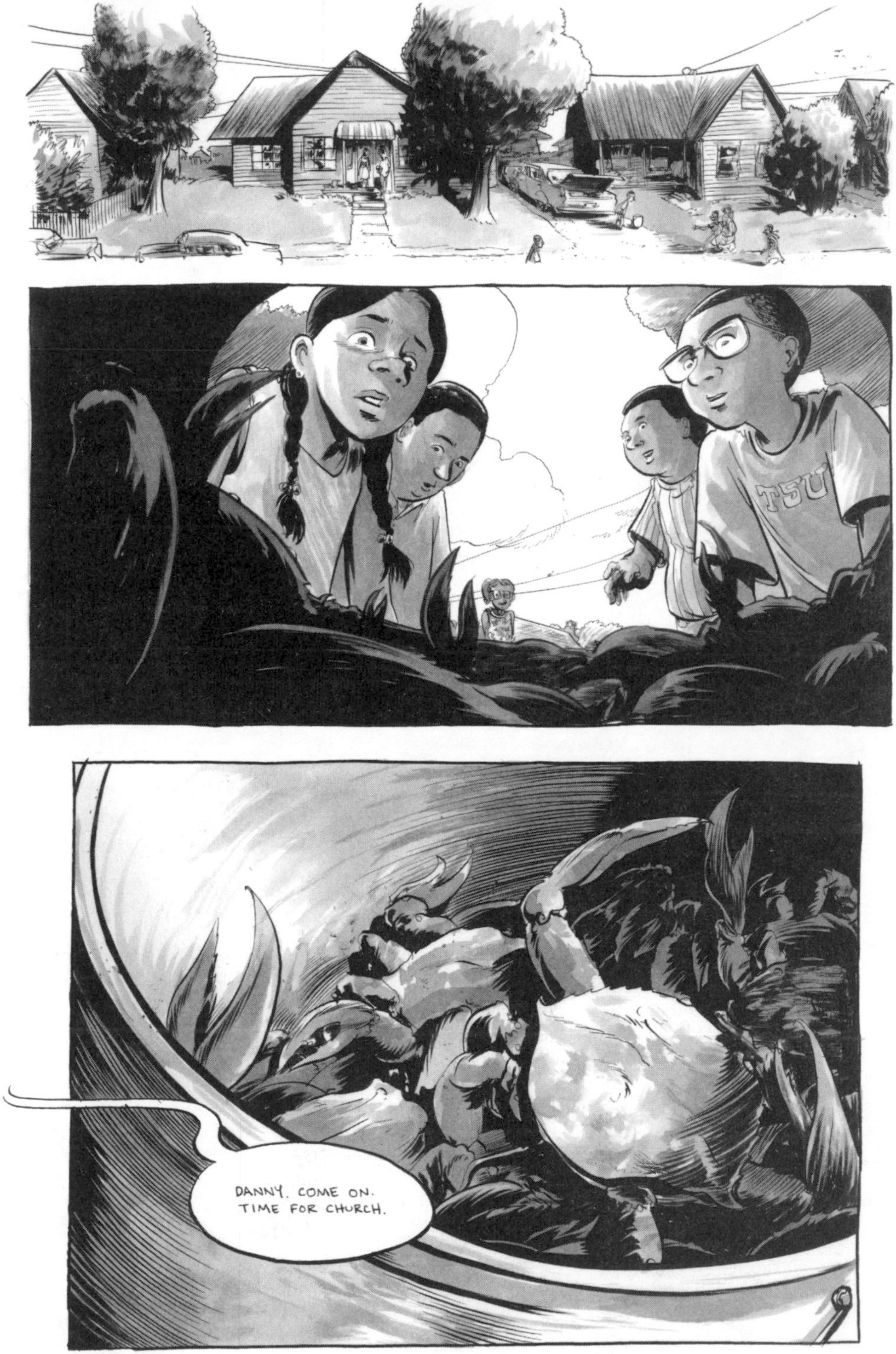
TSU
DANNY. COME ON.
TIME FOR CHURCH.

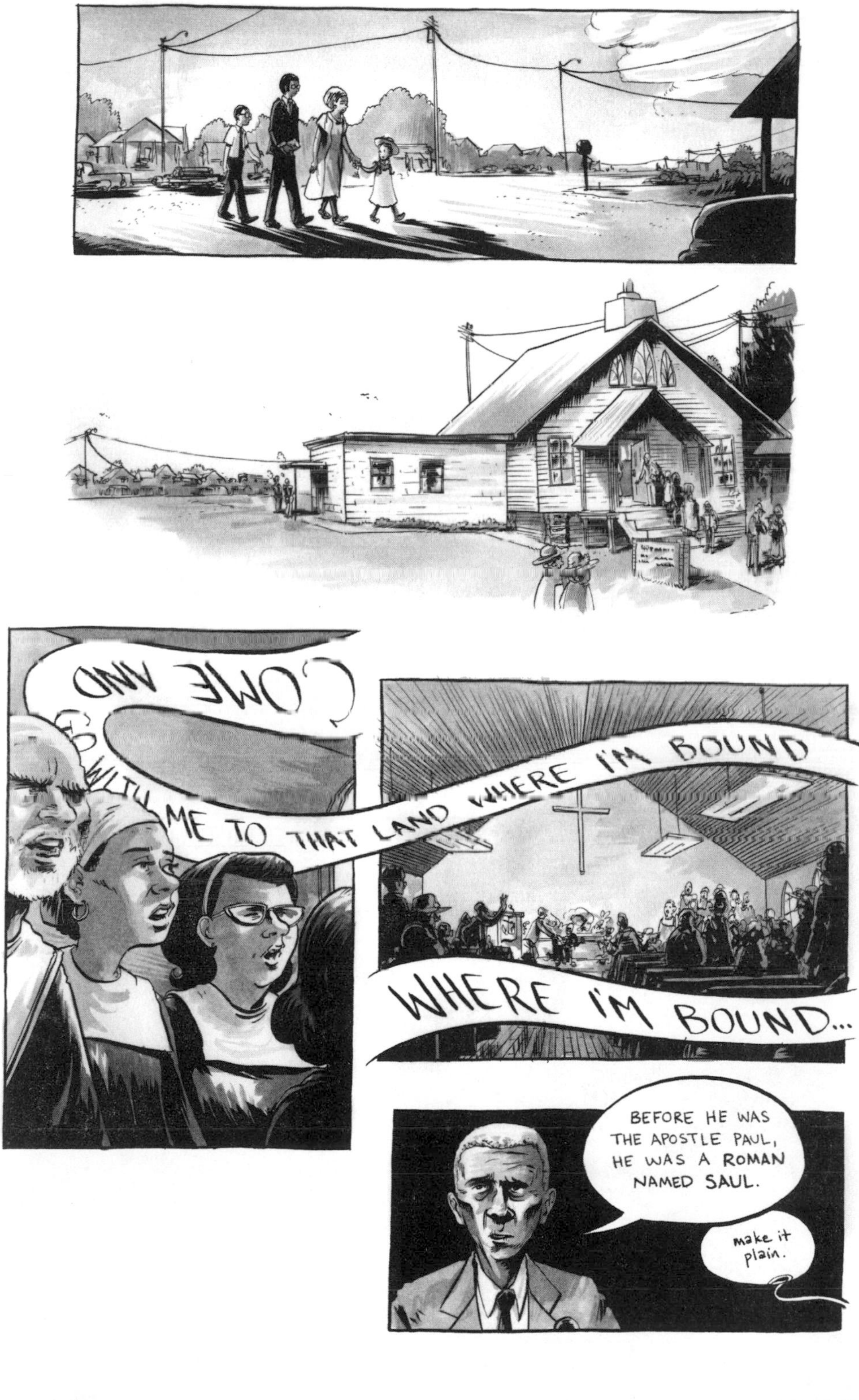
COME AND
GO WITH ME TO THAT LAND WHERE I'M BOUND
WHERE I'M BOUND...
BEFORE HE WAS THE APOSTLE PAUL, HE WAS A ROMAN NAMED SAUL.
make it plain.

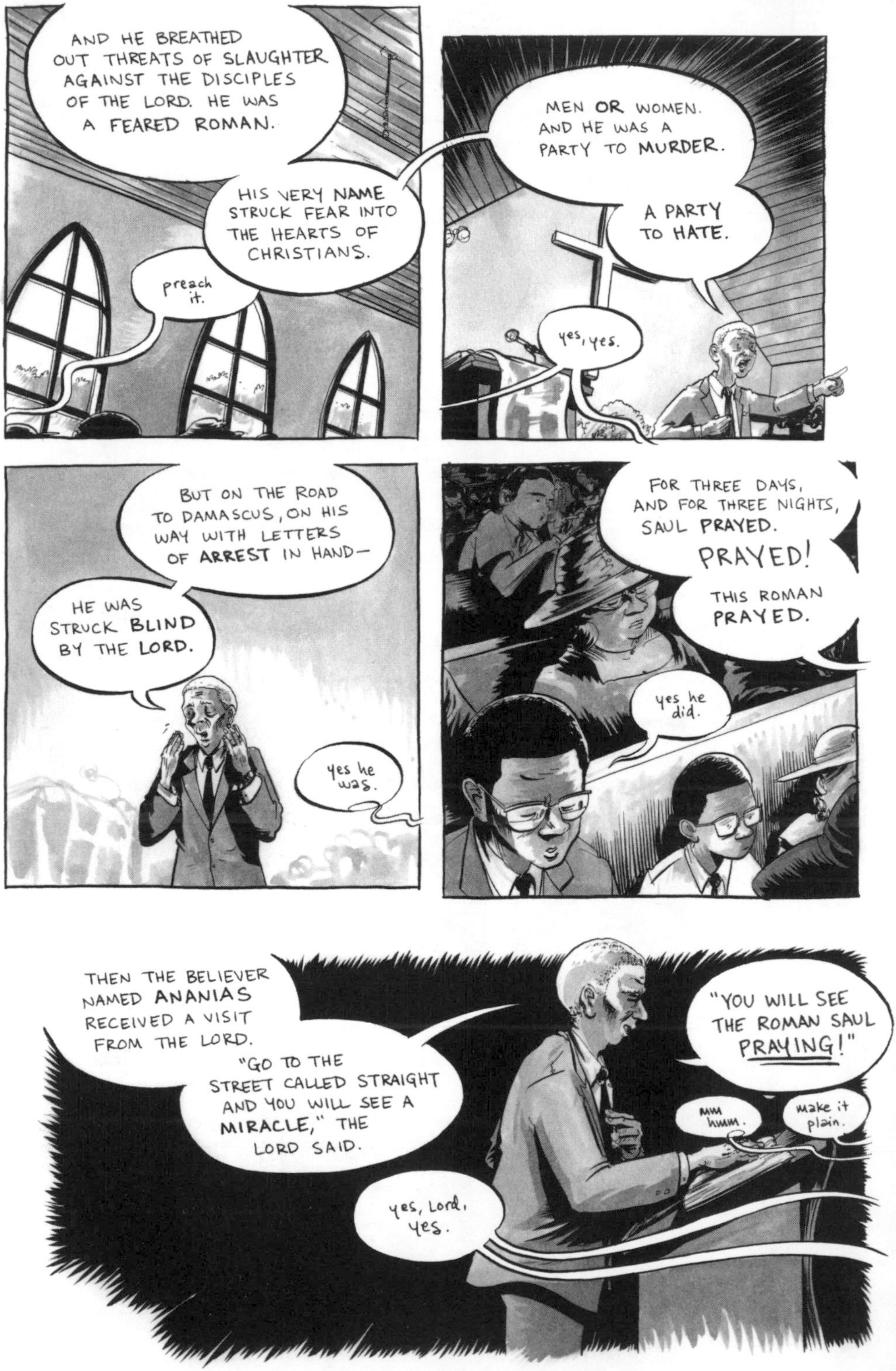
AND HE BREATHED OUT THREATS OF SLAUGHTER AGAINST THE DISCIPLES OF THE LORD. HE WAS A FEARED ROMAN.
HIS VERY NAME STRUCK FEAR INTO THE HEARTS OF CHRISTIANS.
preach it.
MEN OR WOMEN. AND HE WAS A PARTY TO MURDER.
A PARTY TO HATE.
yes, yes.
BUT ON THE ROAD TO DAMASCUS, ON HIS WAY WITH LETTERS OF ARREST IN HAND—
HE WAS STRUCK BLIND BY THE LORD.
yes he was.
FOR THREE DAYS, AND FOR THREE NIGHTS, SAUL PRAYED.
PRAYED!
THIS ROMAN PRAYED.
yes he did.
THEN THE BELIEVER NAMED ANANIAS RECEIVED A VISIT FROM THE LORD.
"GO TO THE STREET CALLED STRAIGHT AND YOU WILL SEE A MIRACLE," THE LORD SAID.
"YOU WILL SEE THE ROMAN SAUL PRAYING!"
mm hmm.
make it plain.
yes, Lord, yes.

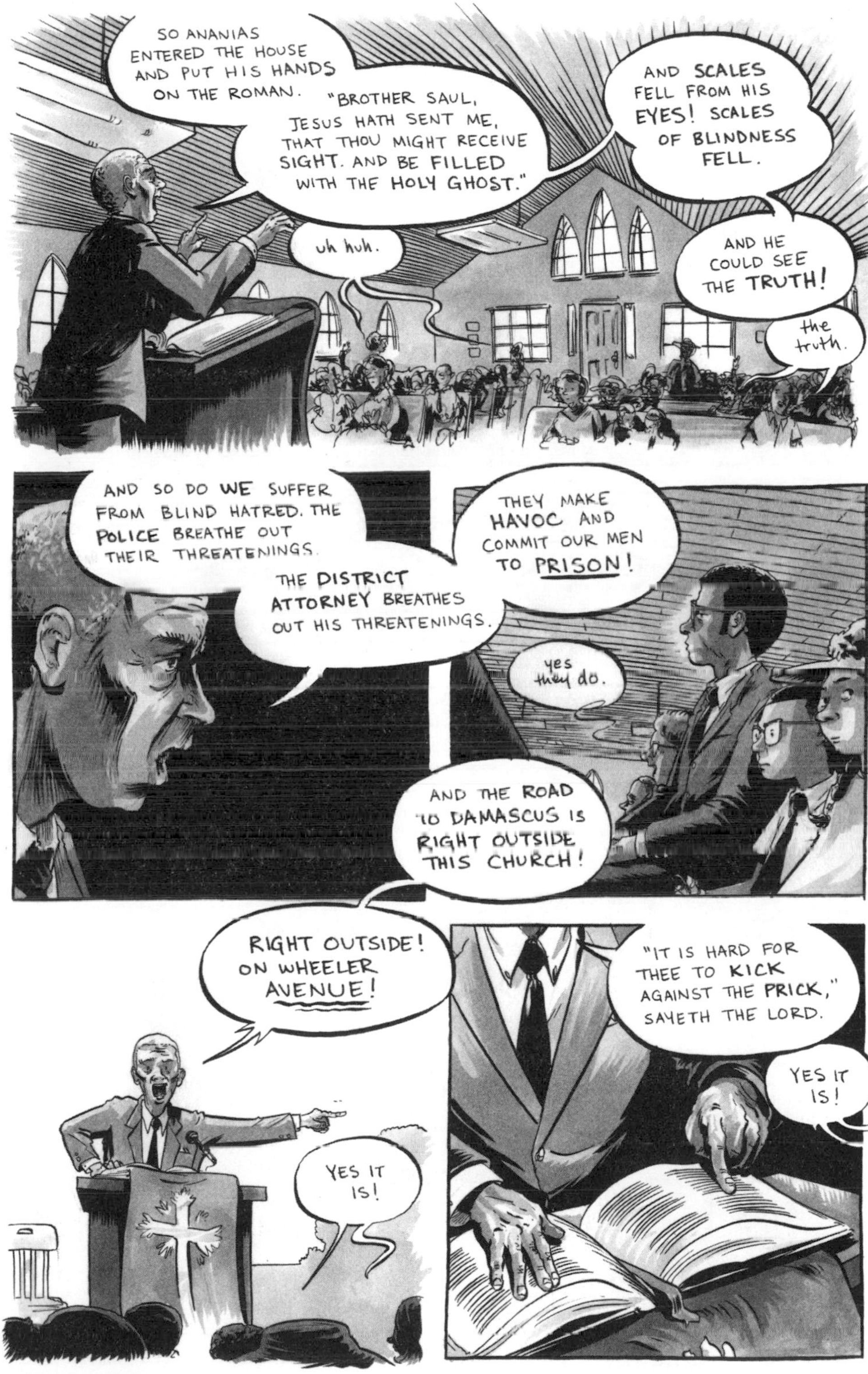

SO ANANIAS ENTERED THE HOUSE AND PUT HIS HANDS ON THE ROMAN.
"BROTHER SAUL, JESUS HATH SENT ME, THAT THOU MIGHT RECEIVE SIGHT. AND BE FILLED WITH THE HOLY GHOST."
uh huh.
AND SCALES FELL FROM HIS EYES! SCALES OF BLINDNESS FELL.
AND HE COULD SEE THE TRUTH!
the truth.
AND SO DO WE SUFFER FROM BLIND HATRED. THE POLICE BREATHE OUT THEIR THREATENINGS.
THE DISTRICT ATTORNEY BREATHES OUT HIS THREATENINGS.
THEY MAKE HAVOC AND COMMIT OUR MEN TO PRISON!
yes they do.
AND THE ROAD TO DAMASCUS IS RIGHT OUTSIDE THIS CHURCH!
RIGHT OUTSIDE! ON WHEELER AVENUE!
YES IT IS!
"IT IS HARD FOR THEE TO KICK AGAINST THE PRICK," SAYETH THE LORD.
YES IT IS!

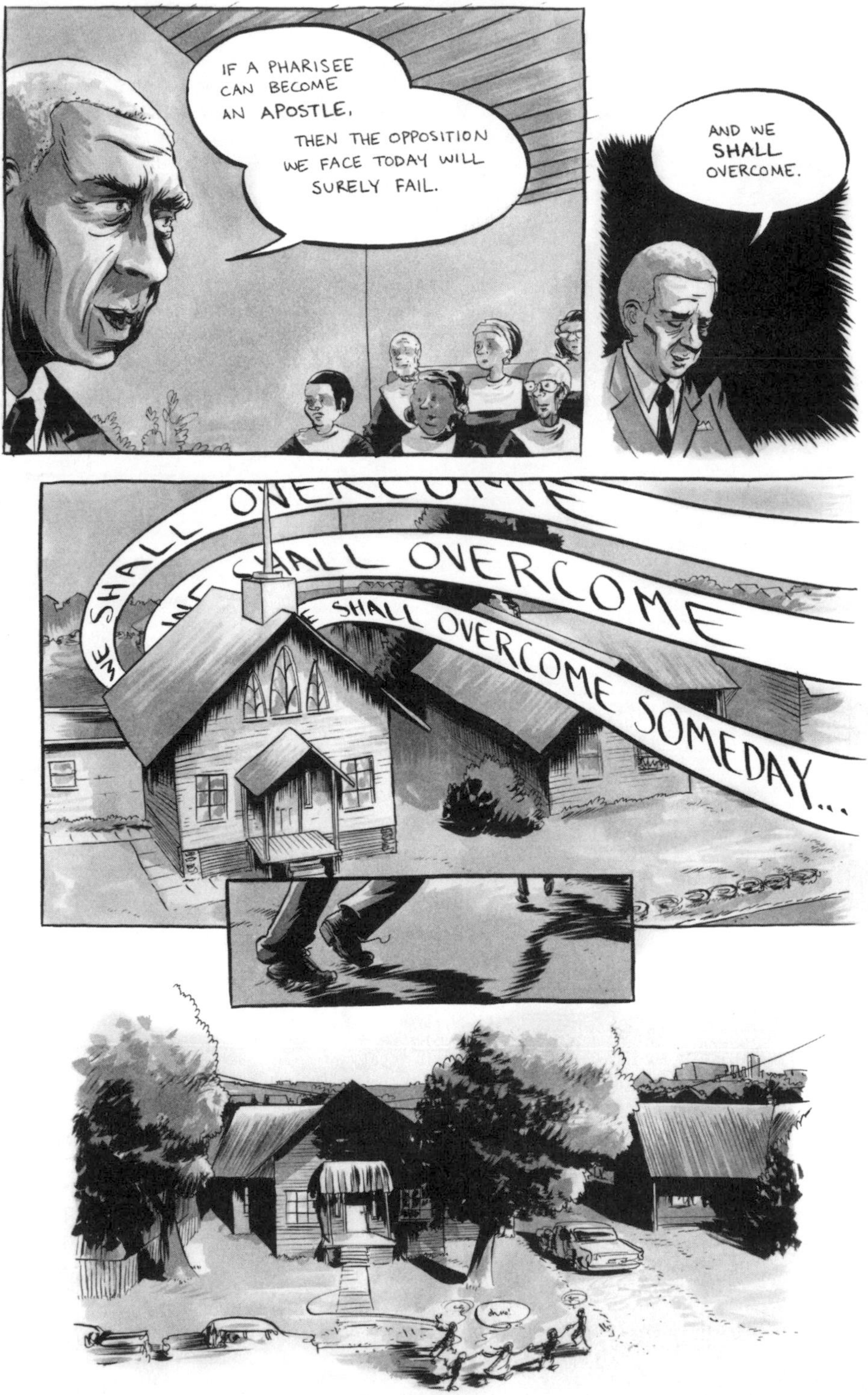
IF A PHARISEE CAN BECOME AN APOSTLE,
THEN THE OPPOSITION WE FACE TODAY WILL SURELY FAIL.
AND WE SHALL OVERCOME.
WE SHALL OVERCOME
SHALL OVERCOME
SHALL OVERCOME SOMEDAY...

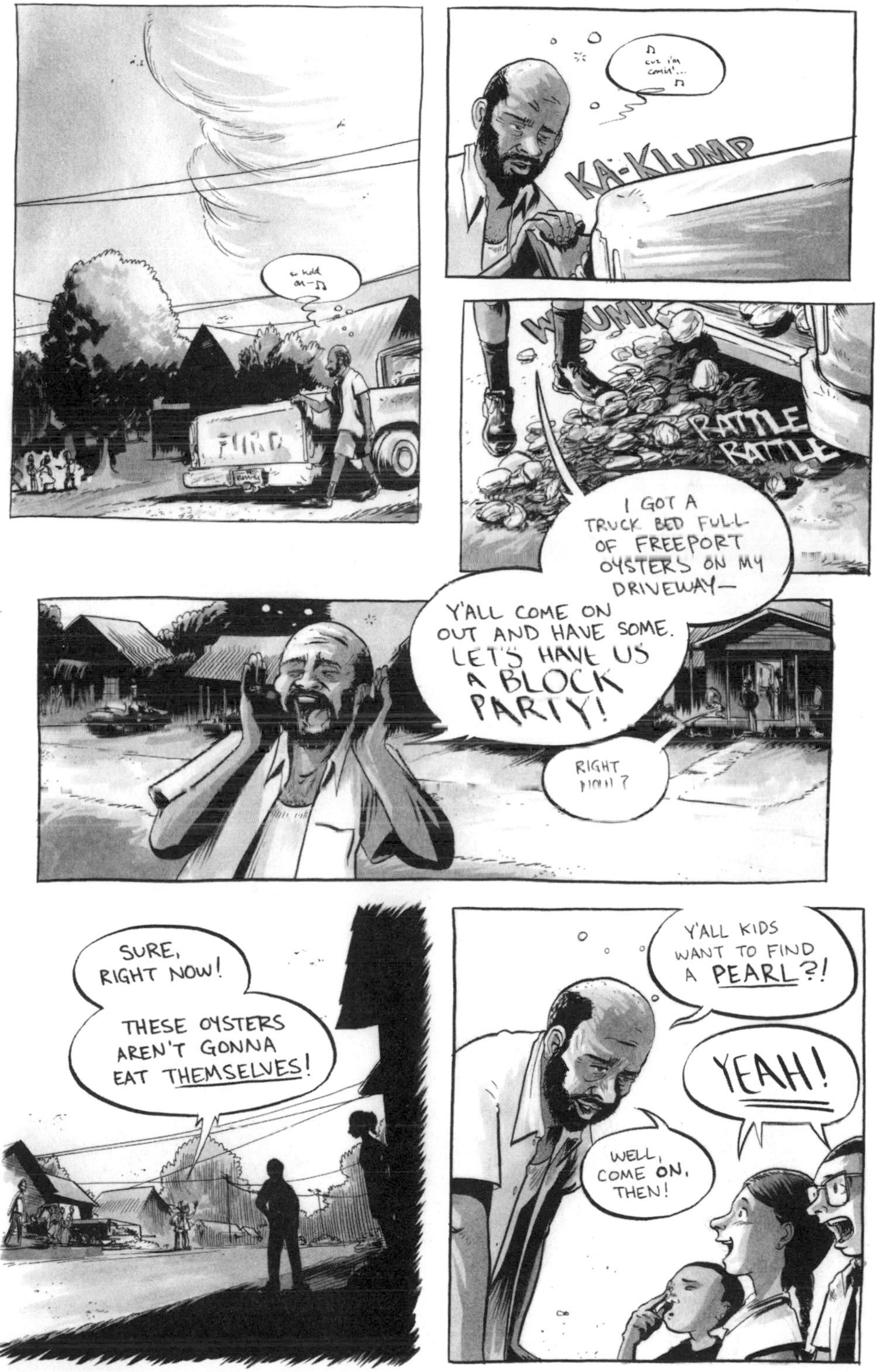
so hold on—♫
FORD
♫ cuz i'm comin'... ♫
KA-KLUMP
WUMP
RATTLE RATTLE
I GOT A TRUCK BED FULL OF FREEPORT OYSTERS ON MY DRIVEWAY—
Y'ALL COME ON OUT AND HAVE SOME. LET'S HAVE US A BLOCK PARTY!
RIGHT NOW?
SURE, RIGHT NOW!
THESE OYSTERS AREN'T GONNA EAT THEMSELVES!
Y'ALL KIDS WANT TO FIND A PEARL?!
YEAH!
WELL, COME ON, THEN!

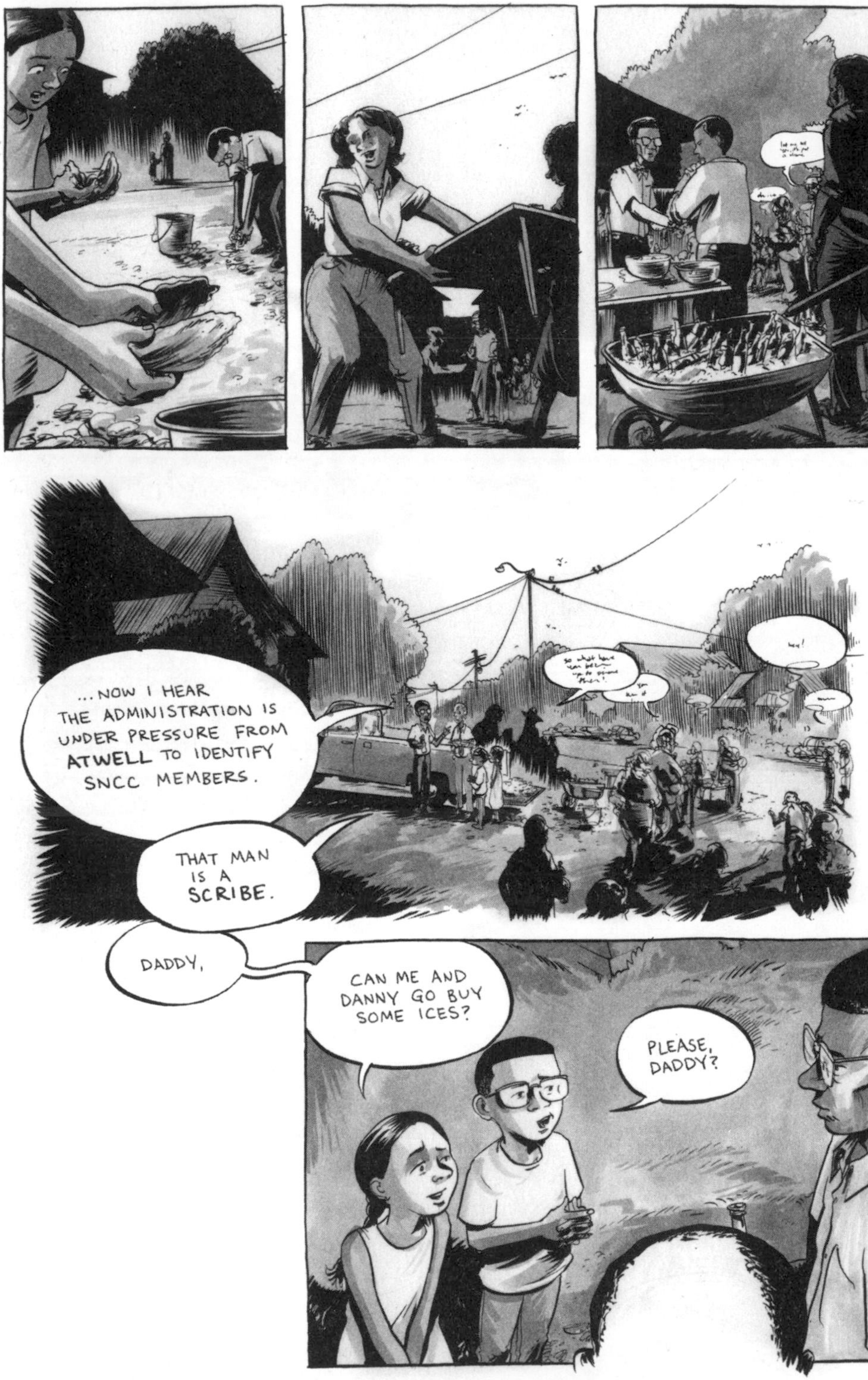
...NOW I HEAR THE ADMINISTRATION IS UNDER PRESSURE FROM ATWELL TO IDENTIFY SNCC MEMBERS.
THAT MAN IS A SCRIBE.
DADDY,
CAN ME AND DANNY GO BUY SOME ICES?
PLEASE, DADDY?

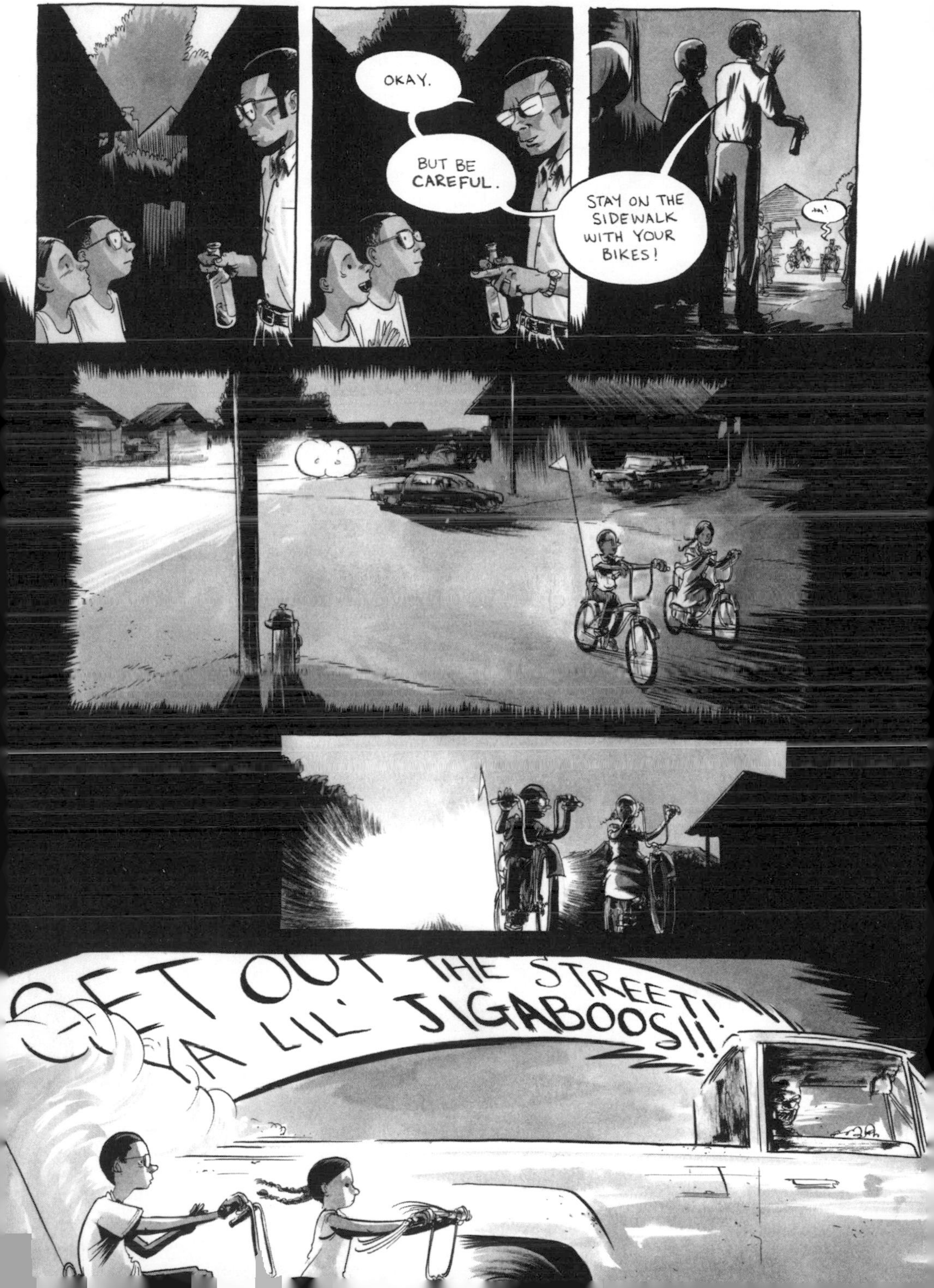
OKAY.
BUT BE CAREFUL.
STAY ON THE SIDEWALK WITH YOUR BIKES!
GET OUT THE STREET, YA LIL' JIGABOOS!!

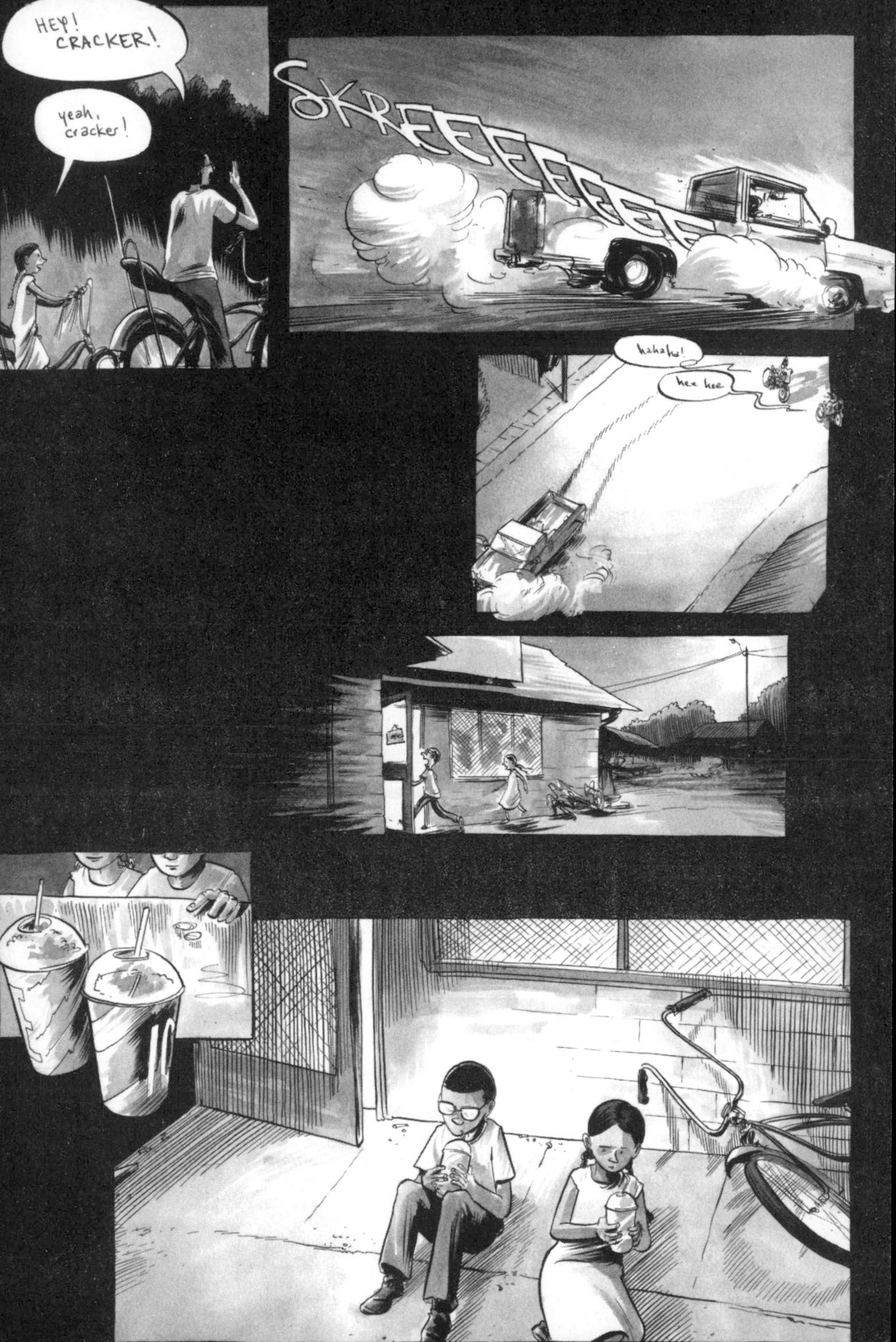
HEY! CRACKER!
yeah, cracker!
SKREEEEEEEEE
hahaha!
hee hee

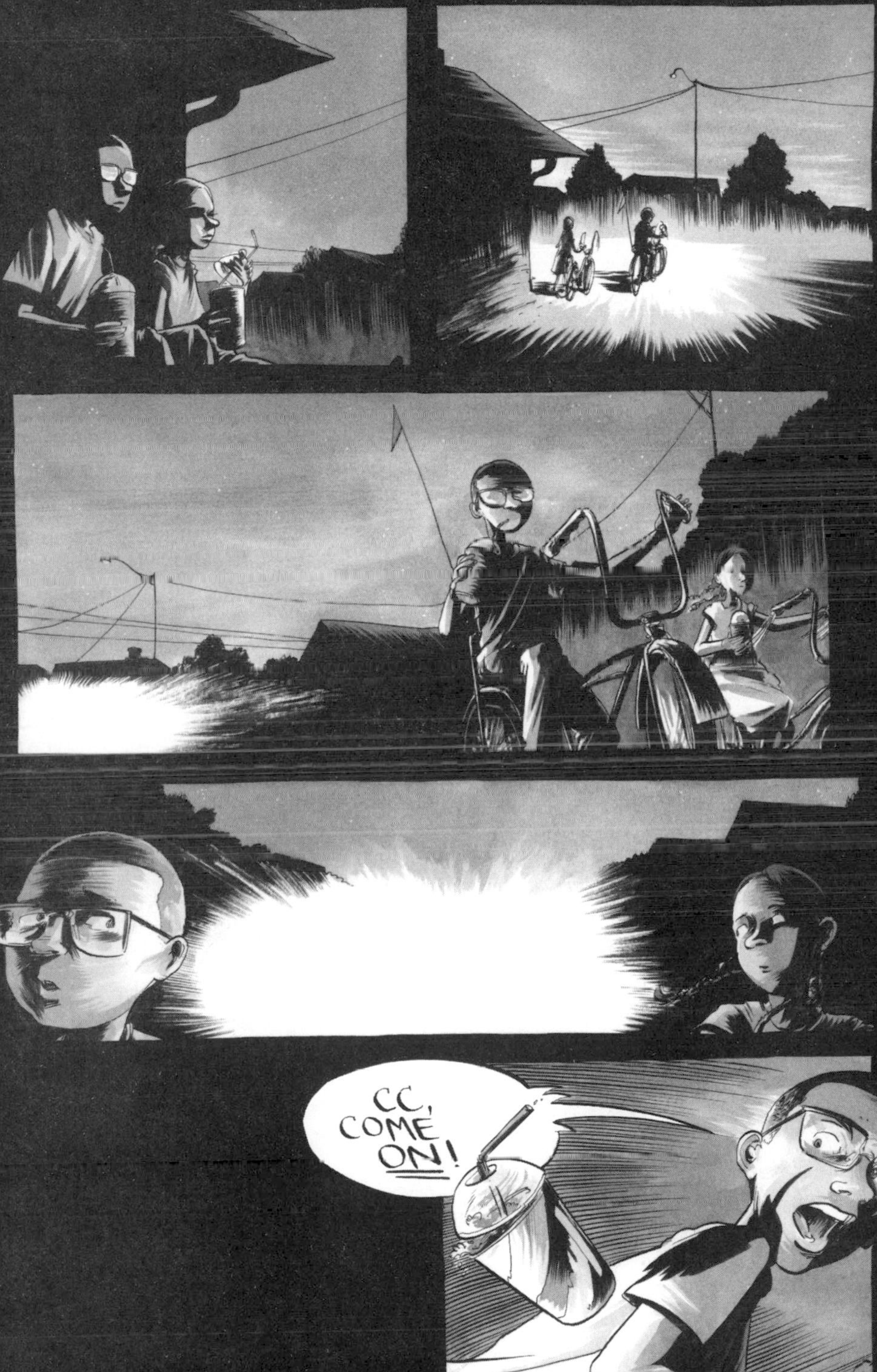
CC, COME ON!

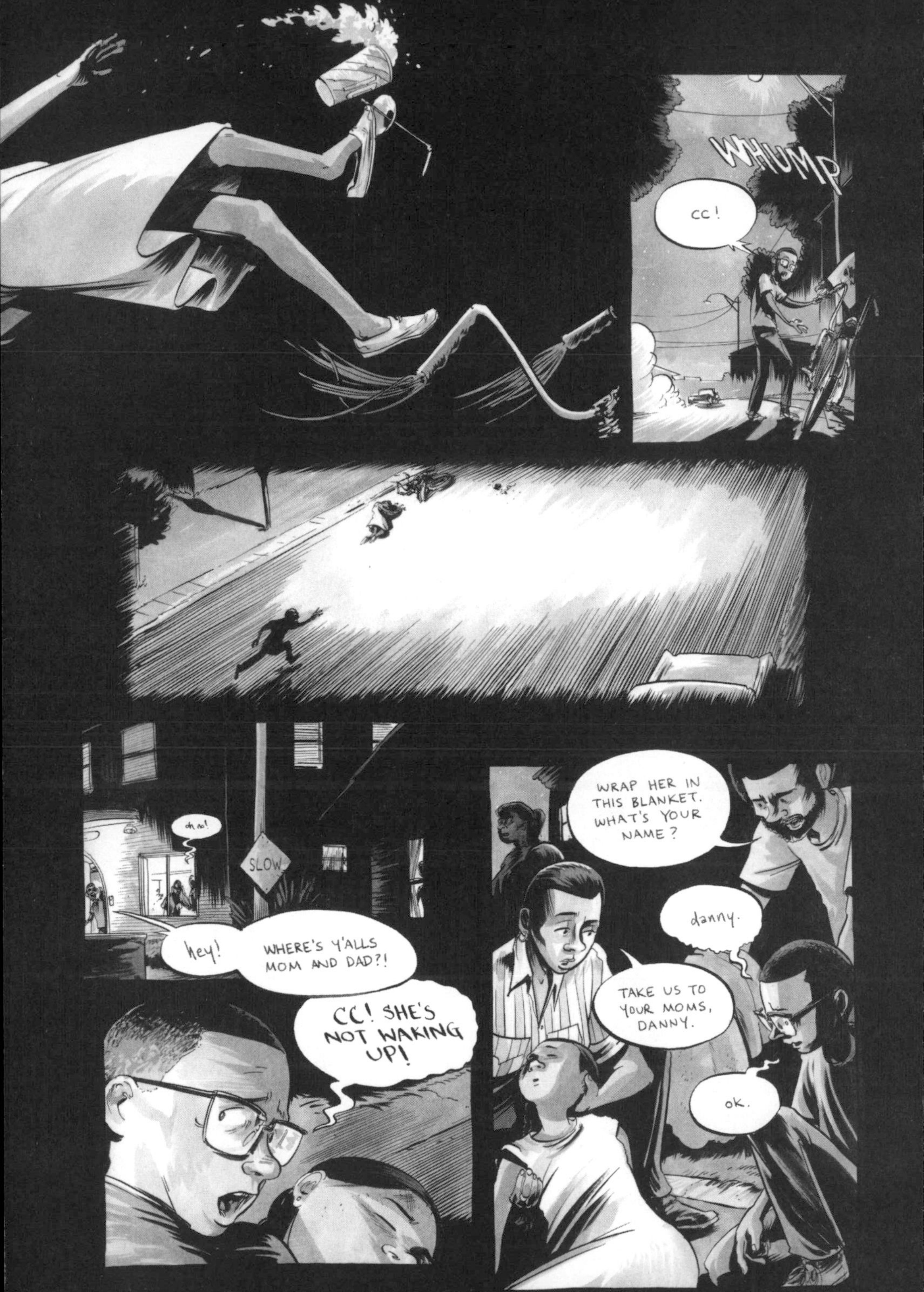
WHUMP
CC!
oh no!
SLOW
hey!
WHERE'S Y'ALLS MOM AND DAD?!
CC! SHE'S NOT WAKING UP!
WRAP HER IN THIS BLANKET. WHAT'S YOUR NAME?
danny.
TAKE US TO YOUR MOMS, DANNY.
ok.

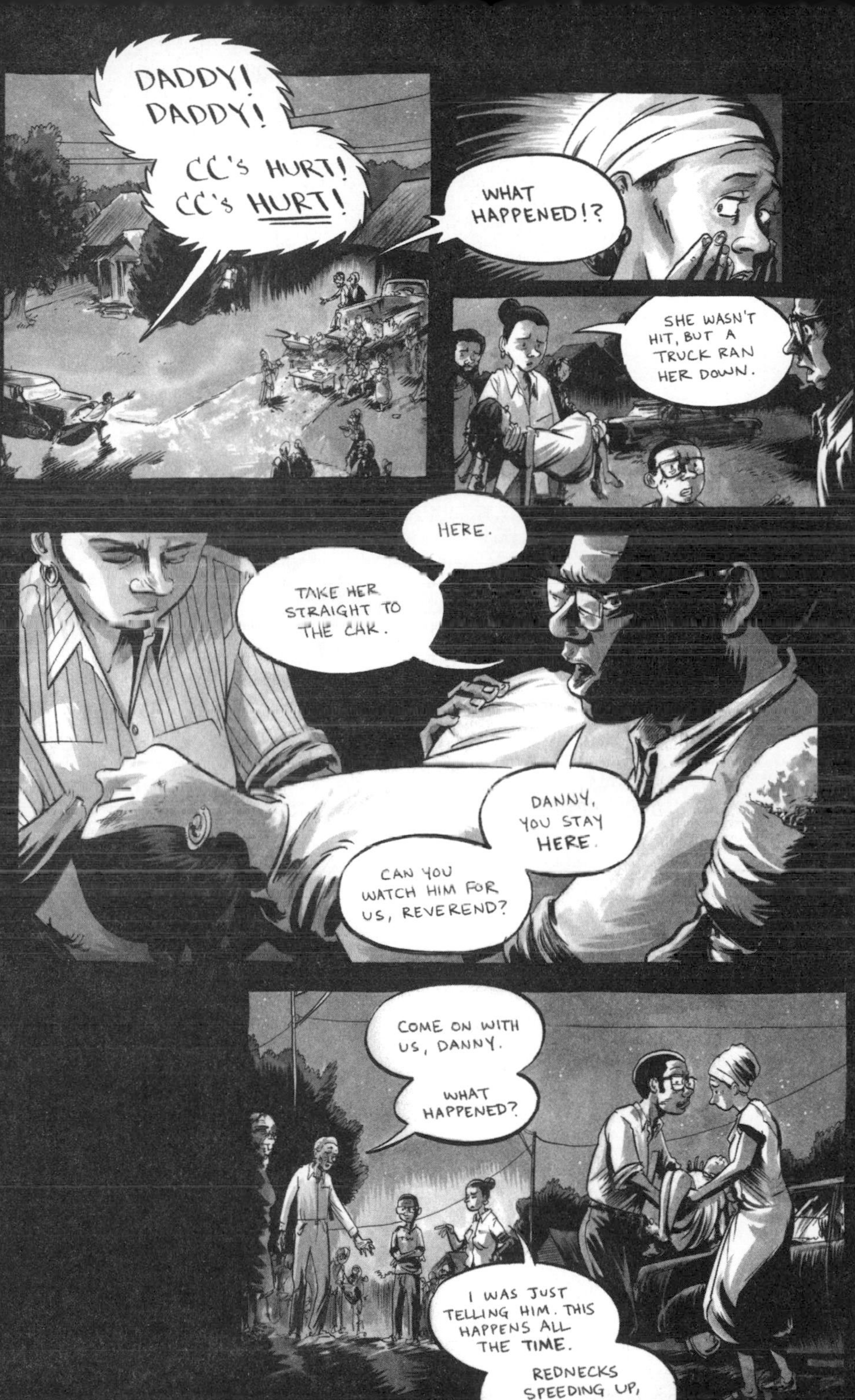
DADDY! DADDY!
CC's HURT! CC's HURT!
WHAT HAPPENED!?
SHE WASN'T HIT, BUT A TRUCK RAN HER DOWN.
HERE.
TAKE HER STRAIGHT TO THE CAR.
DANNY, YOU STAY HERE.
CAN YOU WATCH HIM FOR US, REVEREND?
COME ON WITH US, DANNY.
WHAT HAPPENED?
I WAS JUST TELLING HIM. THIS HAPPENS ALL THE TIME.
REDNECKS SPEEDING UP, NOT CARING.

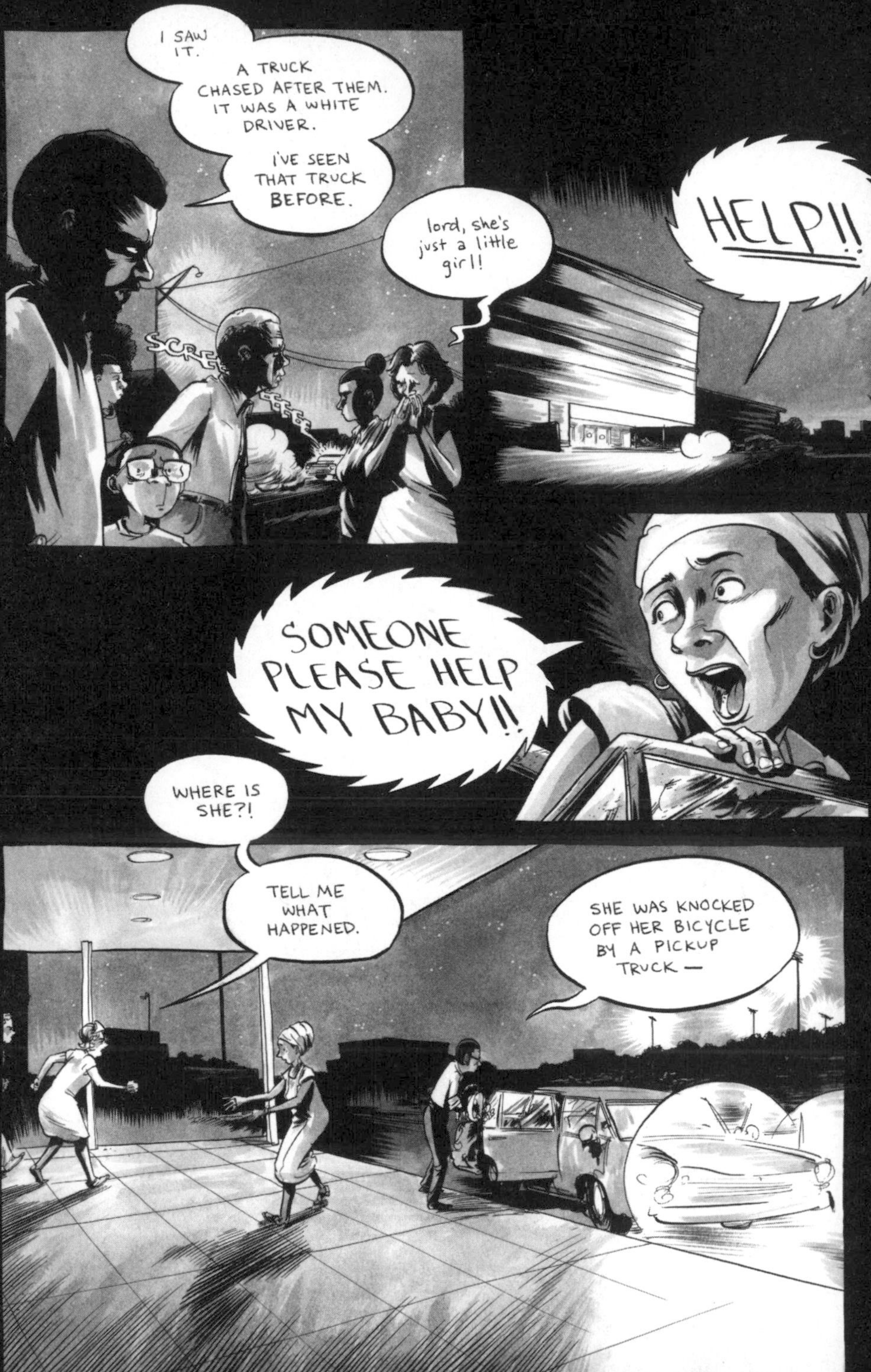
I SAW IT.
A TRUCK CHASED AFTER THEM. IT WAS A WHITE DRIVER.
I'VE SEEN THAT TRUCK BEFORE.
SCREEEEE
lord, she's just a little girl!
HELP!!
SOMEONE PLEASE HELP MY BABY!!
WHERE IS SHE?!
TELL ME WHAT HAPPENED.
SHE WAS KNOCKED OFF HER BICYCLE BY A PICKUP TRUCK —

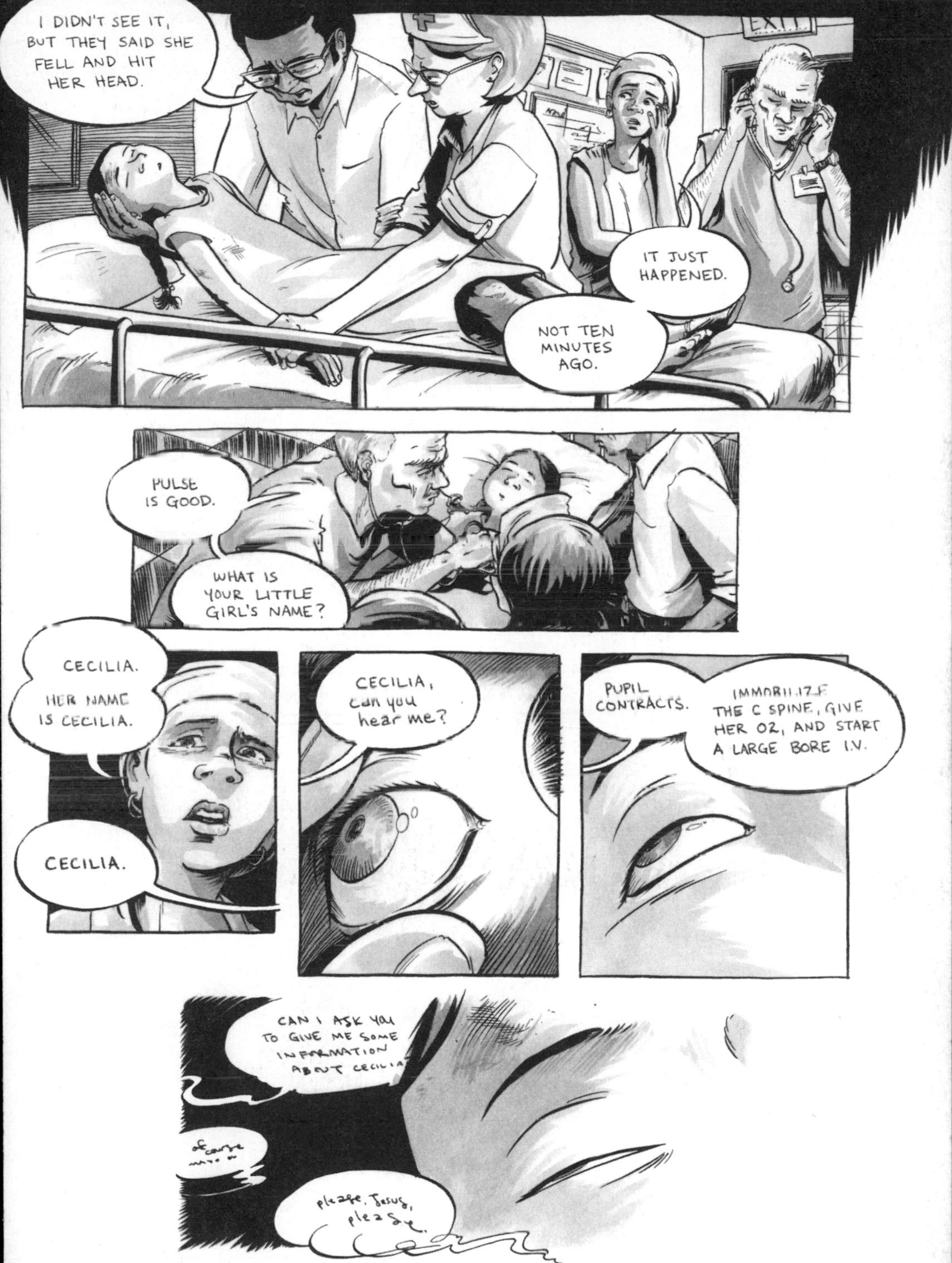
I DIDN'T SEE IT, BUT THEY SAID SHE FELL AND HIT HER HEAD.
IT JUST HAPPENED.
NOT TEN MINUTES AGO.
PULSE IS GOOD.
WHAT IS YOUR LITTLE GIRL'S NAME?
CECILIA.
HER NAME IS CECILIA.
CECILIA.
CECILIA, can you hear me?
PUPIL CONTRACTS.
IMMOBILIZE THE C SPINE, GIVE HER O2, AND START A LARGE BORE I.V.
CAN I ASK YOU TO GIVE ME SOME INFORMATION ABOUT CECILIA
of course
please, Jesus, please.

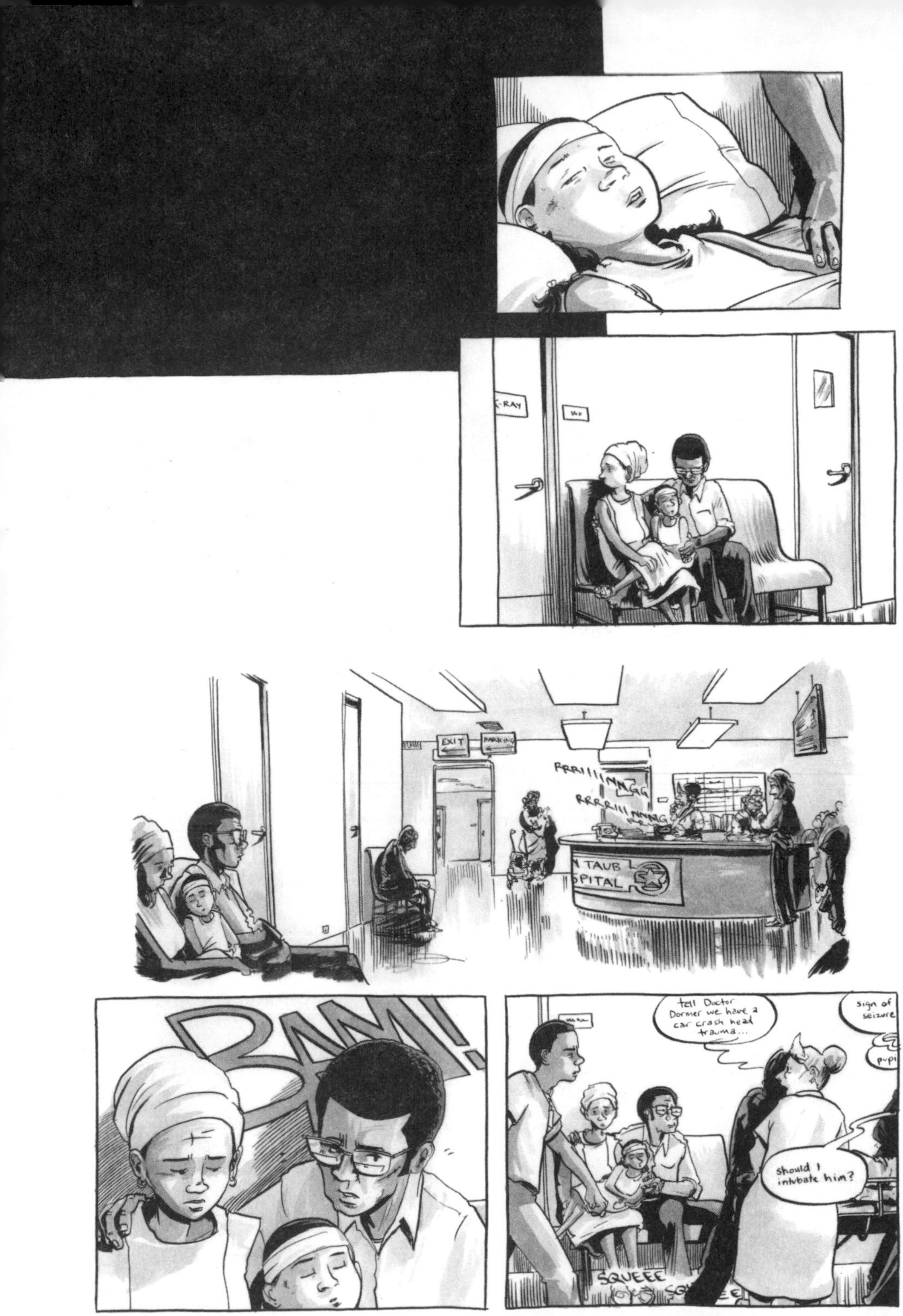
X-RAY
EXIT
PARKING
PRRIIIINNNGG
RRRRIIINNNG
N TAUB
SPITAL
BAM!
tell Doctor Dormer we have a car crash head trauma...
sign of seizure
pupi
should I intubate him?
SQUEEE

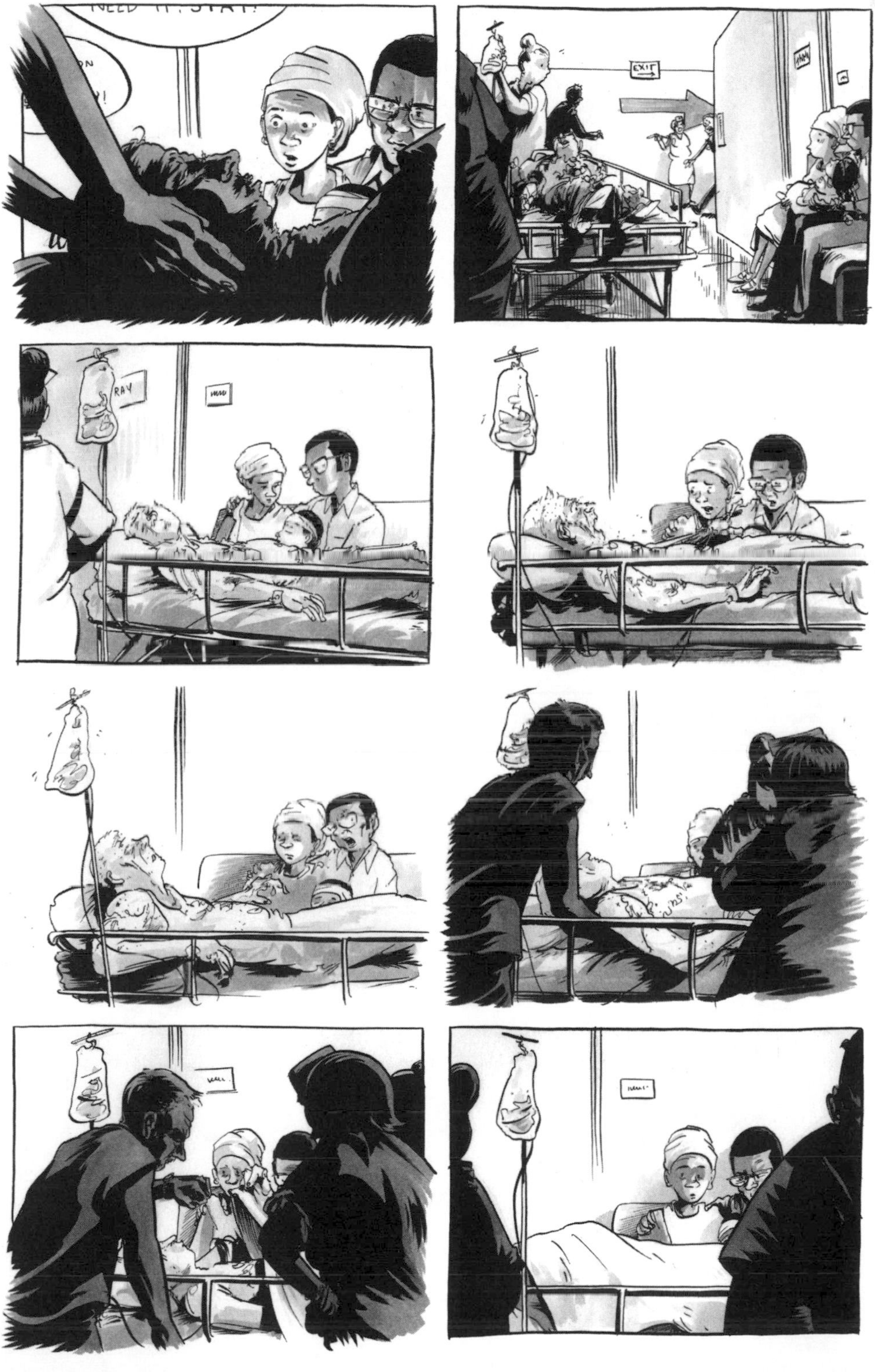
EXIT
RAY

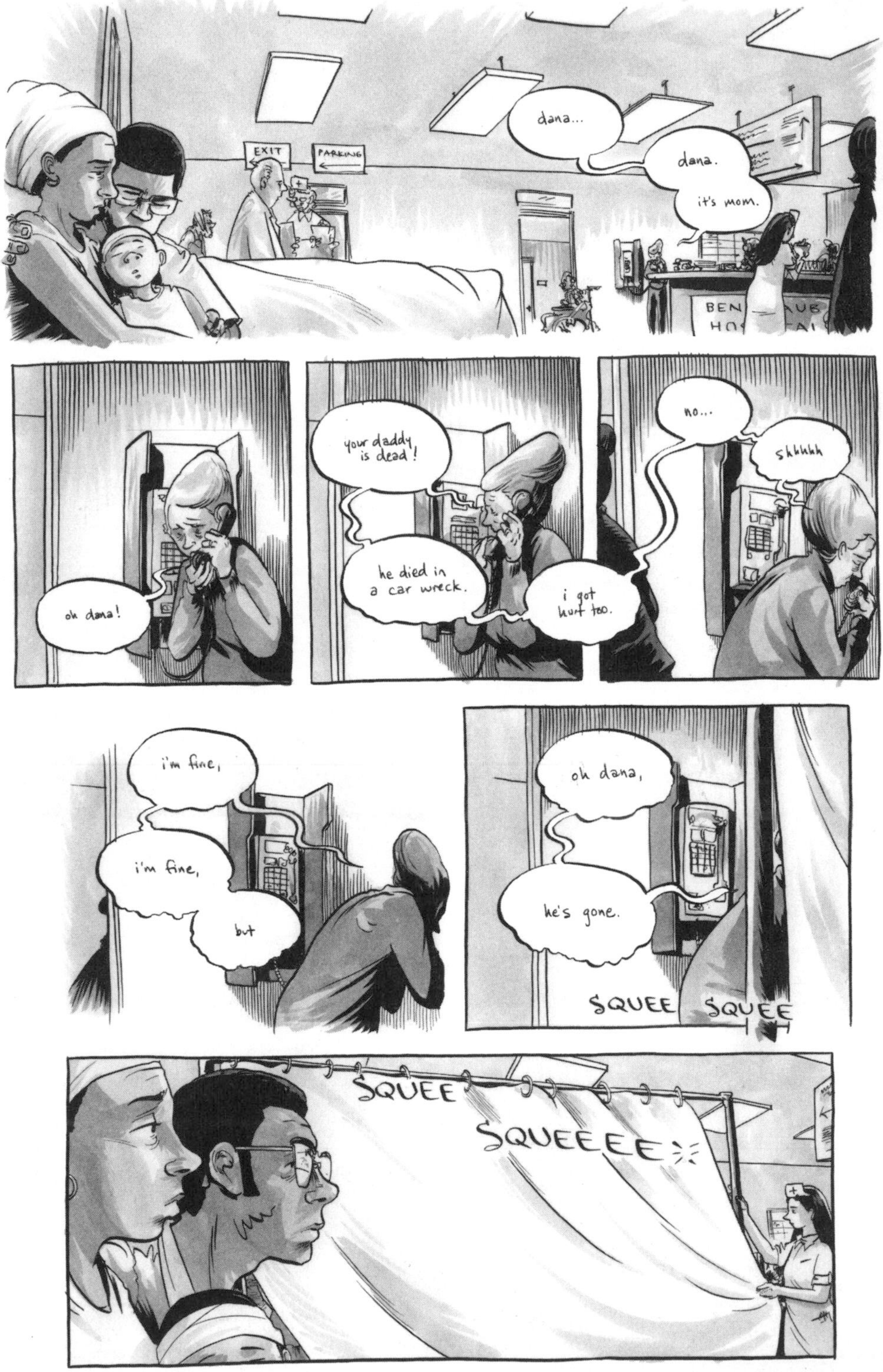
EXIT
PARKING
dana...
dana.
it's mom.
oh dana!
your daddy is dead!
he died in a car wreck.
i got hurt too.
no...
shhhhh
i'm fine,
i'm fine,
but
oh dana,
he's gone.
SQUEE SQUEE
SQUEE
SQUEEEE

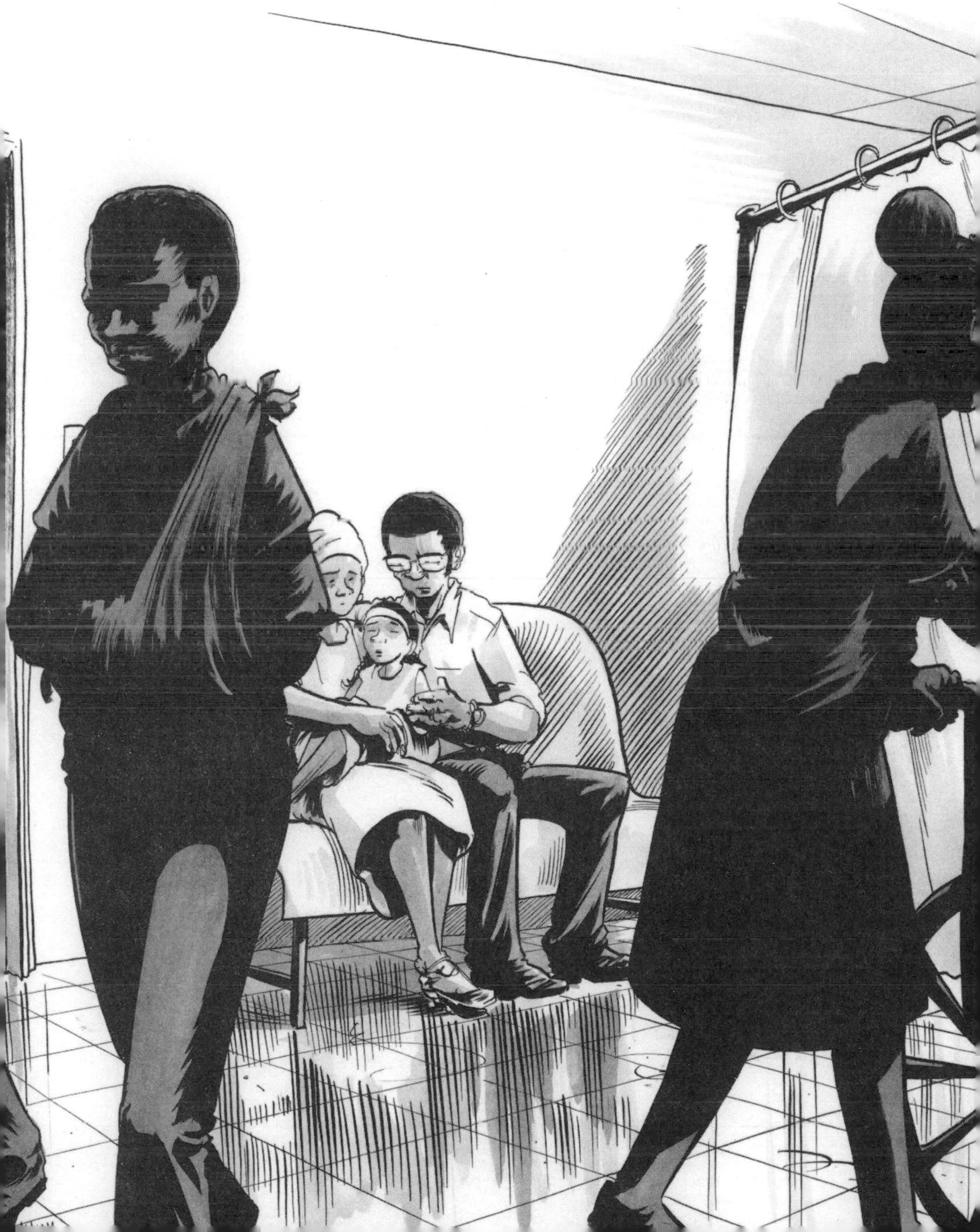

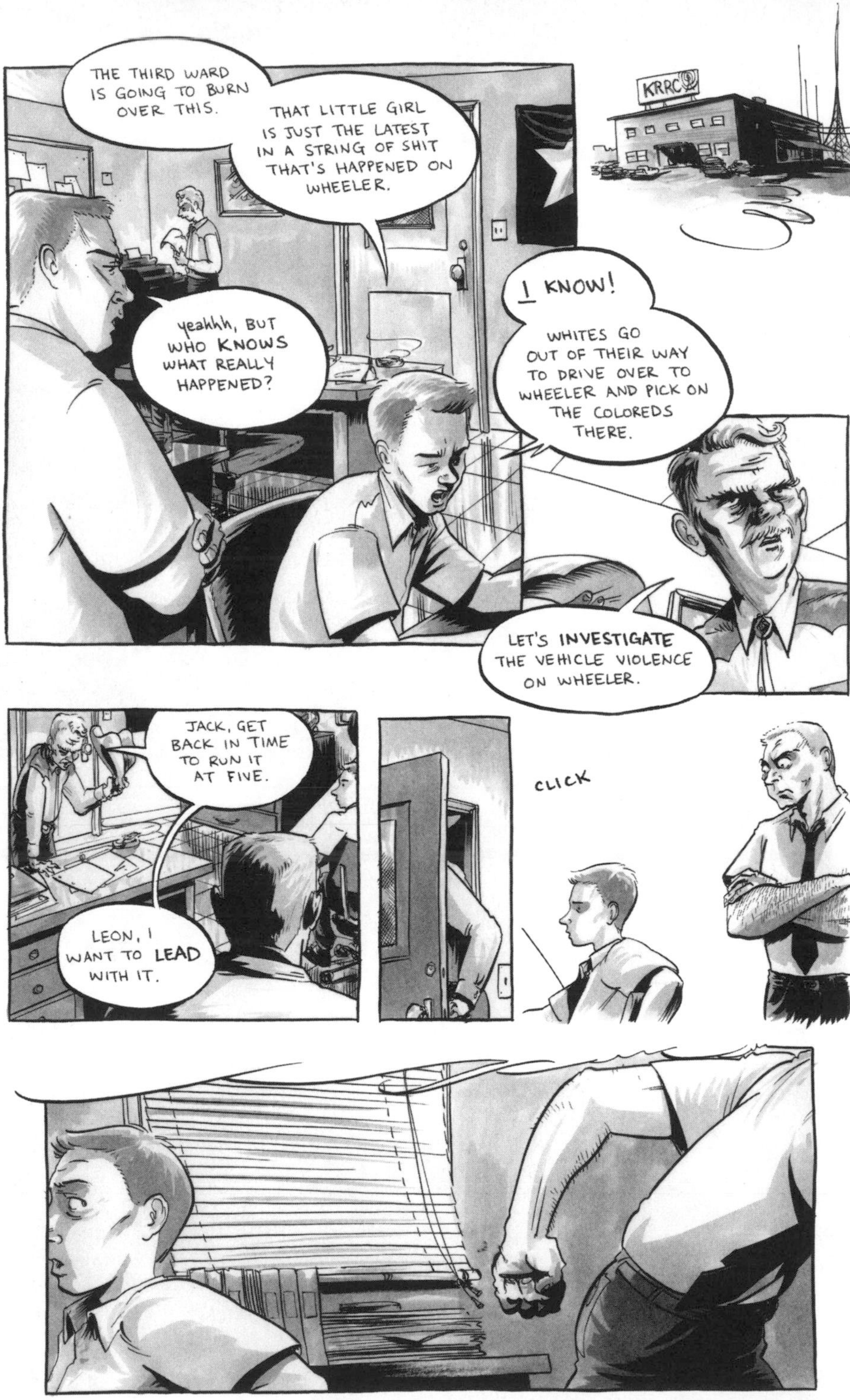
KRRC
THE THIRD WARD IS GOING TO BURN OVER THIS.
THAT LITTLE GIRL IS JUST THE LATEST IN A STRING OF SHIT THAT'S HAPPENED ON WHEELER.
yeahhh, BUT WHO KNOWS WHAT REALLY HAPPENED?
I KNOW!
WHITES GO OUT OF THEIR WAY TO DRIVE OVER TO WHEELER AND PICK ON THE COLOREDS THERE.
LET'S INVESTIGATE THE VEHICLE VIOLENCE ON WHEELER.
JACK, GET BACK IN TIME TO RUN IT AT FIVE.
LEON, I WANT TO LEAD WITH IT.
CLICK

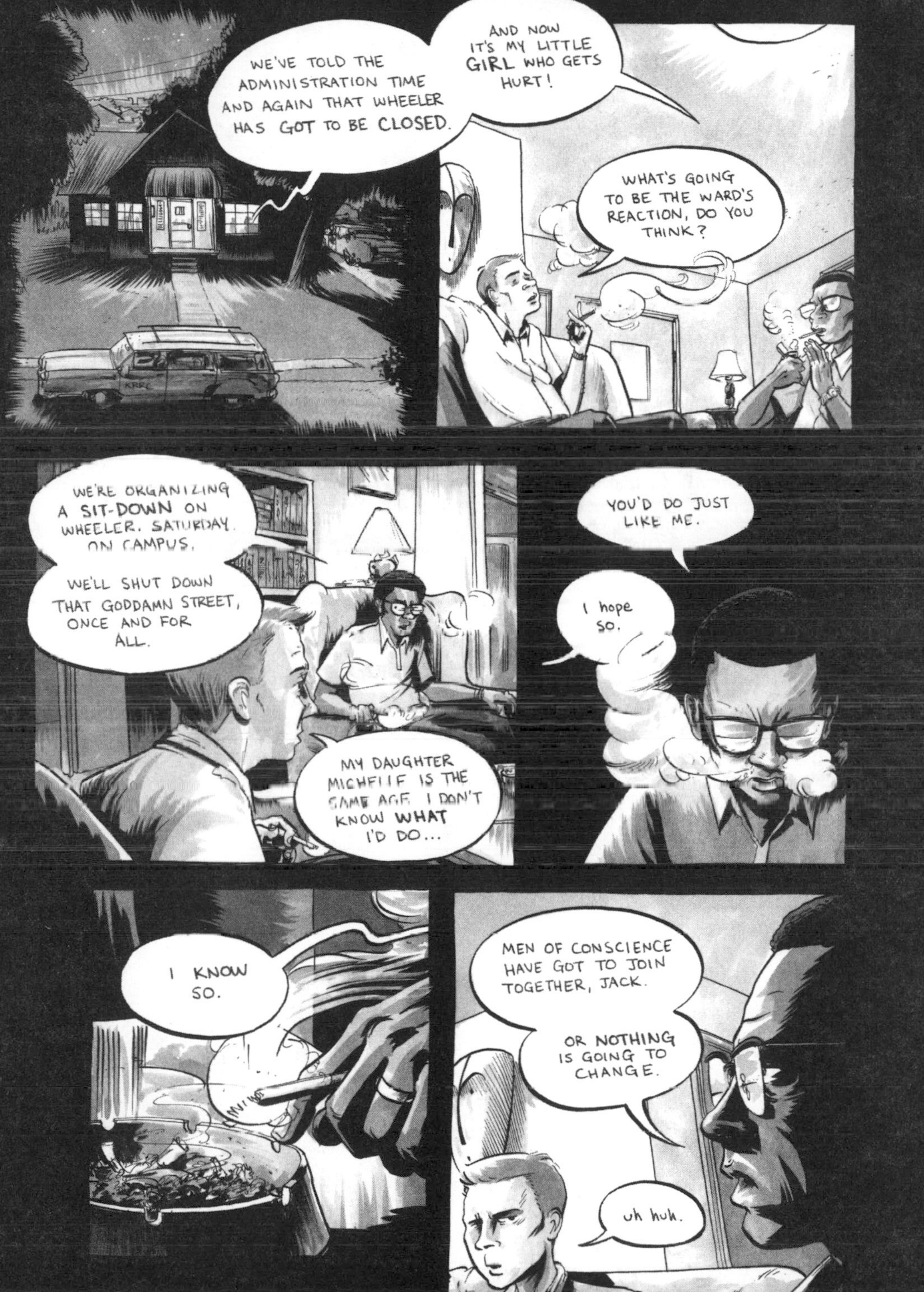
WE'VE TOLD THE ADMINISTRATION TIME AND AGAIN THAT WHEELER HAS GOT TO BE CLOSED.
AND NOW IT'S MY LITTLE GIRL WHO GETS HURT!
WHAT'S GOING TO BE THE WARD'S REACTION, DO YOU THINK?
WE'RE ORGANIZING A SIT-DOWN ON WHEELER. SATURDAY. ON CAMPUS.
WE'LL SHUT DOWN THAT GODDAMN STREET, ONCE AND FOR ALL.
MY DAUGHTER MICHELLE IS THE SAME AGE. I DON'T KNOW WHAT I'D DO...
YOU'D DO JUST LIKE ME.
I hope so.
I KNOW SO.
MEN OF CONSCIENCE HAVE GOT TO JOIN TOGETHER, JACK.
OR NOTHING IS GOING TO CHANGE.
uh huh.

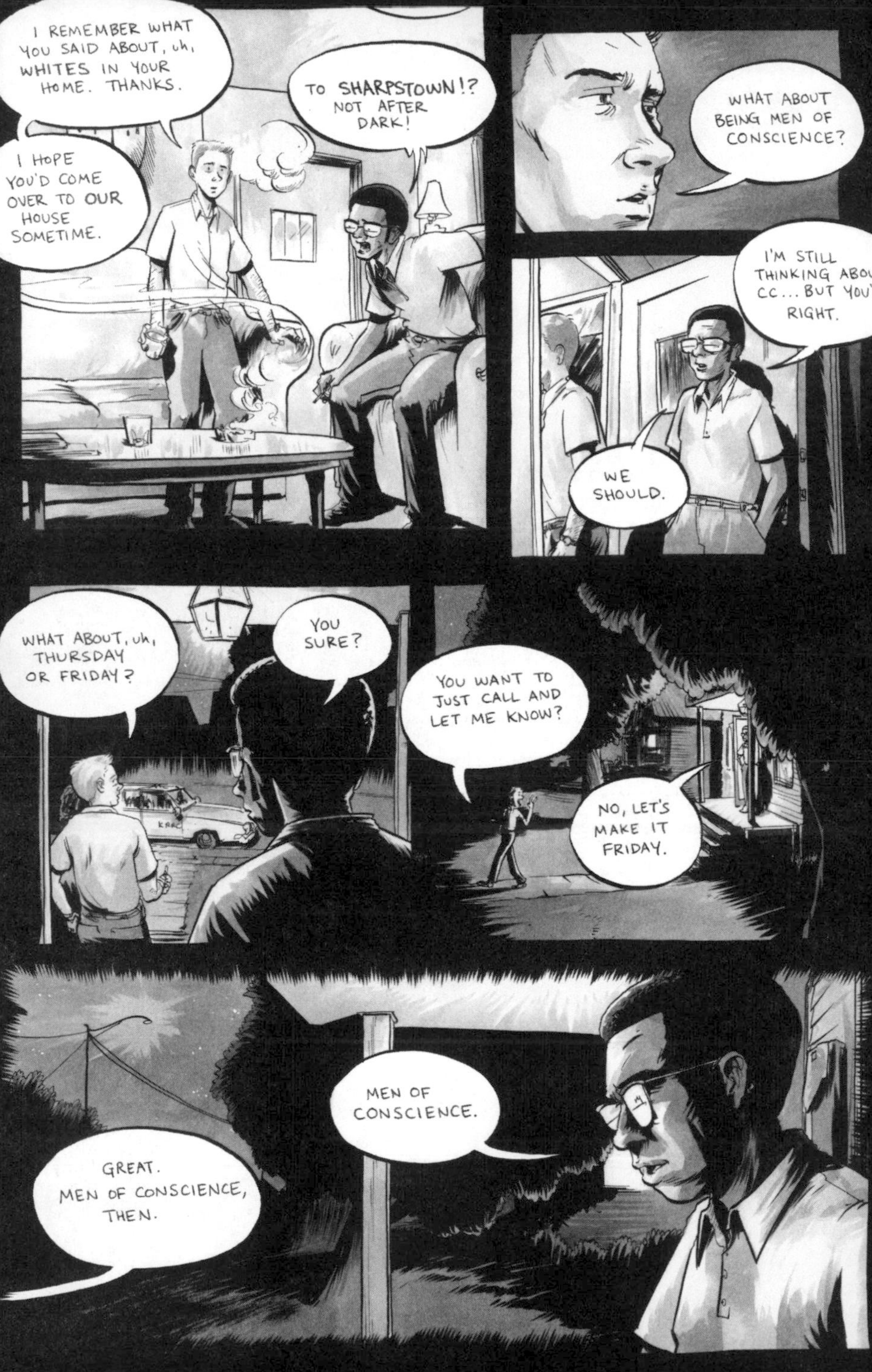
I REMEMBER WHAT YOU SAID ABOUT, uh, WHITES IN YOUR HOME. THANKS.
I HOPE YOU'D COME OVER TO OUR HOUSE SOMETIME.
TO SHARPSTOWN!? NOT AFTER DARK!
WHAT ABOUT BEING MEN OF CONSCIENCE?
I'M STILL THINKING ABOUT CC... BUT YOU'RE RIGHT.
WE SHOULD.
WHAT ABOUT, uh, THURSDAY OR FRIDAY?
YOU SURE?
YOU WANT TO JUST CALL AND LET ME KNOW?
NO, LET'S MAKE IT FRIDAY.
MEN OF CONSCIENCE.
GREAT. MEN OF CONSCIENCE, THEN.

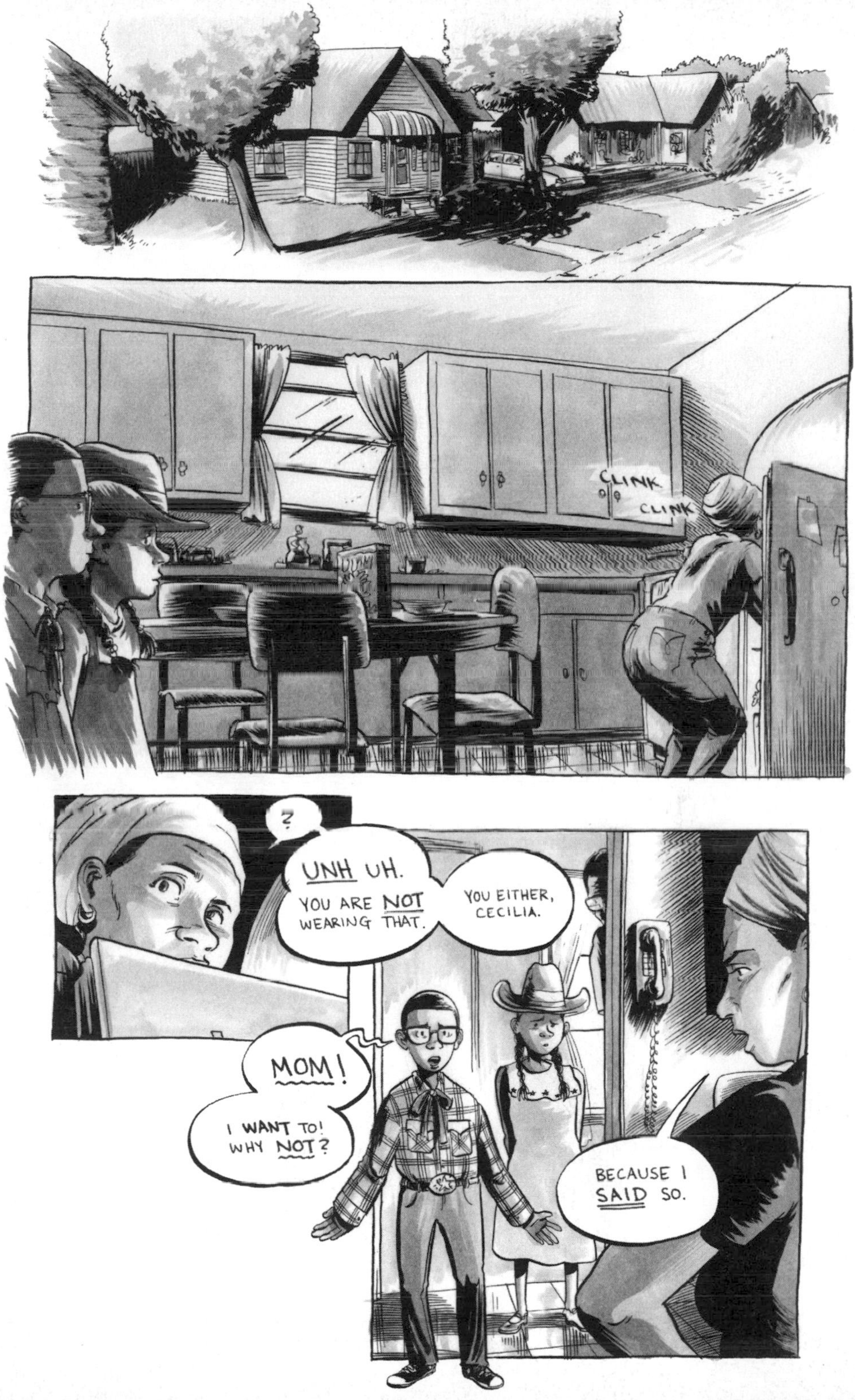
CLINK
CLINK
?
UNH UH. YOU ARE NOT WEARING THAT.
YOU EITHER, CECILIA.
MOM!
I WANT TO! WHY NOT?
BECAUSE I SAID SO.

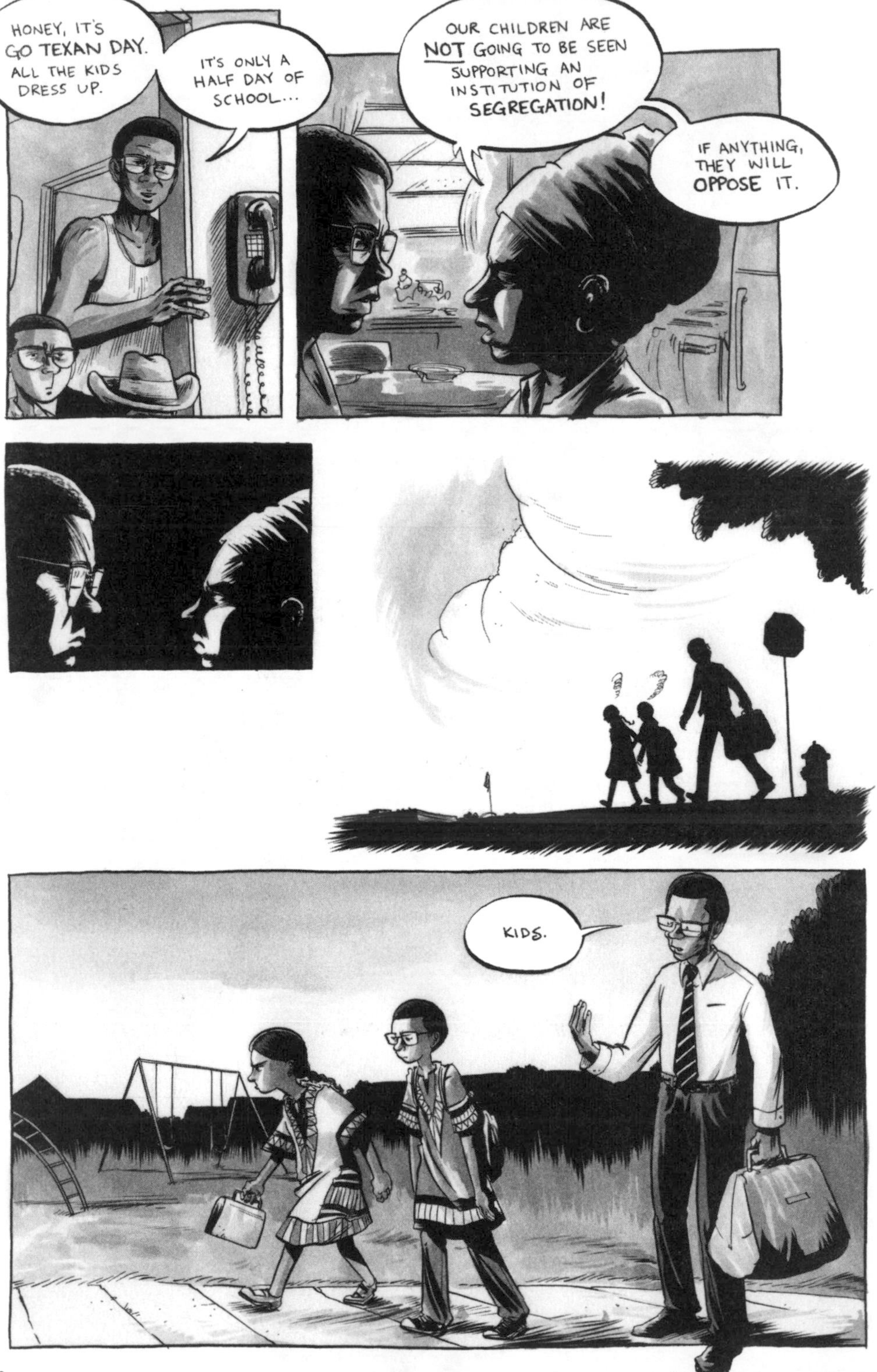
HONEY, IT'S GO TEXAN DAY. ALL THE KIDS DRESS UP.
IT'S ONLY A HALF DAY OF SCHOOL...
OUR CHILDREN ARE NOT GOING TO BE SEEN SUPPORTING AN INSTITUTION OF SEGREGATION!
IF ANYTHING, THEY WILL OPPOSE IT.
KIDS.

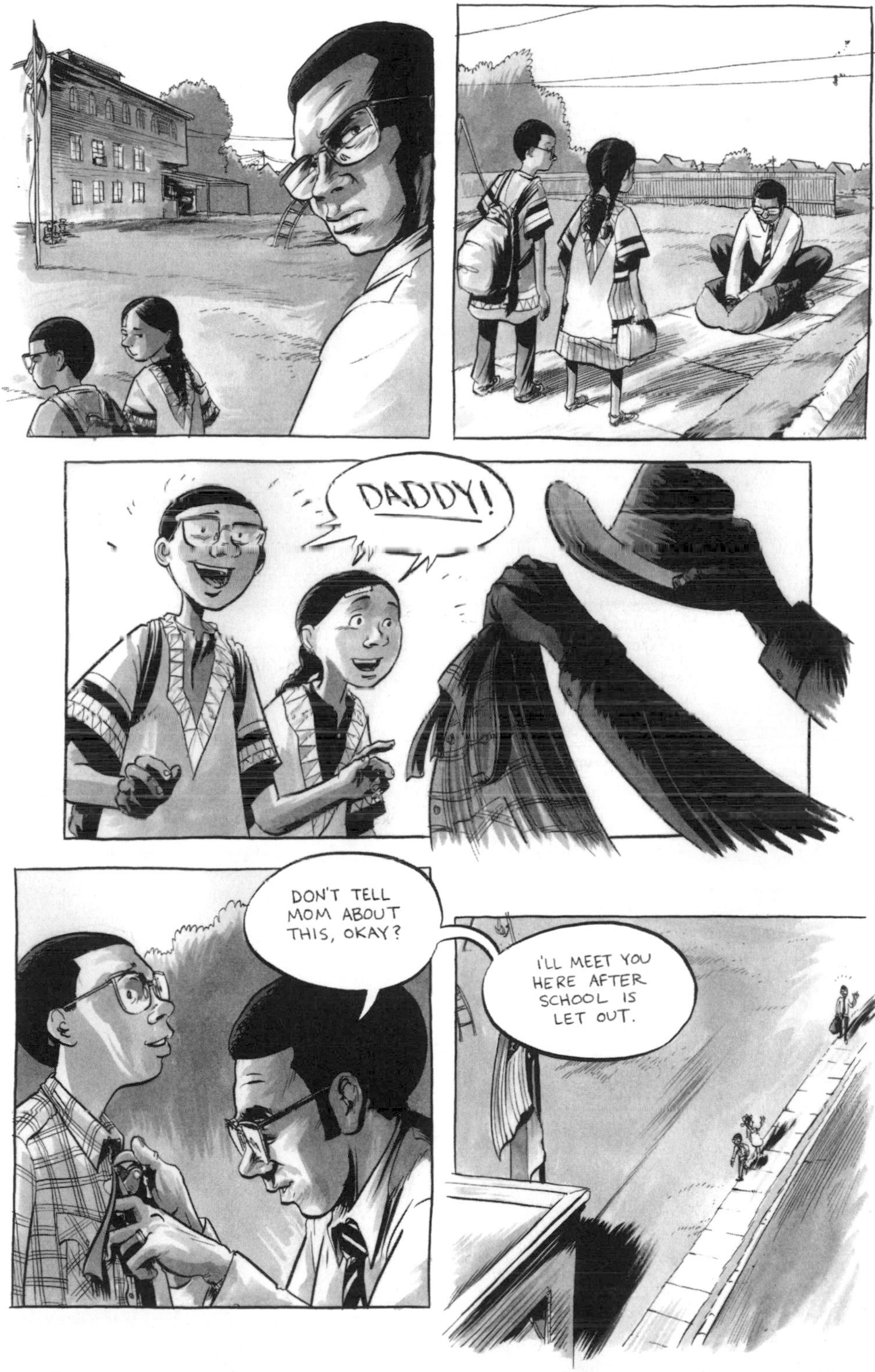
DADDY!
DON'T TELL MOM ABOUT THIS, OKAY?
I'LL MEET YOU HERE AFTER SCHOOL IS LET OUT.

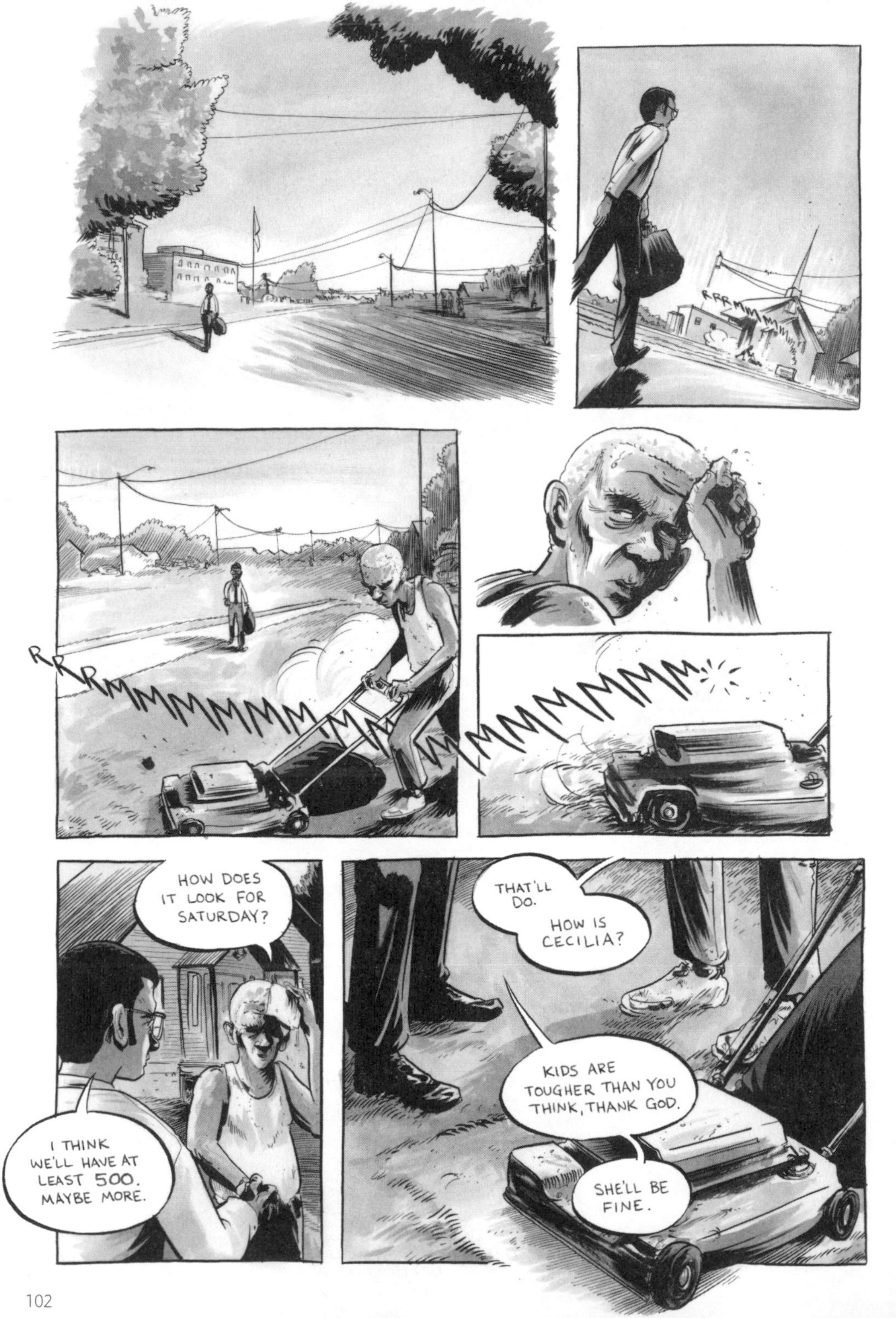
RRRMMMM
RRRMMMMMMMMMMMMMMMMMMMMMM
HOW DOES IT LOOK FOR SATURDAY?
I THINK WE'LL HAVE AT LEAST 500. MAYBE MORE.
THAT'LL DO.
HOW IS CECILIA?
KIDS ARE TOUGHER THAN YOU THINK, THANK GOD.
SHE'LL BE FINE.

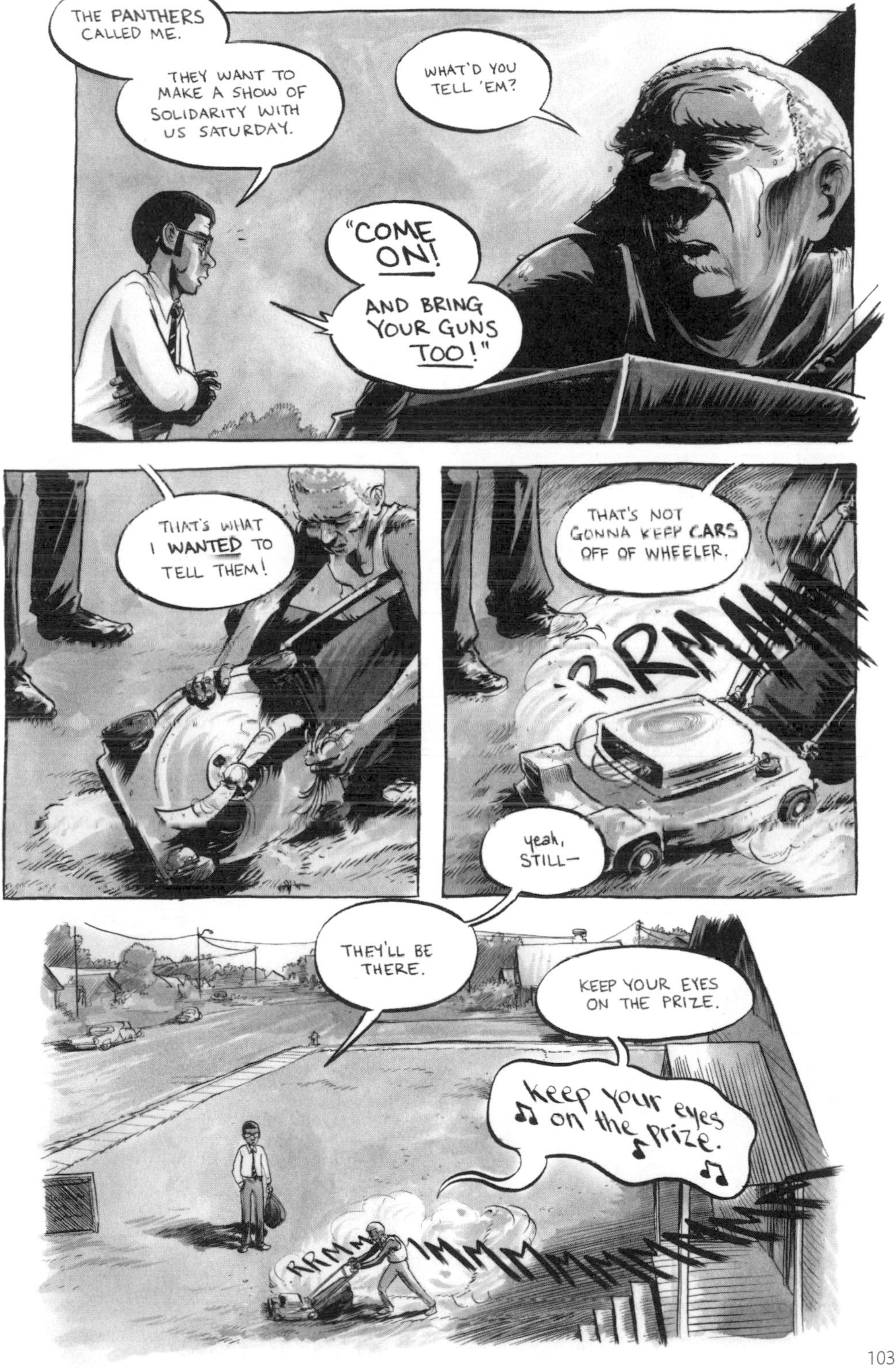
THE PANTHERS CALLED ME.
THEY WANT TO MAKE A SHOW OF SOLIDARITY WITH US SATURDAY.
WHAT'D YOU TELL 'EM?
"COME ON!
AND BRING YOUR GUNS TOO!"
THAT'S WHAT I WANTED TO TELL THEM!
THAT'S NOT GONNA KEEP CARS OFF OF WHEELER.
RRMM
yeah, STILL—
THEY'LL BE THERE.
KEEP YOUR EYES ON THE PRIZE.
keep your eyes on the prize.
RRMMMMMMMMMMMM

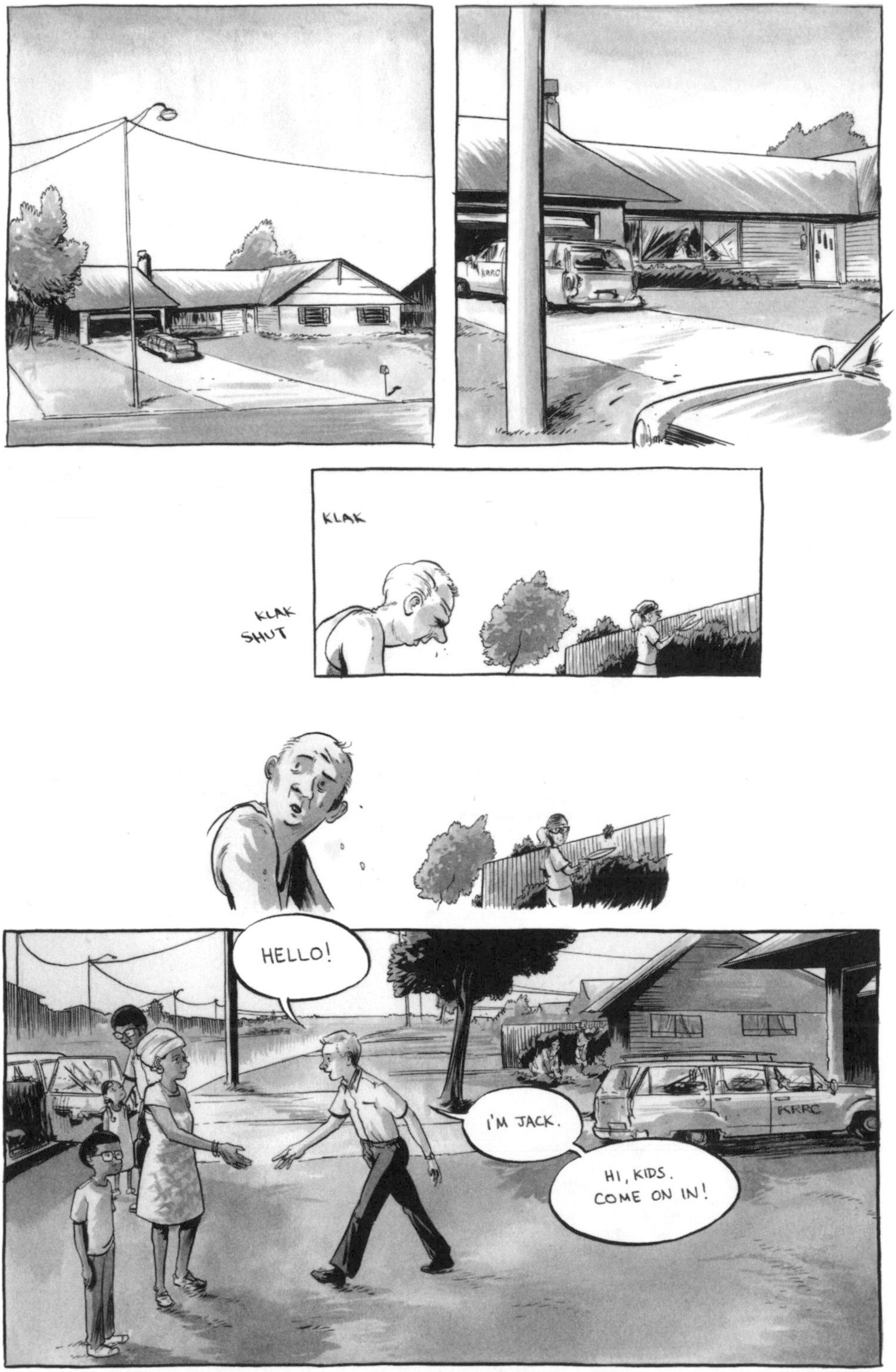
KLAK
KLAK
SHUT
HELLO!
I'M JACK.
HI, KIDS. COME ON IN!

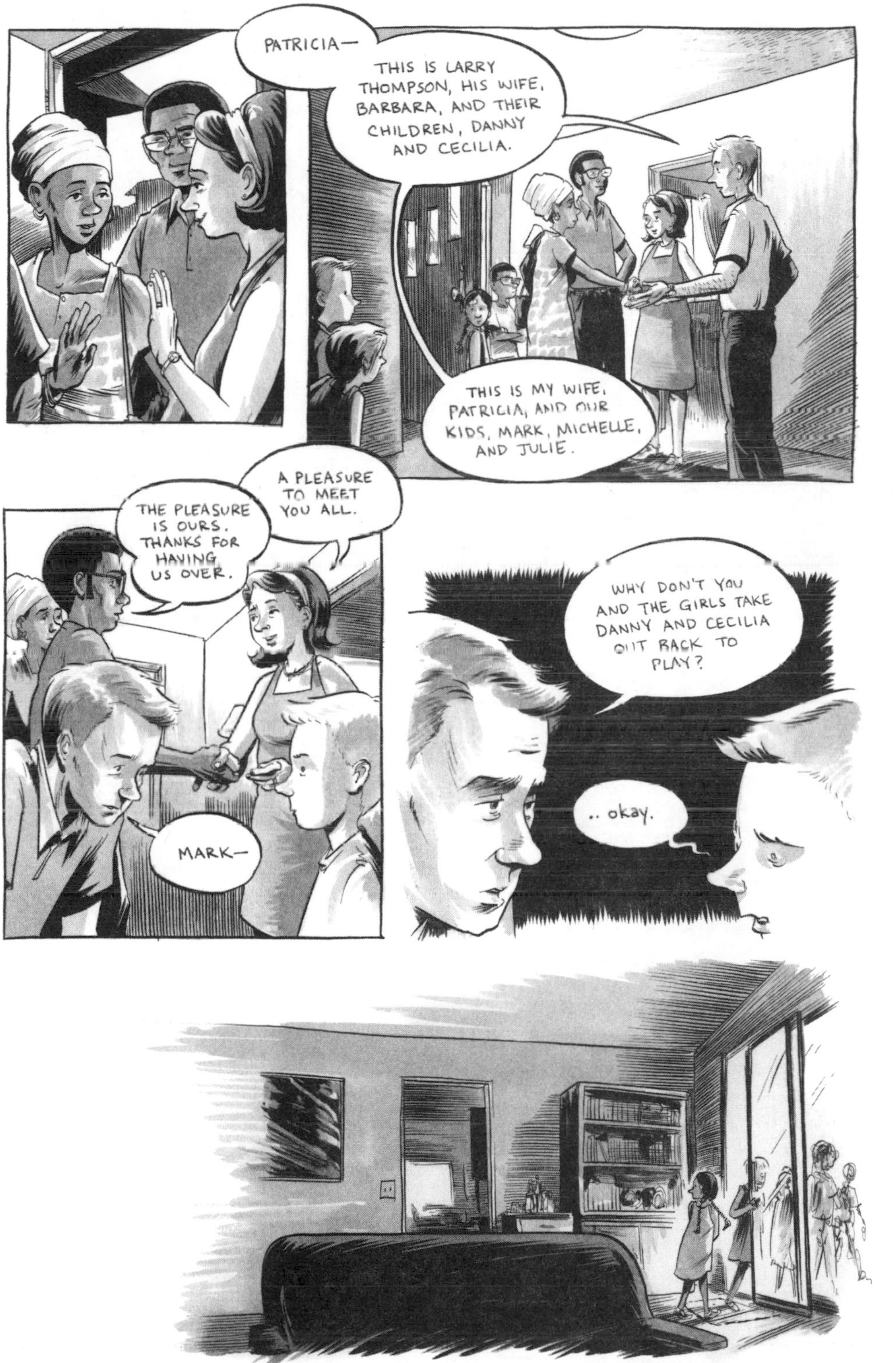
PATRICIA—
THIS IS LARRY THOMPSON, HIS WIFE, BARBARA, AND THEIR CHILDREN, DANNY AND CECILIA.
THIS IS MY WIFE, PATRICIA, AND OUR KIDS, MARK, MICHELLE, AND JULIE.
A PLEASURE TO MEET YOU ALL.
THE PLEASURE IS OURS. THANKS FOR HAVING US OVER.
MARK—
WHY DON'T YOU AND THE GIRLS TAKE DANNY AND CECILIA OUT BACK TO PLAY?
.. okay.

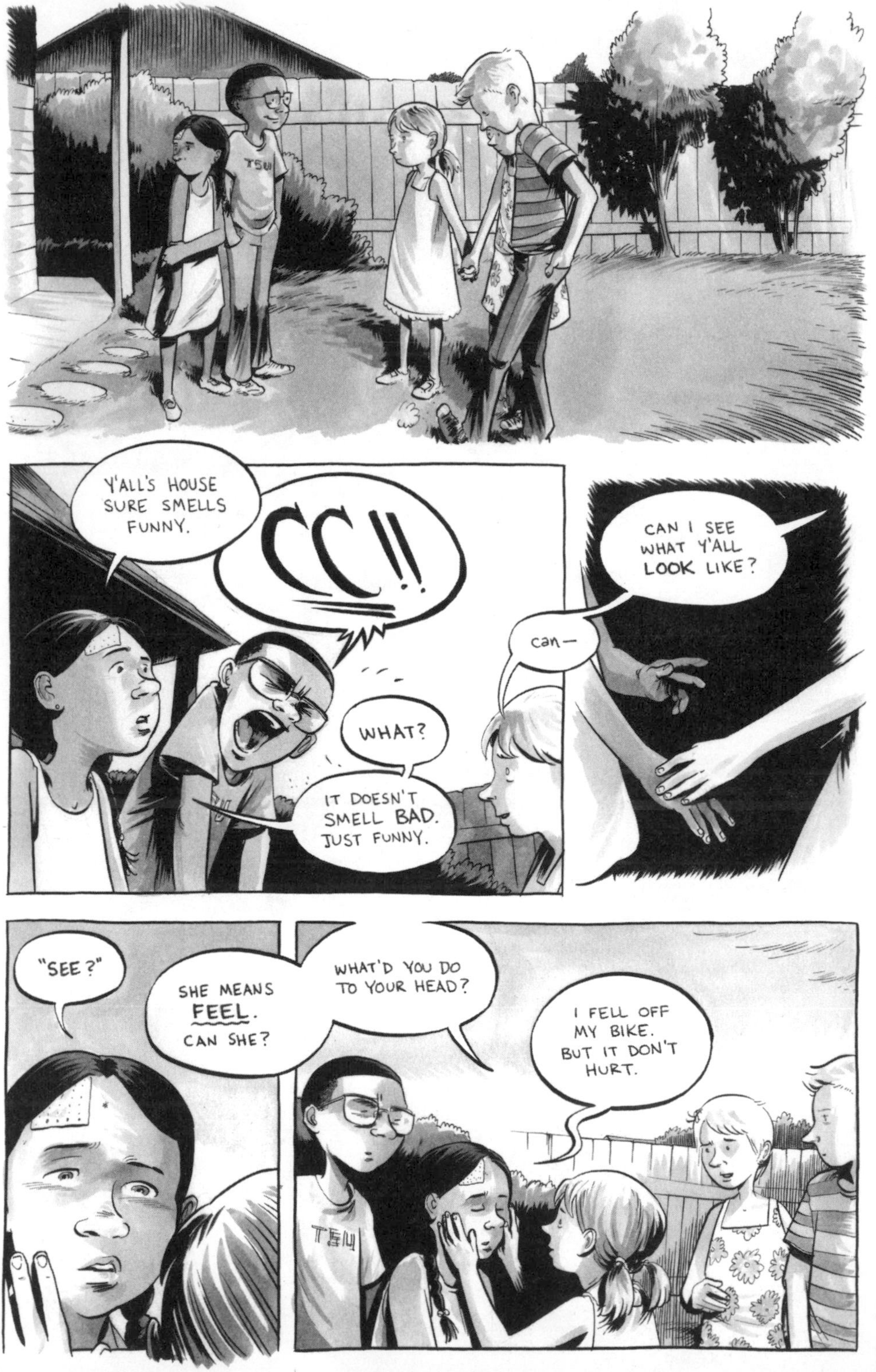

Y'ALL'S HOUSE SURE SMELLS FUNNY.
CC!!
WHAT?
IT DOESN'T SMELL BAD. JUST FUNNY.
can—
CAN I SEE WHAT Y'ALL LOOK LIKE?
"SEE?"
SHE MEANS FEEL. CAN SHE?
WHAT'D YOU DO TO YOUR HEAD?
I FELL OFF MY BIKE. BUT IT DON'T HURT.

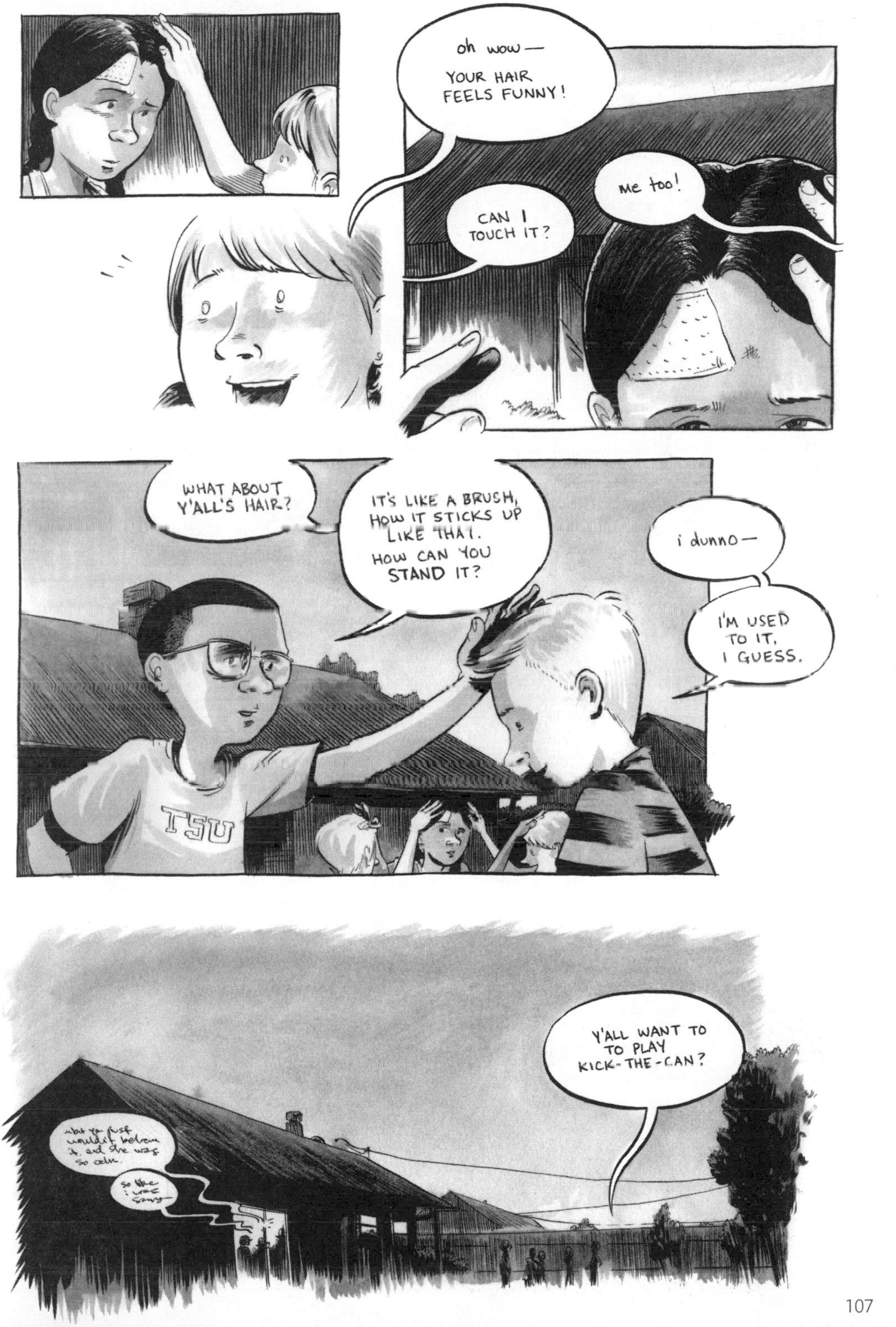
oh wow— YOUR HAIR FEELS FUNNY!
CAN I TOUCH IT?
me too!
WHAT ABOUT Y'ALL'S HAIR?
IT'S LIKE A BRUSH, HOW IT STICKS UP LIKE THAT. HOW CAN YOU STAND IT?
i dunno—
I'M USED TO IT, I GUESS.
TSU
Y'ALL WANT TO TO PLAY KICK-THE-CAN?

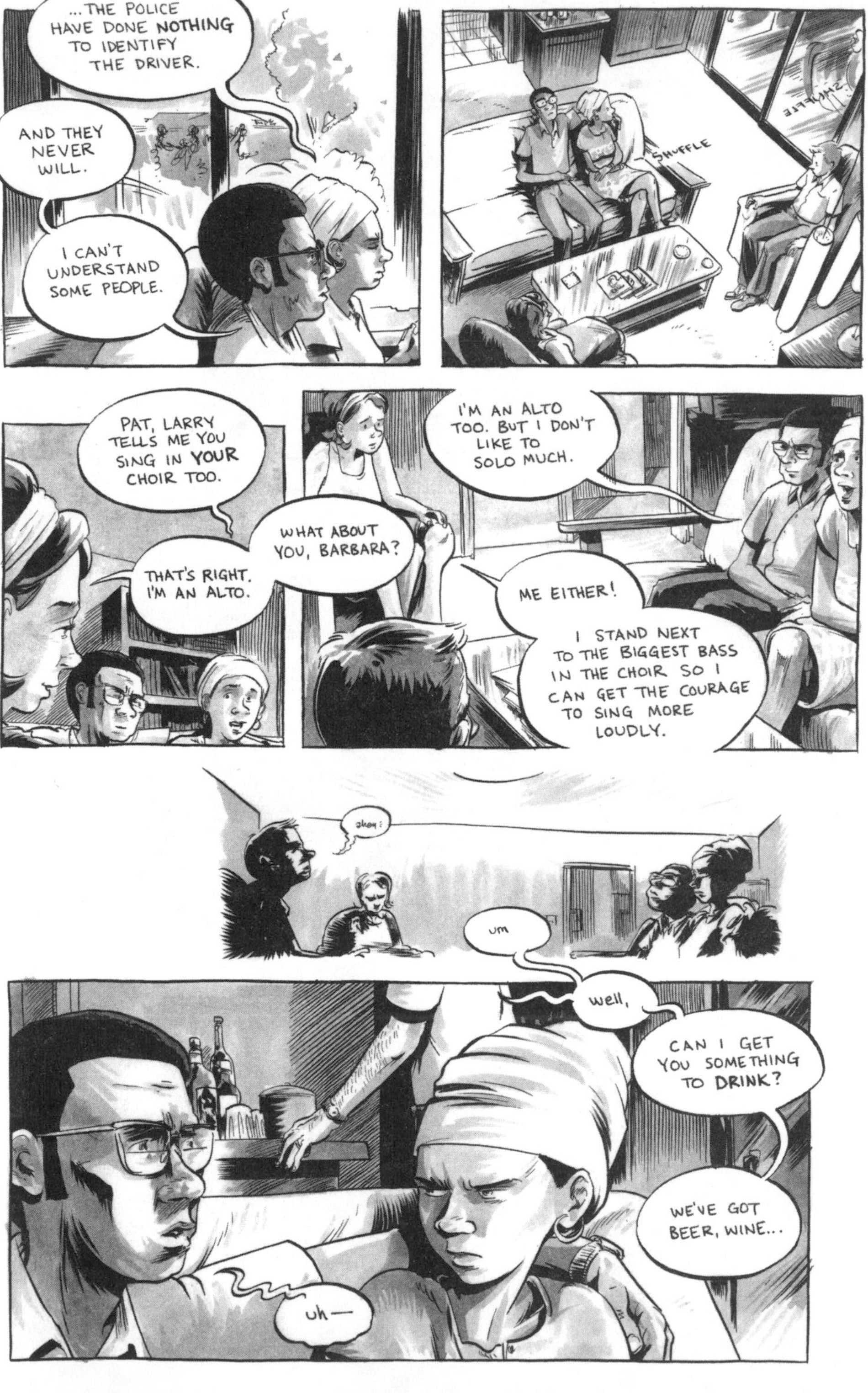
...THE POLICE HAVE DONE NOTHING TO IDENTIFY THE DRIVER.
AND THEY NEVER WILL.
I CAN'T UNDERSTAND SOME PEOPLE.
SHUFFLE
PAT, LARRY TELLS ME YOU SING IN YOUR CHOIR TOO.
THAT'S RIGHT. I'M AN ALTO.
WHAT ABOUT YOU, BARBARA?
I'M AN ALTO TOO. BUT I DON'T LIKE TO SOLO MUCH.
ME EITHER!
I STAND NEXT TO THE BIGGEST BASS IN THE CHOIR SO I CAN GET THE COURAGE TO SING MORE LOUDLY.
um
well,
CAN I GET YOU SOMETHING TO DRINK?
WE'VE GOT BEER, WINE...
uh—

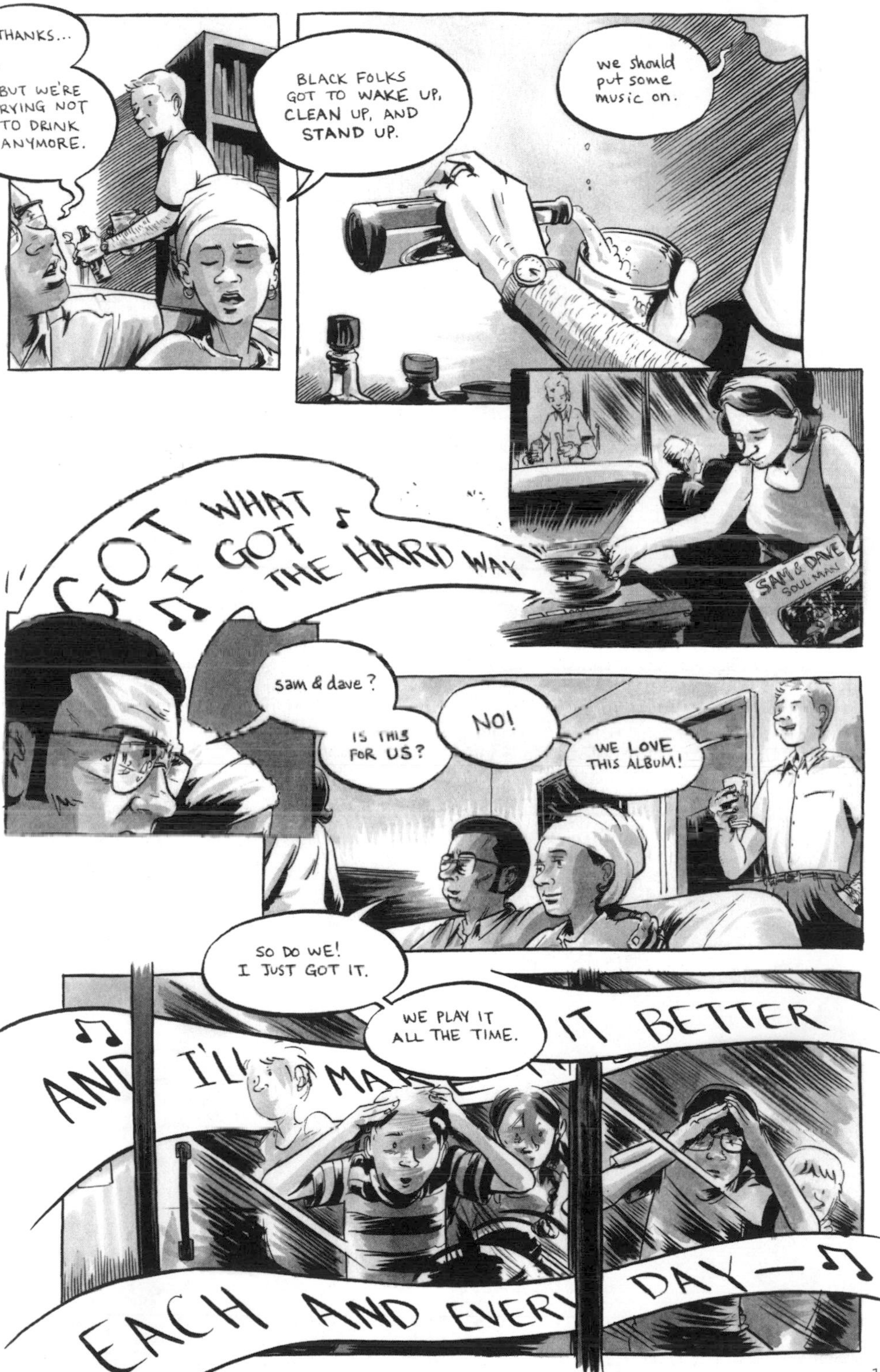
THANKS...
BUT WE'RE TRYING NOT TO DRINK ANYMORE.
BLACK FOLKS GOT TO WAKE UP, CLEAN UP, AND STAND UP.
we should put some music on.
SAM & DAVE SOUL MAN
GOT WHAT I GOT THE HARD WAY
sam & dave?
IS THIS FOR US?
NO!
WE LOVE THIS ALBUM!
SO DO WE! I JUST GOT IT.
WE PLAY IT ALL THE TIME.
IT BETTER
EACH AND EVERY DAY—

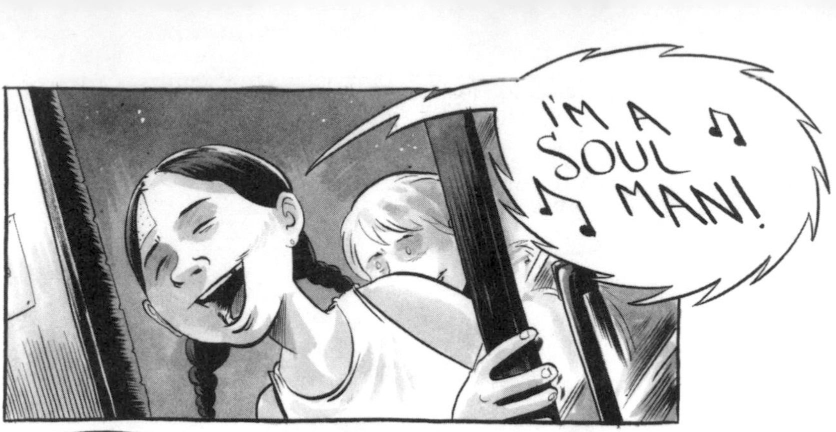
I'M A SOUL MAN!

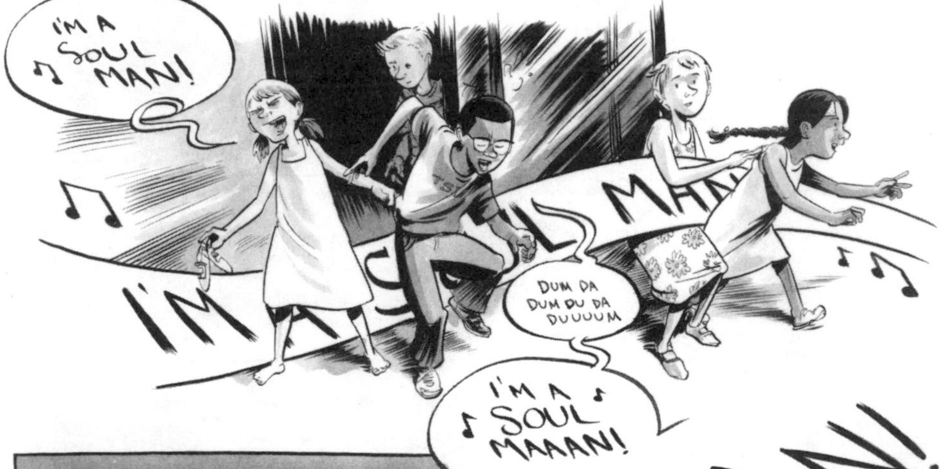
I'M A SOUL MAN!
I'M A SOUL MAN
DUM DA DUM DU DA DUUUUM
I'M A SOUL MAAAN!

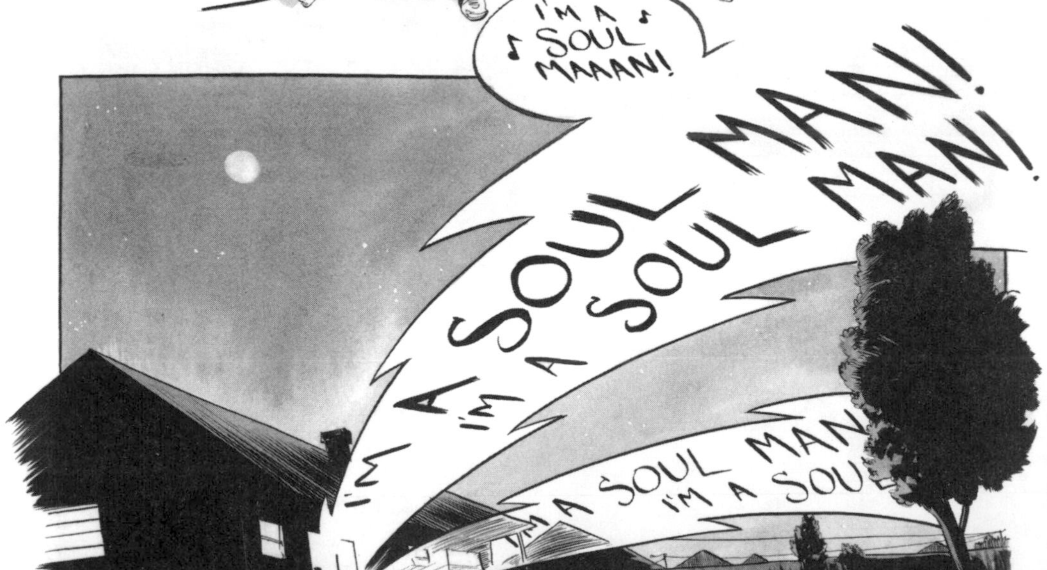
I'M A SOUL MAN!
I'M A SOUL MAN!
I'M A SOUL MAN
I'M A SOU

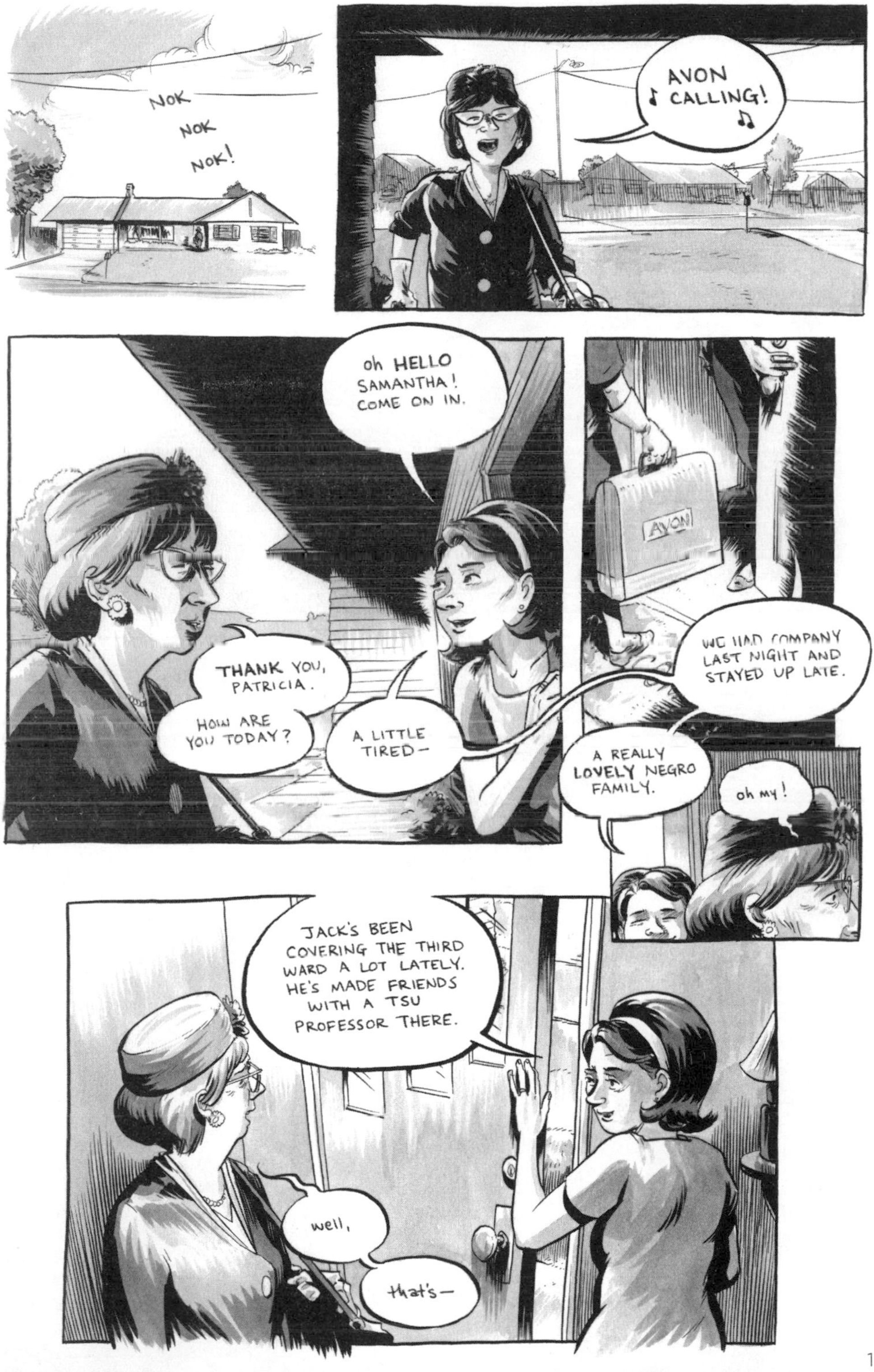
NOK
NOK
NOK!
AVON CALLING!
oh HELLO SAMANTHA! COME ON IN.
THANK YOU, PATRICIA.
HOW ARE YOU TODAY?
A LITTLE TIRED—
WE HAD COMPANY LAST NIGHT AND STAYED UP LATE.
AVON
A REALLY LOVELY NEGRO FAMILY.
oh my!
JACK'S BEEN COVERING THE THIRD WARD A LOT LATELY. HE'S MADE FRIENDS WITH A TSU PROFESSOR THERE.
well,
that's—

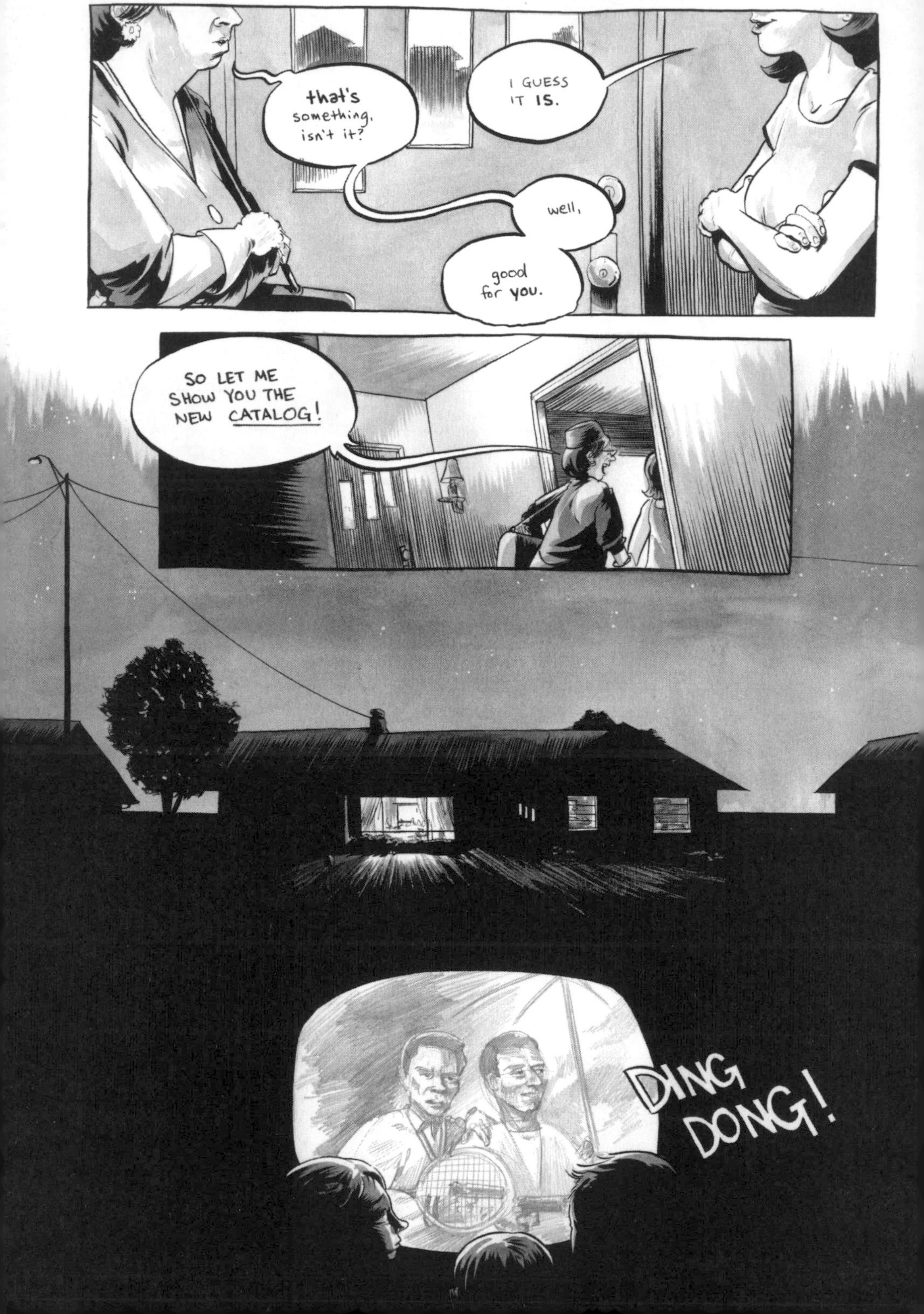
that's something, isn't it?
I GUESS IT IS.
well,
good for you.
SO LET ME SHOW YOU THE NEW CATALOG!
DING DONG!

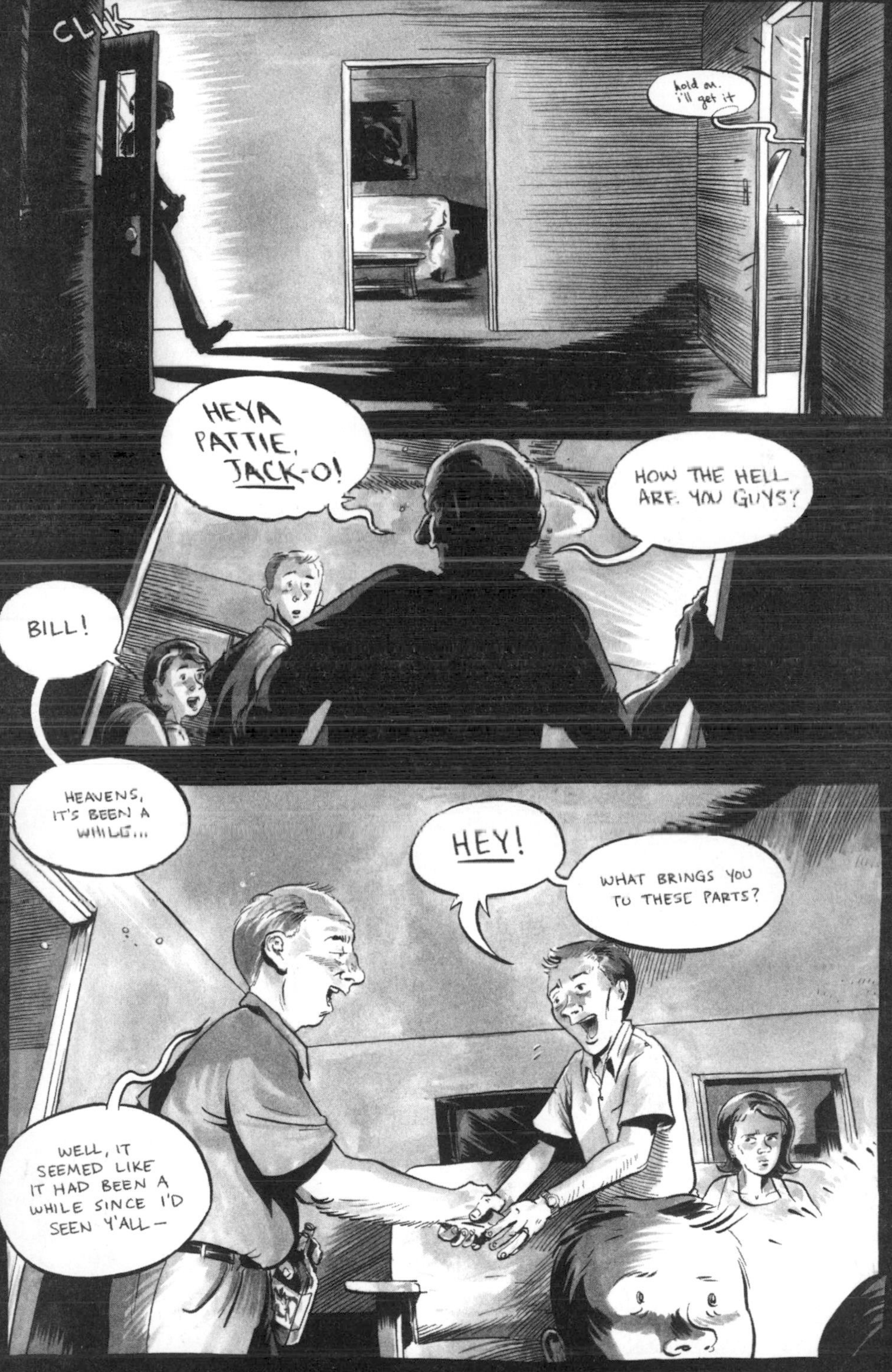
CLIK
hold on. i'll get it
HEYA PATTIE, JACK-O!
HOW THE HELL ARE YOU GUYS?
BILL!
HEAVENS, IT'S BEEN A WHILE...
HEY!
WHAT BRINGS YOU TO THESE PARTS?
WELL, IT SEEMED LIKE IT HAD BEEN A WHILE SINCE I'D SEEN Y'ALL—

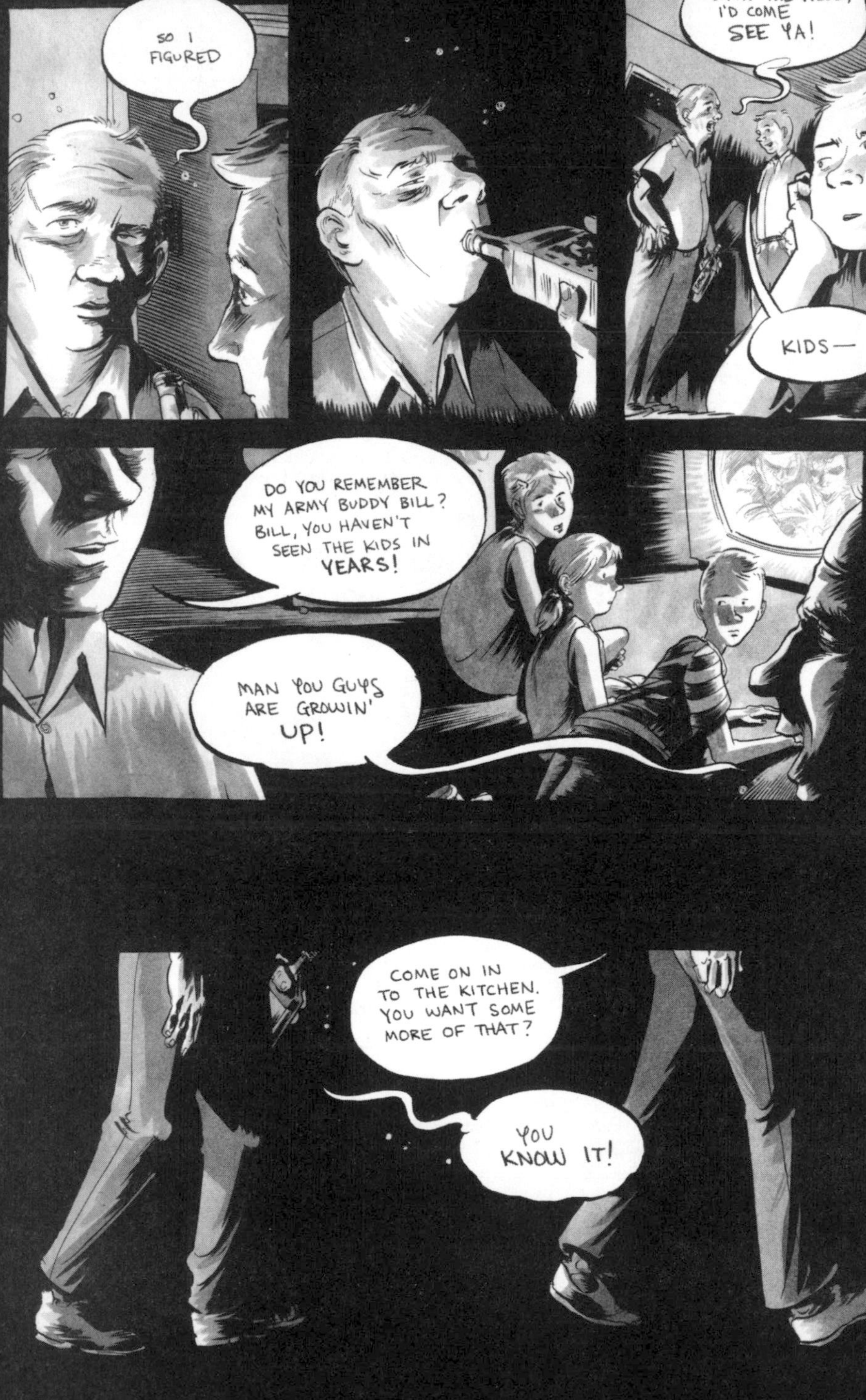
SO I FIGURED
WHAT THE HELL, I'D COME SEE YA!
KIDS—
DO YOU REMEMBER MY ARMY BUDDY BILL? BILL, YOU HAVEN'T SEEN THE KIDS IN YEARS!
MAN YOU GUYS ARE GROWIN' UP!
COME ON IN TO THE KITCHEN. YOU WANT SOME MORE OF THAT?
YOU KNOW IT!

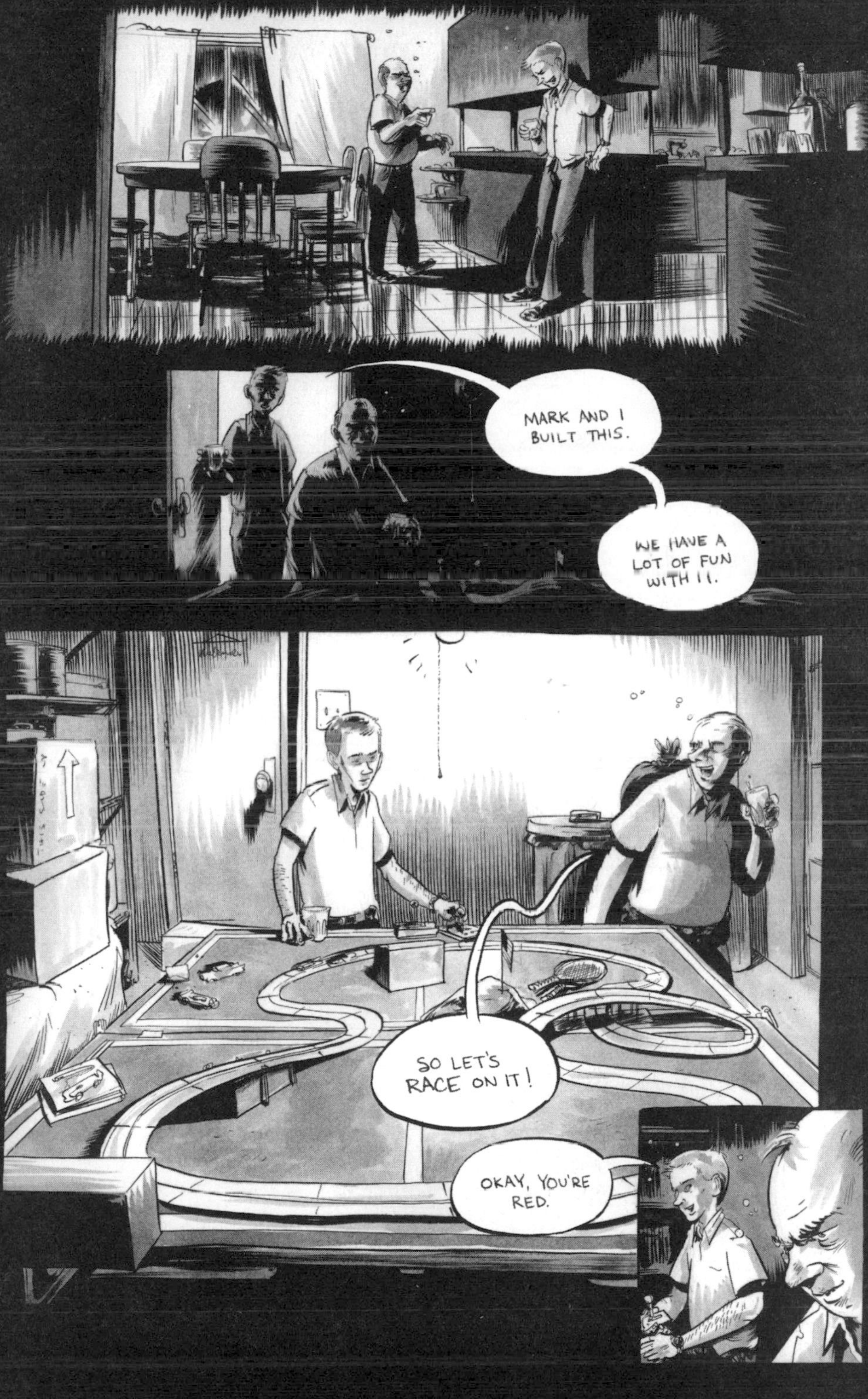
MARK AND I BUILT THIS.
WE HAVE A LOT OF FUN WITH IT.
SO LET'S RACE ON IT!
OKAY, YOU'RE RED.

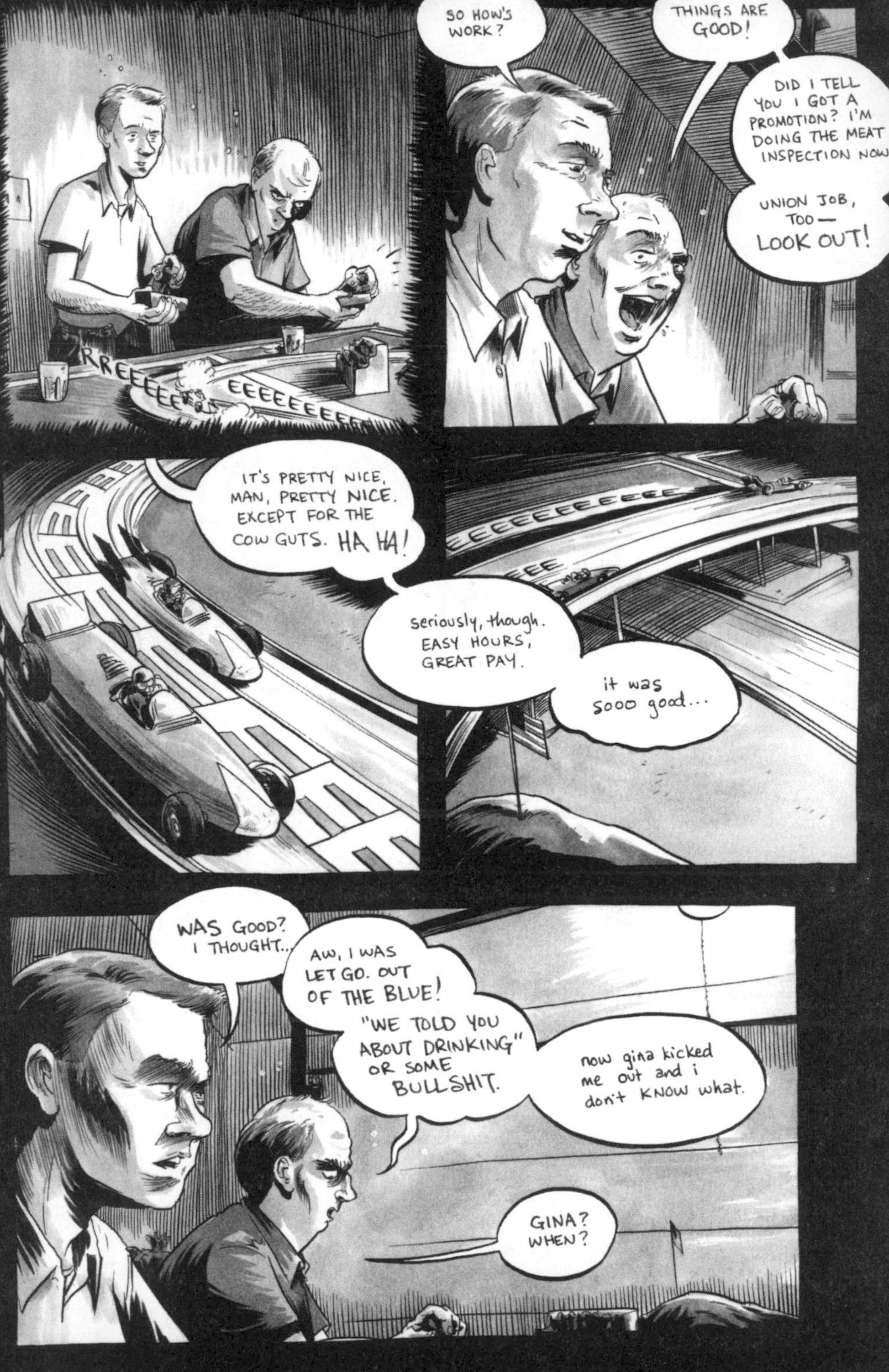
RREEEEEEEEEEEEEEEEEEE
SO HOW'S WORK?
THINGS ARE GOOD!
DID I TELL YOU I GOT A PROMOTION? I'M DOING THE MEAT INSPECTION NOW.
UNION JOB, TOO— LOOK OUT!
IT'S PRETTY NICE, MAN, PRETTY NICE. EXCEPT FOR THE COW GUTS. HA HA!
seriously, though. EASY HOURS, GREAT PAY.
it was sooo good...
WAS GOOD? I THOUGHT...
AW, I WAS LET GO. OUT OF THE BLUE!
"WE TOLD YOU ABOUT DRINKING" OR SOME BULLSHIT.
now gina kicked me out and i don't KNOW what.
GINA? WHEN?

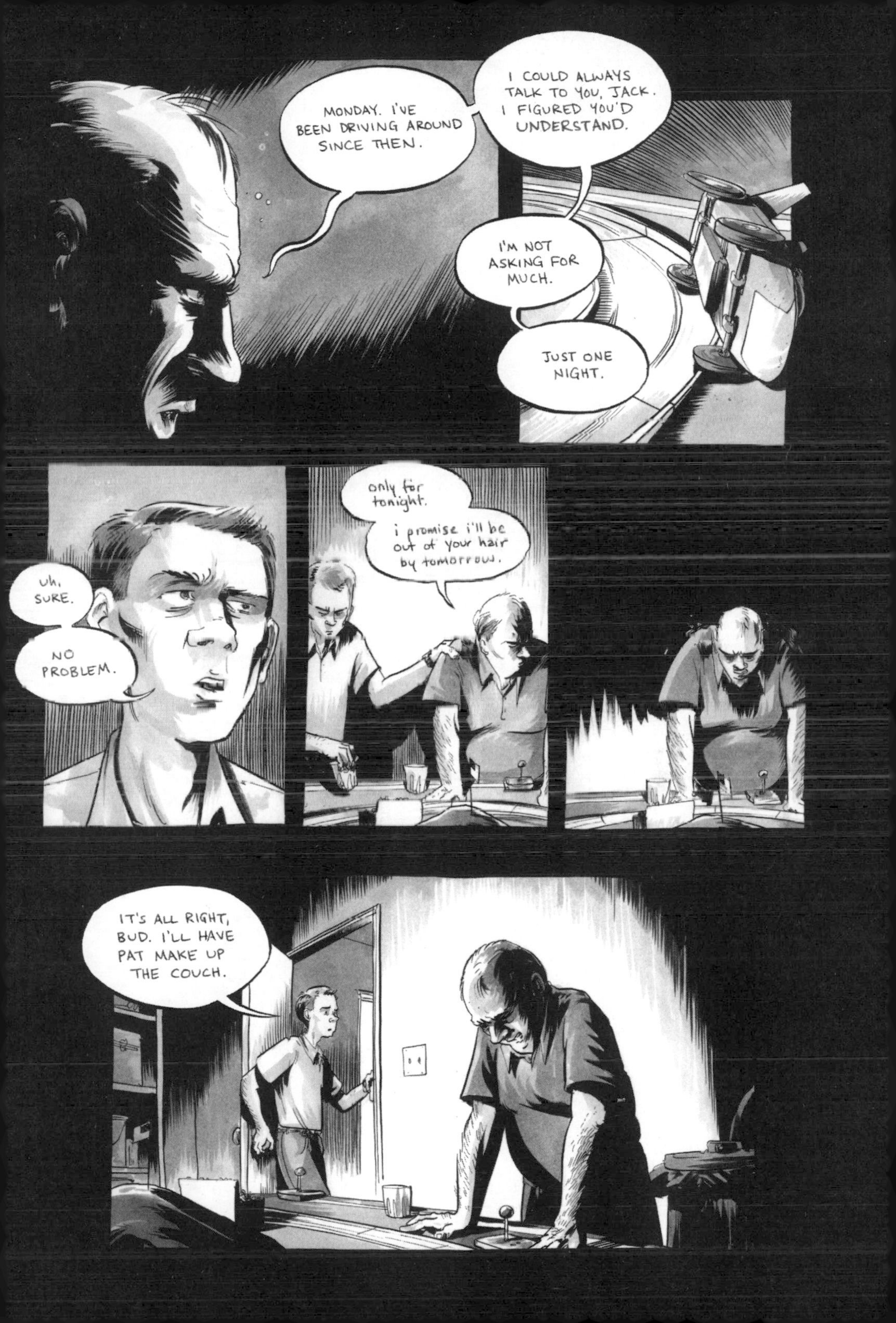
MONDAY. I'VE BEEN DRIVING AROUND SINCE THEN.
I COULD ALWAYS TALK TO YOU, JACK. I FIGURED YOU'D UNDERSTAND.
I'M NOT ASKING FOR MUCH.
JUST ONE NIGHT.
uh, SURE.
NO PROBLEM.
only for tonight.
i promise i'll be out of your hair by tomorrow.
IT'S ALL RIGHT, BUD. I'LL HAVE PAT MAKE UP THE COUCH.

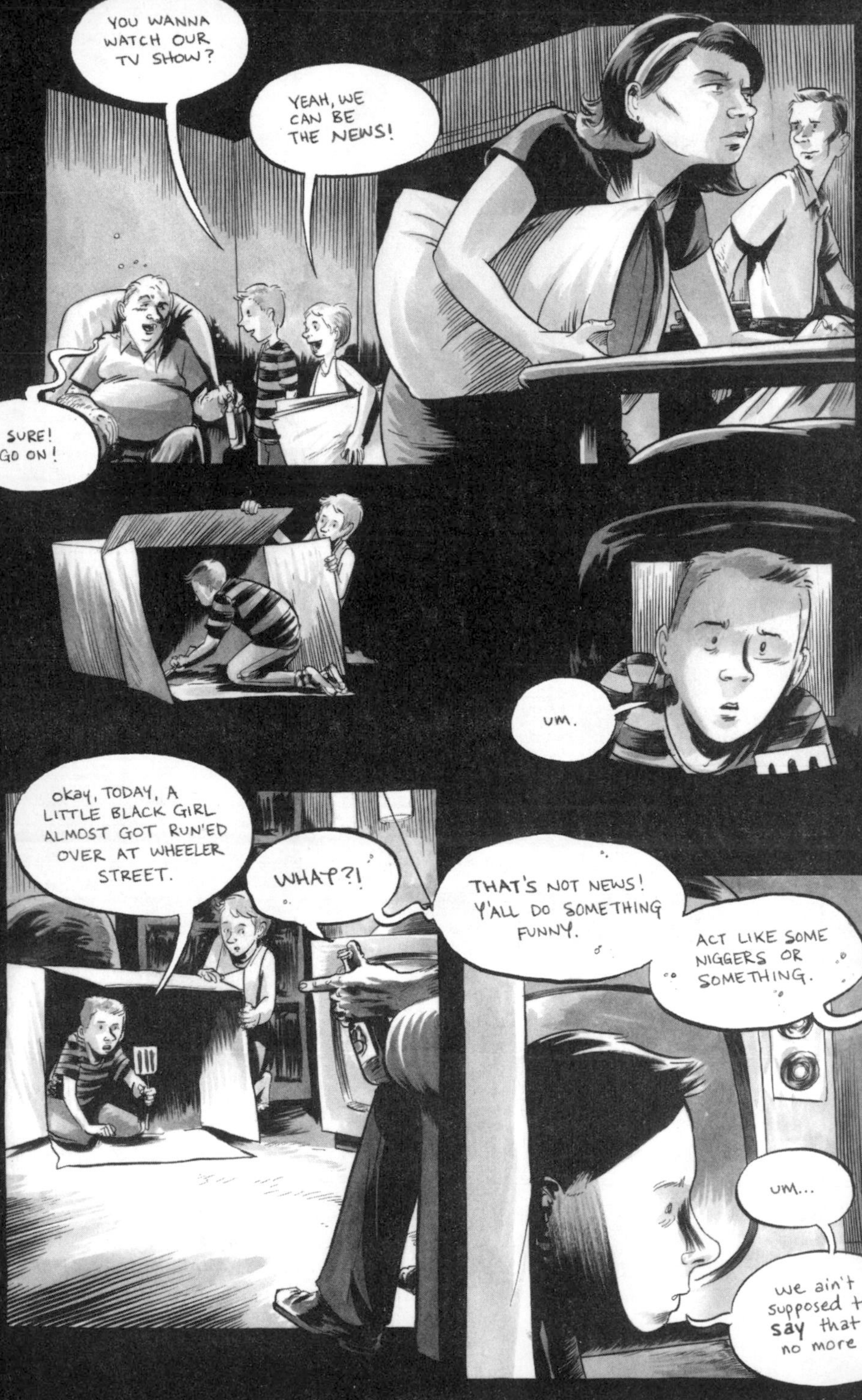
YOU WANNA WATCH OUR TV SHOW?
YEAH, WE CAN BE THE NEWS!
SURE! GO ON!
UM.
okay, TODAY, A LITTLE BLACK GIRL ALMOST GOT RUN'ED OVER AT WHEELER STREET.
WHAT?!
THAT'S NOT NEWS! Y'ALL DO SOMETHING FUNNY.
ACT LIKE SOME NIGGERS OR SOMETHING.
UM...
we ain't supposed to say that no more.

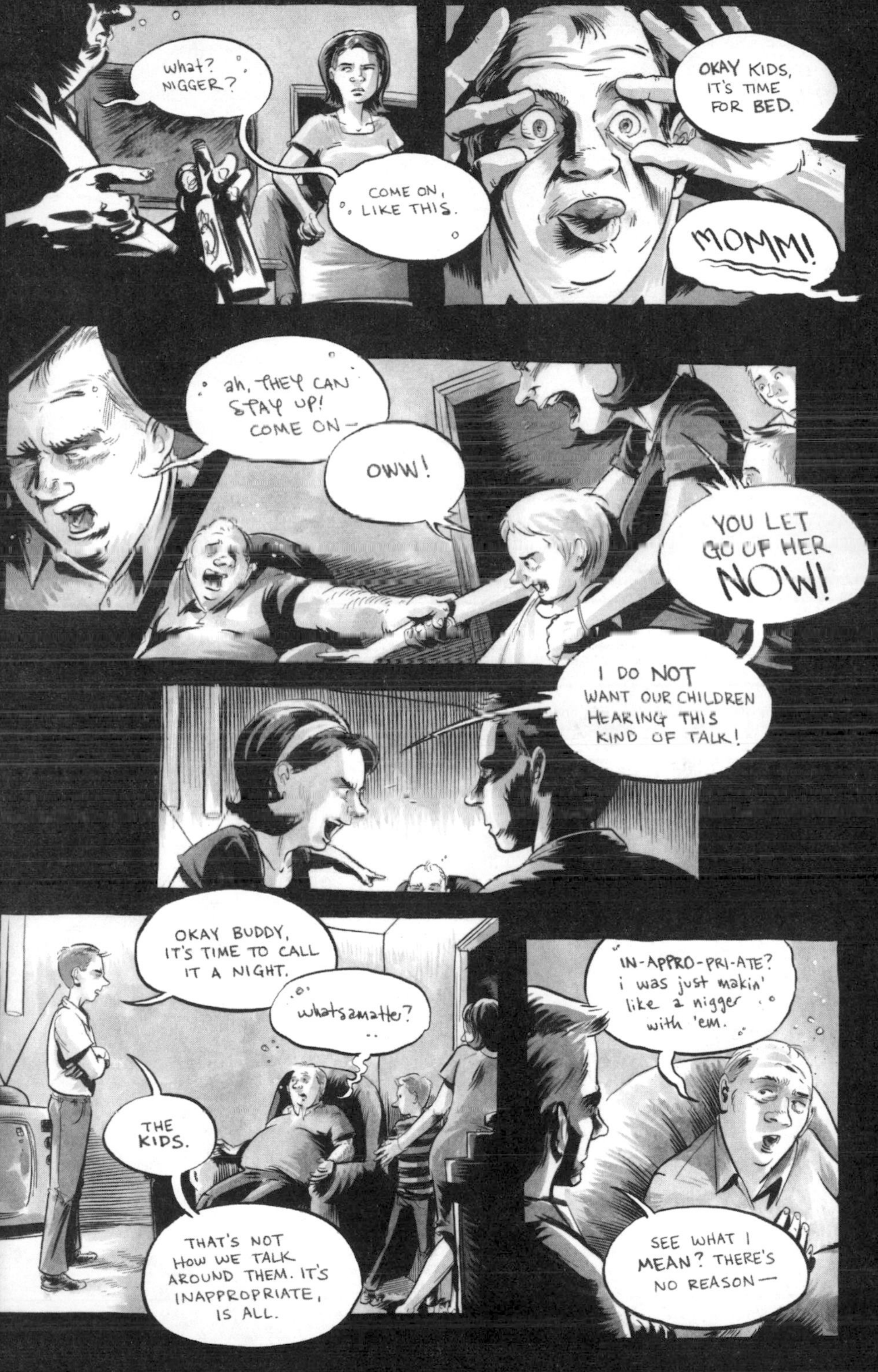
what? NIGGER?
COME ON, LIKE THIS.
OKAY KIDS, IT'S TIME FOR BED.
MOMM!
ah, THEY CAN STAY UP! COME ON—
OWW!
YOU LET GO OF HER NOW!
I DO NOT WANT OUR CHILDREN HEARING THIS KIND OF TALK!
OKAY BUDDY, IT'S TIME TO CALL IT A NIGHT.
whatsamatter?
THE KIDS.
THAT'S NOT HOW WE TALK AROUND THEM. IT'S INAPPROPRIATE, IS ALL.
IN-APPRO-PRI-ATE? i was just makin' like a nigger with 'em.
SEE WHAT I MEAN? THERE'S NO REASON—

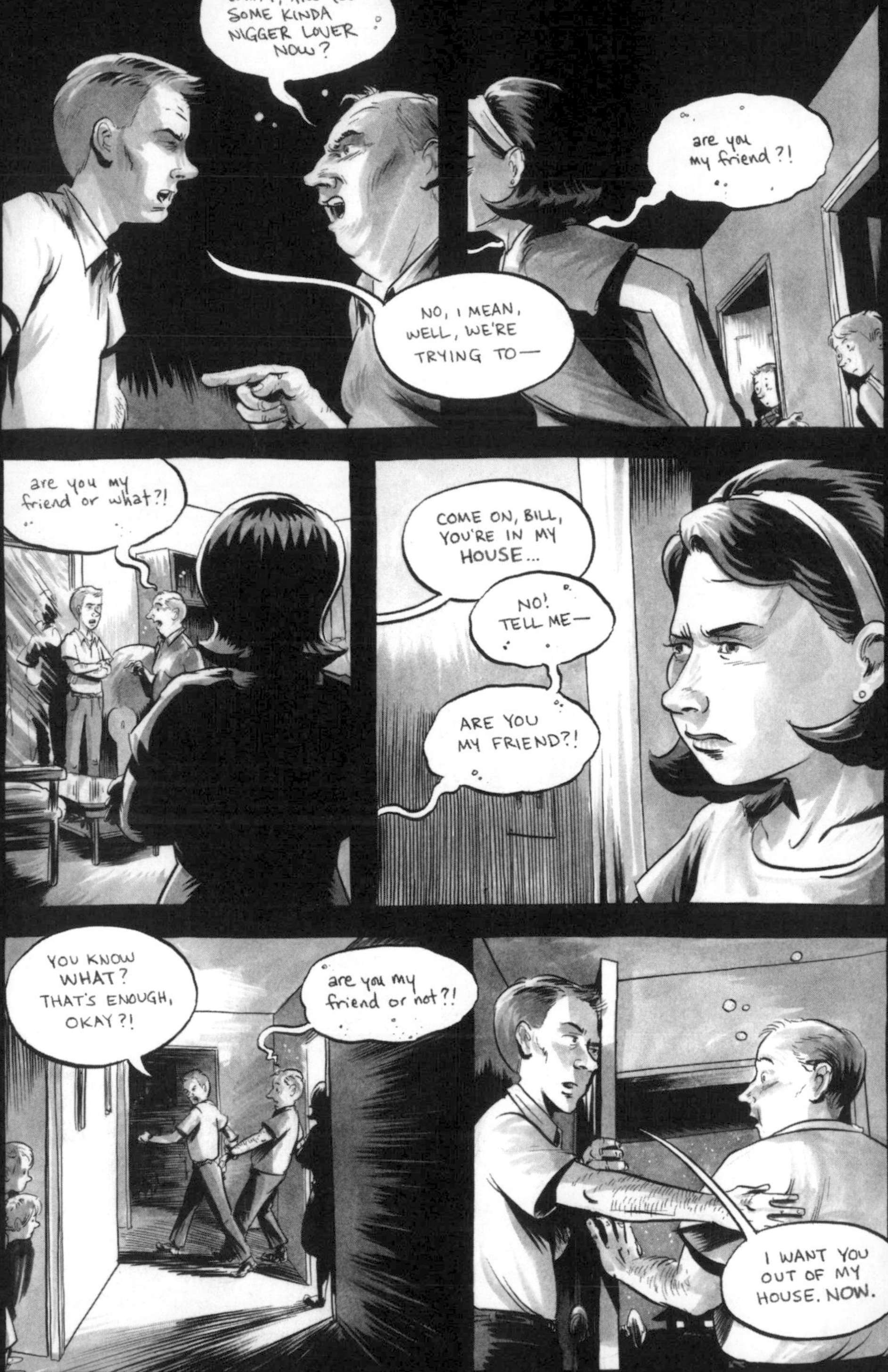
WHAT, ARE YOU SOME KINDA NIGGER LOVER NOW?
are you my friend?!
NO, I MEAN, WELL, WE'RE TRYING TO—
are you my friend or what?!
COME ON, BILL, YOU'RE IN MY HOUSE...
NO! TELL ME—
ARE YOU MY FRIEND?!
YOU KNOW WHAT? THAT'S ENOUGH, OKAY?!
are you my friend or not?!
I WANT YOU OUT OF MY HOUSE. NOW.

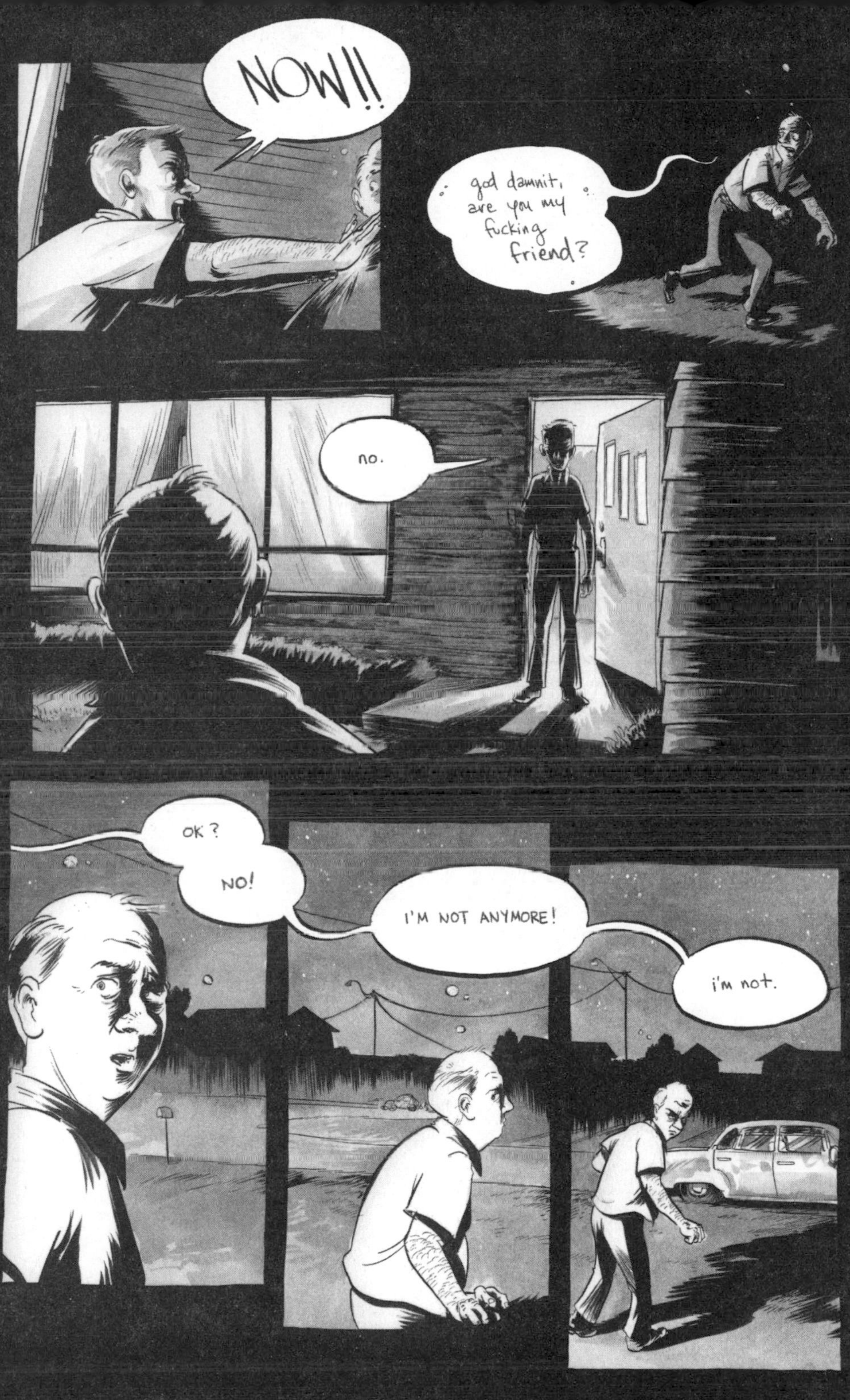
NOW!!
god damnit, are you my fucking friend?
no.
OK?
NO!
I'M NOT ANYMORE!
i'm not.

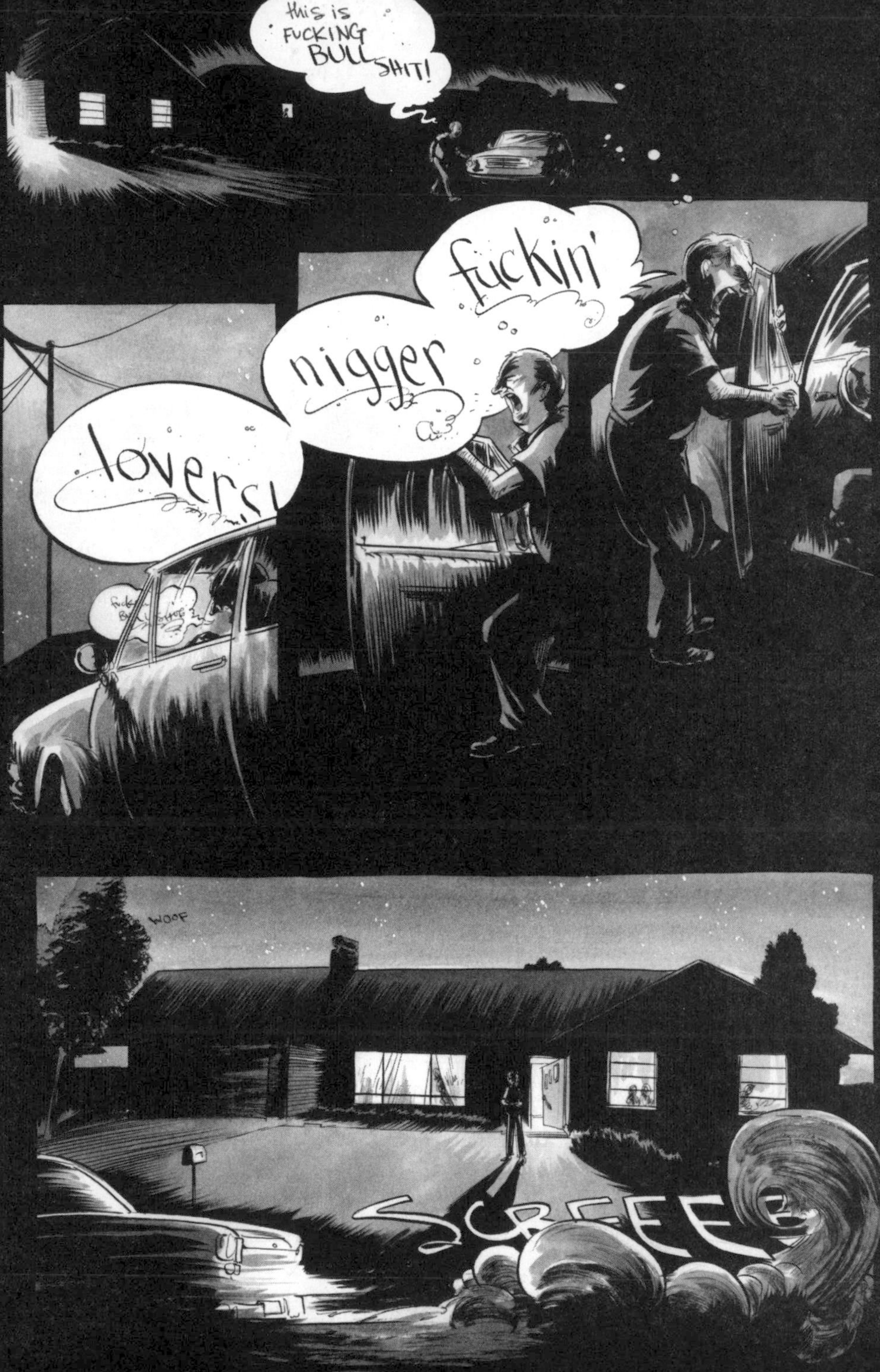
this is FUCKING BULL SHIT!
fuckin'
nigger
lovers!
WOOF
SCREEE

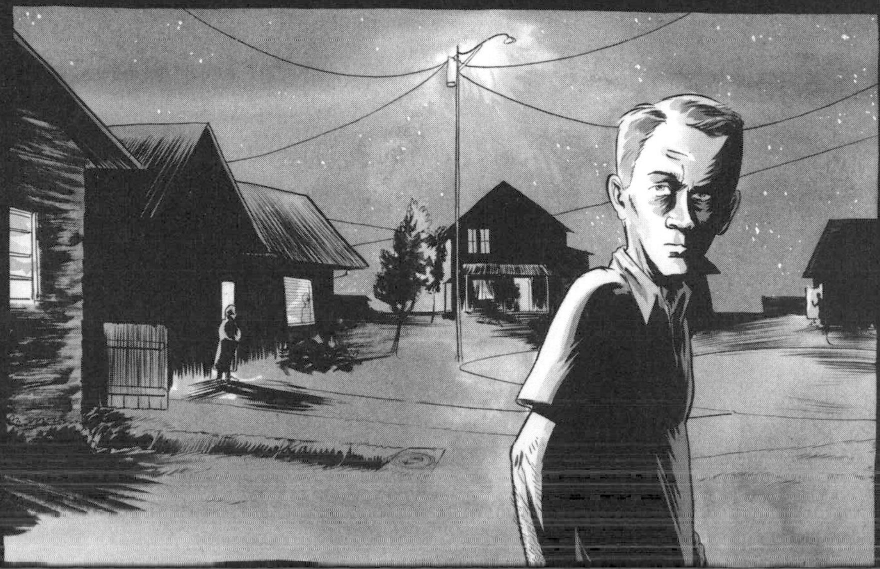
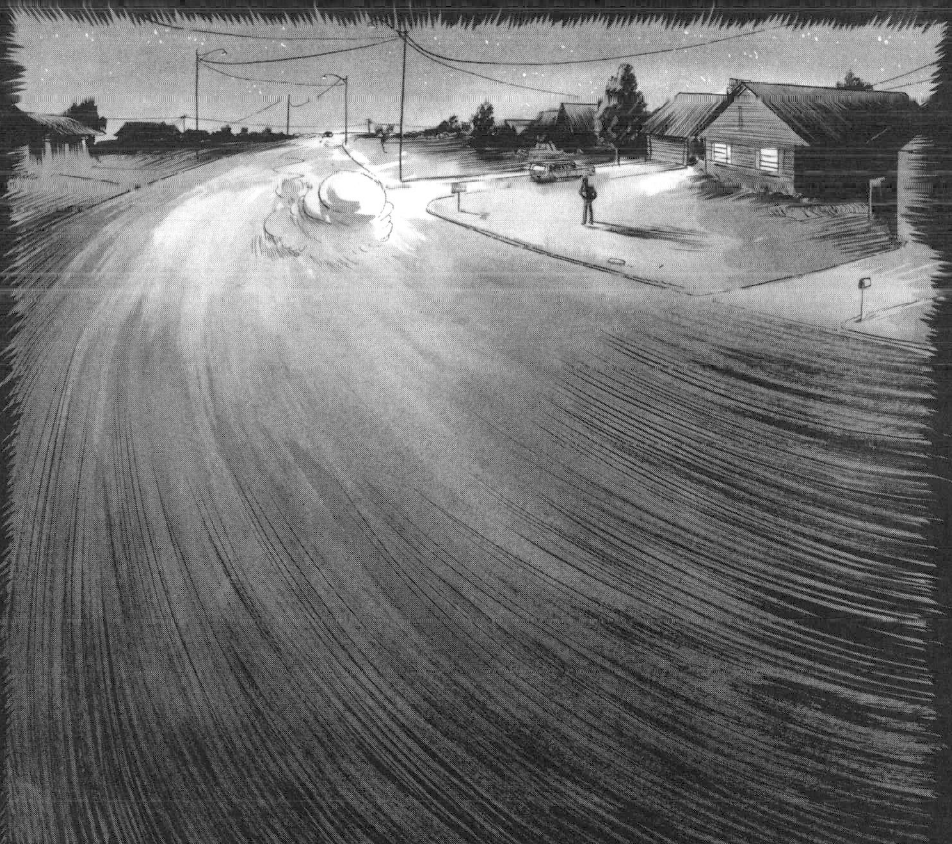

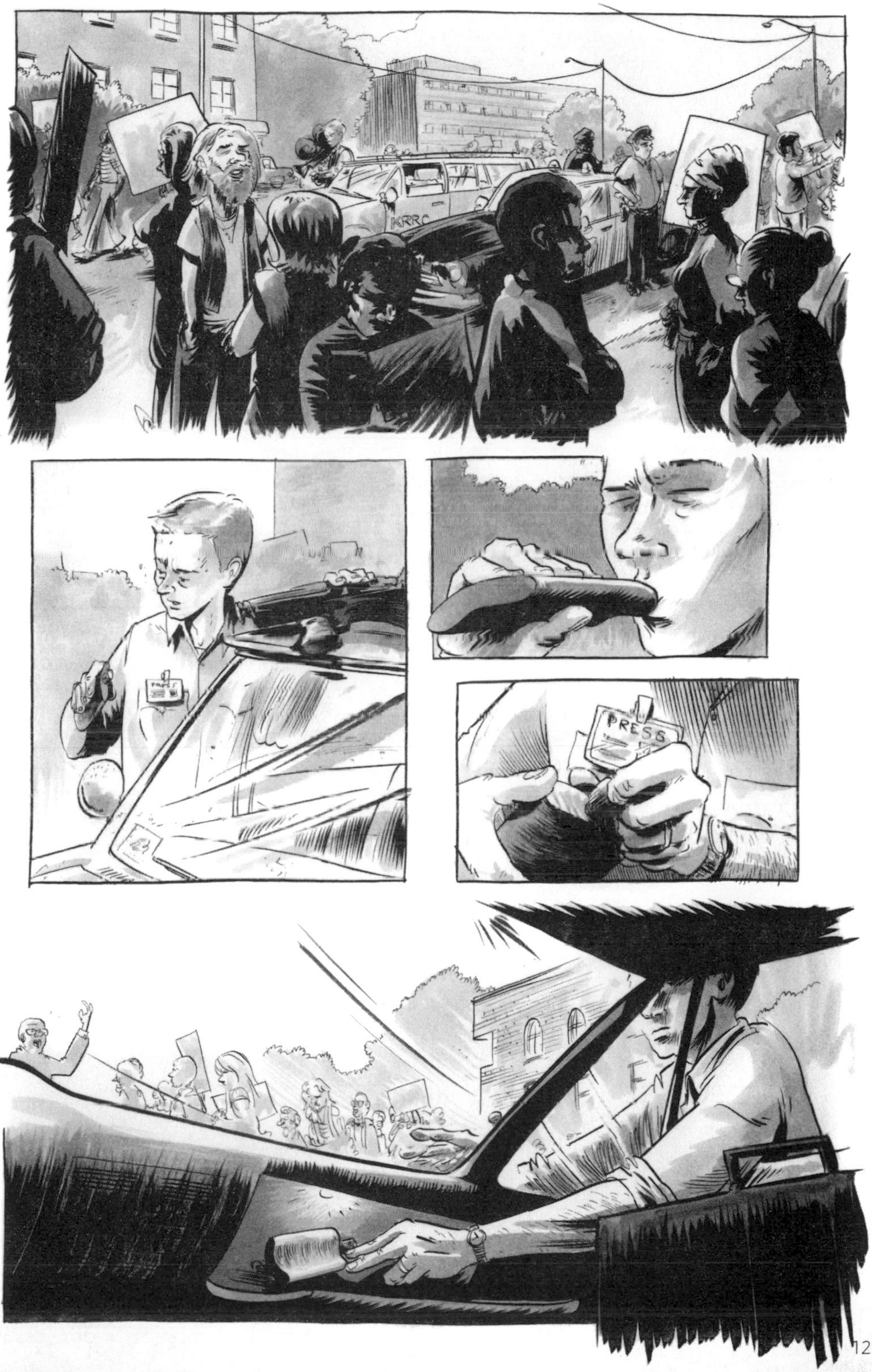
KRRC
PRESS

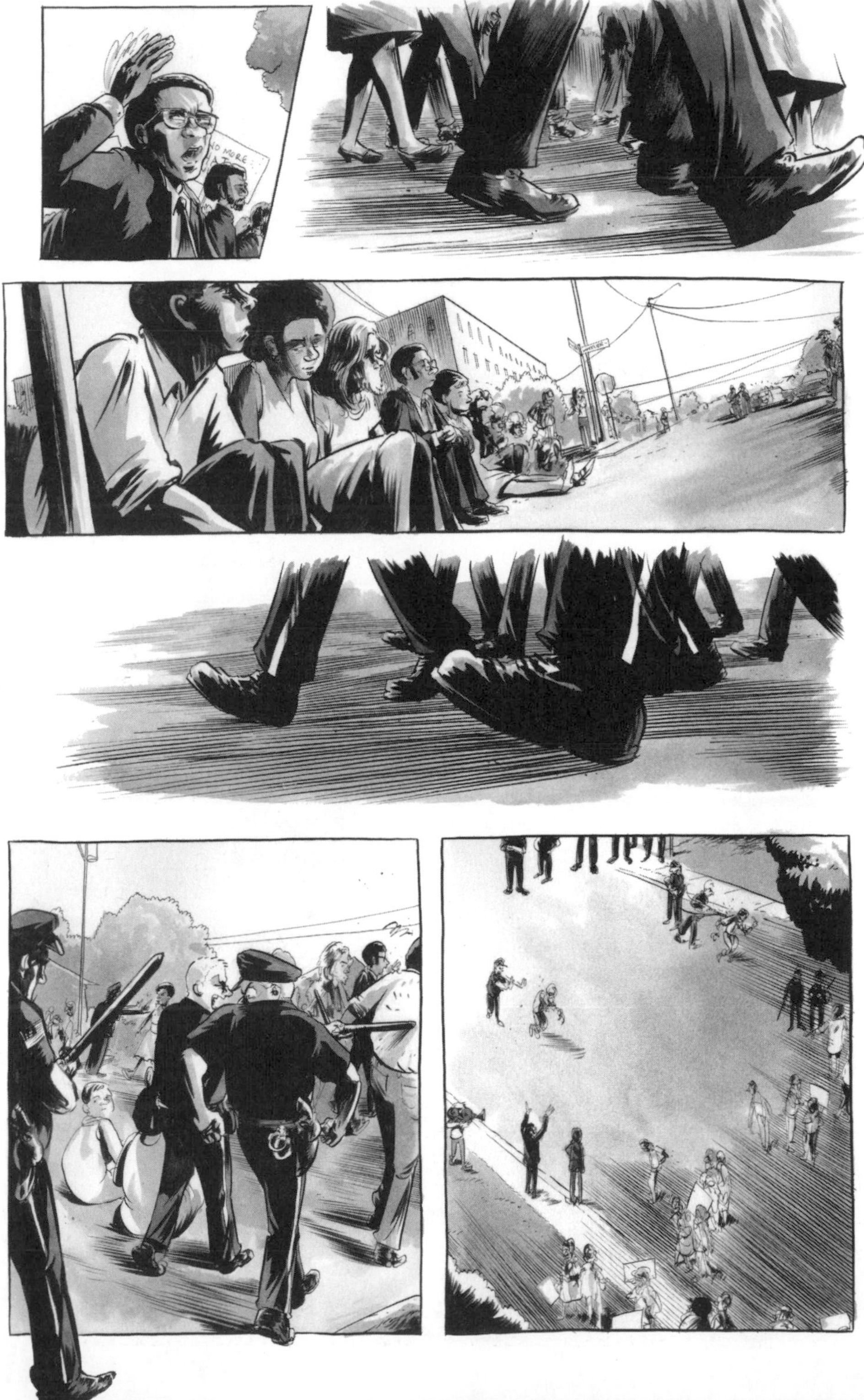
NO MORE

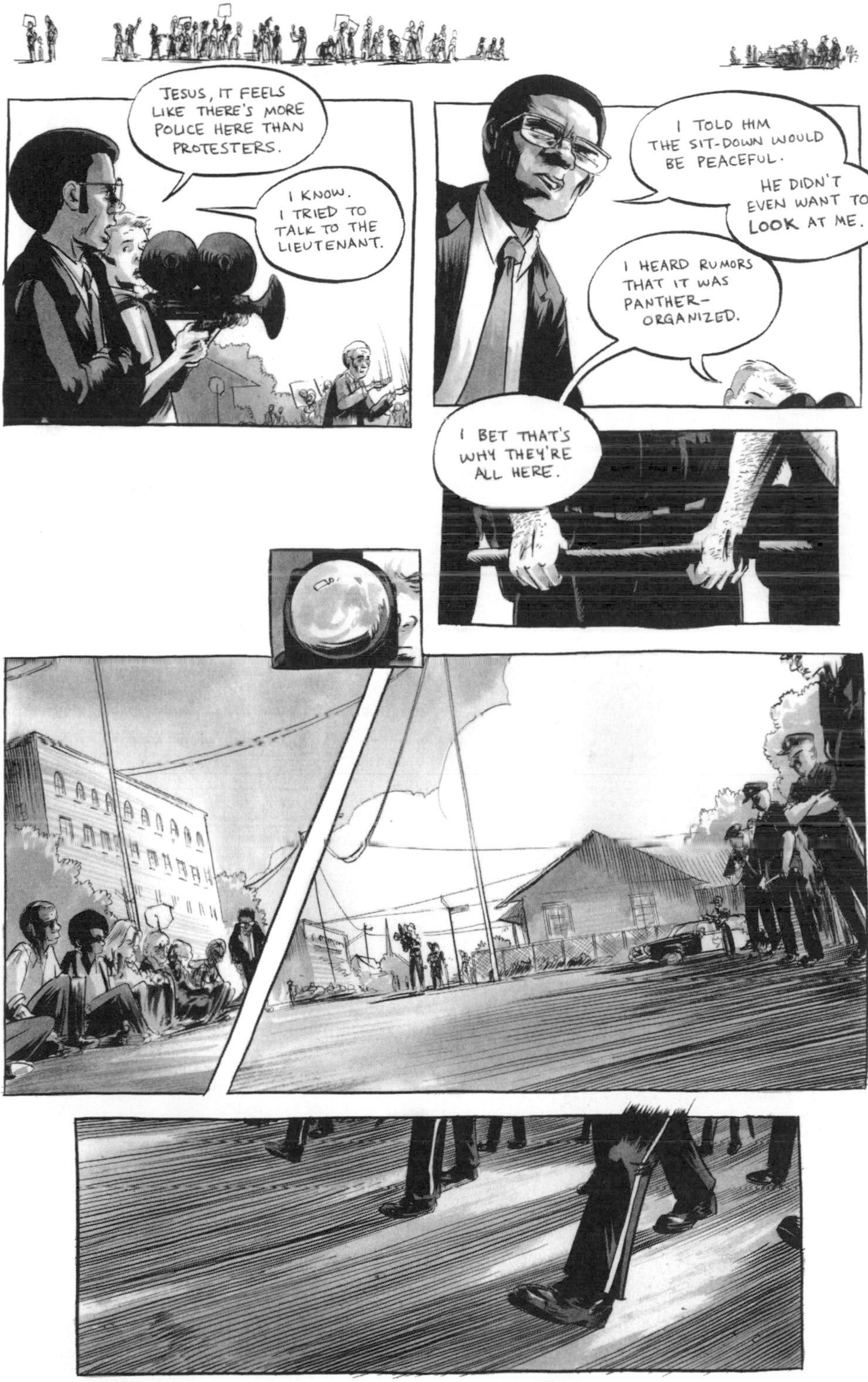

JESUS, IT FEELS LIKE THERE'S MORE POLICE HERE THAN PROTESTERS.
I KNOW. I TRIED TO TALK TO THE LIEUTENANT.
I TOLD HIM THE SIT-DOWN WOULD BE PEACEFUL.
HE DIDN'T EVEN WANT TO LOOK AT ME.
I HEARD RUMORS THAT IT WAS PANTHER-ORGANIZED.
I BET THAT'S WHY THEY'RE ALL HERE.

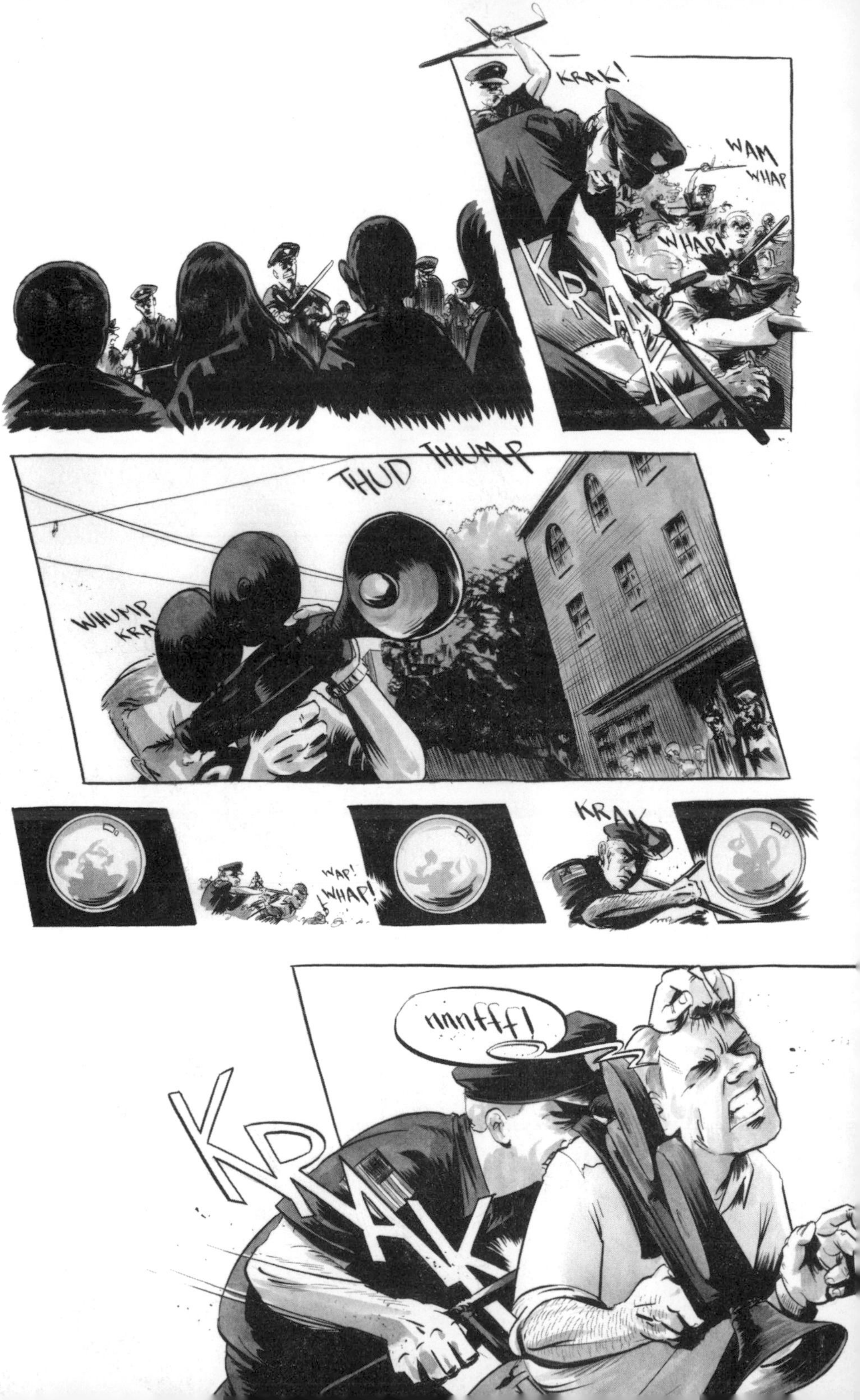
KRAK!
WAM
WHAP
WHAP!
KRAAK
THUD THUMP
WHUMP
KRA
WAP!
WHAP!
KRAK
nnnfff!
KRAK

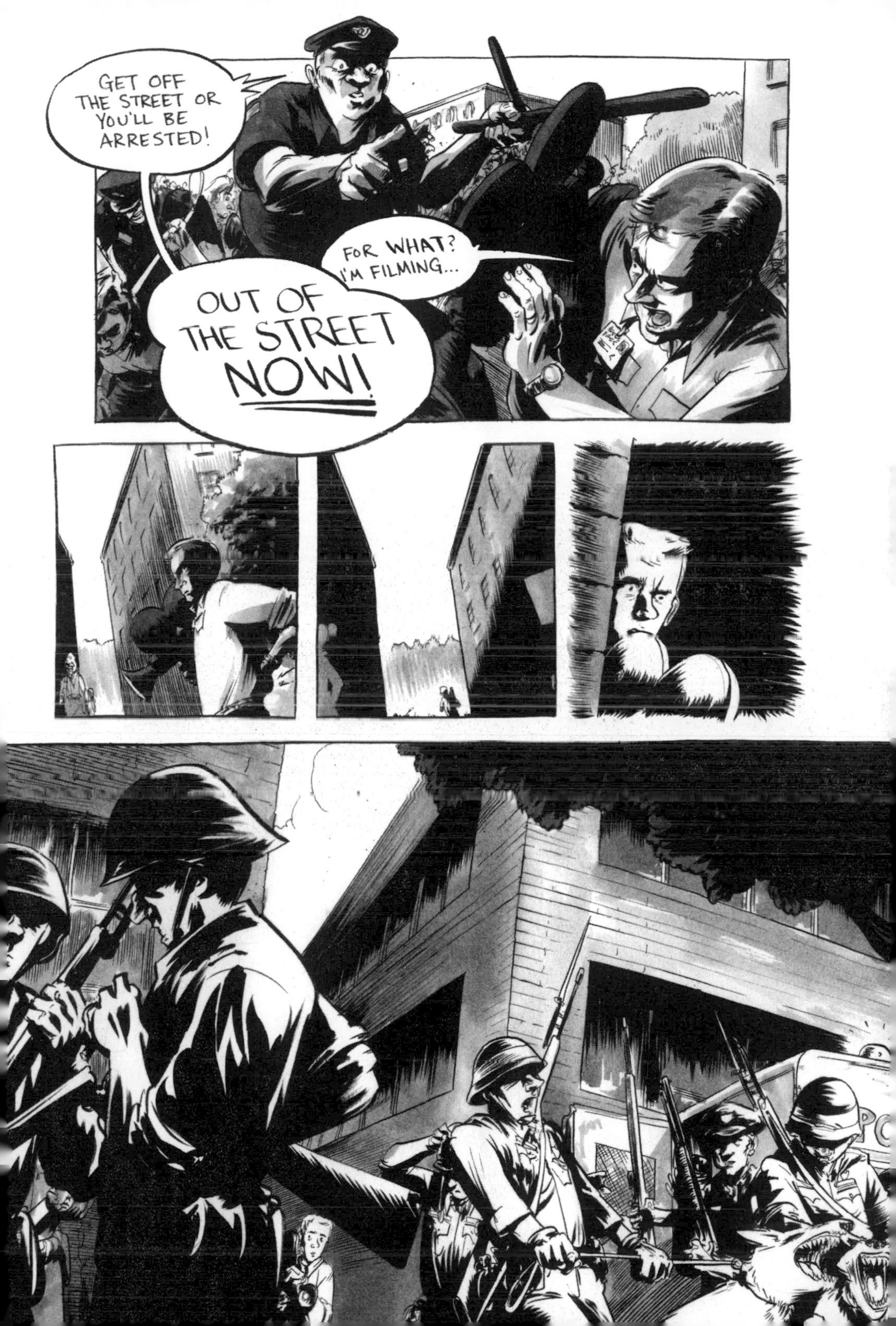
GET OFF THE STREET OR YOU'LL BE ARRESTED!
FOR WHAT? I'M FILMING...
OUT OF THE STREET NOW!

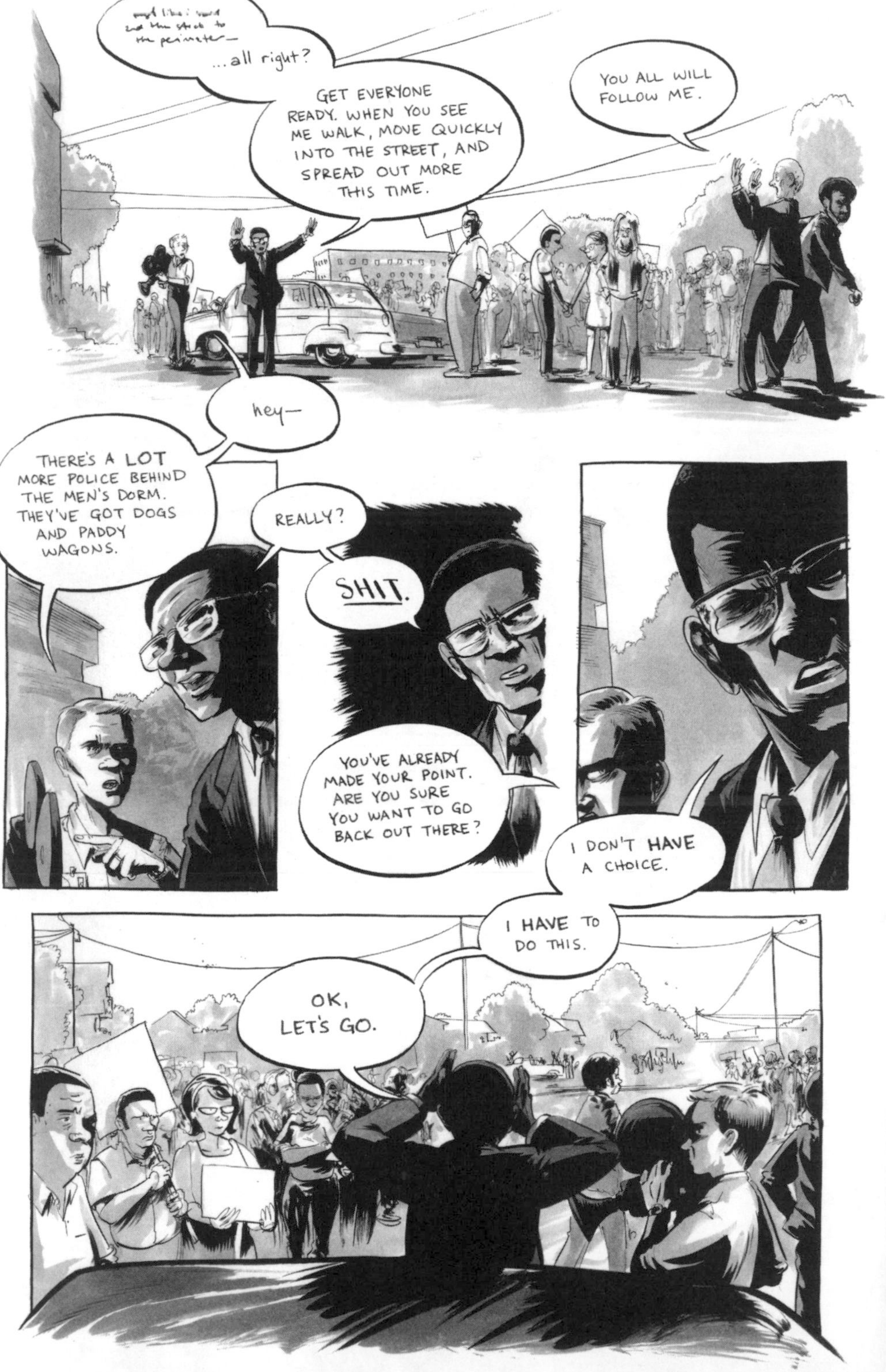
...all right?
GET EVERYONE READY. WHEN YOU SEE ME WALK, MOVE QUICKLY INTO THE STREET, AND SPREAD OUT MORE THIS TIME.
YOU ALL WILL FOLLOW ME.
hey—
THERE'S A LOT MORE POLICE BEHIND THE MEN'S DORM. THEY'VE GOT DOGS AND PADDY WAGONS.
REALLY?
SHIT.
YOU'VE ALREADY MADE YOUR POINT. ARE YOU SURE YOU WANT TO GO BACK OUT THERE?
I DON'T HAVE A CHOICE.
I HAVE TO DO THIS.
OK, LET'S GO.

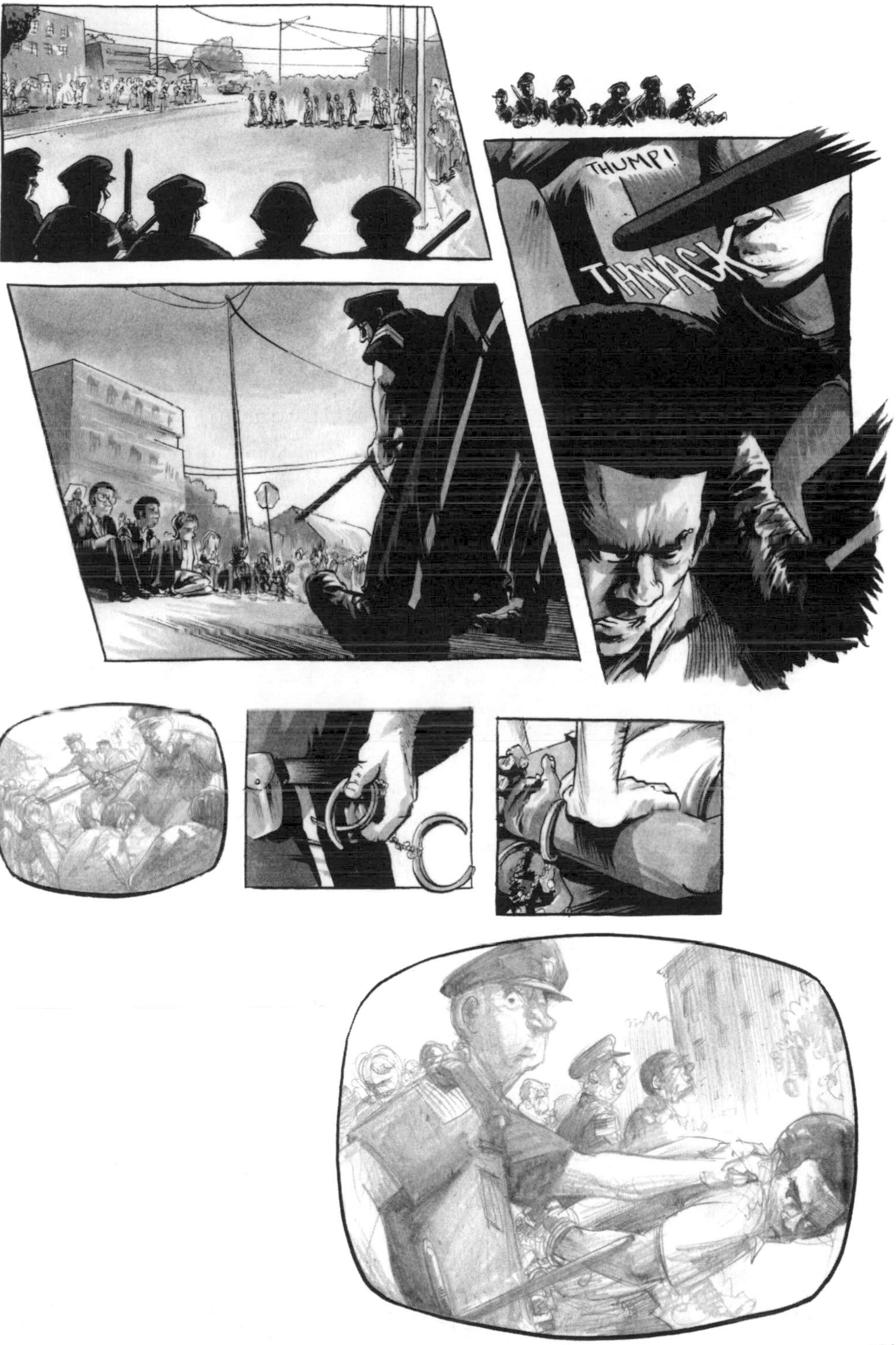
THUMP!
THWACK

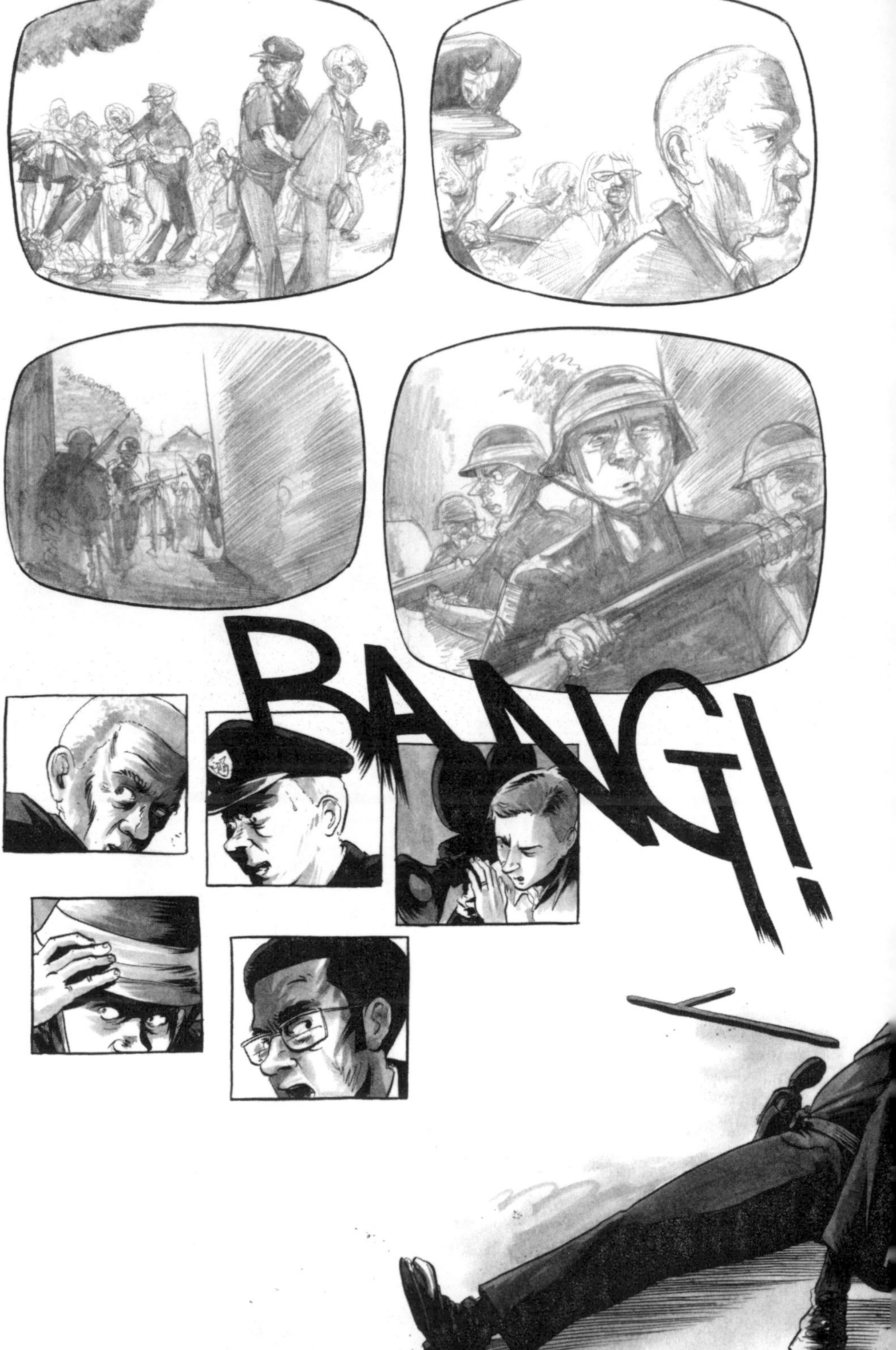
BANG!

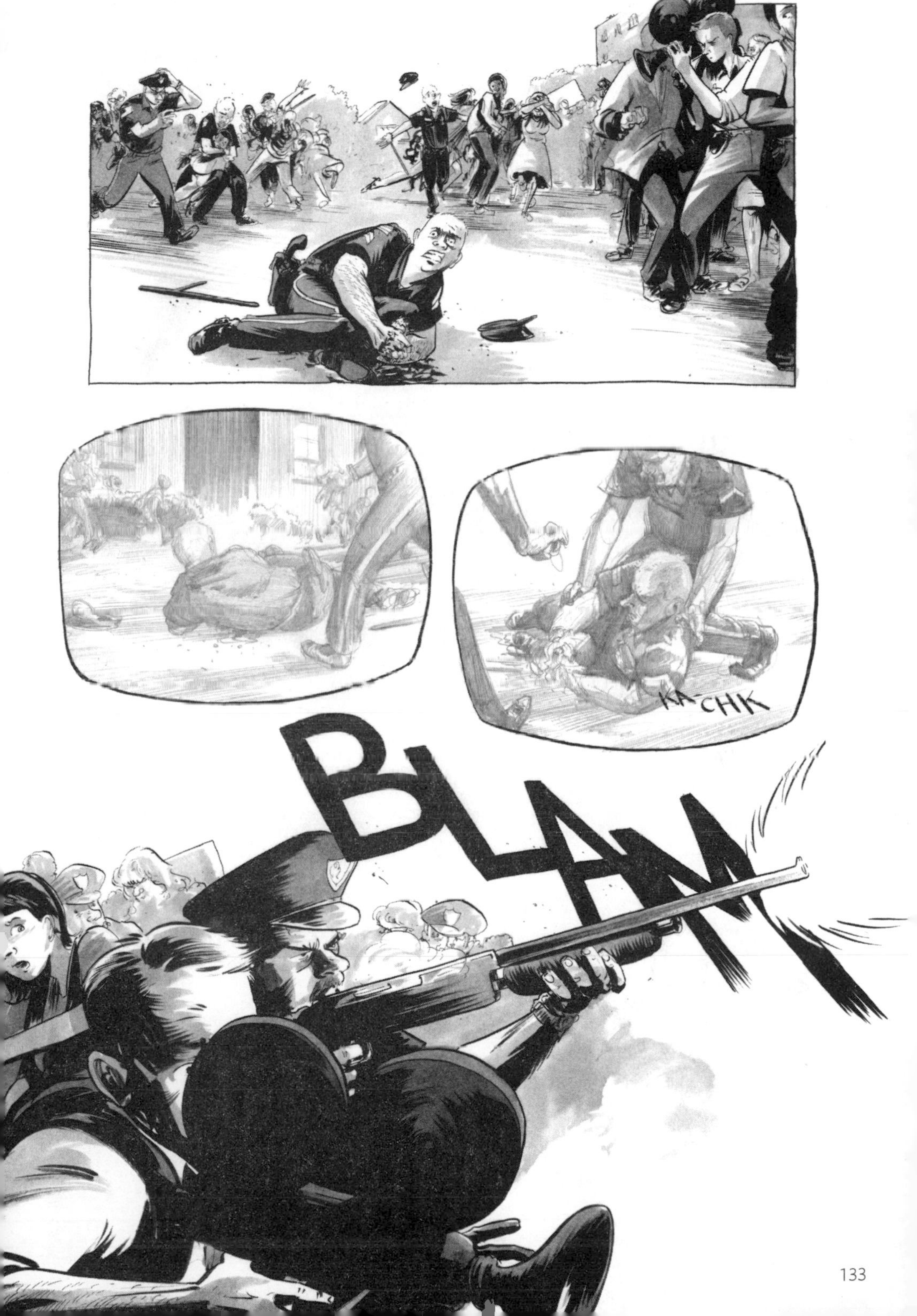
KA-CHK
BLAM

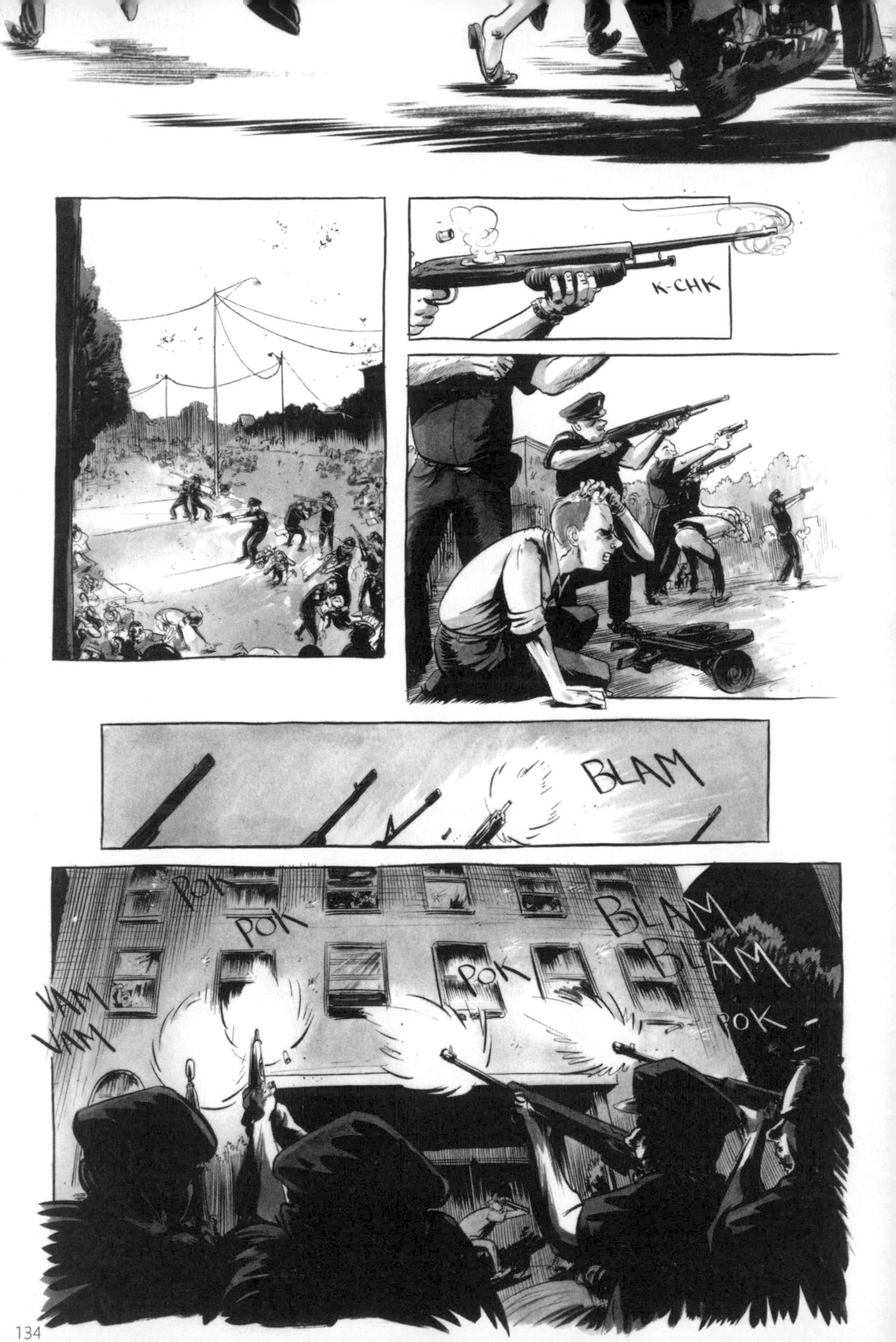
K-CHK
BLAM
POK
POK
BLAM
BLAM
POK
VAM
VAM
POK

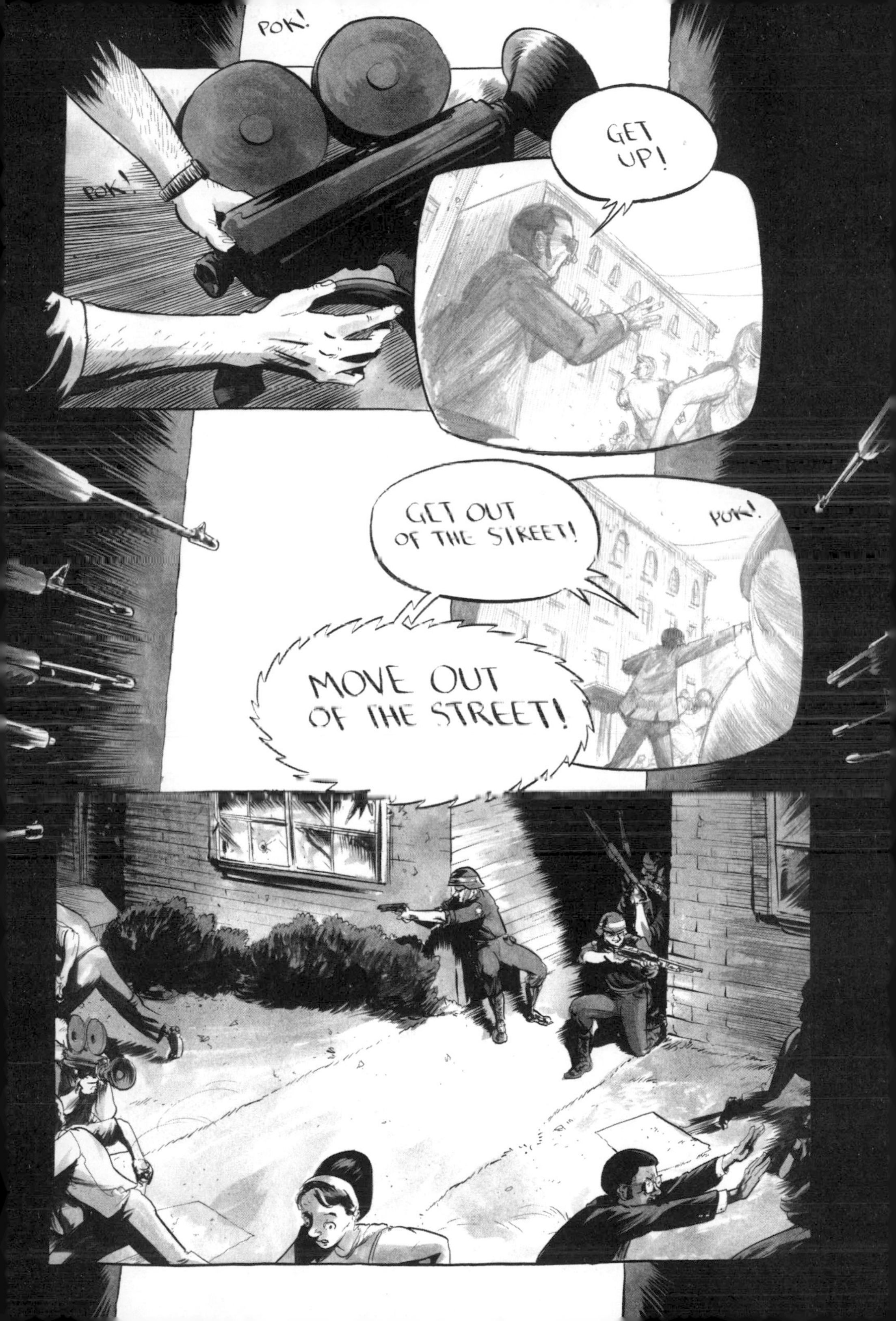
POK!
POK!
GET UP!
GET OUT OF THE STREET!
POK!
MOVE OUT OF THE STREET!

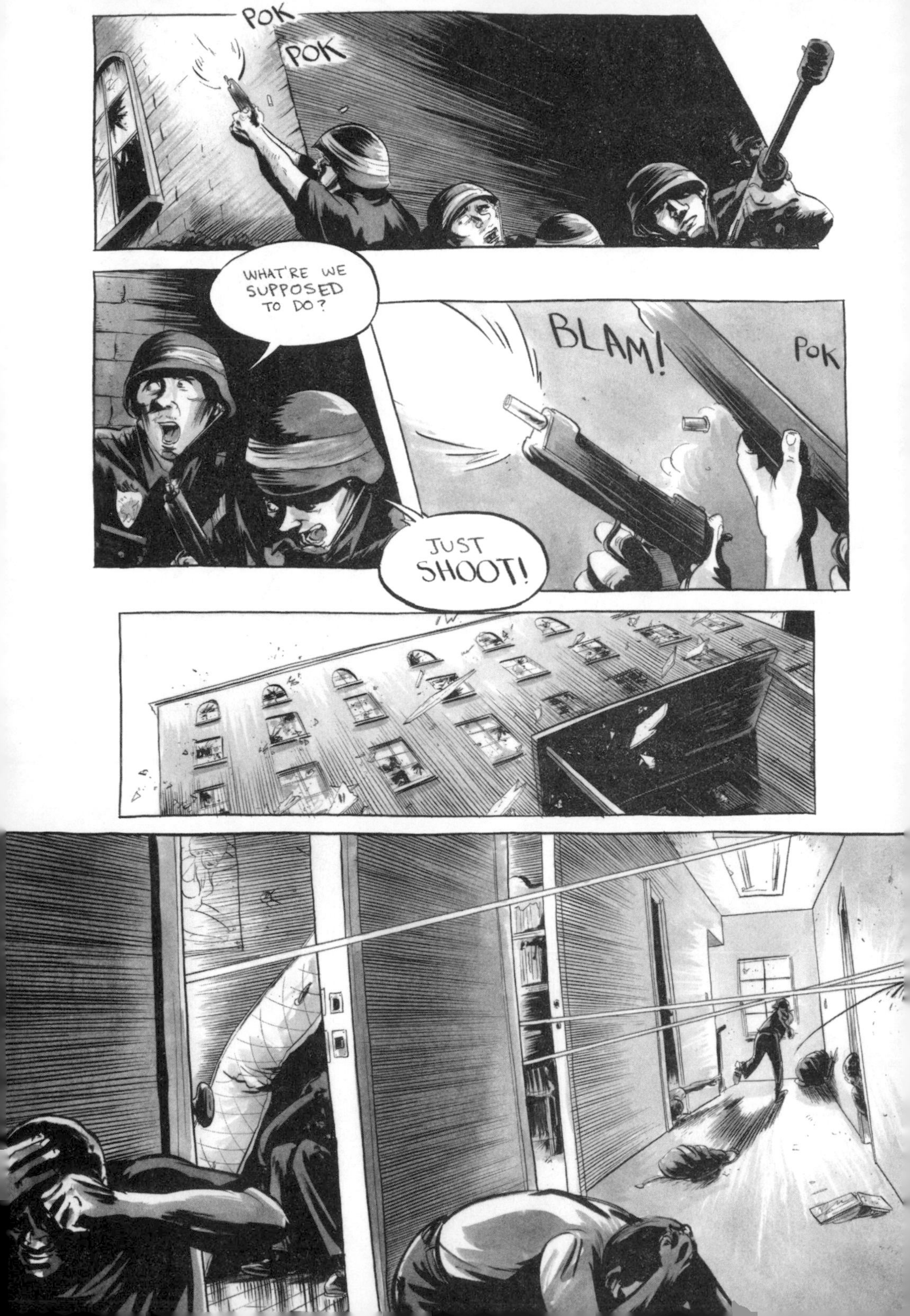
POK
POK
WHAT'RE WE SUPPOSED TO DO?
BLAM!
POK
JUST SHOOT!

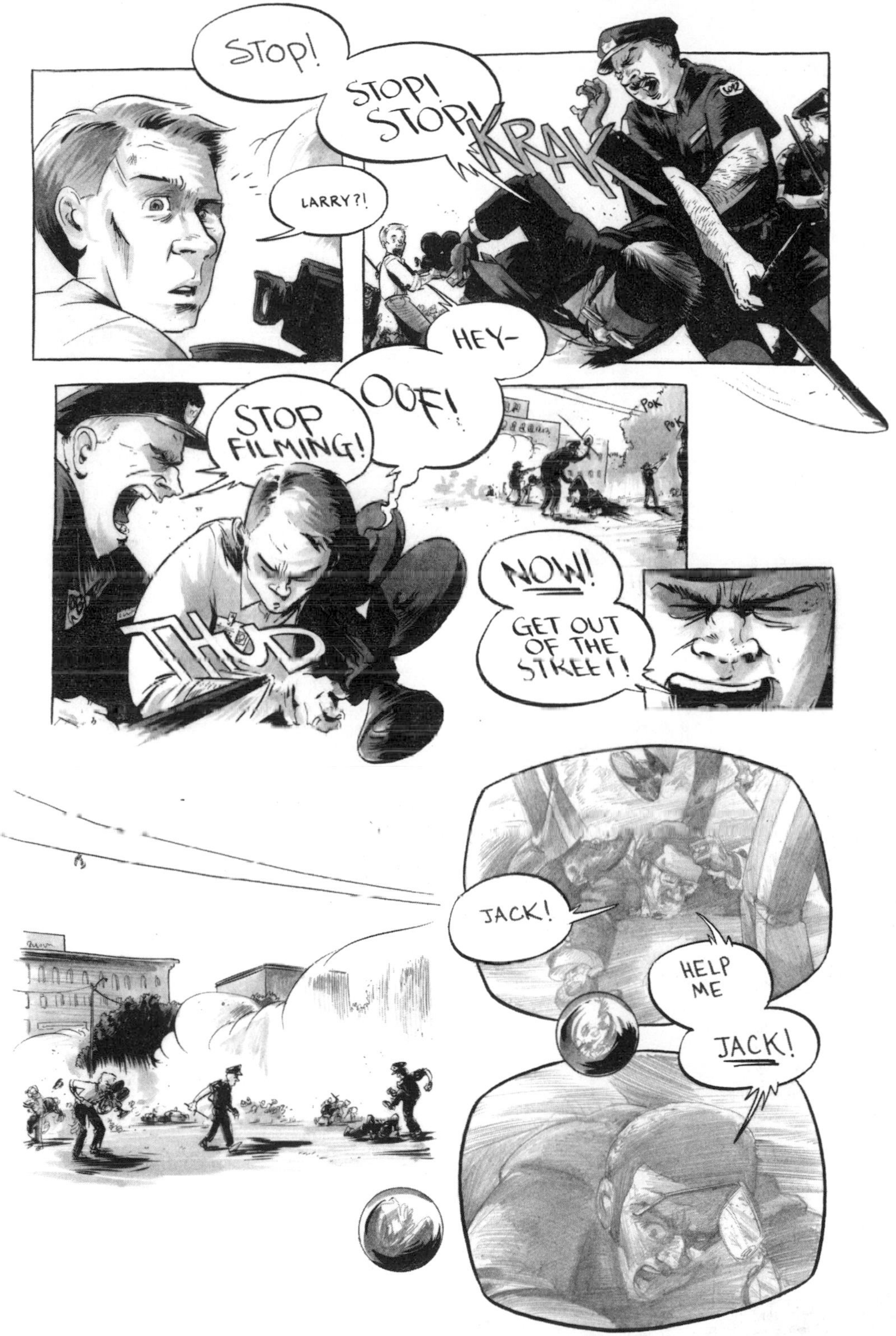

STOP!
STOP! STOP!
LARRY?!
KRAK
HEY-
OOF!
STOP FILMING!
THUD
POK
POK
NOW!
GET OUT OF THE STREET!
JACK!
HELP ME
JACK!

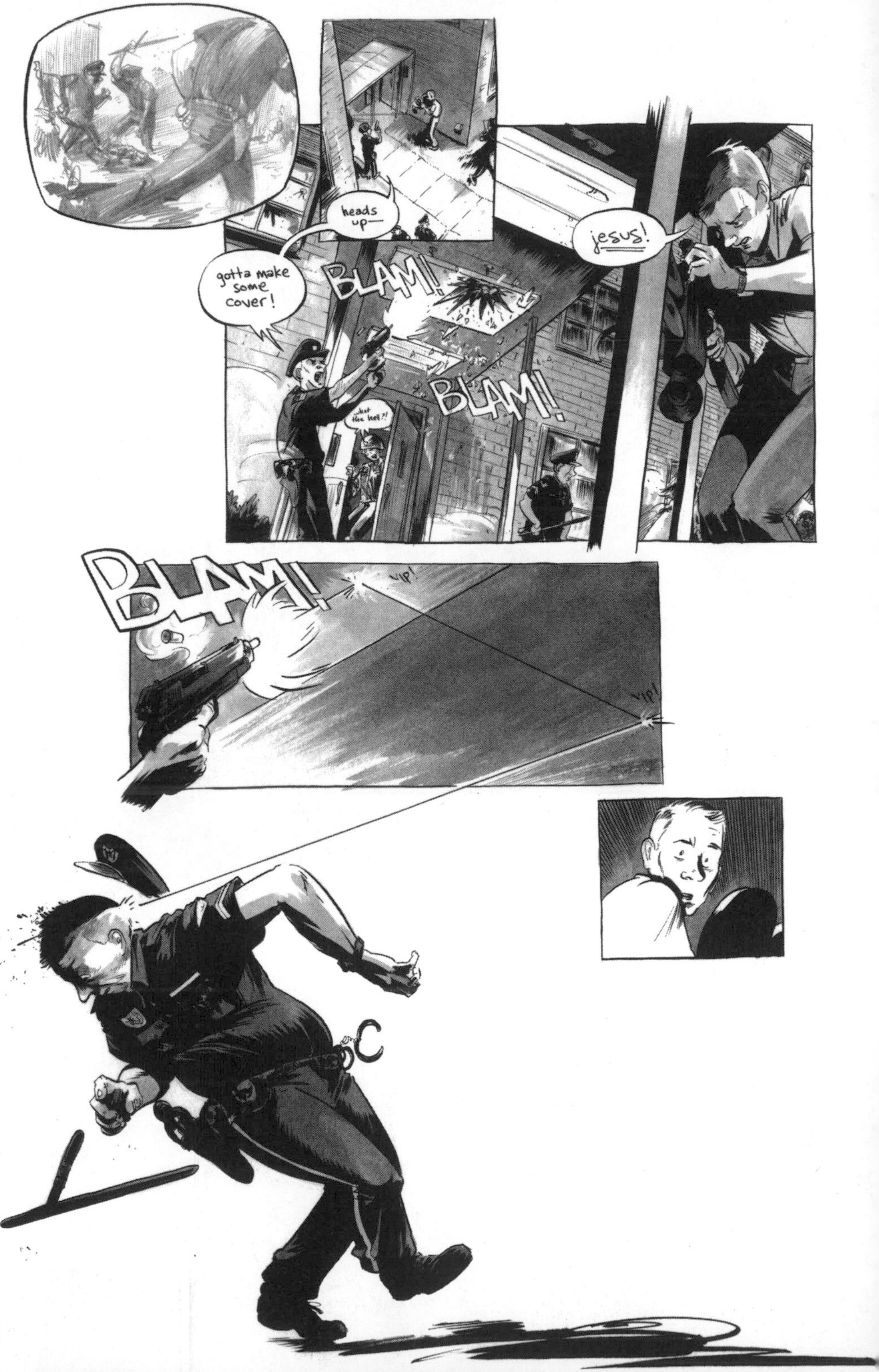
heads up—
gotta make some cover!
BLAM!
BLAM!
what the hell?!
jesus!
BLAM!
VIP!
VIP!

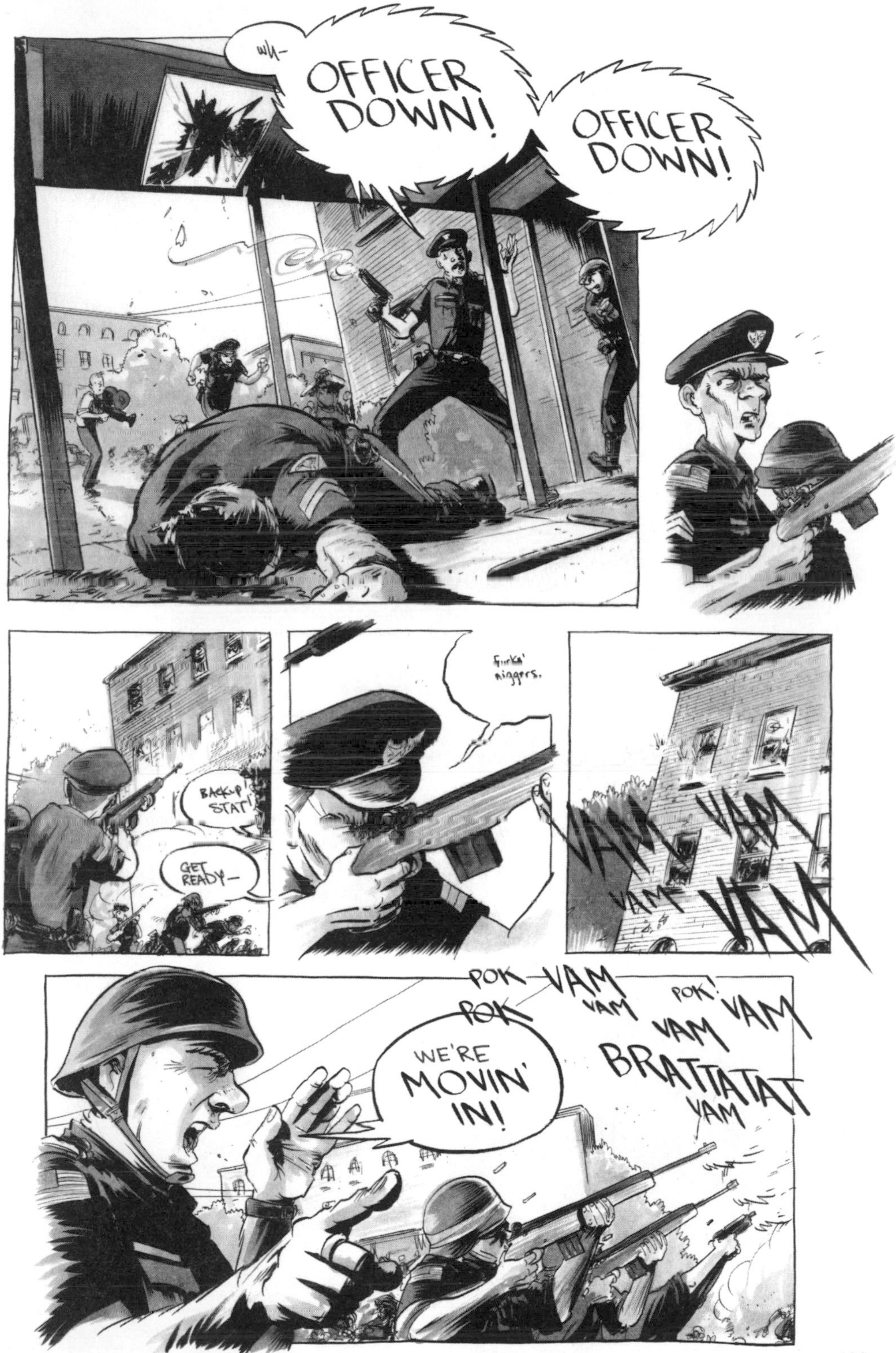
wh-
OFFICER DOWN!
OFFICER DOWN!
BACK-UP STAT!
GET READY—
Fuckn' niggers.
VAM VAM VAM VAM
WE'RE MOVIN' IN!
POK VAM
POK VAM
POK! VAM
VAM
BRATTATAT
VAM

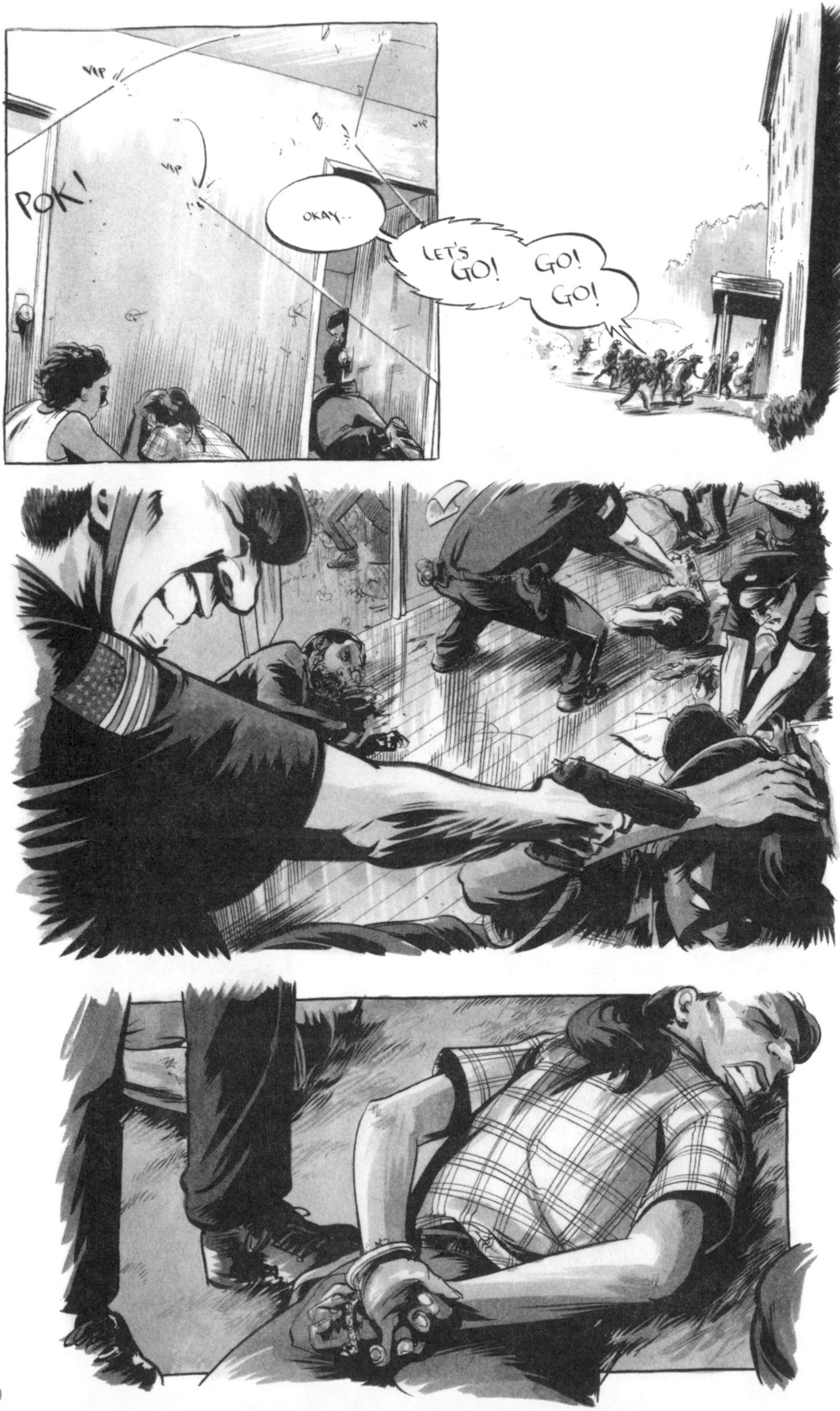
VIP
VIP
VIP
POK!
OKAY--
LET'S GO!
GO! GO!

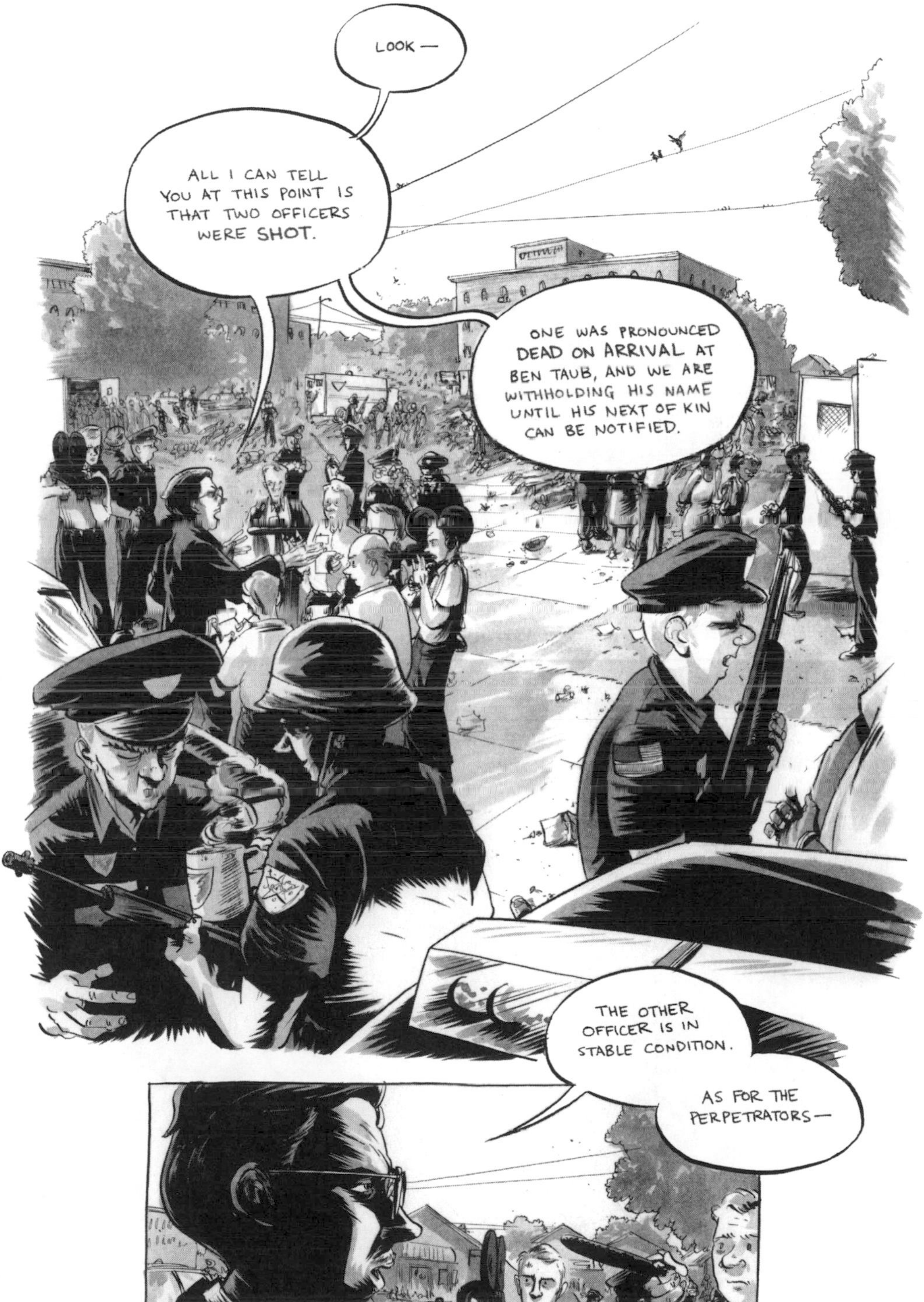
LOOK —
ALL I CAN TELL YOU AT THIS POINT IS THAT TWO OFFICERS WERE SHOT.
ONE WAS PRONOUNCED DEAD ON ARRIVAL AT BEN TAUB, AND WE ARE WITHHOLDING HIS NAME UNTIL HIS NEXT OF KIN CAN BE NOTIFIED.
THE OTHER OFFICER IS IN STABLE CONDITION.
AS FOR THE PERPETRATORS —

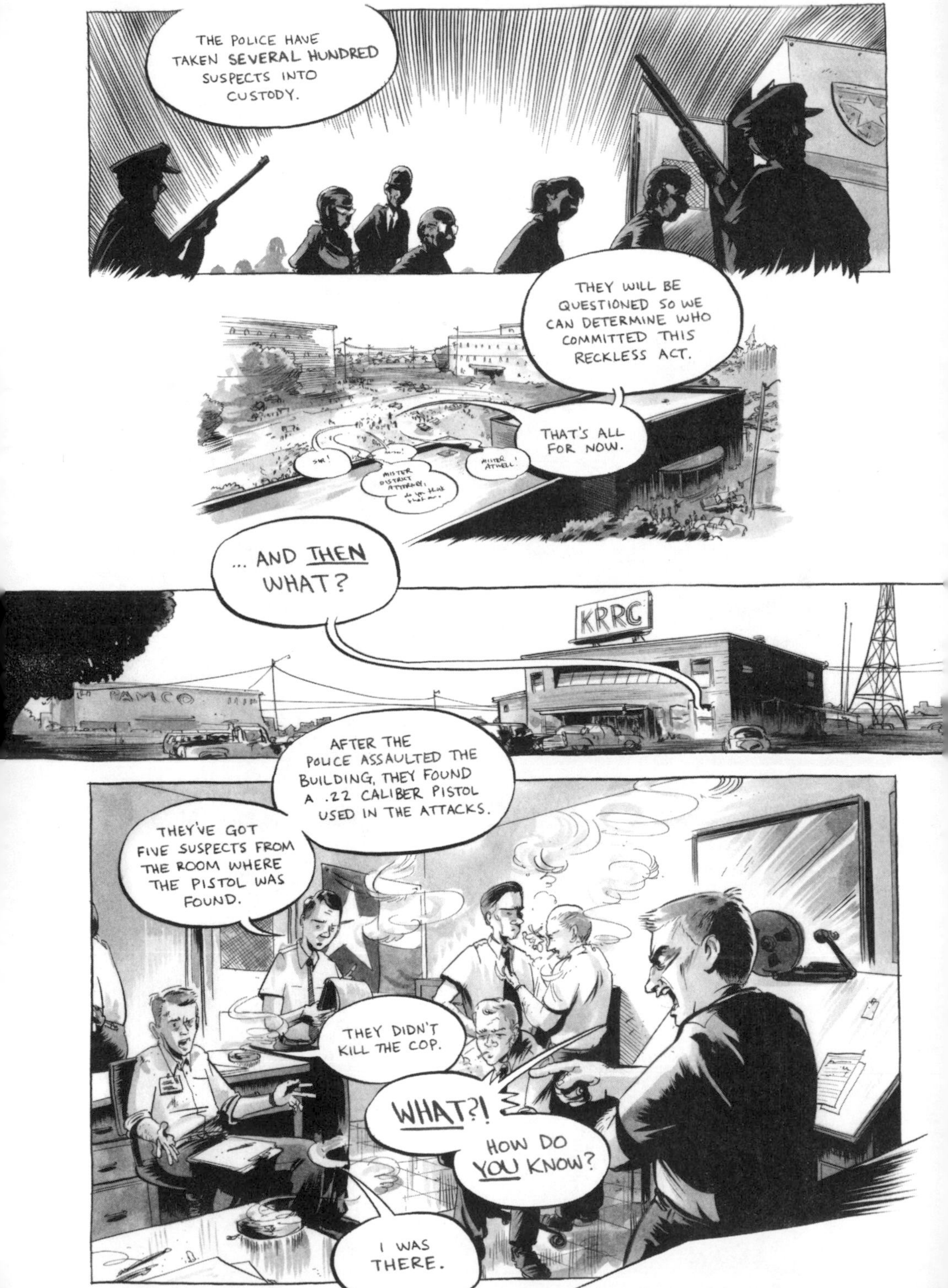
THE POLICE HAVE TAKEN SEVERAL HUNDRED SUSPECTS INTO CUSTODY.
THEY WILL BE QUESTIONED SO WE CAN DETERMINE WHO COMMITTED THIS RECKLESS ACT.
THAT'S ALL FOR NOW.
... AND THEN WHAT?
KRRC
AFTER THE POLICE ASSAULTED THE BUILDING, THEY FOUND A .22 CALIBER PISTOL USED IN THE ATTACKS.
THEY'VE GOT FIVE SUSPECTS FROM THE ROOM WHERE THE PISTOL WAS FOUND.
THEY DIDN'T KILL THE COP.
WHAT?!
HOW DO YOU KNOW?
I WAS THERE.

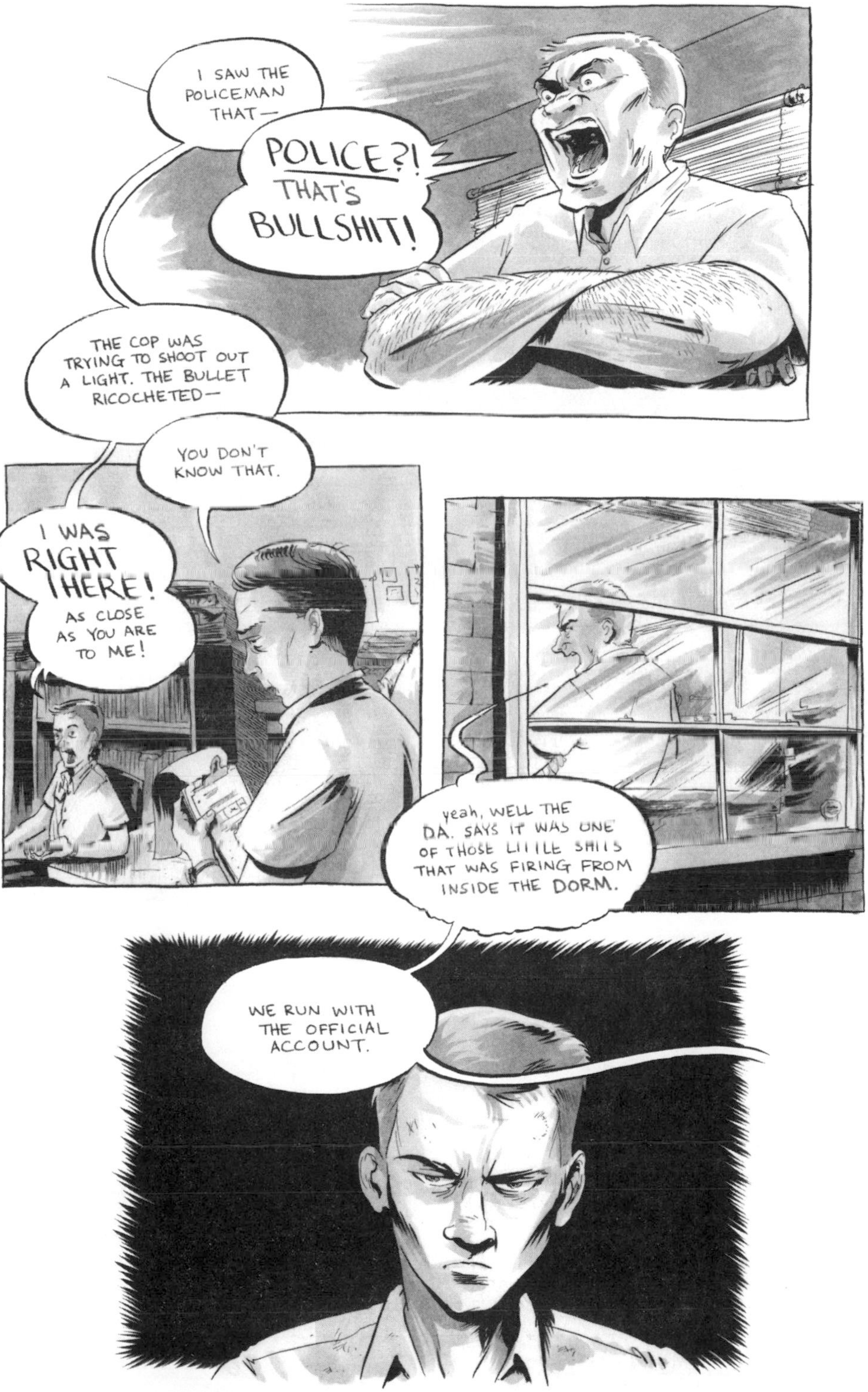
I SAW THE POLICEMAN THAT—
POLICE?! THAT'S BULLSHIT!
THE COP WAS TRYING TO SHOOT OUT A LIGHT. THE BULLET RICOCHETED—
YOU DON'T KNOW THAT.
I WAS RIGHT THERE! AS CLOSE AS YOU ARE TO ME!
yeah, WELL THE DA. SAYS IT WAS ONE OF THOSE LITTLE SHITS THAT WAS FIRING FROM INSIDE THE DORM.
WE RUN WITH THE OFFICIAL ACCOUNT.

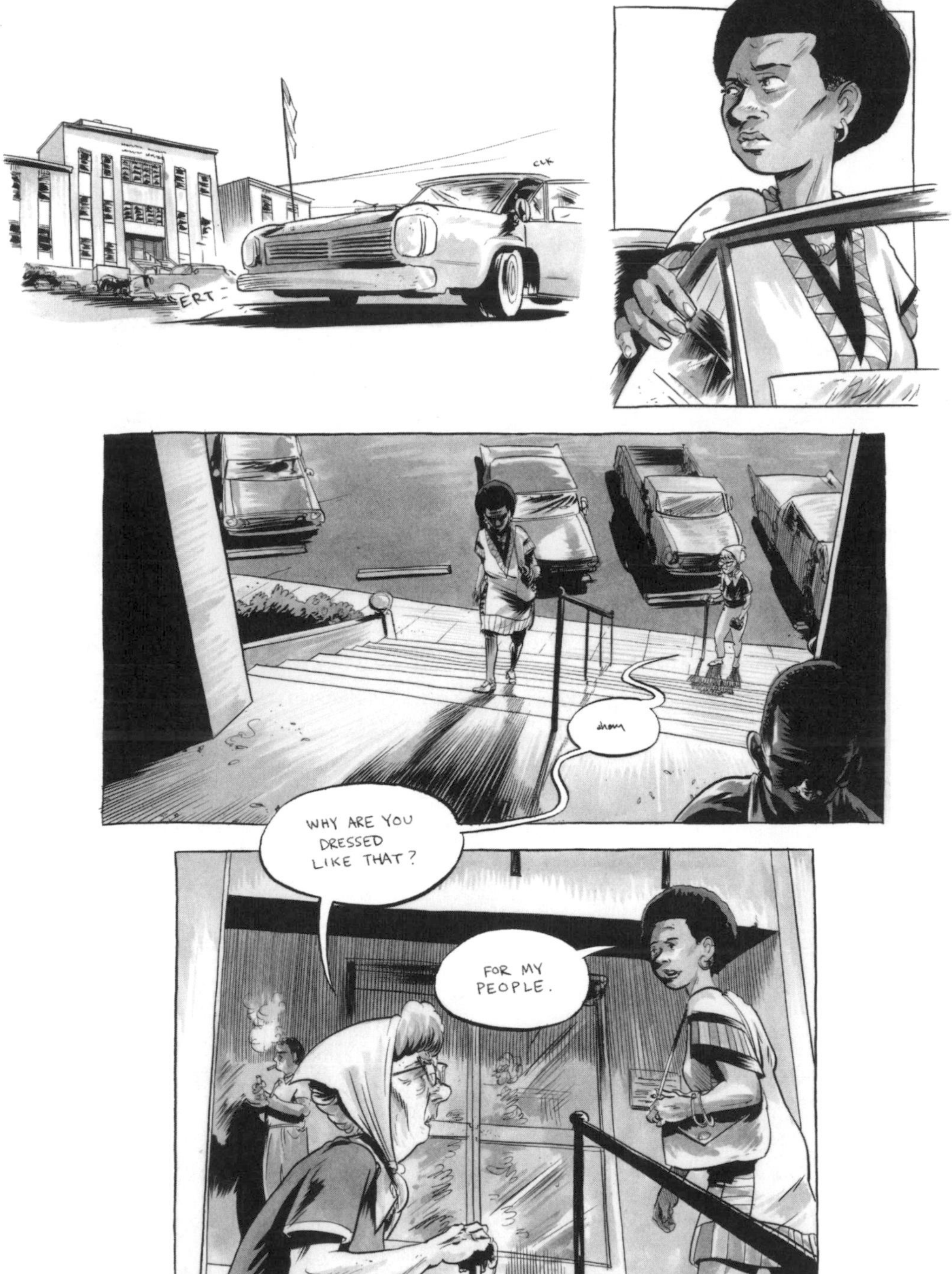
ERT
CLK
ahem
WHY ARE YOU DRESSED LIKE THAT?
FOR MY PEOPLE.

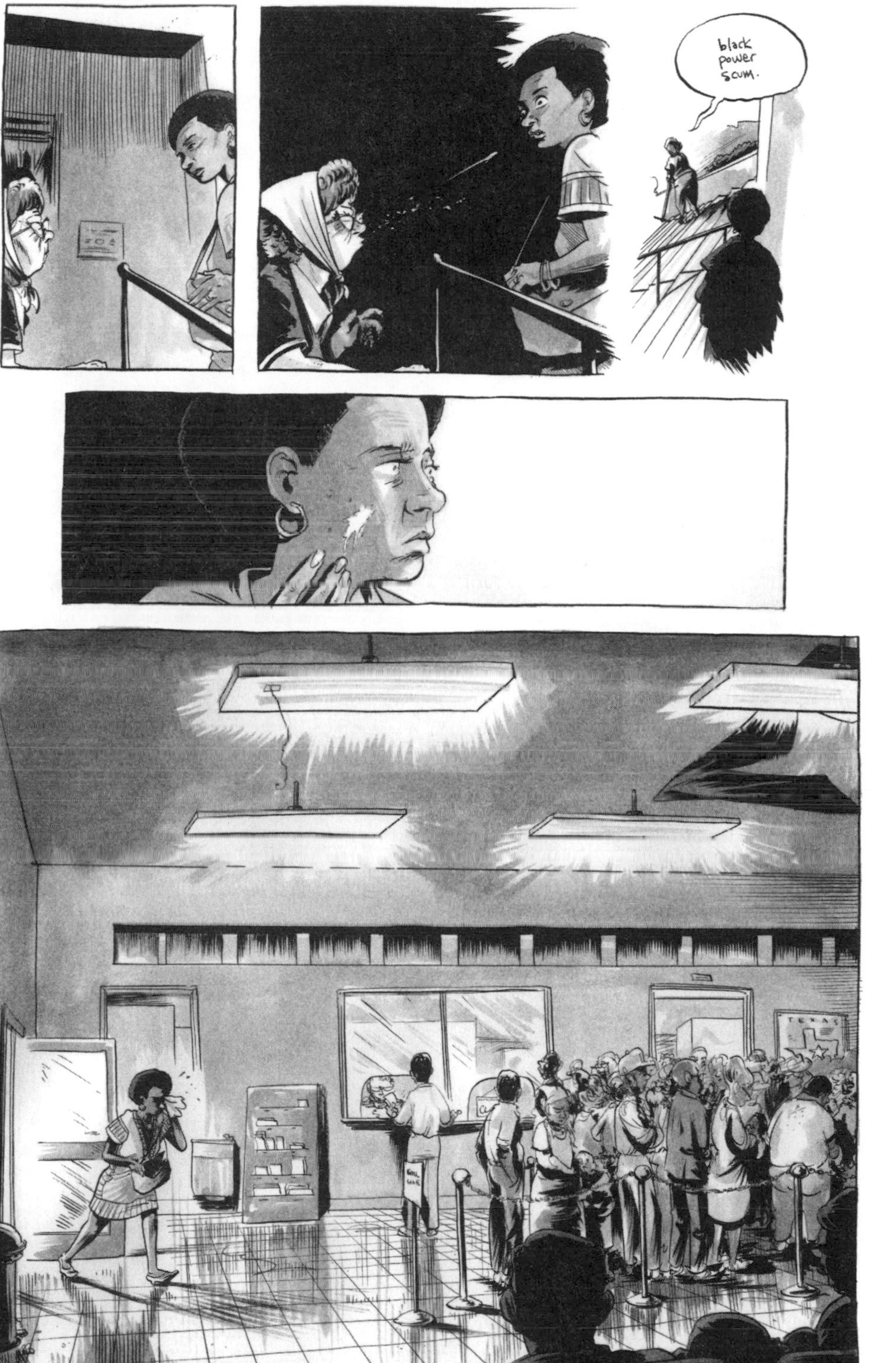
black power scum.

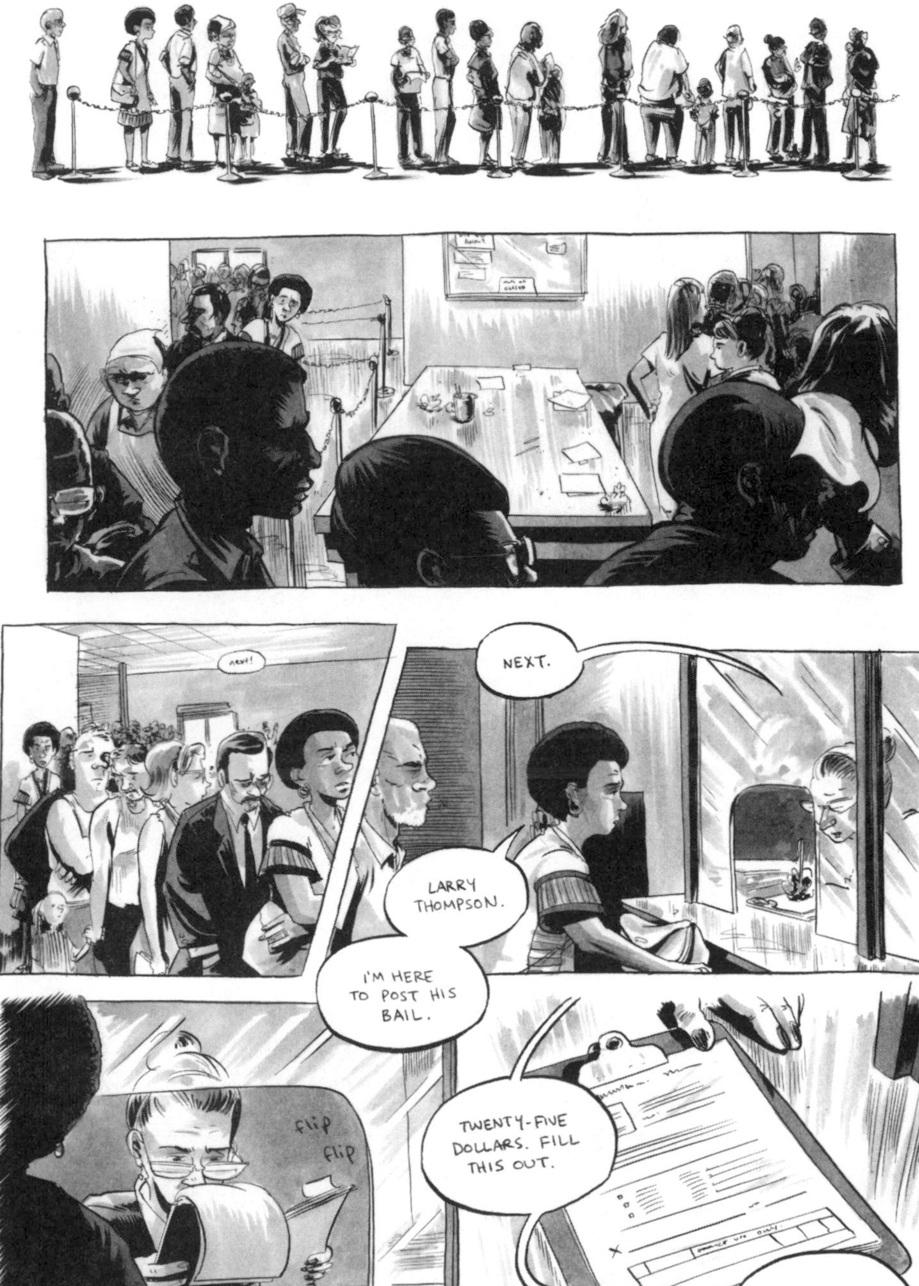
next!
NEXT.
LARRY THOMPSON.
I'M HERE TO POST HIS BAIL.
flip
flip
TWENTY-FIVE DOLLARS. FILL THIS OUT.
NEXT!

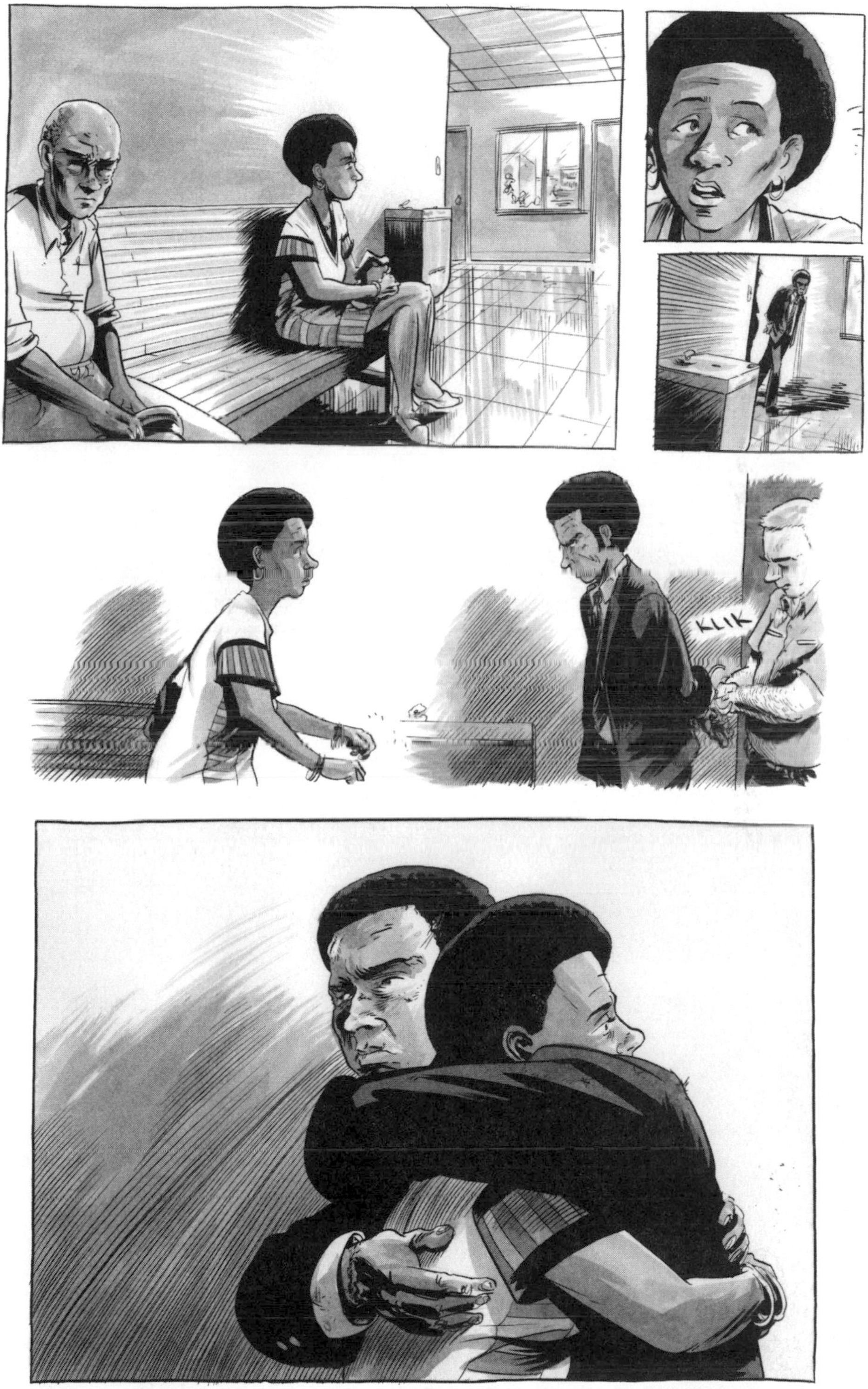
KLIK

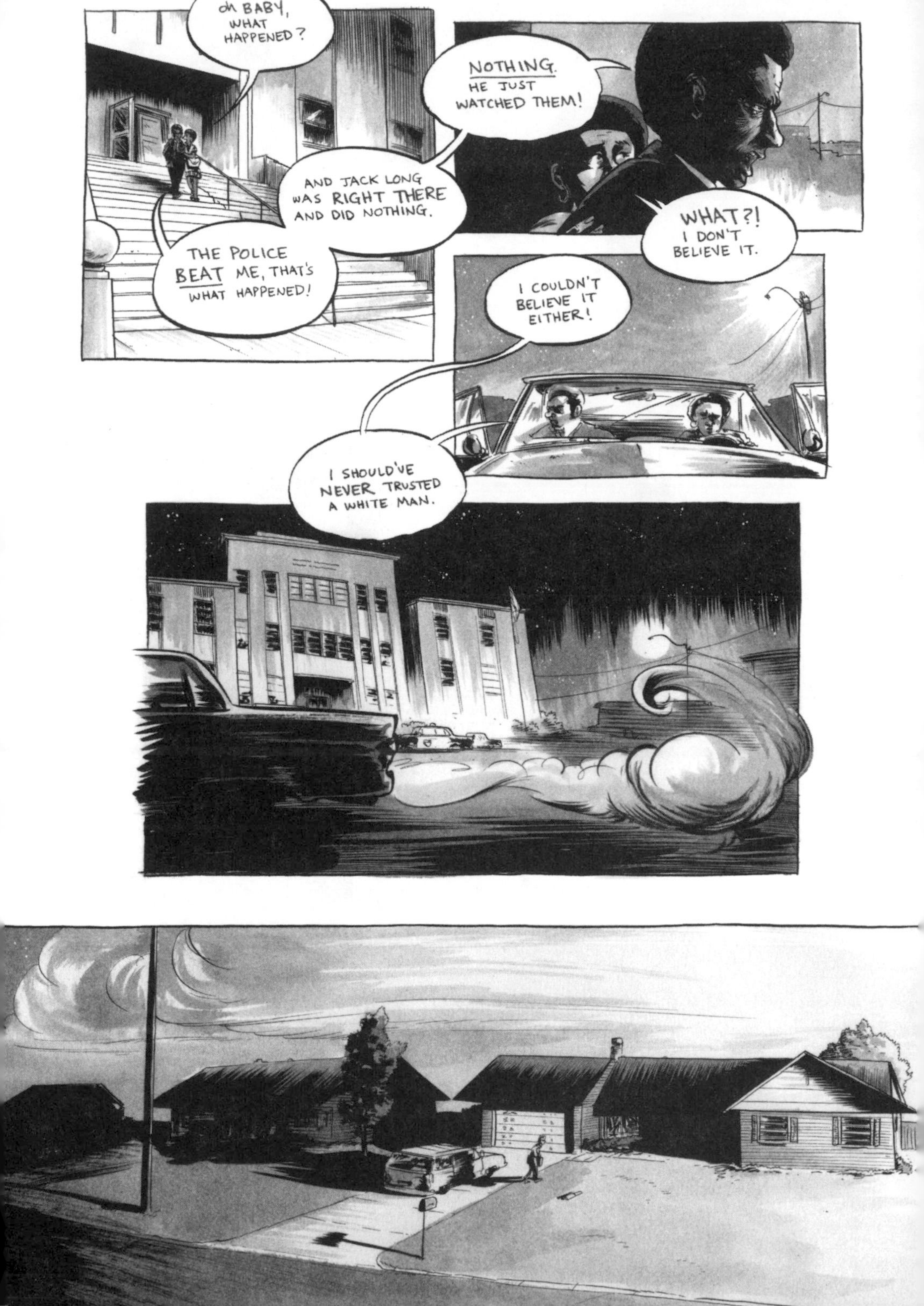

oh BABY, WHAT HAPPENED?
THE POLICE BEAT ME, THAT'S WHAT HAPPENED!
AND JACK LONG WAS RIGHT THERE AND DID NOTHING.
NOTHING. HE JUST WATCHED THEM!
WHAT?! I DON'T BELIEVE IT.
I COULDN'T BELIEVE IT EITHER!
I SHOULD'VE NEVER TRUSTED A WHITE MAN.

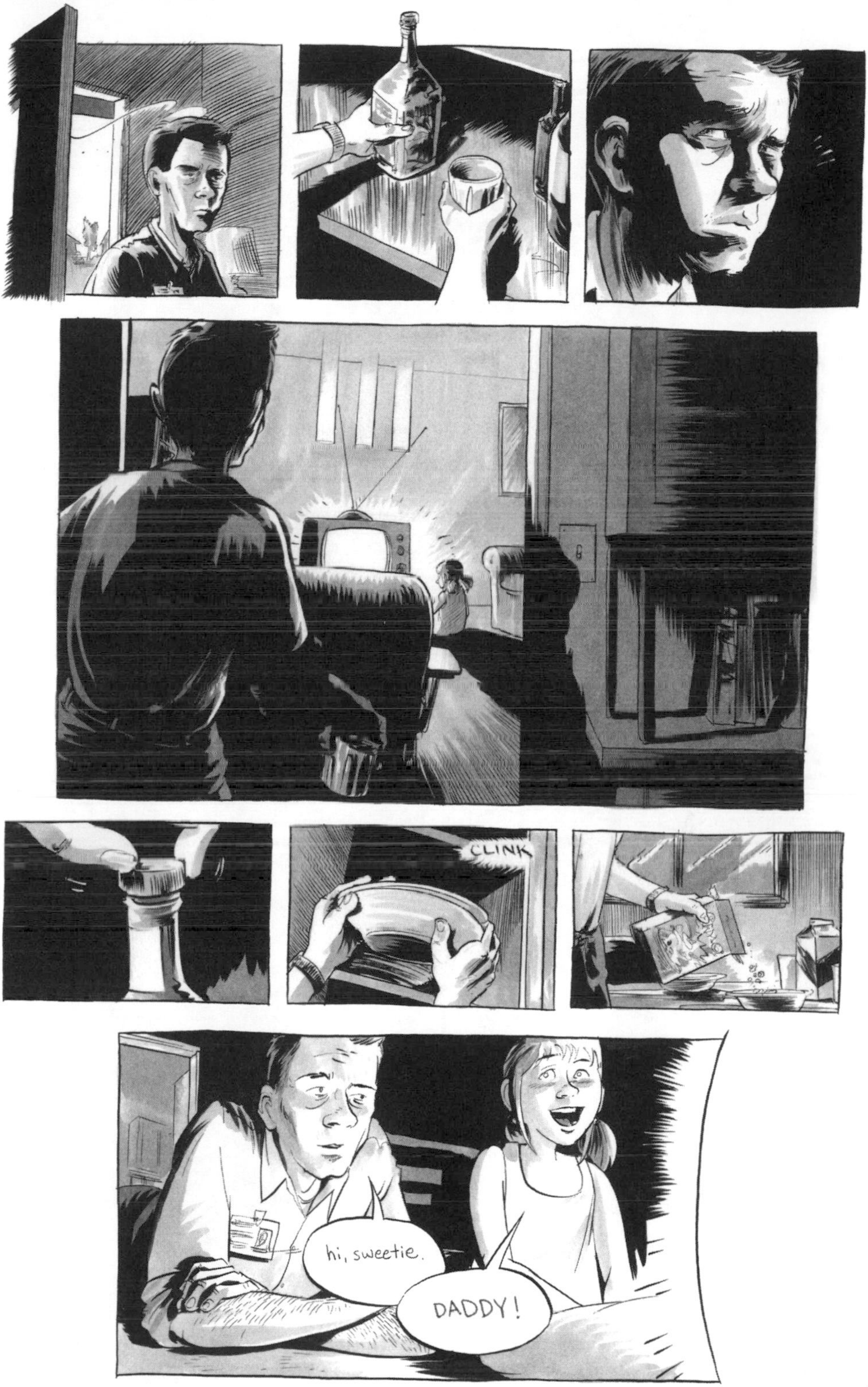
CLINK
hi, sweetie.
DADDY!

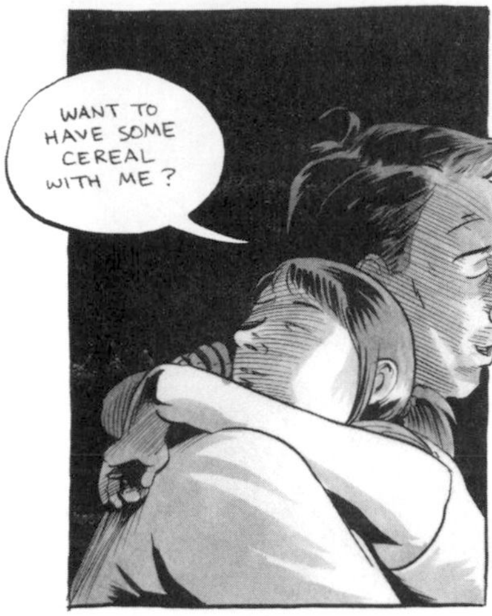
WANT TO HAVE SOME CEREAL WITH ME?

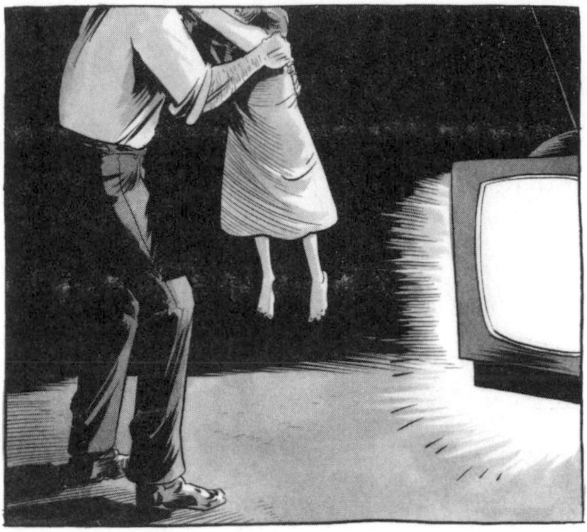

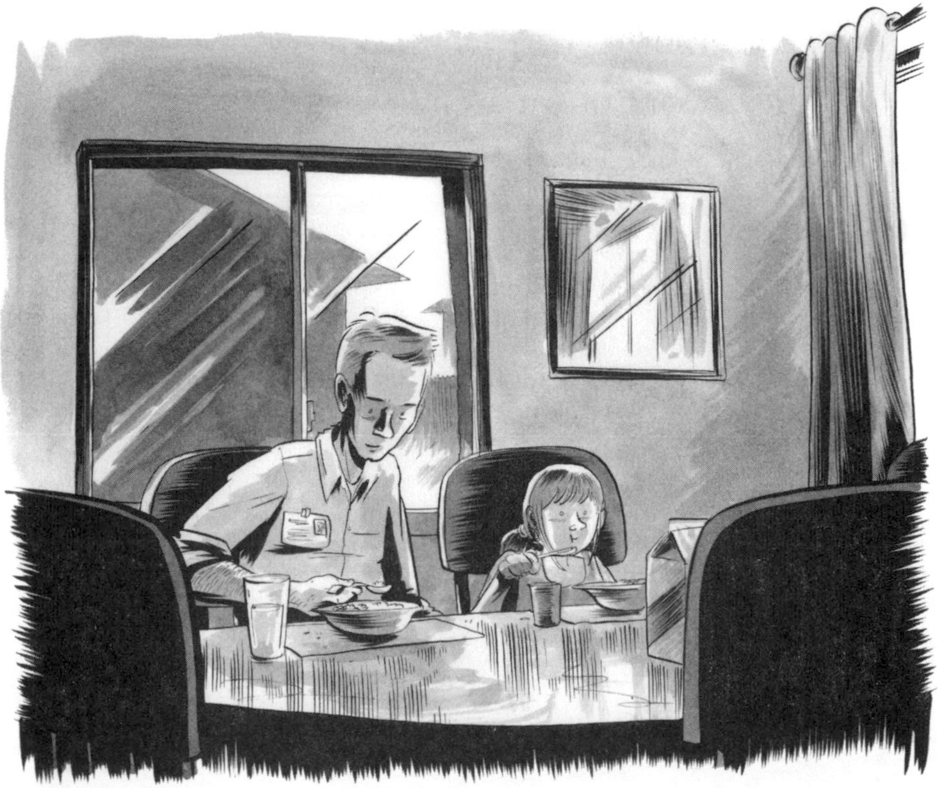

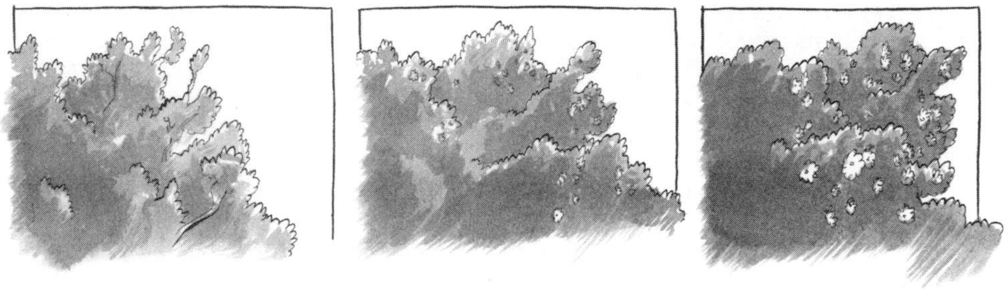

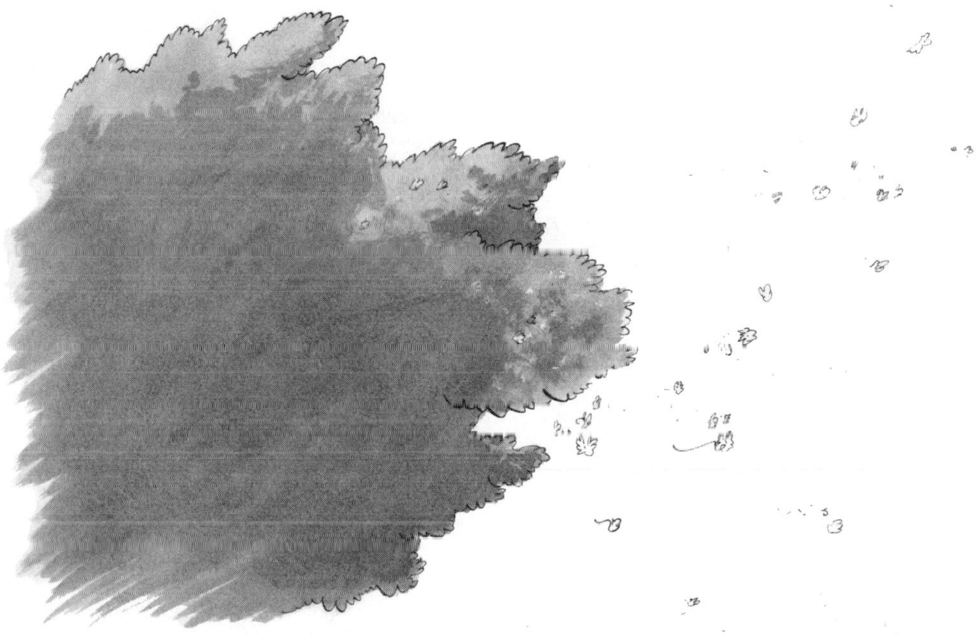

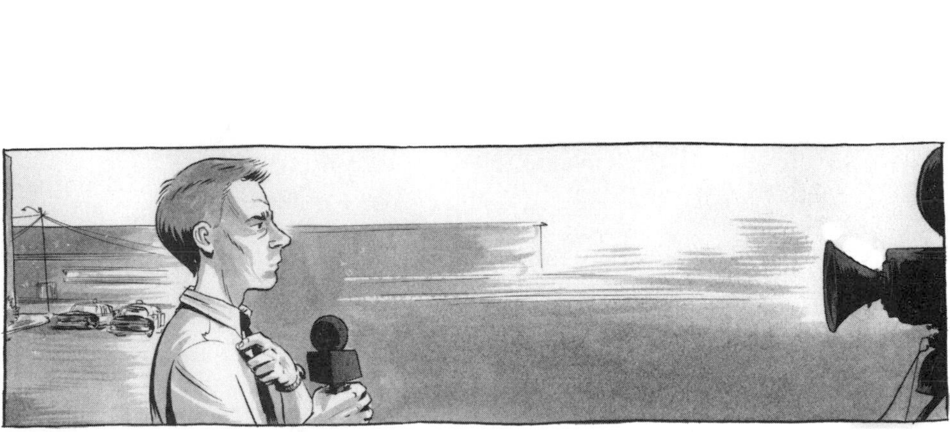

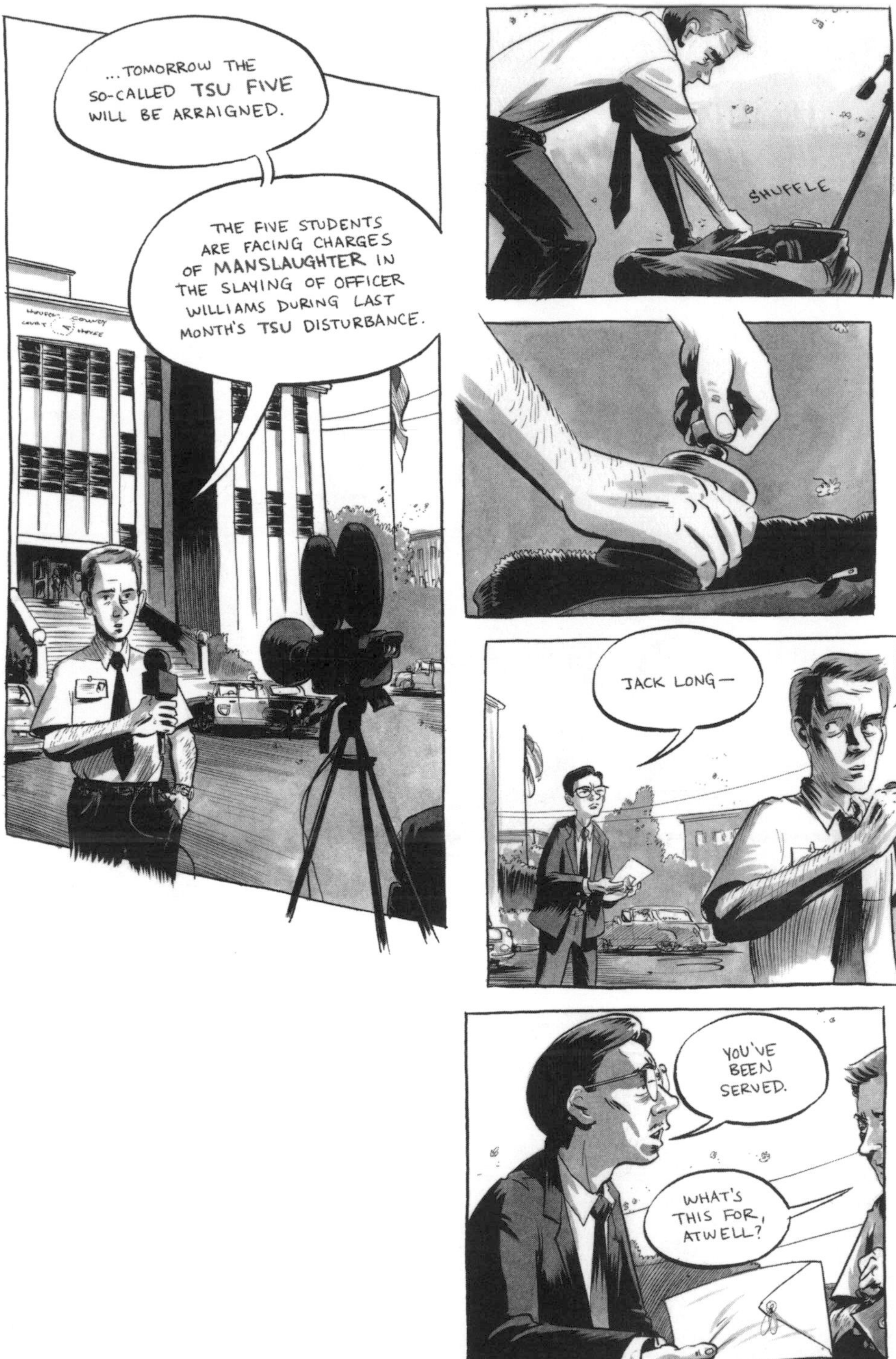
...TOMORROW THE SO-CALLED TSU FIVE WILL BE ARRAIGNED.
THE FIVE STUDENTS ARE FACING CHARGES OF MANSLAUGHTER IN THE SLAYING OF OFFICER WILLIAMS DURING LAST MONTH'S TSU DISTURBANCE.
SHUFFLE
JACK LONG—
YOU'VE BEEN SERVED.
WHAT'S THIS FOR, ATWELL?

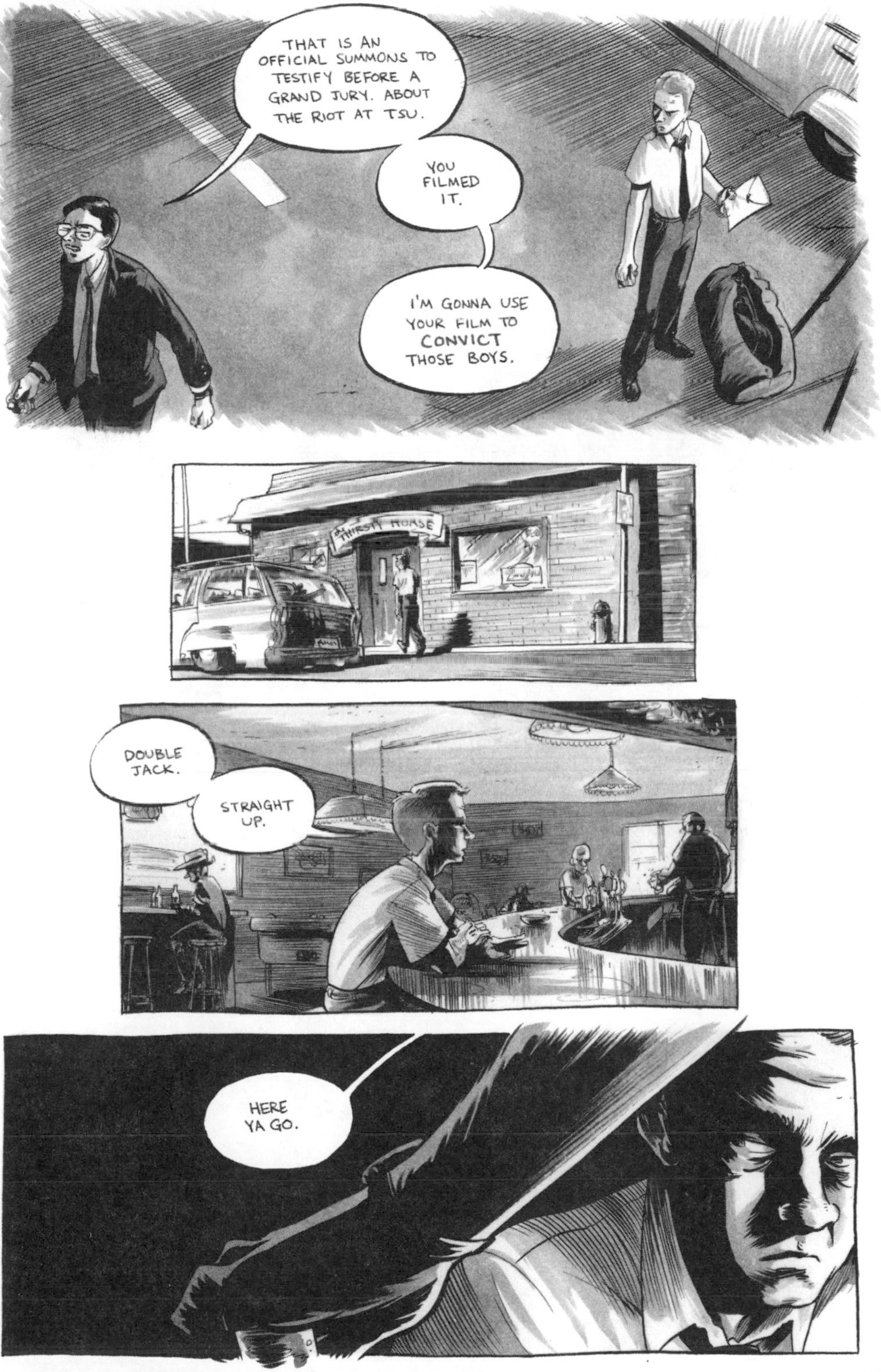
THAT IS AN OFFICIAL SUMMONS TO TESTIFY BEFORE A GRAND JURY. ABOUT THE RIOT AT TSU.
YOU FILMED IT.
I'M GONNA USE YOUR FILM TO CONVICT THOSE BOYS.
THIRSTY HORSE
DOUBLE JACK.
STRAIGHT UP.
HERE YA GO.

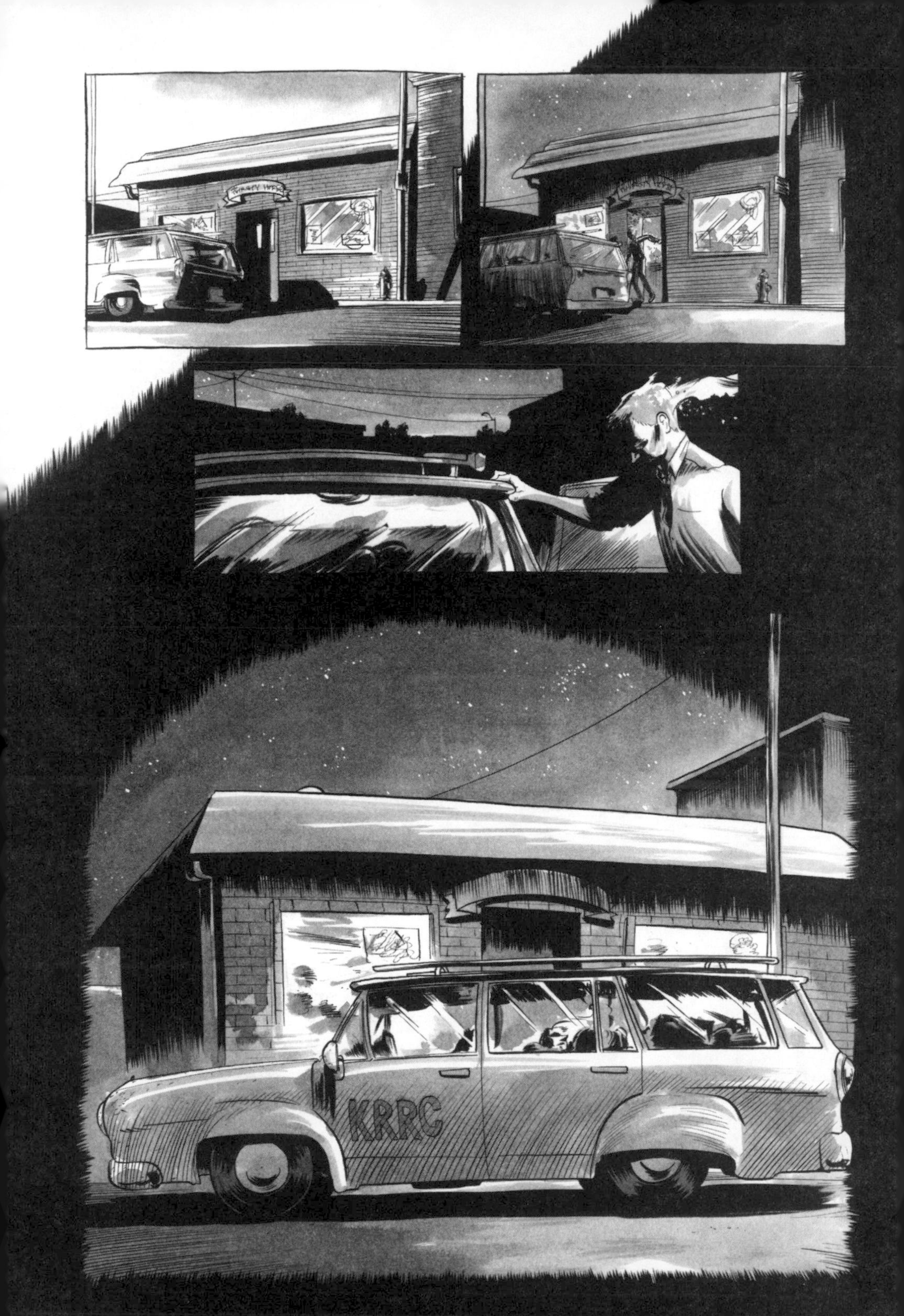
KRRC

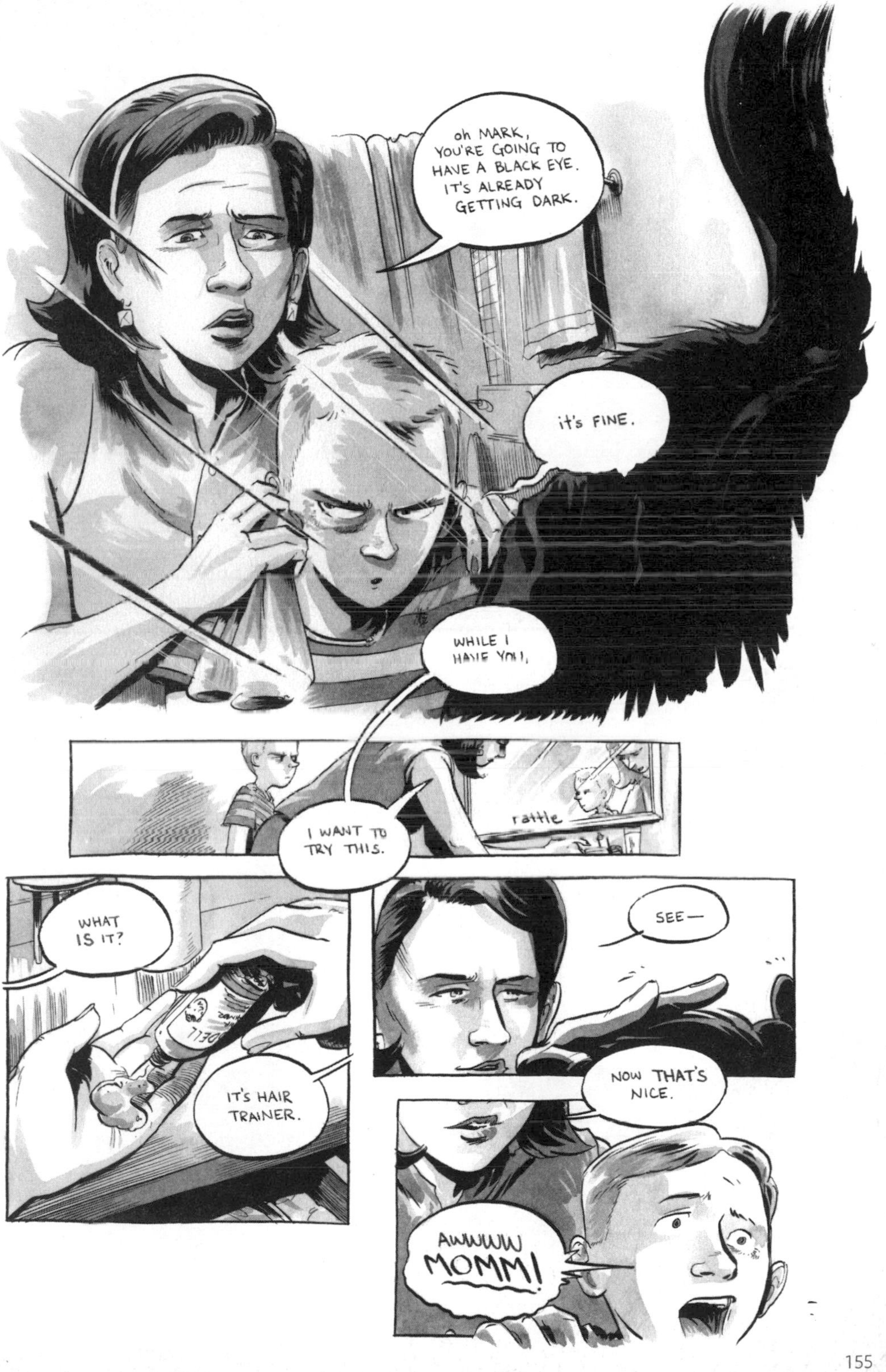
oh MARK, YOU'RE GOING TO HAVE A BLACK EYE. IT'S ALREADY GETTING DARK.
it's FINE.
WHILE I HAVE YOU,
I WANT TO TRY THIS.
rattle
WHAT IS IT?
IT'S HAIR TRAINER.
SEE—
NOW THAT'S NICE.
AWWWW MOMM!

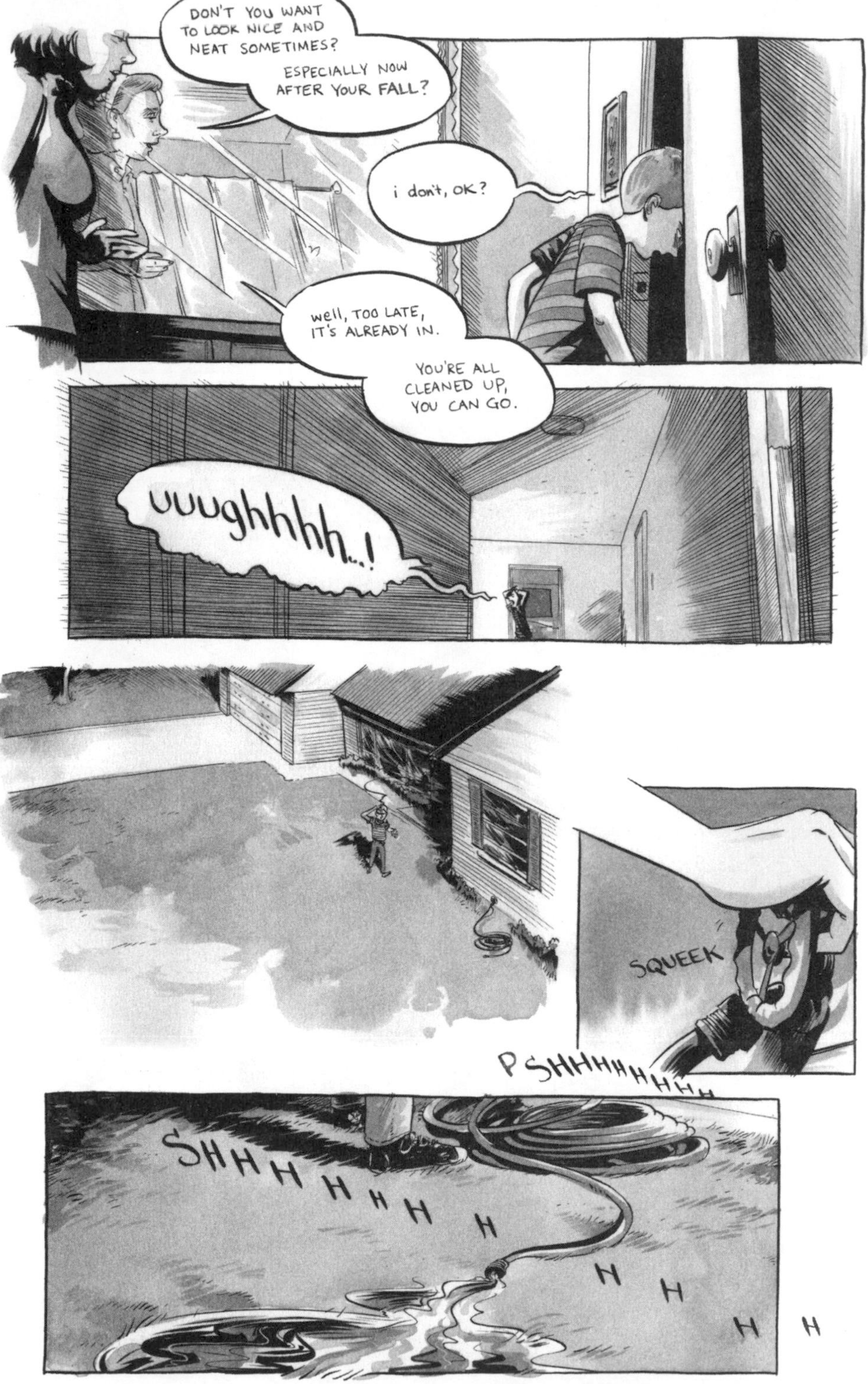
DON'T YOU WANT TO LOOK NICE AND NEAT SOMETIMES?
ESPECIALLY NOW AFTER YOUR FALL?
i don't, OK?
well, TOO LATE, IT'S ALREADY IN.
YOU'RE ALL CLEANED UP, YOU CAN GO.
uuughhhh..!
SQUEEK
PSHHHHHHHHHH
SHHHHHHHHHHH

SPPSH H H H H H

H H H H H H H H H H

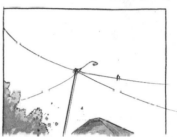
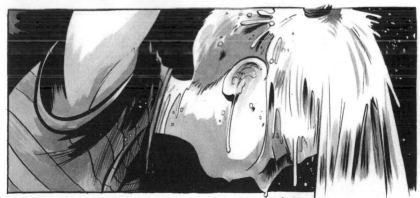

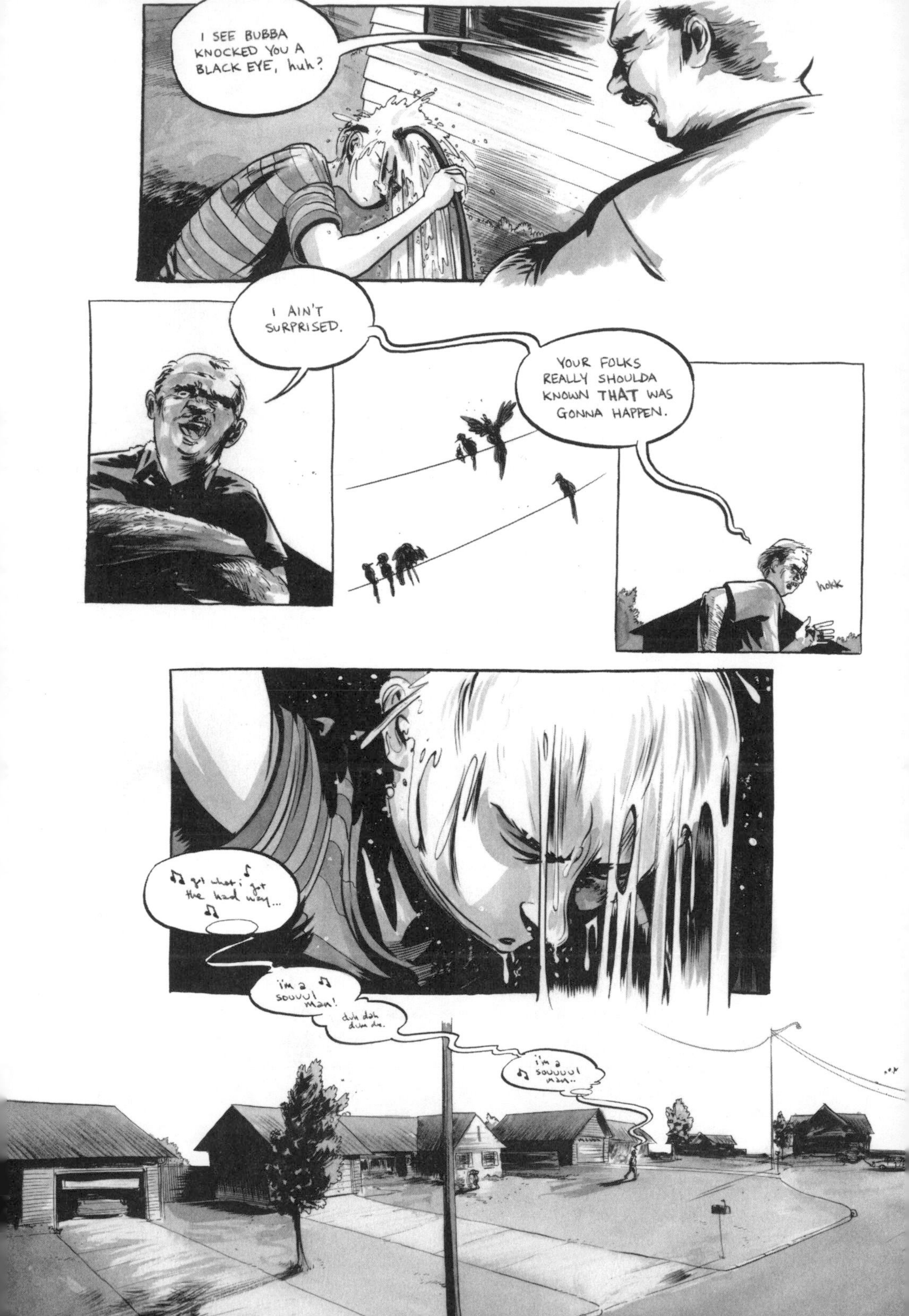
I SEE BUBBA KNOCKED YOU A BLACK EYE, huh?
I AIN'T SURPRISED.
YOUR FOLKS REALLY SHOULDA KNOWN THAT WAS GONNA HAPPEN.
hokk
♫ got what i got the had way... ♫
i'm a ♫ souuul man!
duh dah dum de.
♫ i'm a souuuul man..

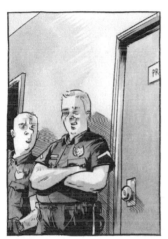

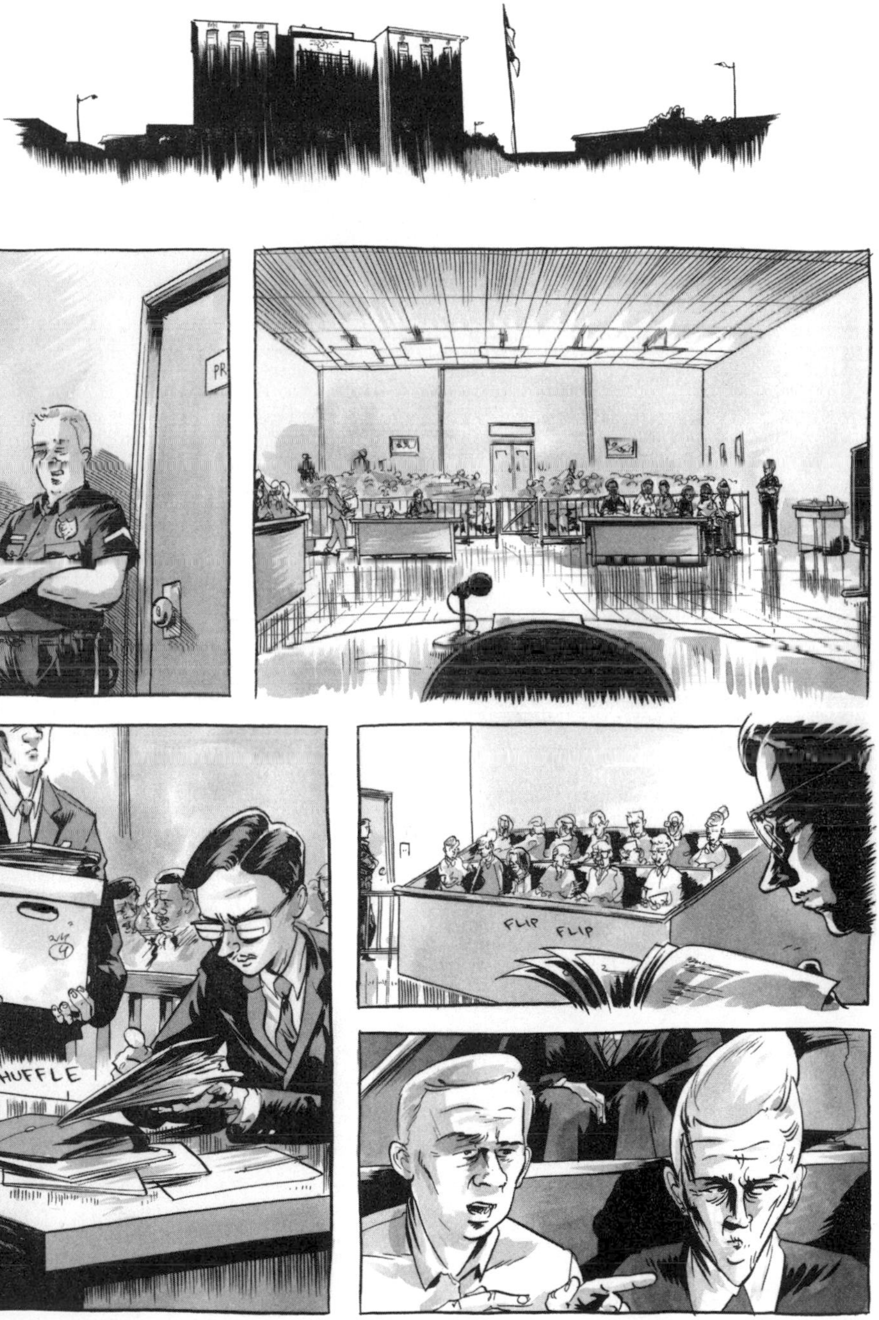
SHUFFLE
FLIP FLIP

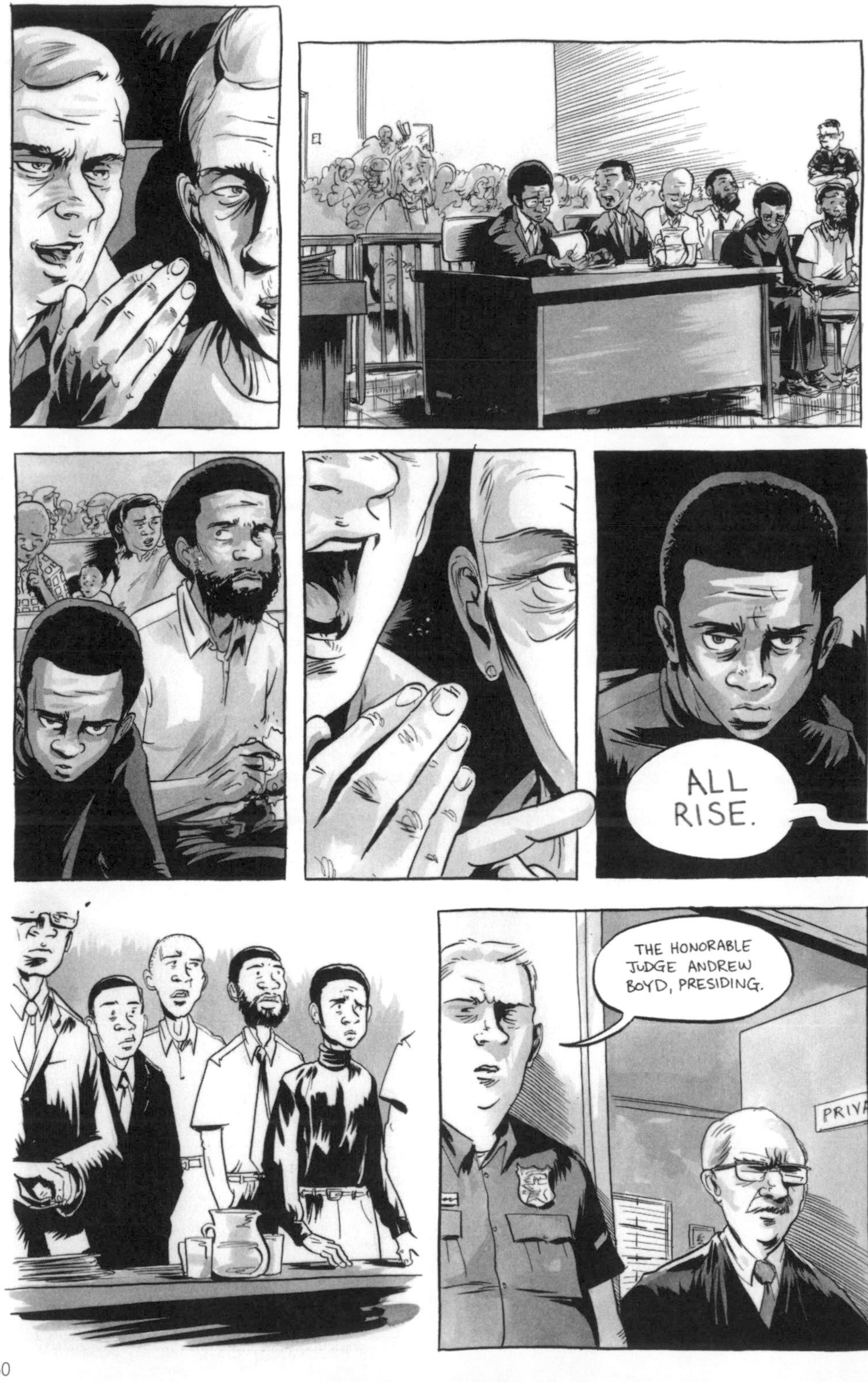
ALL RISE.
THE HONORABLE JUDGE ANDREW BOYD, PRESIDING.
PRIVA

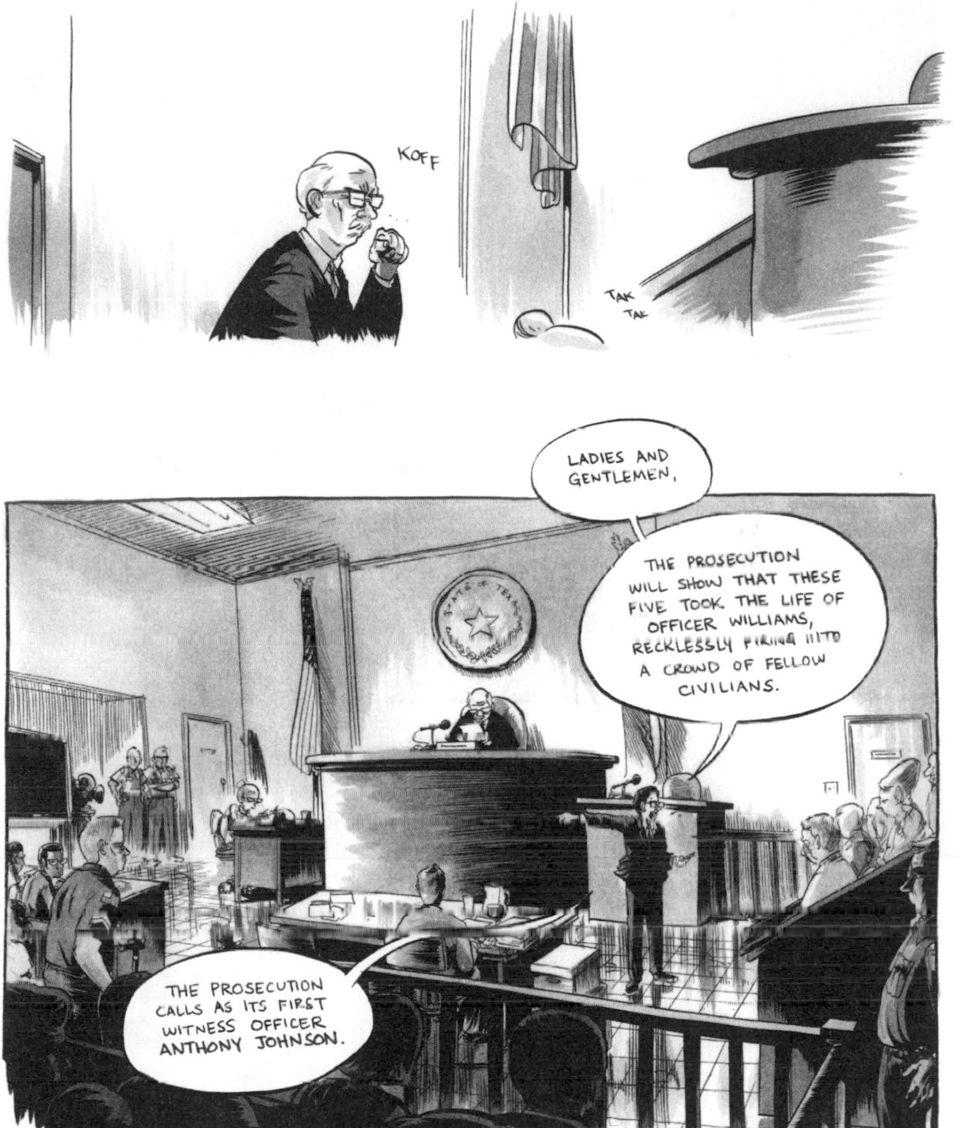
KOFF
TAK TAK
LADIES AND GENTLEMEN,
THE PROSECUTION WILL SHOW THAT THESE FIVE TOOK THE LIFE OF OFFICER WILLIAMS, RECKLESSLY FIRING INTO A CROWD OF FELLOW CIVILIANS.
THE PROSECUTION CALLS AS ITS FIRST WITNESS OFFICER ANTHONY JOHNSON.
CLUNK
PIK PIK
WHAT DID YOU SEE WHEN YOU FIRST ARRIVED, OFFICER JOHNSON?

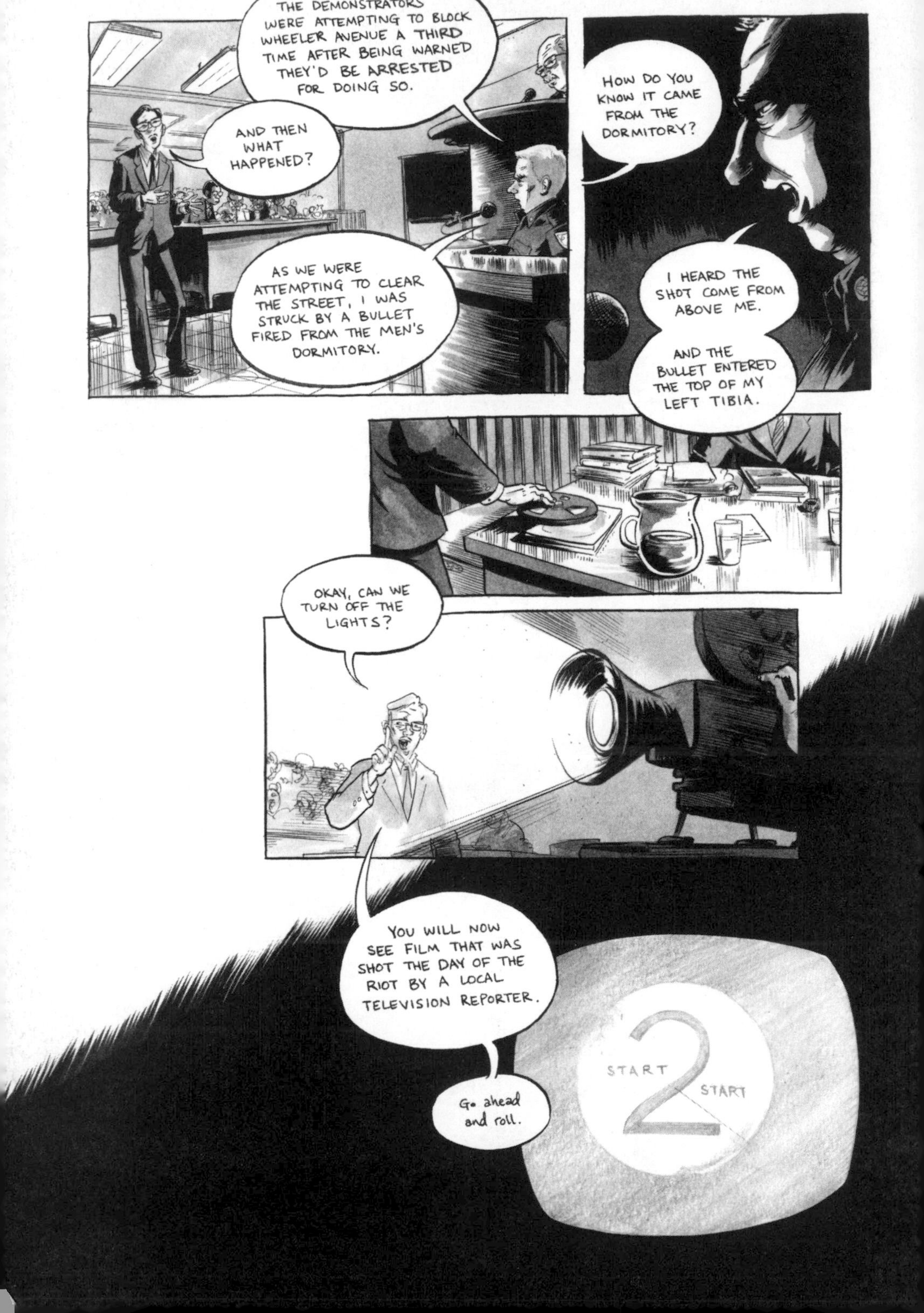
THE DEMONSTRATORS WERE ATTEMPTING TO BLOCK WHEELER AVENUE A THIRD TIME AFTER BEING WARNED THEY'D BE ARRESTED FOR DOING SO.
AND THEN WHAT HAPPENED?
AS WE WERE ATTEMPTING TO CLEAR THE STREET, I WAS STRUCK BY A BULLET FIRED FROM THE MEN'S DORMITORY.
HOW DO YOU KNOW IT CAME FROM THE DORMITORY?
I HEARD THE SHOT COME FROM ABOVE ME.
AND THE BULLET ENTERED THE TOP OF MY LEFT TIBIA.
OKAY, CAN WE TURN OFF THE LIGHTS?
YOU WILL NOW SEE FILM THAT WAS SHOT THE DAY OF THE RIOT BY A LOCAL TELEVISION REPORTER.
Go ahead and roll.
START
2
START

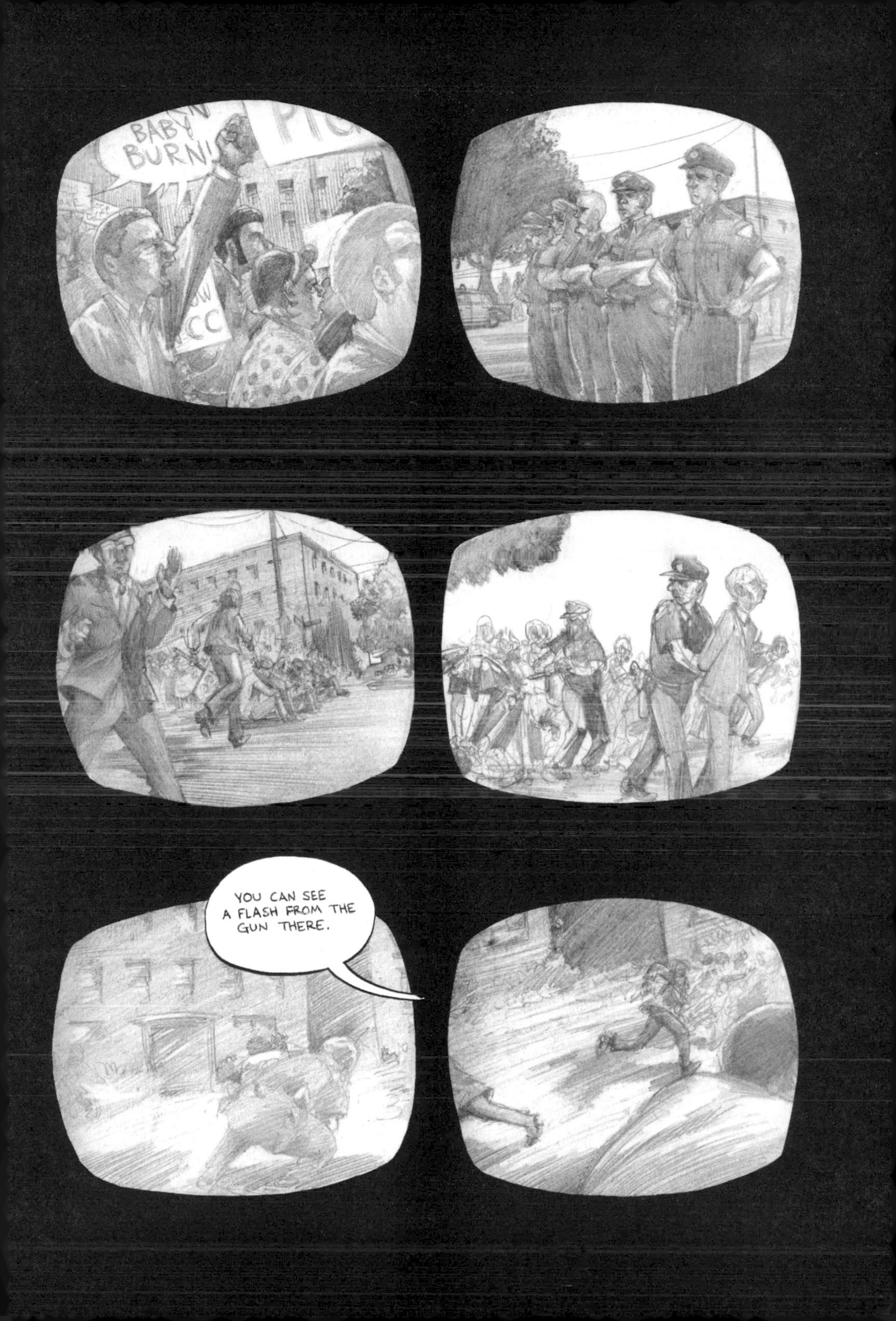
BABY BURN!
YOU CAN SEE A FLASH FROM THE GUN THERE.

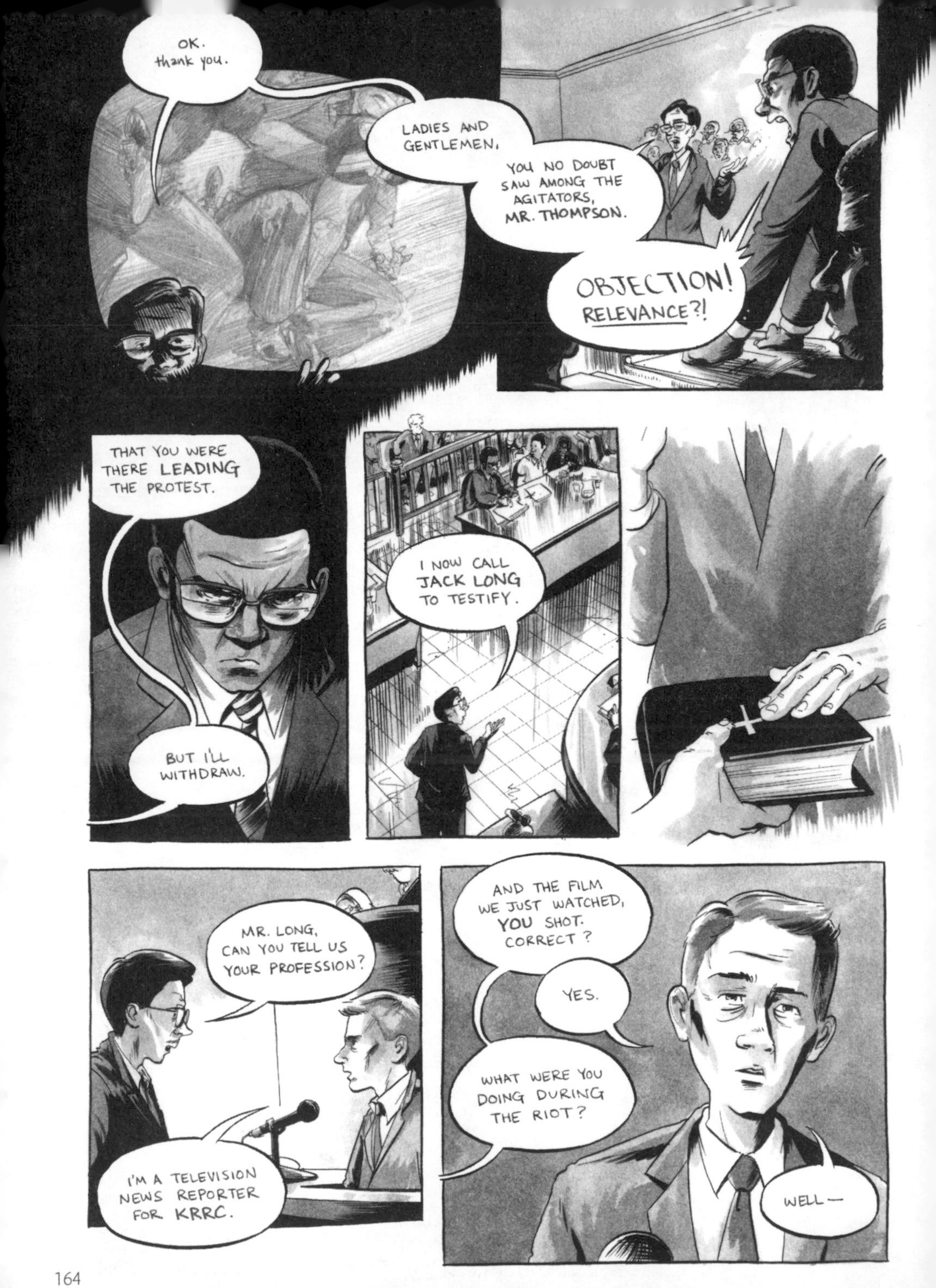
OK. thank you.
LADIES AND GENTLEMEN,
YOU NO DOUBT SAW AMONG THE AGITATORS, MR. THOMPSON.
OBJECTION! RELEVANCE?!
THAT YOU WERE THERE LEADING THE PROTEST.
BUT I'LL WITHDRAW.
I NOW CALL JACK LONG TO TESTIFY.
MR. LONG, CAN YOU TELL US YOUR PROFESSION?
I'M A TELEVISION NEWS REPORTER FOR KRRC.
AND THE FILM WE JUST WATCHED, YOU SHOT. CORRECT?
YES.
WHAT WERE YOU DOING DURING THE RIOT?
WELL—

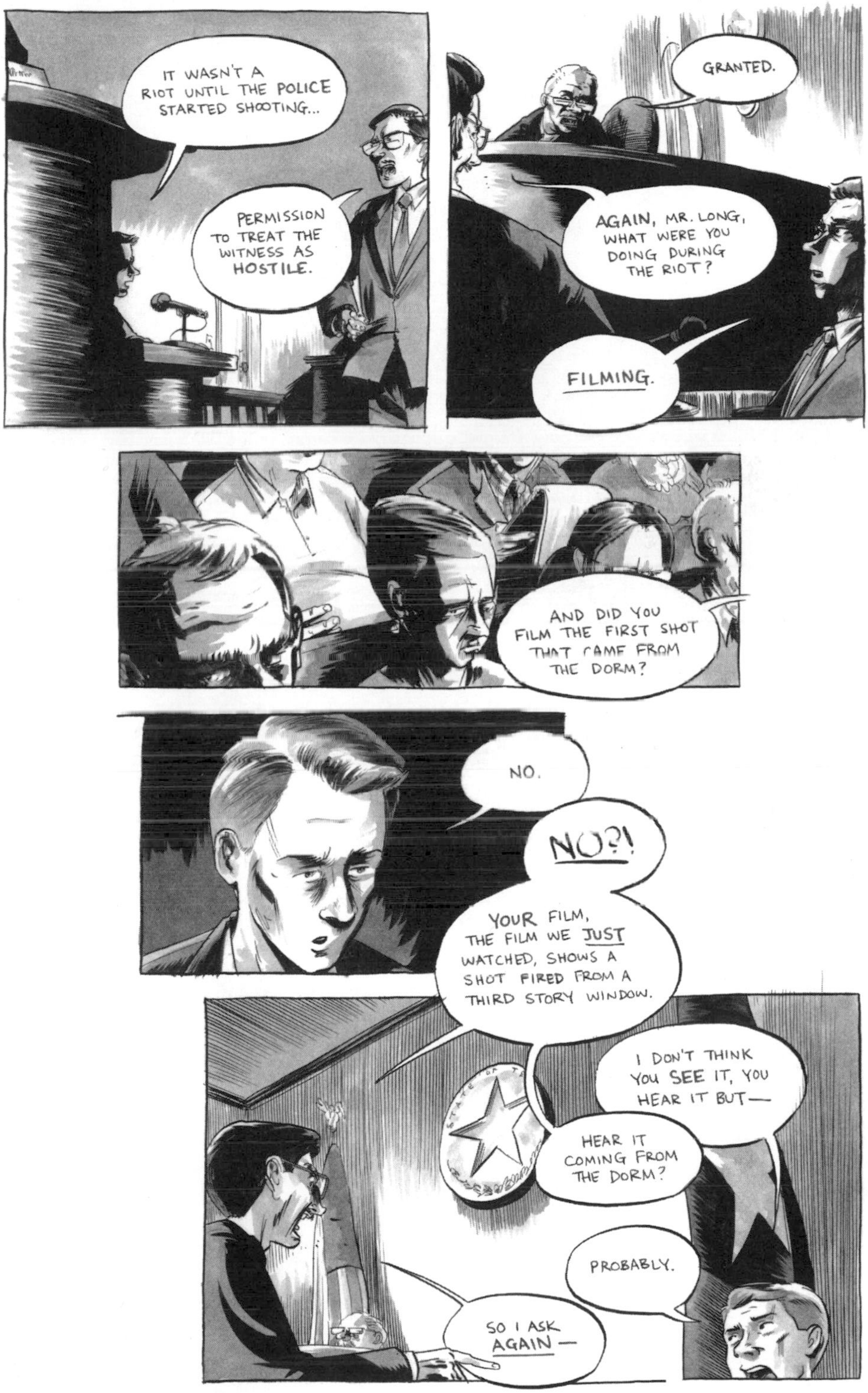
IT WASN'T A RIOT UNTIL THE POLICE STARTED SHOOTING...
PERMISSION TO TREAT THE WITNESS AS HOSTILE.
GRANTED.
AGAIN, MR. LONG, WHAT WERE YOU DOING DURING THE RIOT?
FILMING.
AND DID YOU FILM THE FIRST SHOT THAT CAME FROM THE DORM?
NO.
NO?!
YOUR FILM, THE FILM WE JUST WATCHED, SHOWS A SHOT FIRED FROM A THIRD STORY WINDOW.
I DON'T THINK YOU SEE IT, YOU HEAR IT BUT—
HEAR IT COMING FROM THE DORM?
PROBABLY.
SO I ASK AGAIN—

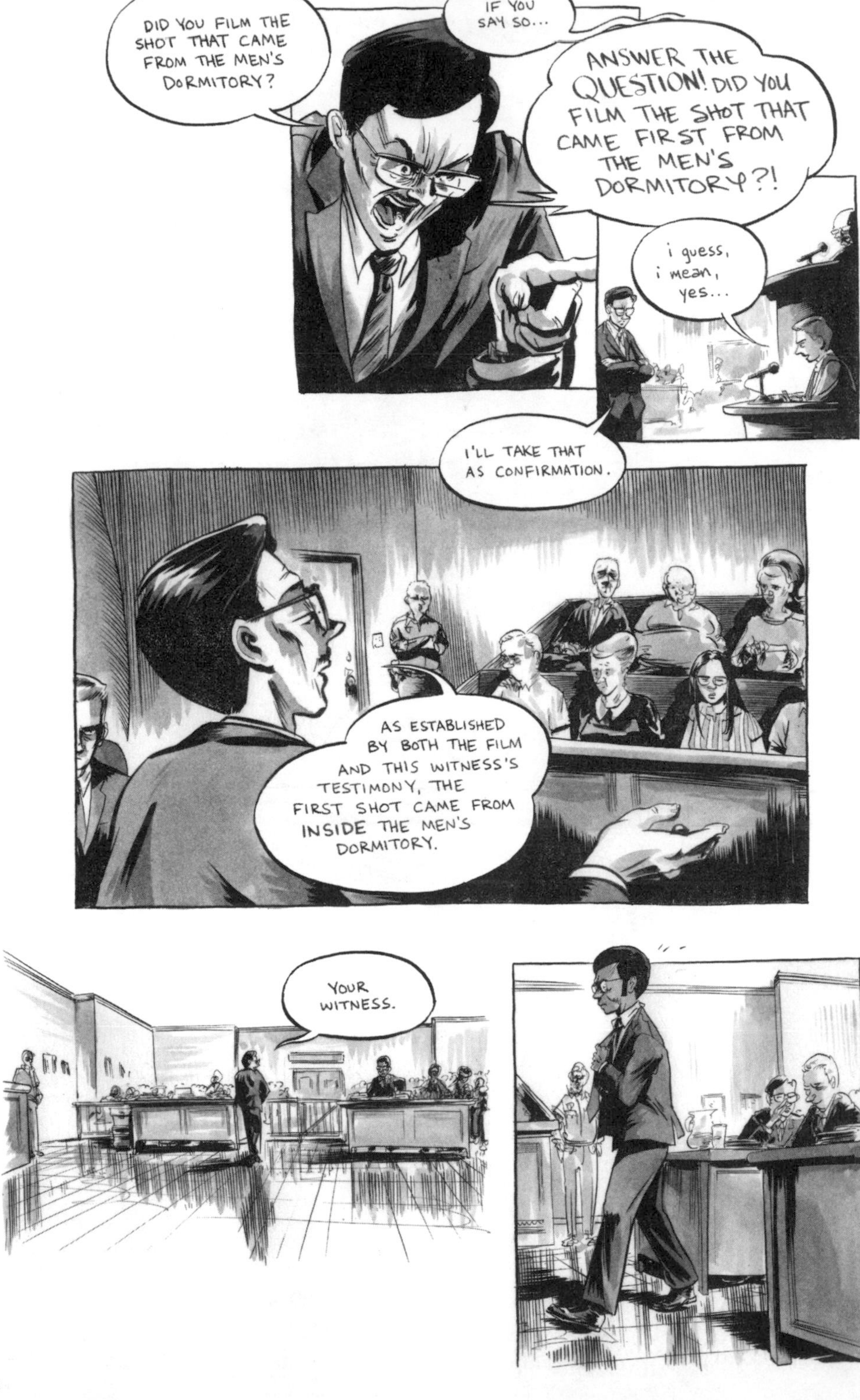
DID YOU FILM THE SHOT THAT CAME FROM THE MEN'S DORMITORY?
IF YOU SAY SO...
ANSWER THE QUESTION! DID YOU FILM THE SHOT THAT CAME FIRST FROM THE MEN'S DORMITORY?!
i guess, i mean, yes...
I'LL TAKE THAT AS CONFIRMATION.
AS ESTABLISHED BY BOTH THE FILM AND THIS WITNESS'S TESTIMONY, THE FIRST SHOT CAME FROM INSIDE THE MEN'S DORMITORY.
YOUR WITNESS.

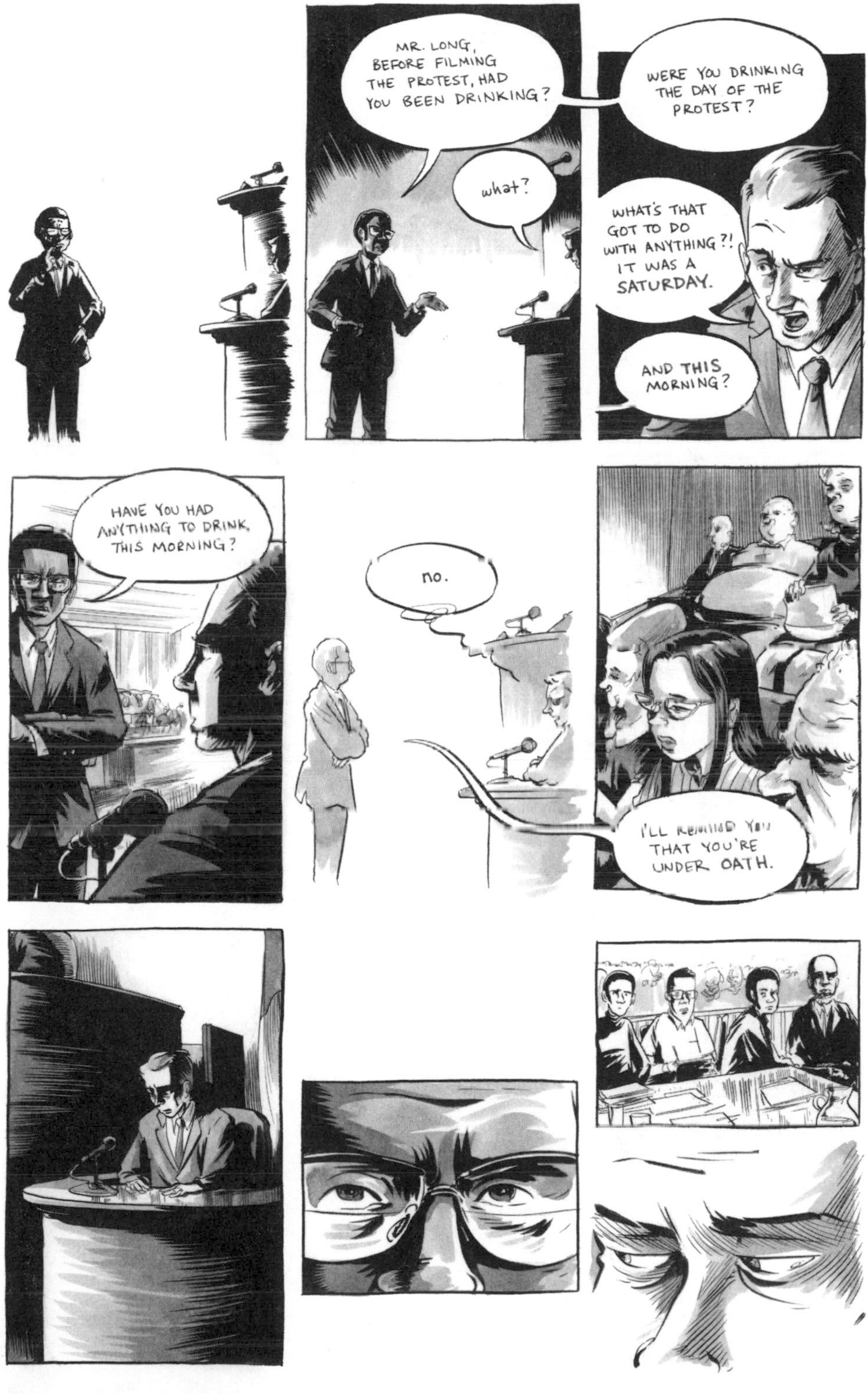
MR. LONG, BEFORE FILMING THE PROTEST, HAD YOU BEEN DRINKING?
what?
WERE YOU DRINKING THE DAY OF THE PROTEST?
WHAT'S THAT GOT TO DO WITH ANYTHING?! IT WAS A SATURDAY.
AND THIS MORNING?
HAVE YOU HAD ANYTHING TO DRINK THIS MORNING?
no.
I'LL REMIND YOU THAT YOU'RE UNDER OATH.

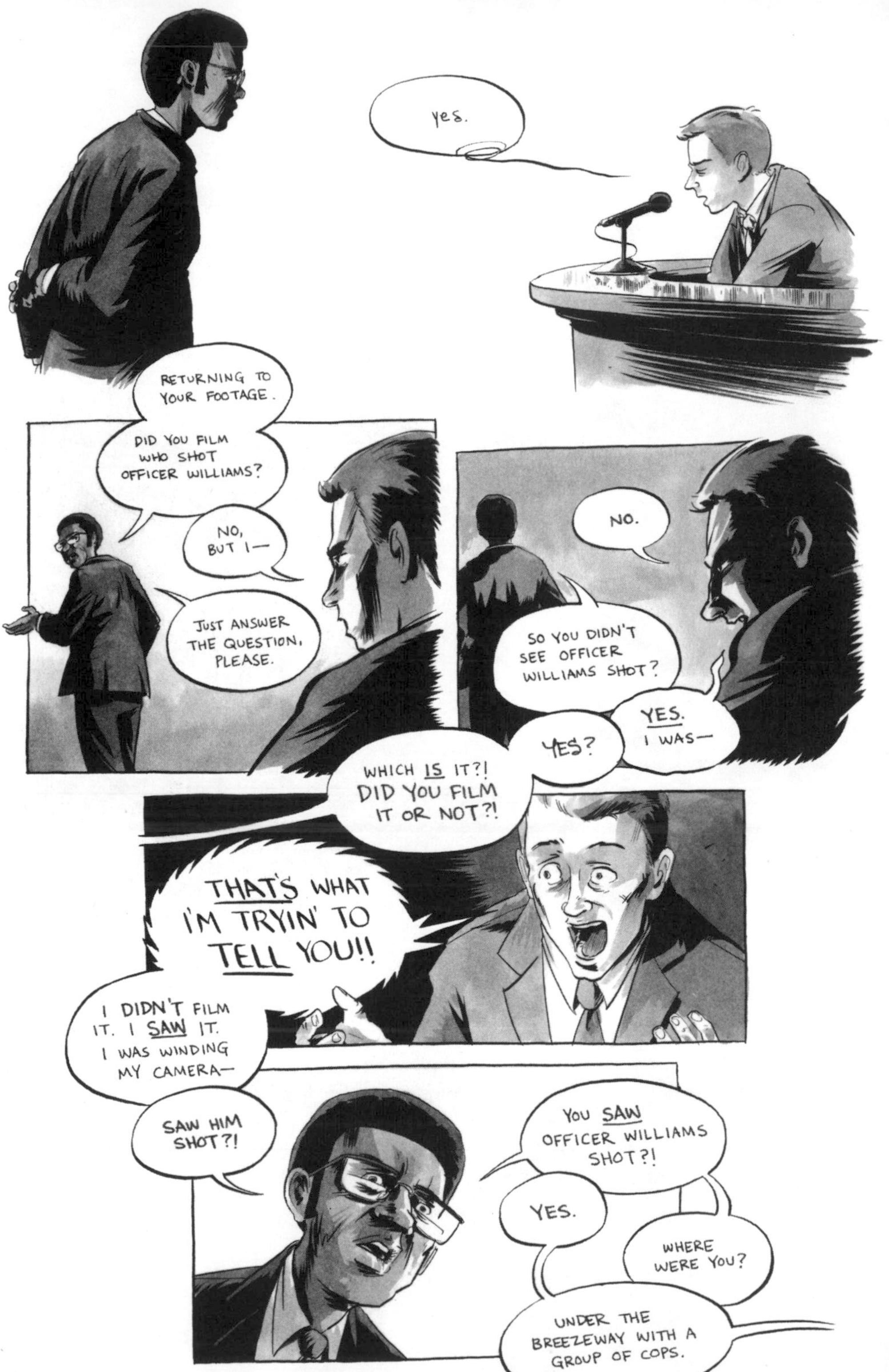
yes.
RETURNING TO YOUR FOOTAGE.
DID YOU FILM WHO SHOT OFFICER WILLIAMS?
NO, BUT I—
JUST ANSWER THE QUESTION, PLEASE.
NO.
SO YOU DIDN'T SEE OFFICER WILLIAMS SHOT?
YES. I WAS—
YES?
WHICH IS IT?! DID YOU FILM IT OR NOT?!
THAT'S WHAT I'M TRYIN' TO TELL YOU!!
I DIDN'T FILM IT. I SAW IT. I WAS WINDING MY CAMERA—
SAW HIM SHOT?!
YOU SAW OFFICER WILLIAMS SHOT?!
YES.
WHERE WERE YOU?
UNDER THE BREEZEWAY WITH A GROUP OF COPS.

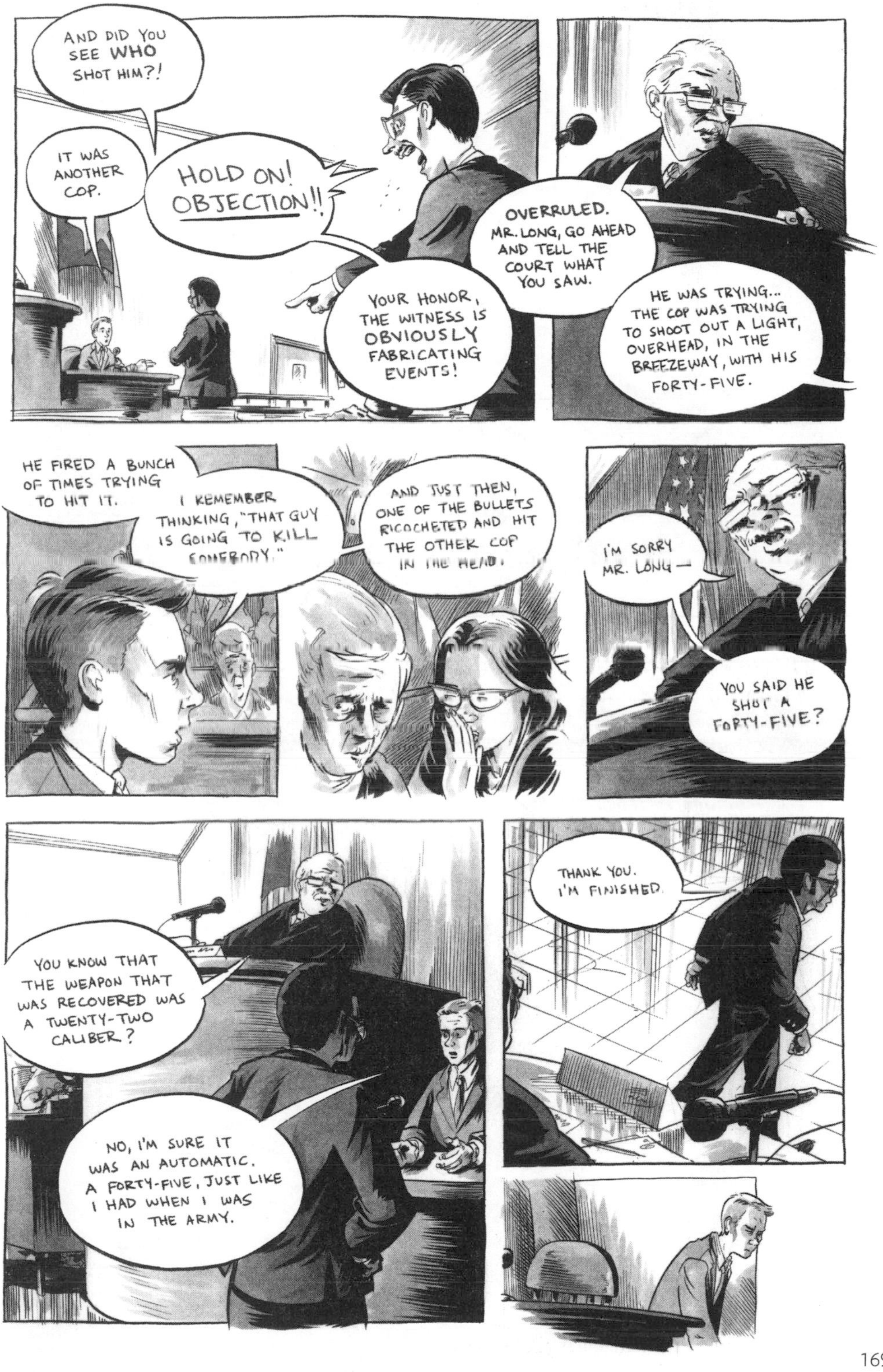
AND DID YOU SEE WHO SHOT HIM?!
IT WAS ANOTHER COP.
HOLD ON! OBJECTION!!
YOUR HONOR, THE WITNESS IS OBVIOUSLY FABRICATING EVENTS!
OVERRULED. MR. LONG, GO AHEAD AND TELL THE COURT WHAT YOU SAW.
HE WAS TRYING... THE COP WAS TRYING TO SHOOT OUT A LIGHT, OVERHEAD, IN THE BREEZEWAY, WITH HIS FORTY-FIVE.
HE FIRED A BUNCH OF TIMES TRYING TO HIT IT.
I REMEMBER THINKING, "THAT GUY IS GOING TO KILL SOMEBODY."
AND JUST THEN, ONE OF THE BULLETS RICOCHETED AND HIT THE OTHER COP IN THE HEAD.
I'M SORRY MR. LONG—
YOU SAID HE SHOT A FORTY-FIVE?
YOU KNOW THAT THE WEAPON THAT WAS RECOVERED WAS A TWENTY-TWO CALIBER?
NO, I'M SURE IT WAS AN AUTOMATIC. A FORTY-FIVE, JUST LIKE I HAD WHEN I WAS IN THE ARMY.
THANK YOU. I'M FINISHED.

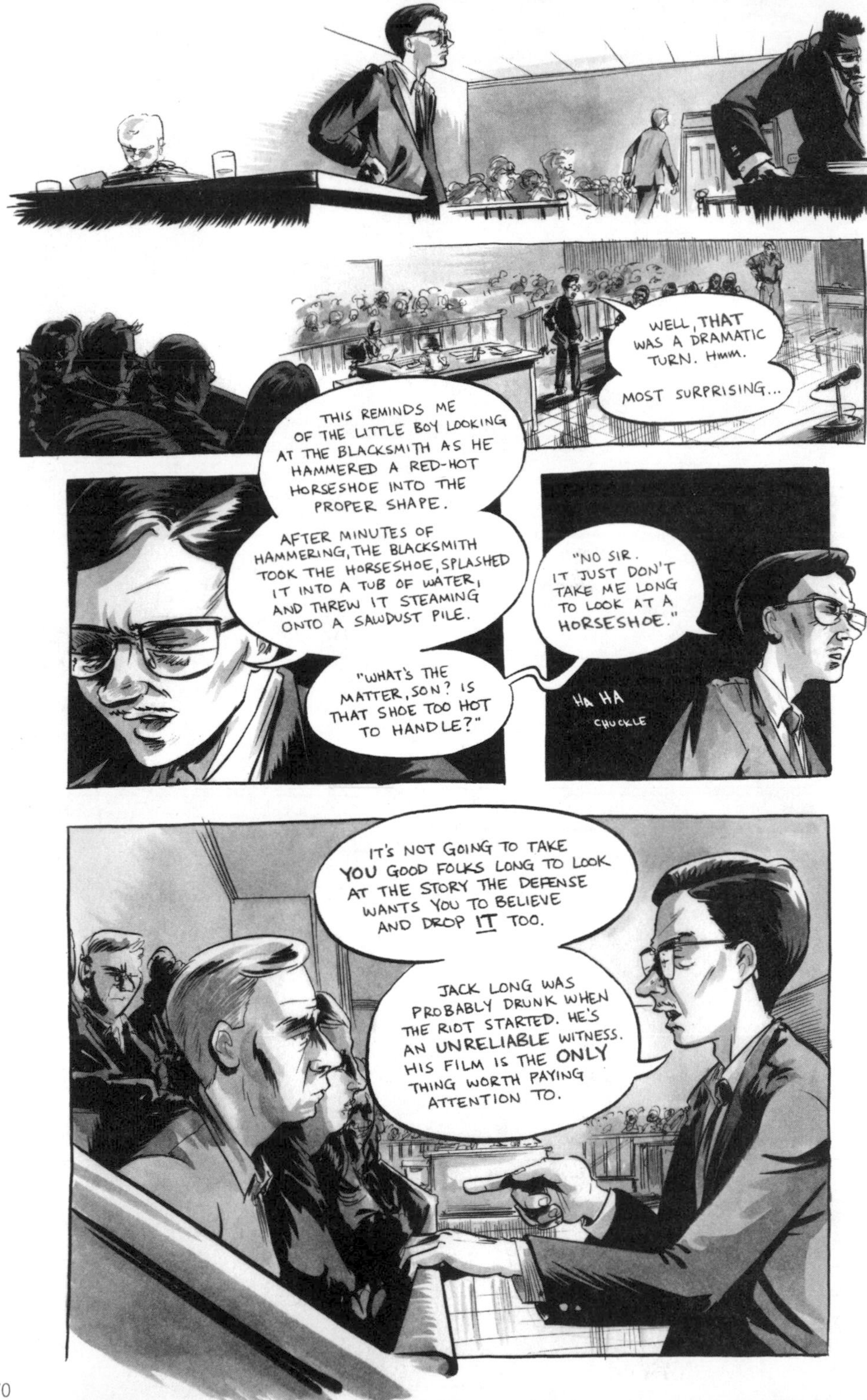
WELL, THAT WAS A DRAMATIC TURN. Hmm.
MOST SURPRISING...
THIS REMINDS ME OF THE LITTLE BOY LOOKING AT THE BLACKSMITH AS HE HAMMERED A RED-HOT HORSESHOE INTO THE PROPER SHAPE.
AFTER MINUTES OF HAMMERING, THE BLACKSMITH TOOK THE HORSESHOE, SPLASHED IT INTO A TUB OF WATER, AND THREW IT STEAMING ONTO A SAWDUST PILE.
"WHAT'S THE MATTER, SON? IS THAT SHOE TOO HOT TO HANDLE?"
"NO SIR. IT JUST DON'T TAKE ME LONG TO LOOK AT A HORSESHOE."
HA HA
CHUCKLE
IT'S NOT GOING TO TAKE YOU GOOD FOLKS LONG TO LOOK AT THE STORY THE DEFENSE WANTS YOU TO BELIEVE AND DROP IT TOO.
JACK LONG WAS PROBABLY DRUNK WHEN THE RIOT STARTED. HE'S AN UNRELIABLE WITNESS. HIS FILM IS THE ONLY THING WORTH PAYING ATTENTION TO.

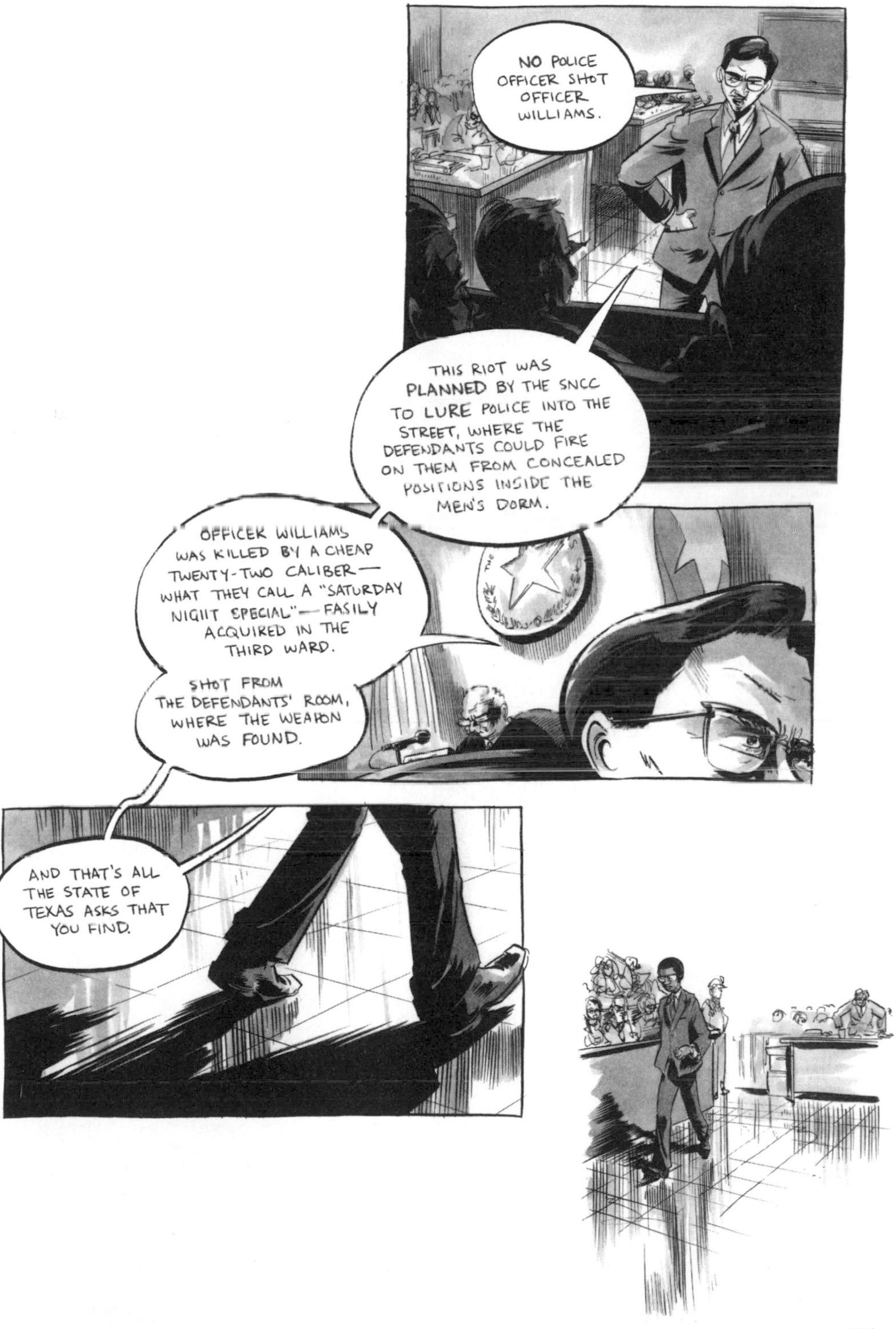
NO POLICE OFFICER SHOT OFFICER WILLIAMS.
THIS RIOT WAS PLANNED BY THE SNCC TO LURE POLICE INTO THE STREET, WHERE THE DEFENDANTS COULD FIRE ON THEM FROM CONCEALED POSITIONS INSIDE THE MEN'S DORM.
OFFICER WILLIAMS WAS KILLED BY A CHEAP TWENTY-TWO CALIBER— WHAT THEY CALL A "SATURDAY NIGHT SPECIAL"— EASILY ACQUIRED IN THE THIRD WARD.
SHOT FROM THE DEFENDANTS' ROOM, WHERE THE WEAPON WAS FOUND.
AND THAT'S ALL THE STATE OF TEXAS ASKS THAT YOU FIND.

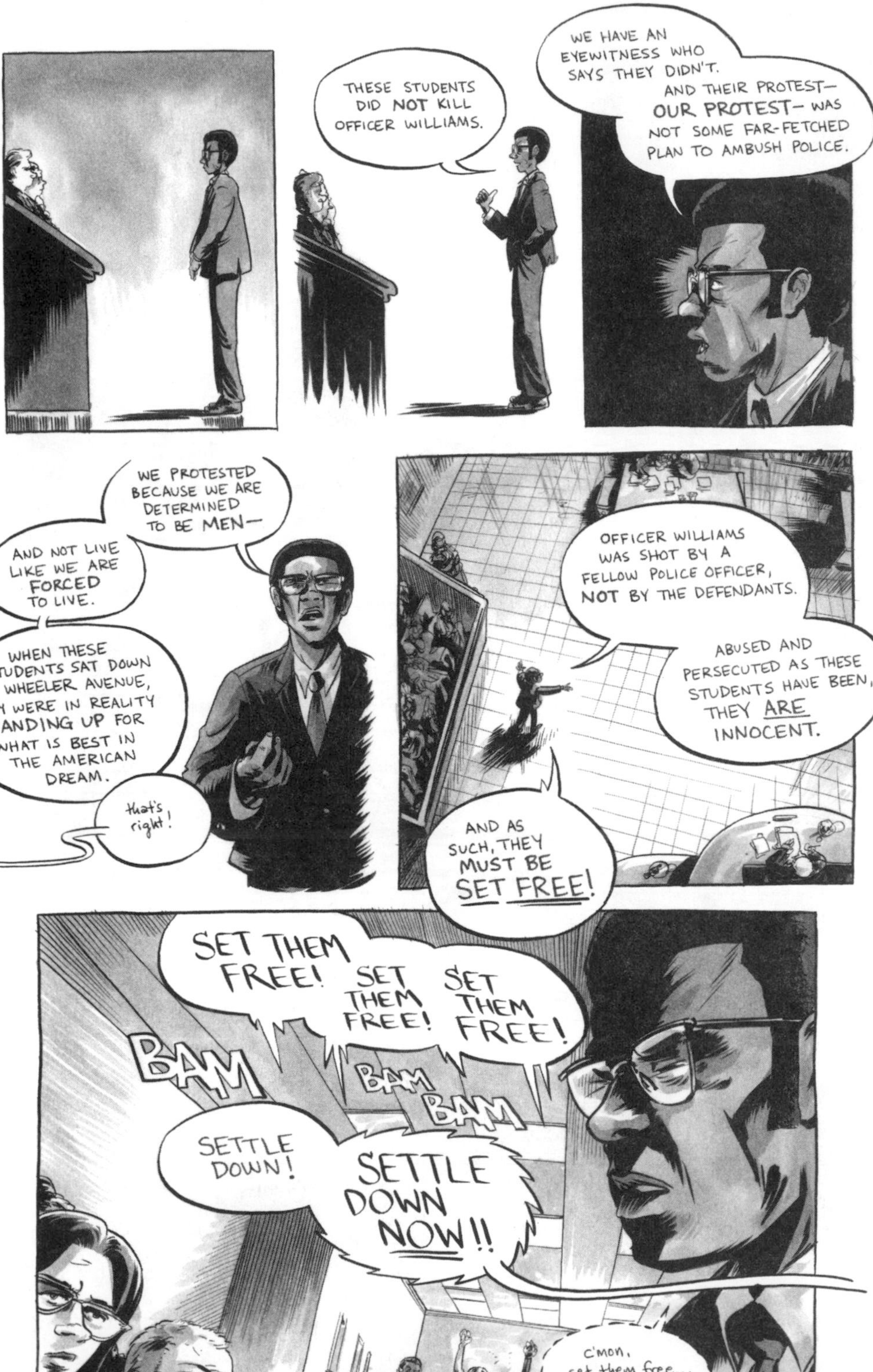
THESE STUDENTS DID **NOT** KILL OFFICER WILLIAMS.
WE HAVE AN EYEWITNESS WHO SAYS THEY DIDN'T.
AND THEIR PROTEST— **OUR PROTEST**— WAS NOT SOME FAR-FETCHED PLAN TO AMBUSH POLICE.
WE PROTESTED BECAUSE WE ARE DETERMINED TO BE **MEN**—
AND NOT LIVE LIKE WE ARE **FORCED** TO LIVE.
WHEN THESE STUDENTS SAT DOWN ON WHEELER AVENUE, THEY WERE IN REALITY **STANDING UP** FOR WHAT IS BEST IN THE AMERICAN DREAM.
that's right!
OFFICER WILLIAMS WAS SHOT BY A FELLOW POLICE OFFICER, **NOT** BY THE DEFENDANTS.
ABUSED AND PERSECUTED AS THESE STUDENTS HAVE BEEN, THEY ARE INNOCENT.
AND AS SUCH, THEY **MUST BE SET FREE!**
SET THEM FREE!
SET THEM FREE!
SET THEM FREE!
BAM
BAM
BAM
SETTLE DOWN!
SETTLE DOWN NOW!!
c'mon, set them free...

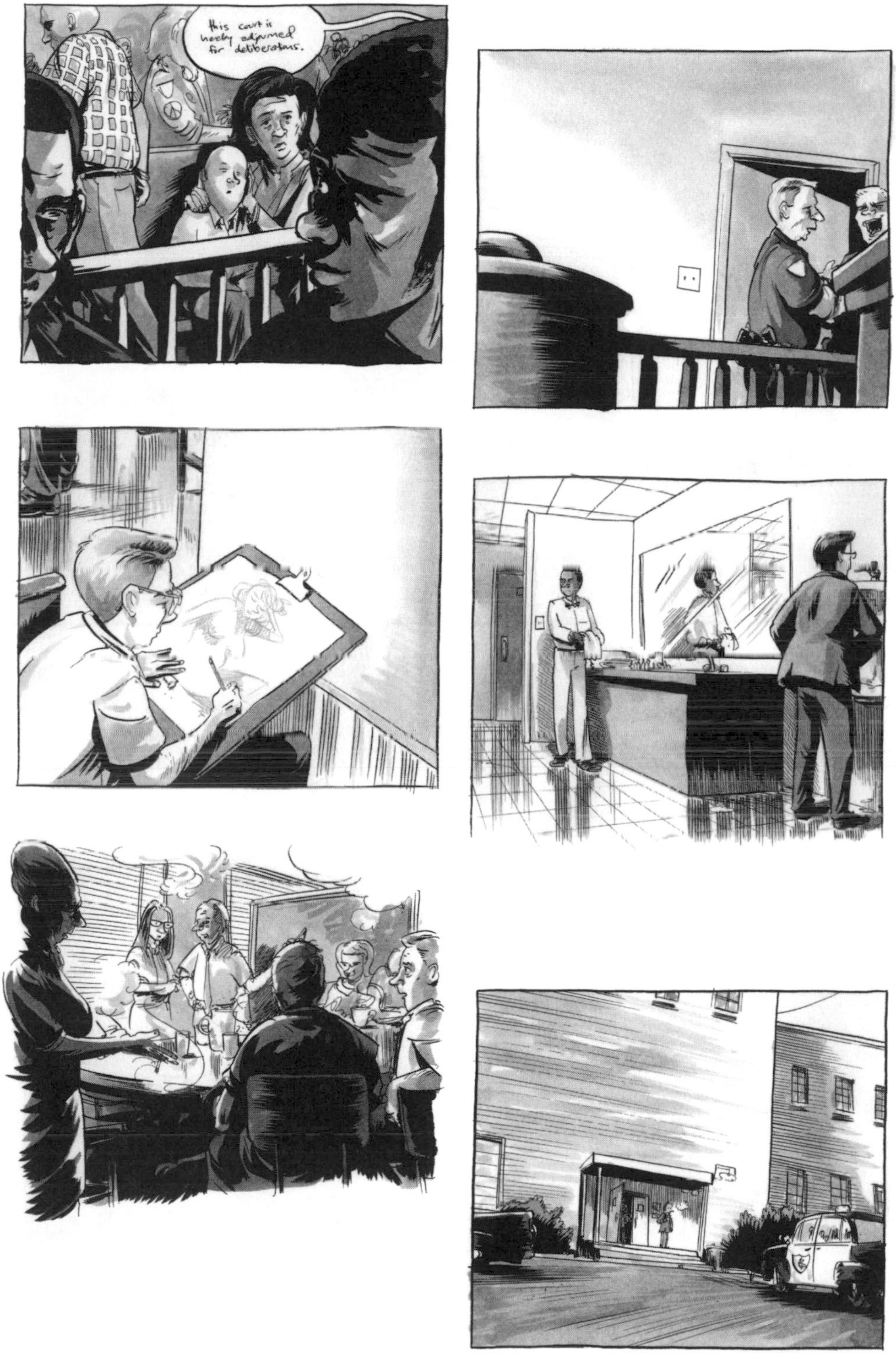
This court is hereby adjourned for deliberations.

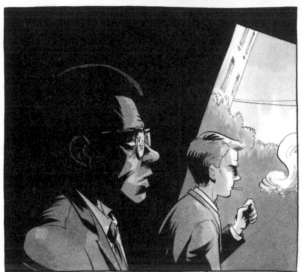

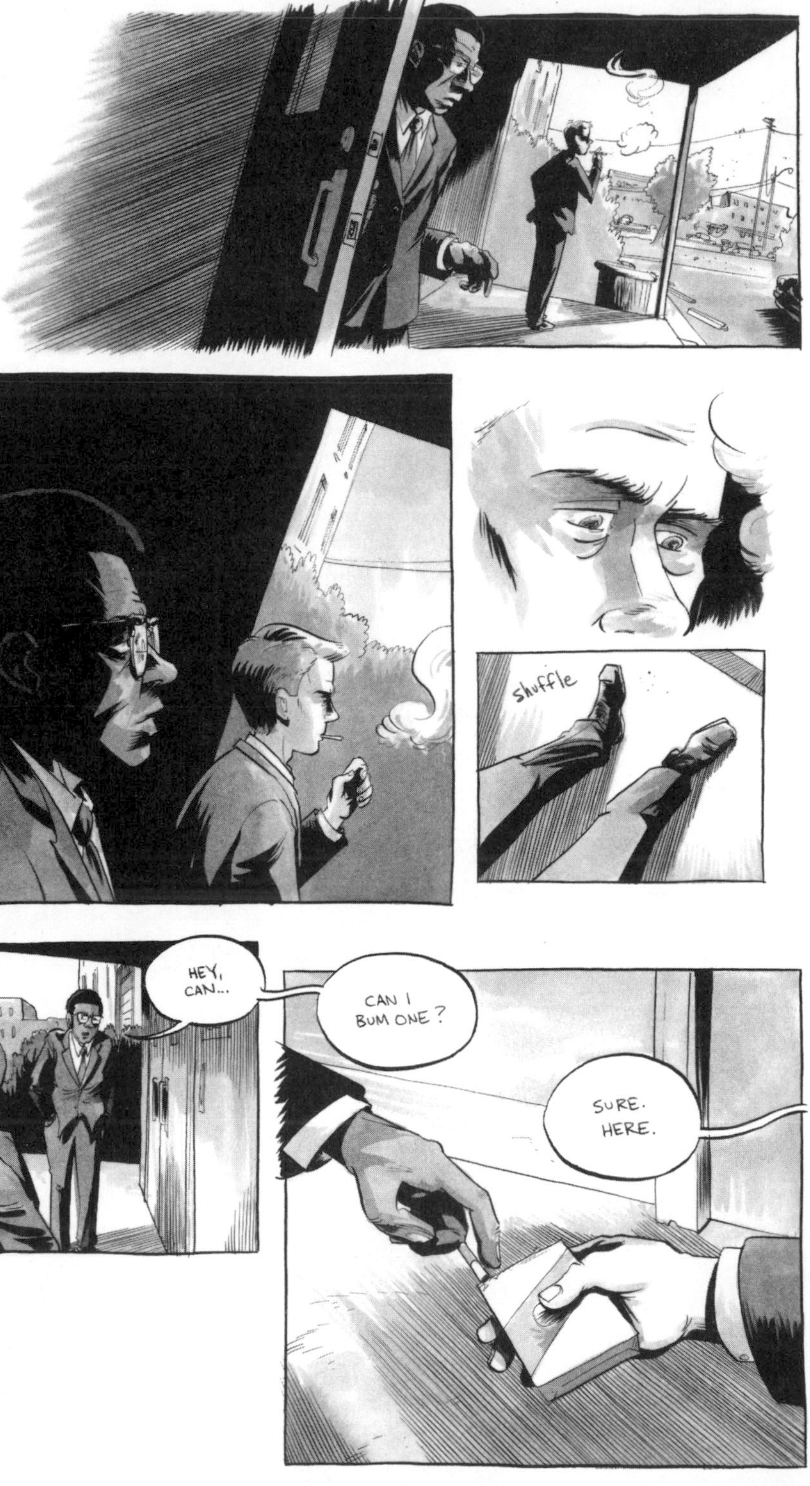
shuffle
HEY, CAN...
CAN I BUM ONE?
SURE. HERE.

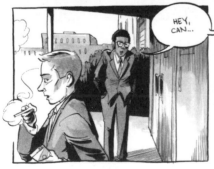

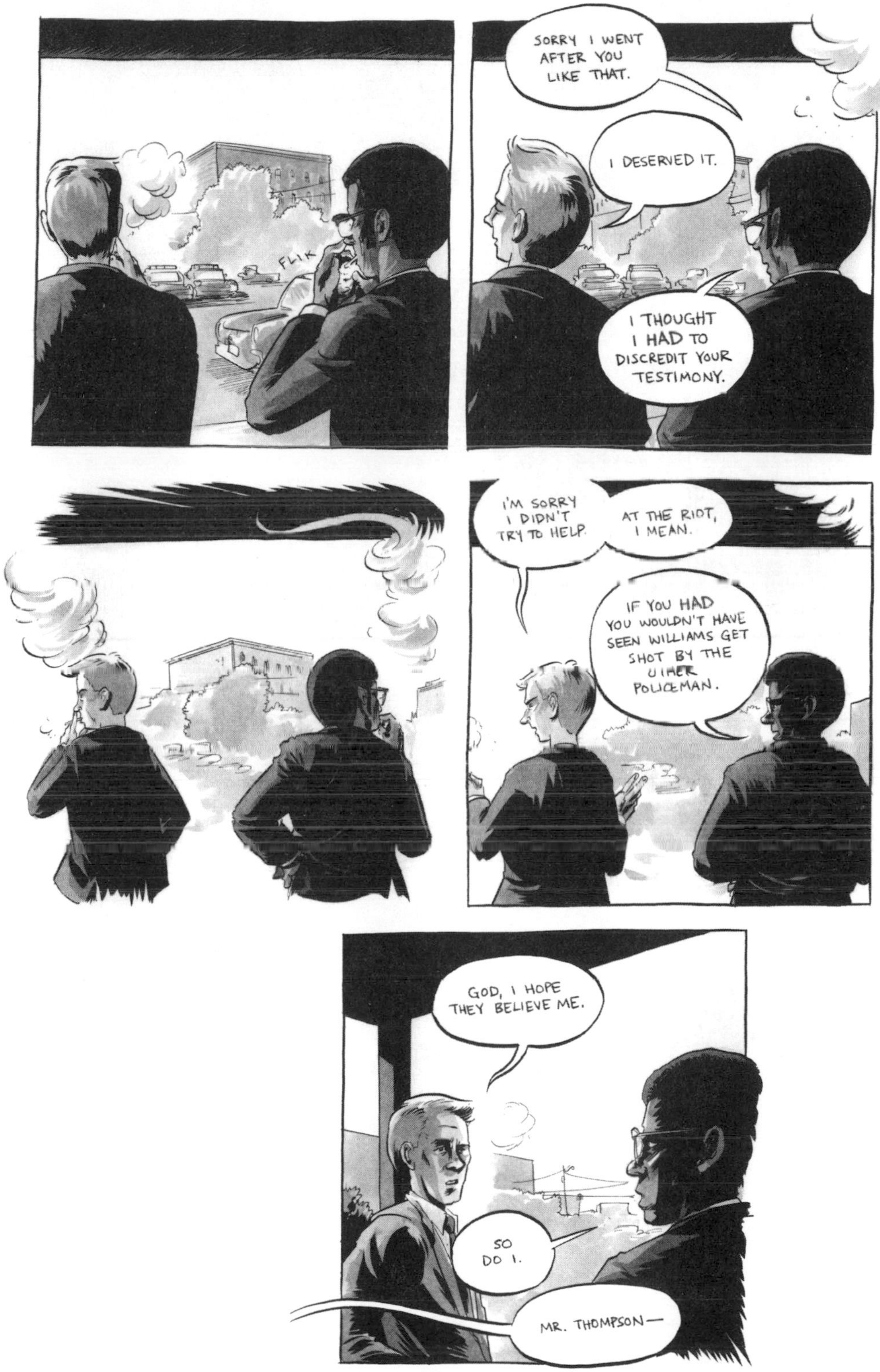
FLIK
SORRY I WENT AFTER YOU LIKE THAT.
I DESERVED IT.
I THOUGHT I HAD TO DISCREDIT YOUR TESTIMONY.
I'M SORRY I DIDN'T TRY TO HELP.
AT THE RIOT, I MEAN.
IF YOU HAD YOU WOULDN'T HAVE SEEN WILLIAMS GET SHOT BY THE OTHER POLICEMAN.
GOD, I HOPE THEY BELIEVE ME.
SO DO I.
MR. THOMPSON—

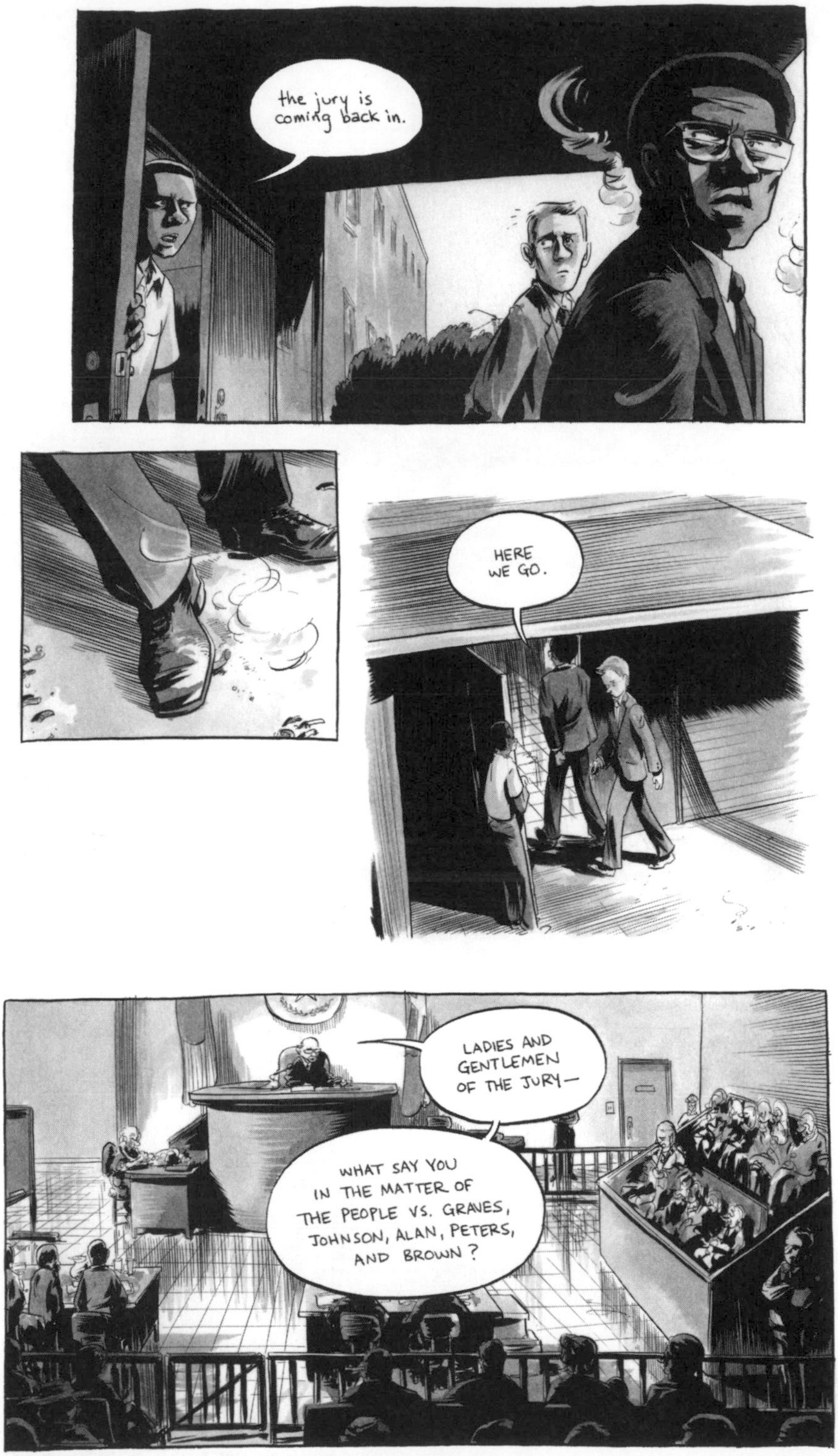
the jury is coming back in.
HERE WE GO.
LADIES AND GENTLEMEN OF THE JURY—
WHAT SAY YOU IN THE MATTER OF THE PEOPLE VS. GRAVES, JOHNSON, ALAN, PETERS, AND BROWN?

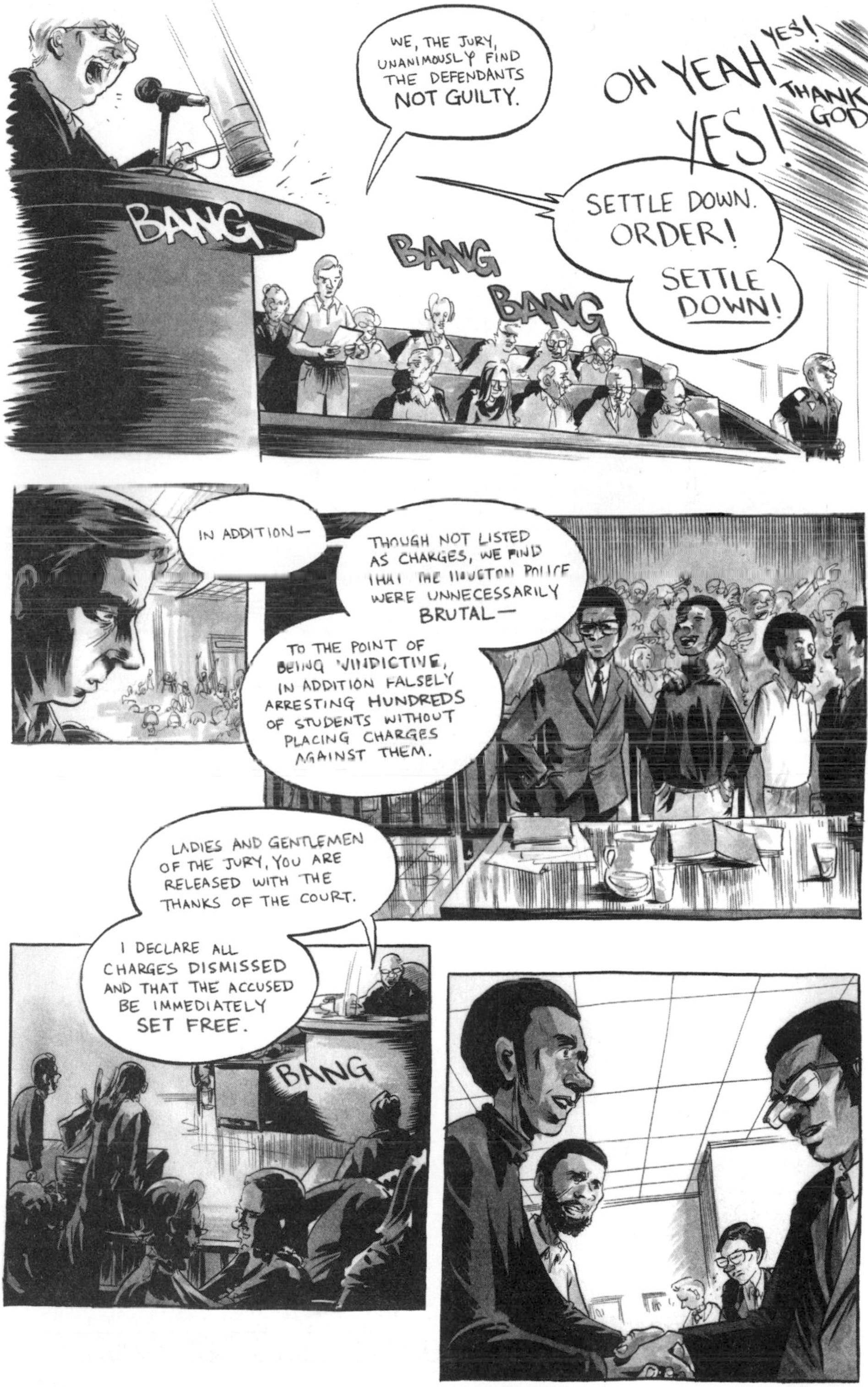
BANG
WE, THE JURY, UNANIMOUSLY FIND THE DEFENDANTS NOT GUILTY.
OH YEAH
YES!
YES!
THANK GOD
SETTLE DOWN. ORDER!
SETTLE DOWN!
BANG
BANG
IN ADDITION—
THOUGH NOT LISTED AS CHARGES, WE FIND THAT THE HOUSTON POLICE WERE UNNECESSARILY BRUTAL—
TO THE POINT OF BEING VINDICTIVE, IN ADDITION FALSELY ARRESTING HUNDREDS OF STUDENTS WITHOUT PLACING CHARGES AGAINST THEM.
LADIES AND GENTLEMEN OF THE JURY, YOU ARE RELEASED WITH THE THANKS OF THE COURT.
I DECLARE ALL CHARGES DISMISSED AND THAT THE ACCUSED BE IMMEDIATELY SET FREE.
BANG

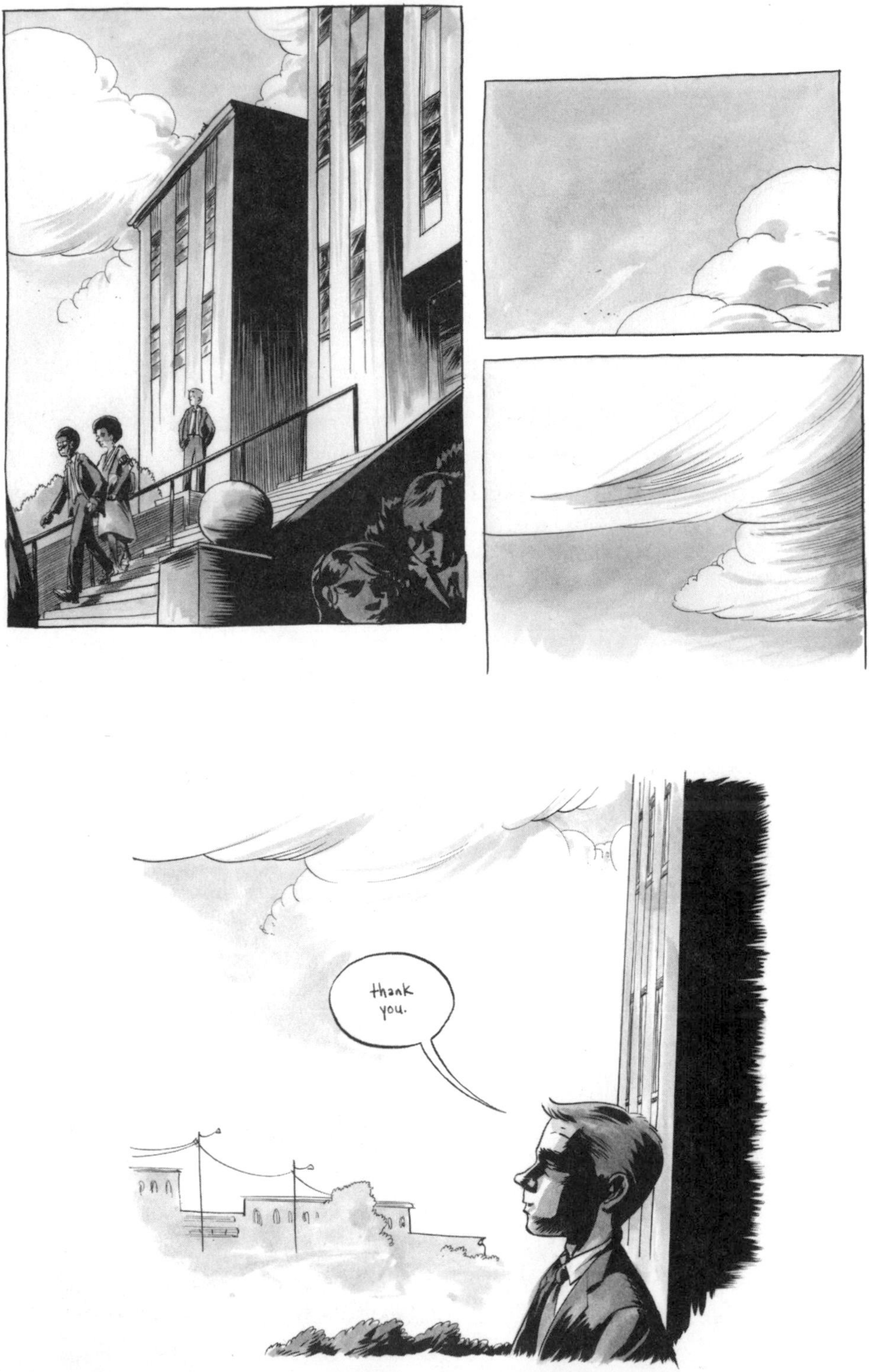
thank you.

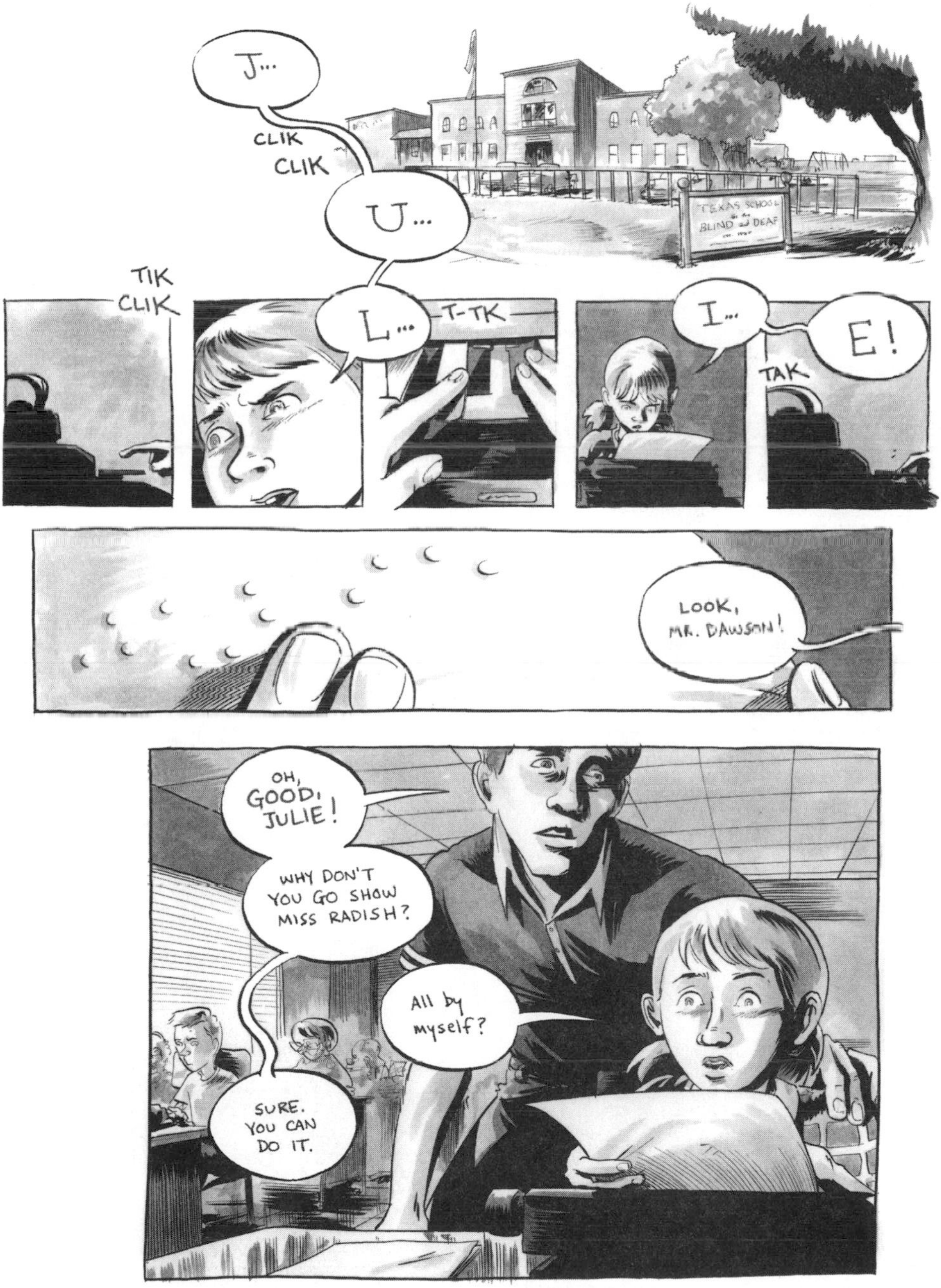
J...
CLIK
CLIK
U...
TIK
CLIK
L...
T-TK
I...
TAK
E!
LOOK, MR. DAWSON!
OH, GOOD, JULIE!
WHY DON'T YOU GO SHOW MISS RADISH?
All by myself?
SURE. YOU CAN DO IT.

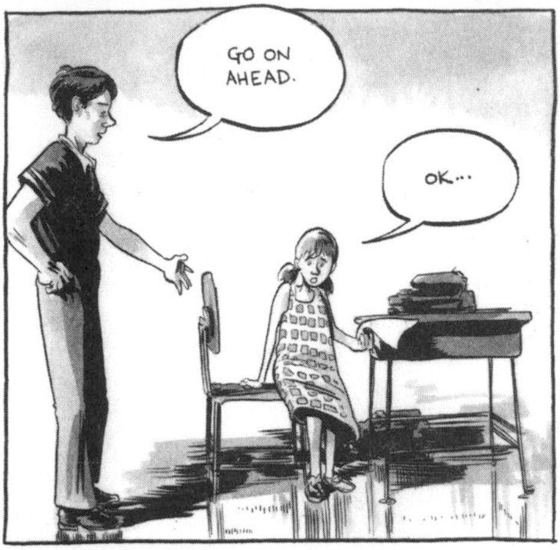
GO ON AHEAD.
OK...

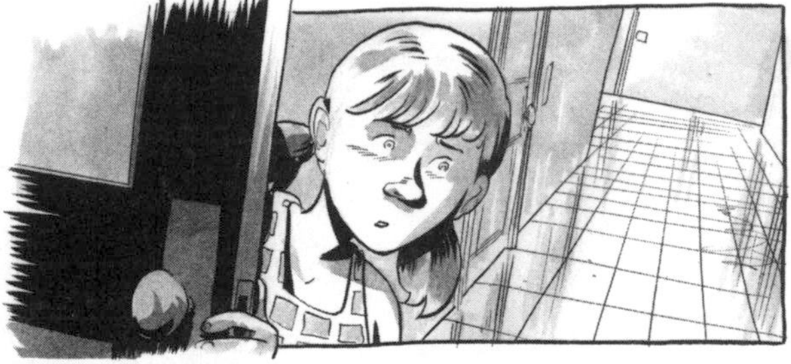

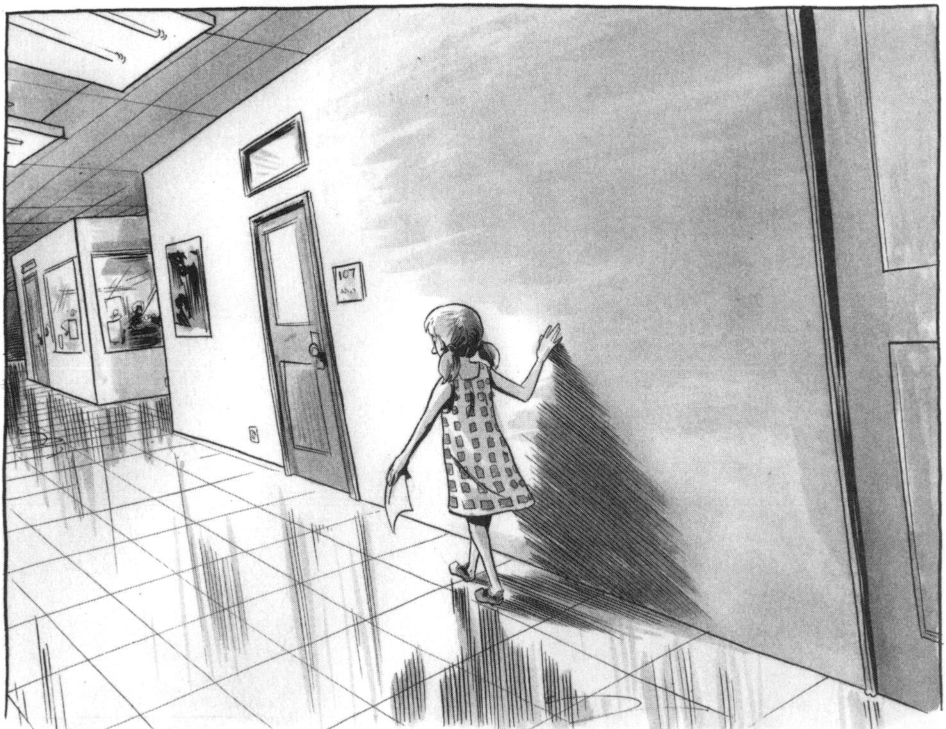
107

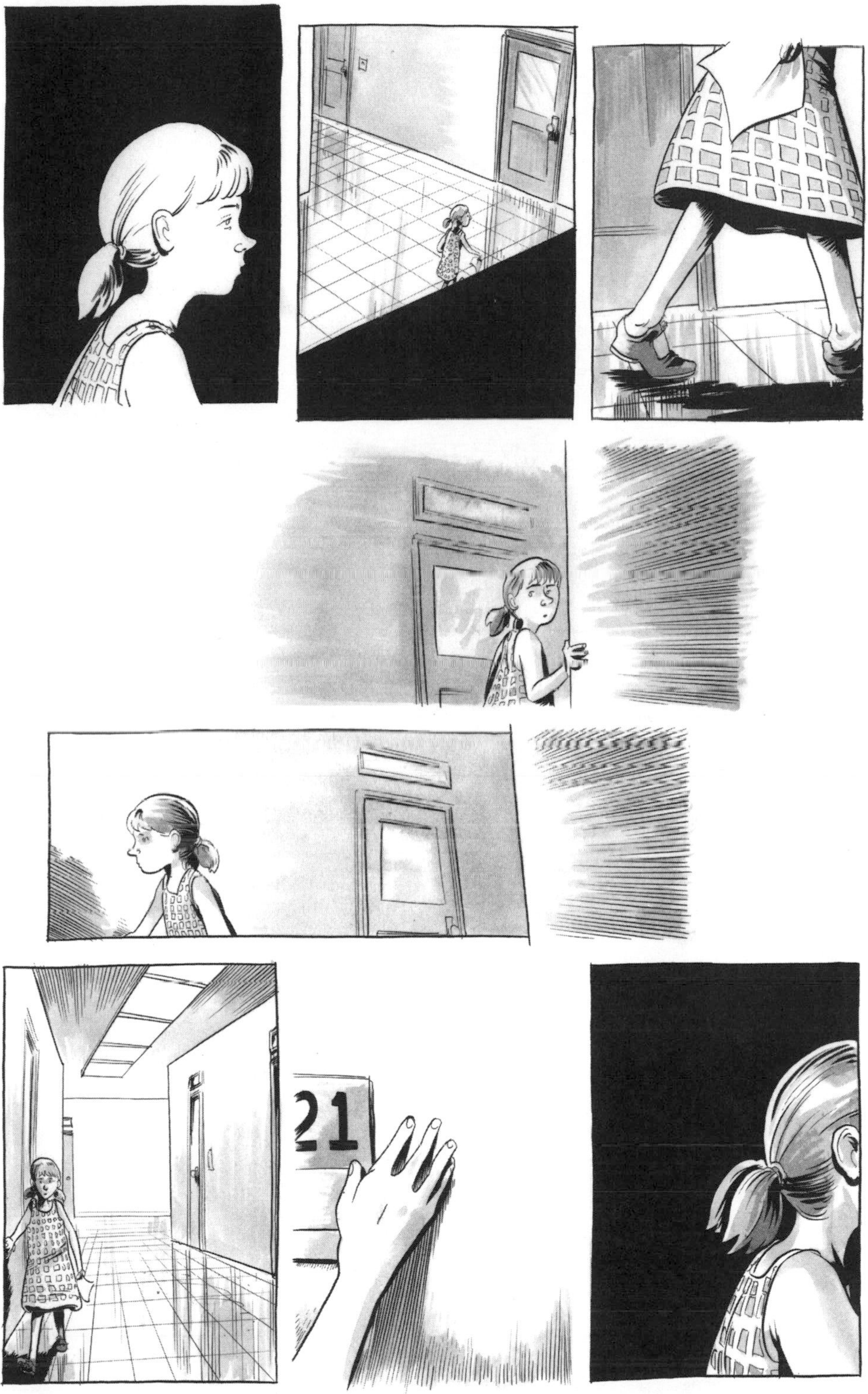
21

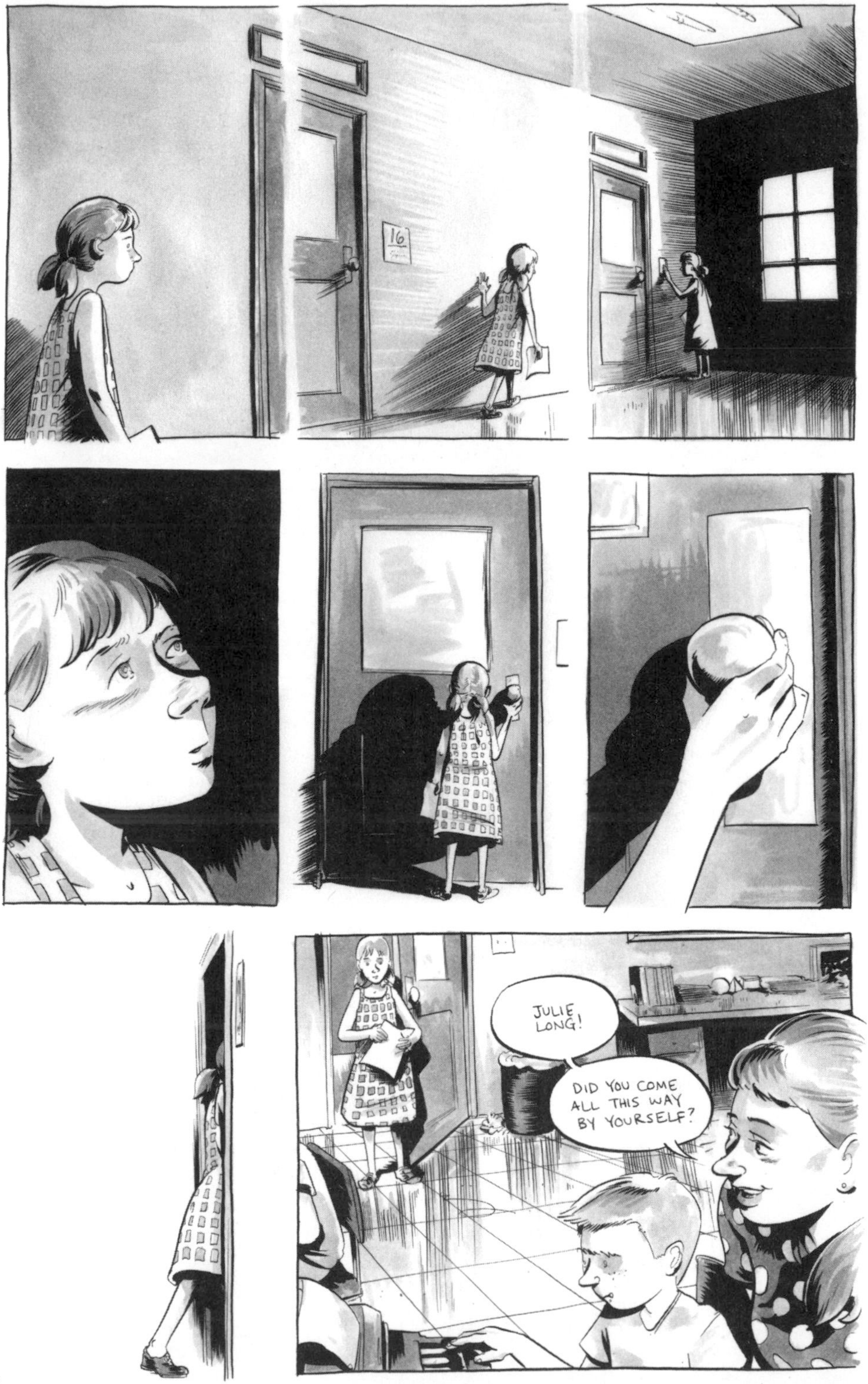
JULIE LONG!
DID YOU COME ALL THIS WAY BY YOURSELF?

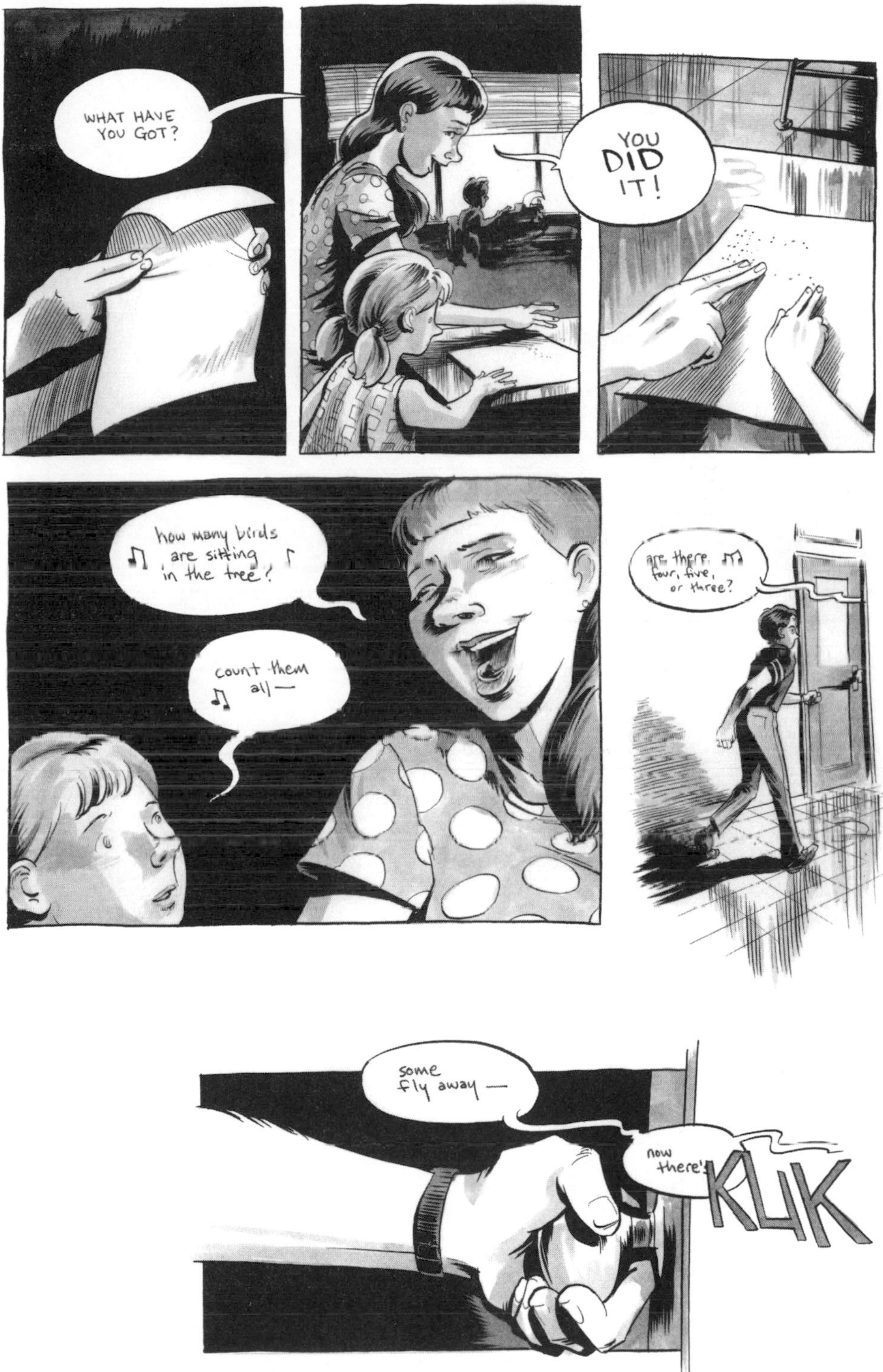
WHAT HAVE YOU GOT?
YOU DID IT!
how many birds are sitting in the tree?
count them all—
are there, four, five, or three?
some fly away—
now there's
KLIK

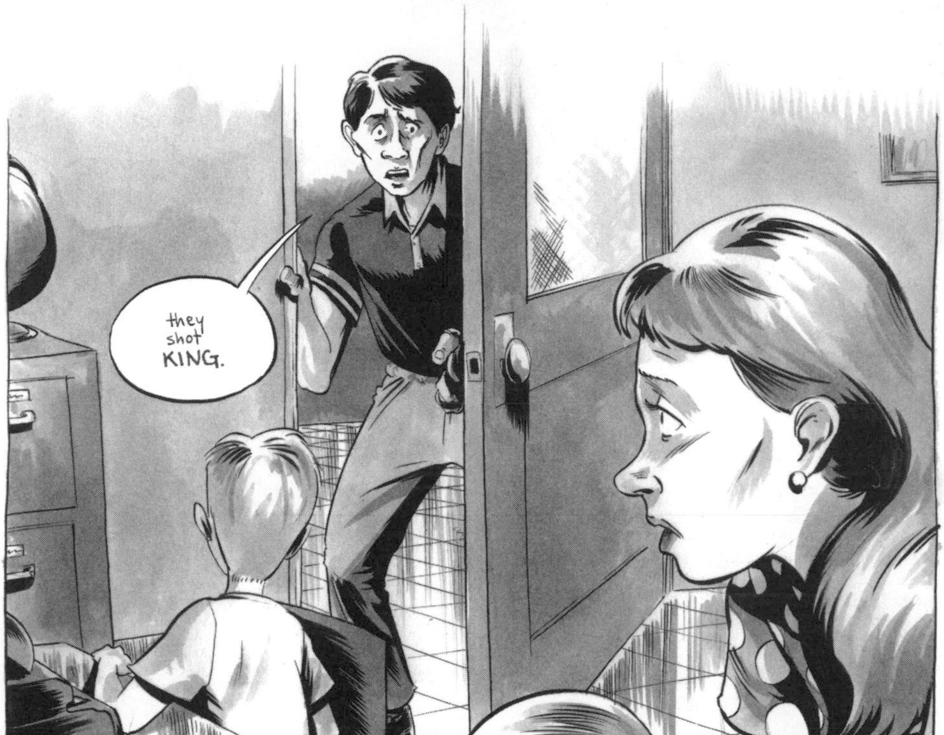
they shot KING.

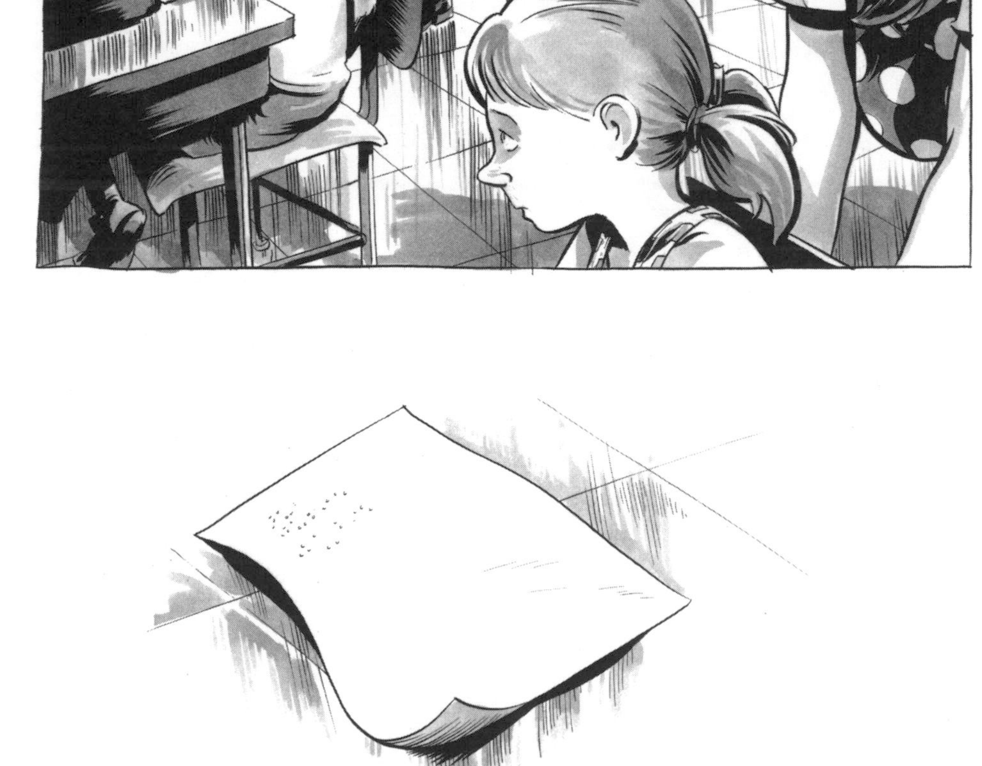

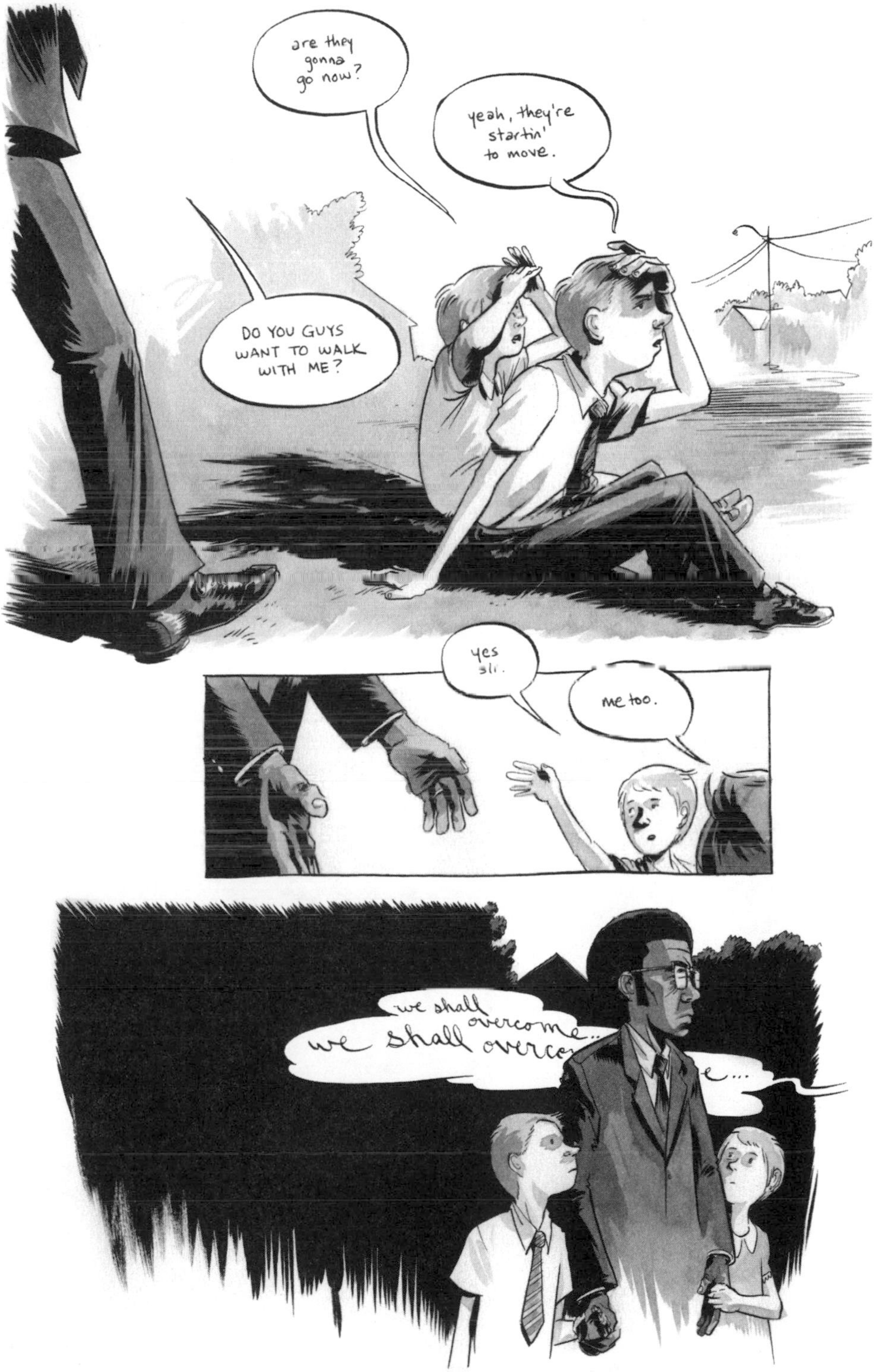
are they gonna go now?
yeah, they're startin' to move.
DO YOU GUYS WANT TO WALK WITH ME?
yes sir.
me too.
we shall overcome...
we shall overco...e...

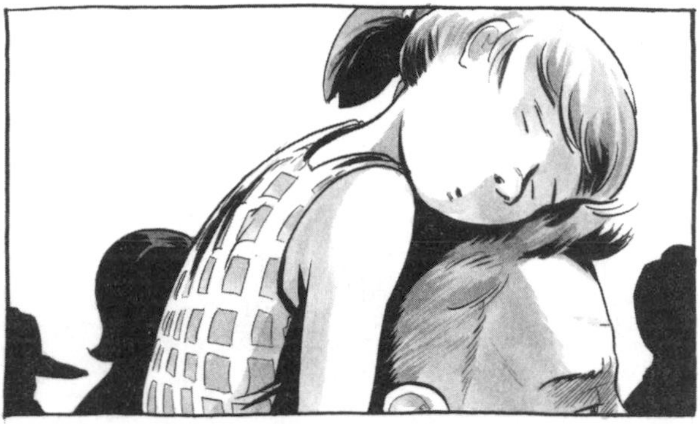

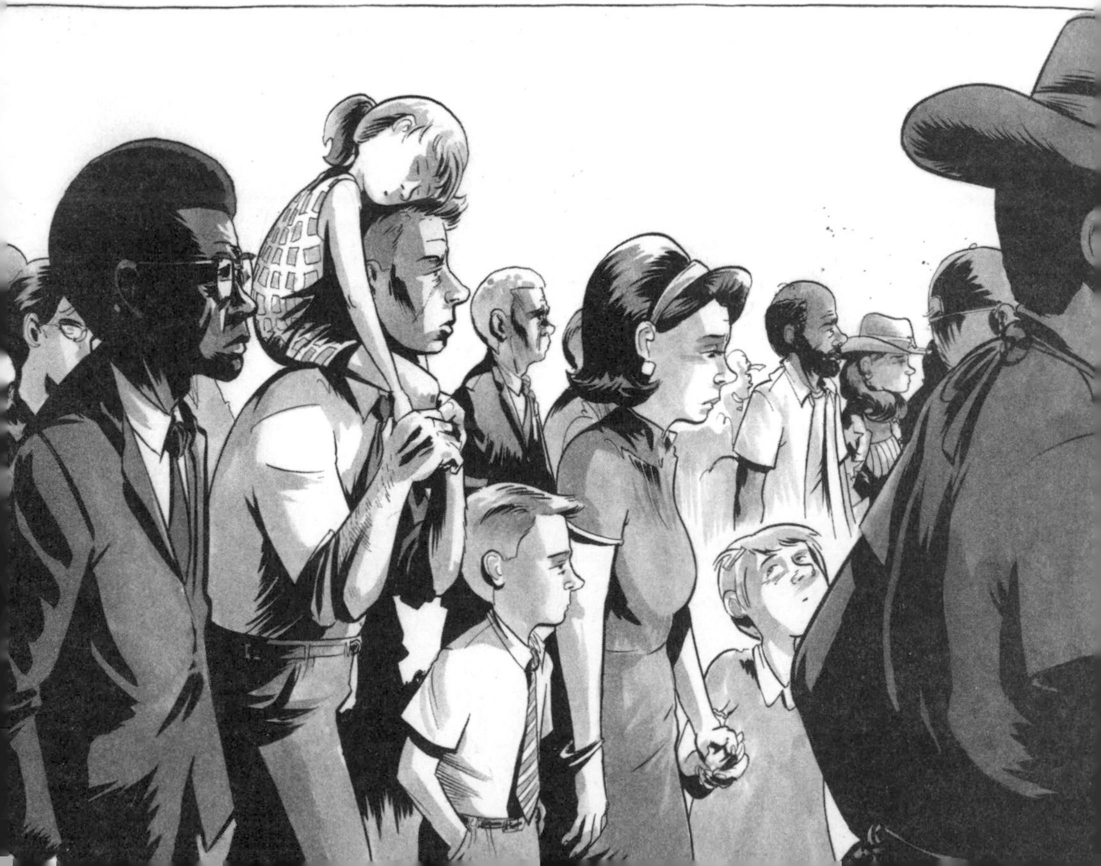

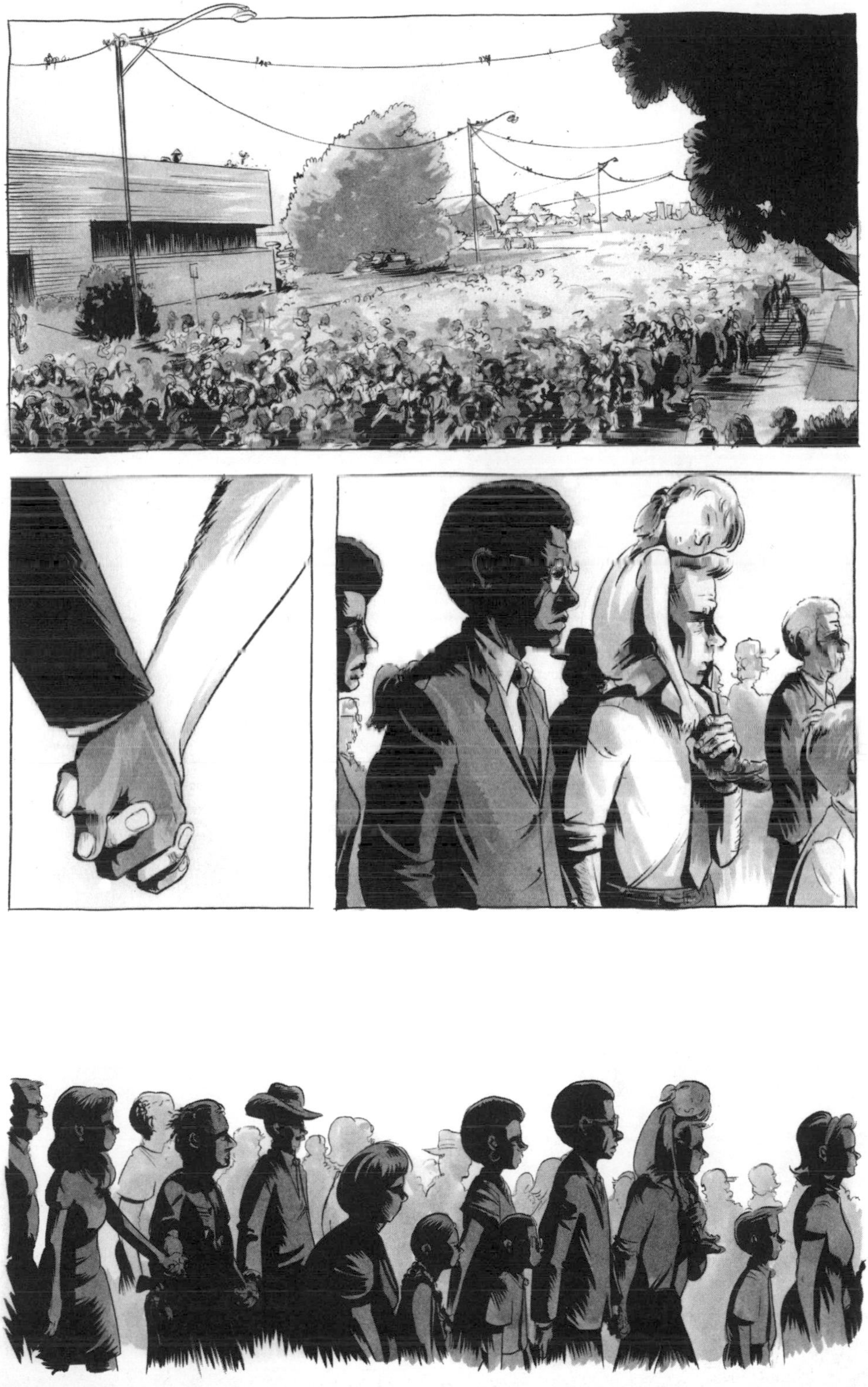

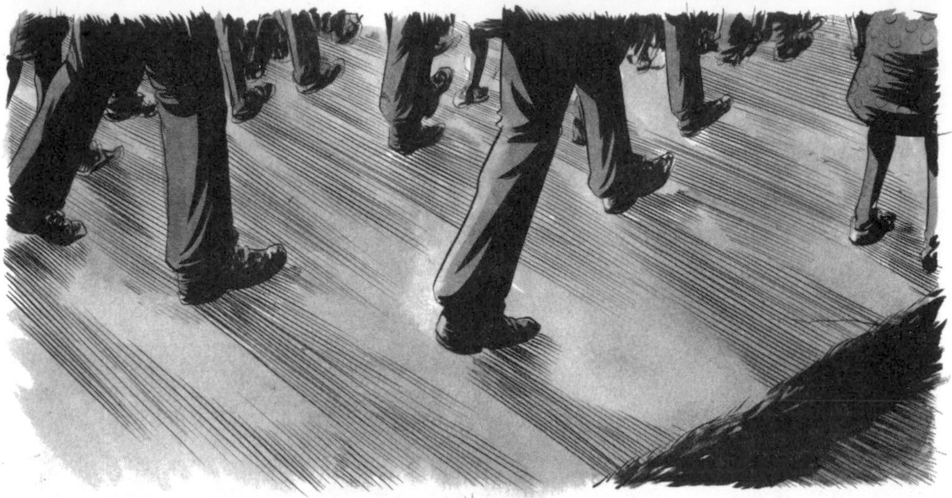

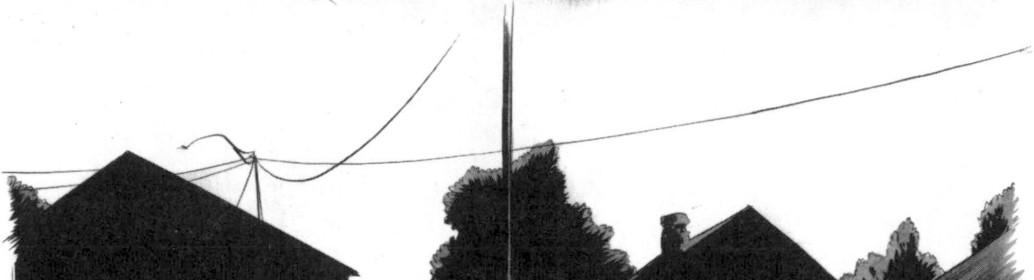

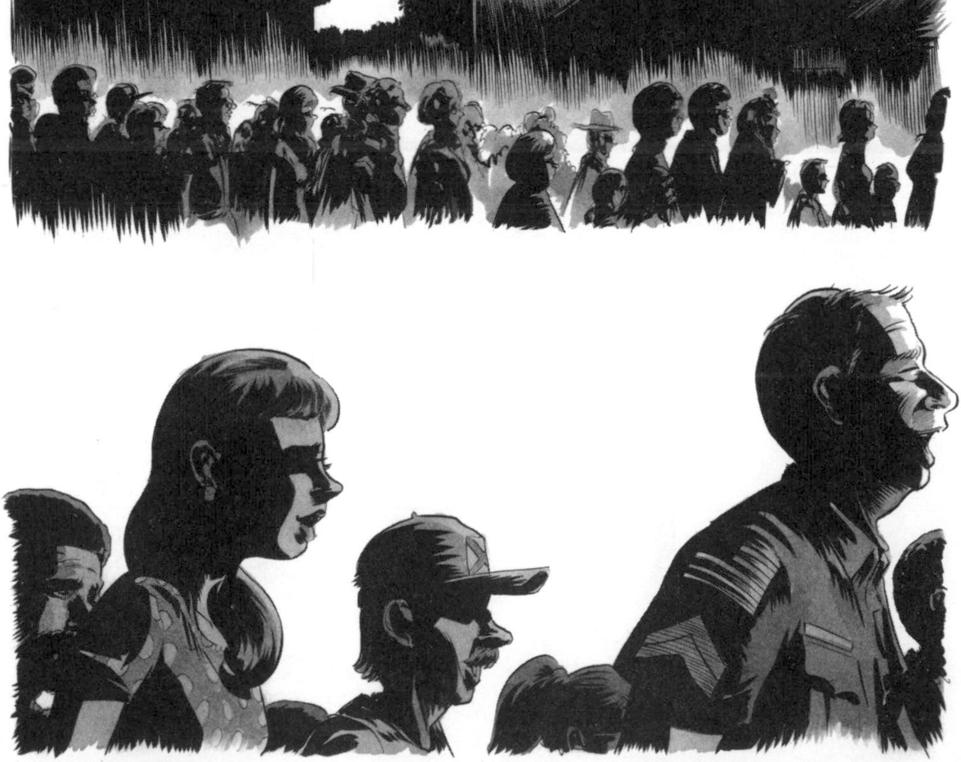

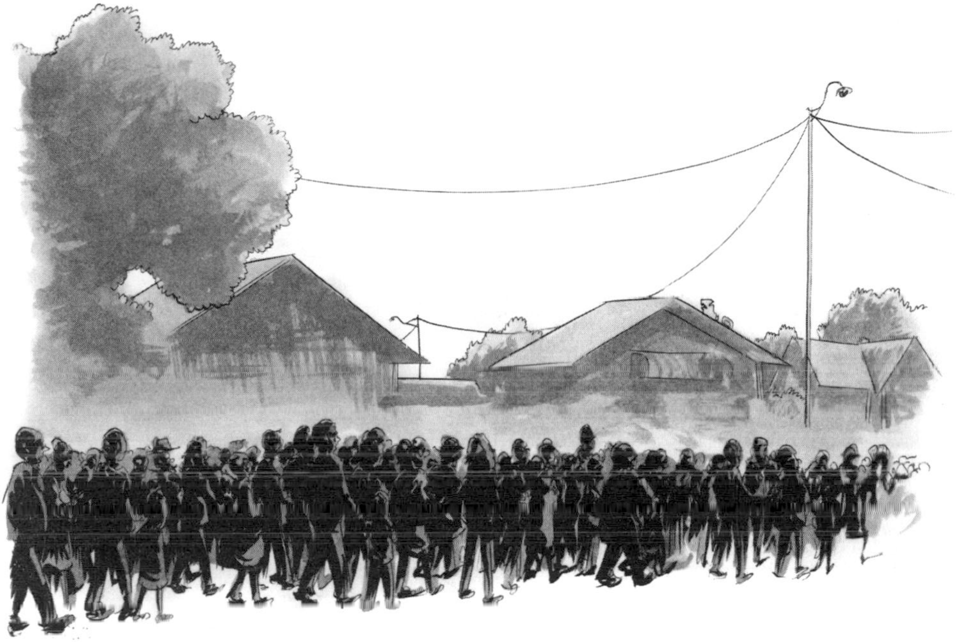

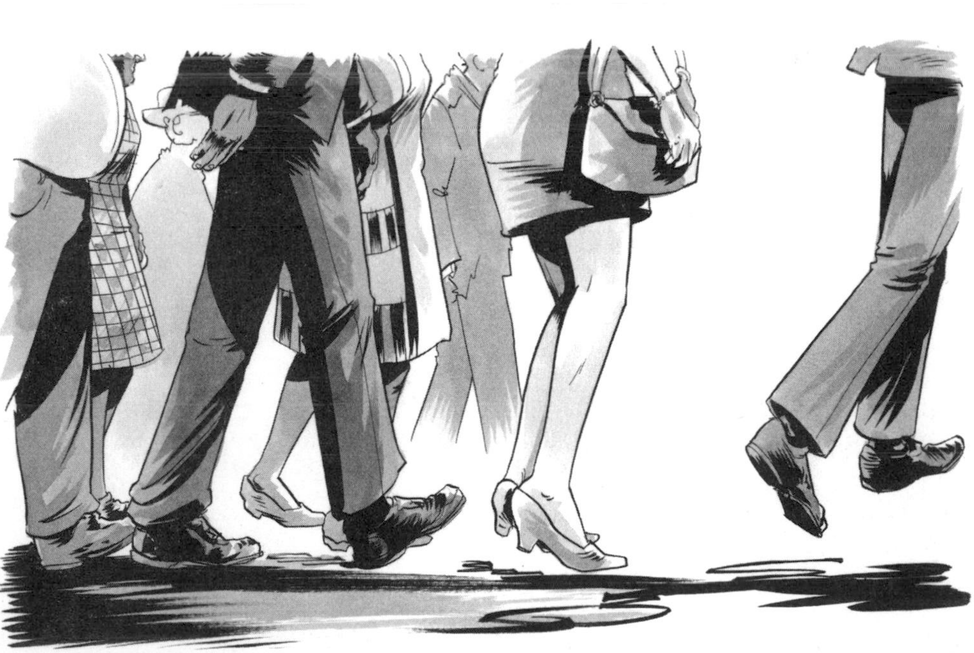

"IN THE END,
WE WILL REMEMBER NOT
THE WORDS OF OUR ENEMIES...

...BUT THE SILENCE OF OUR FRIENDS."

-Dr. Martin Luther King, Jr.

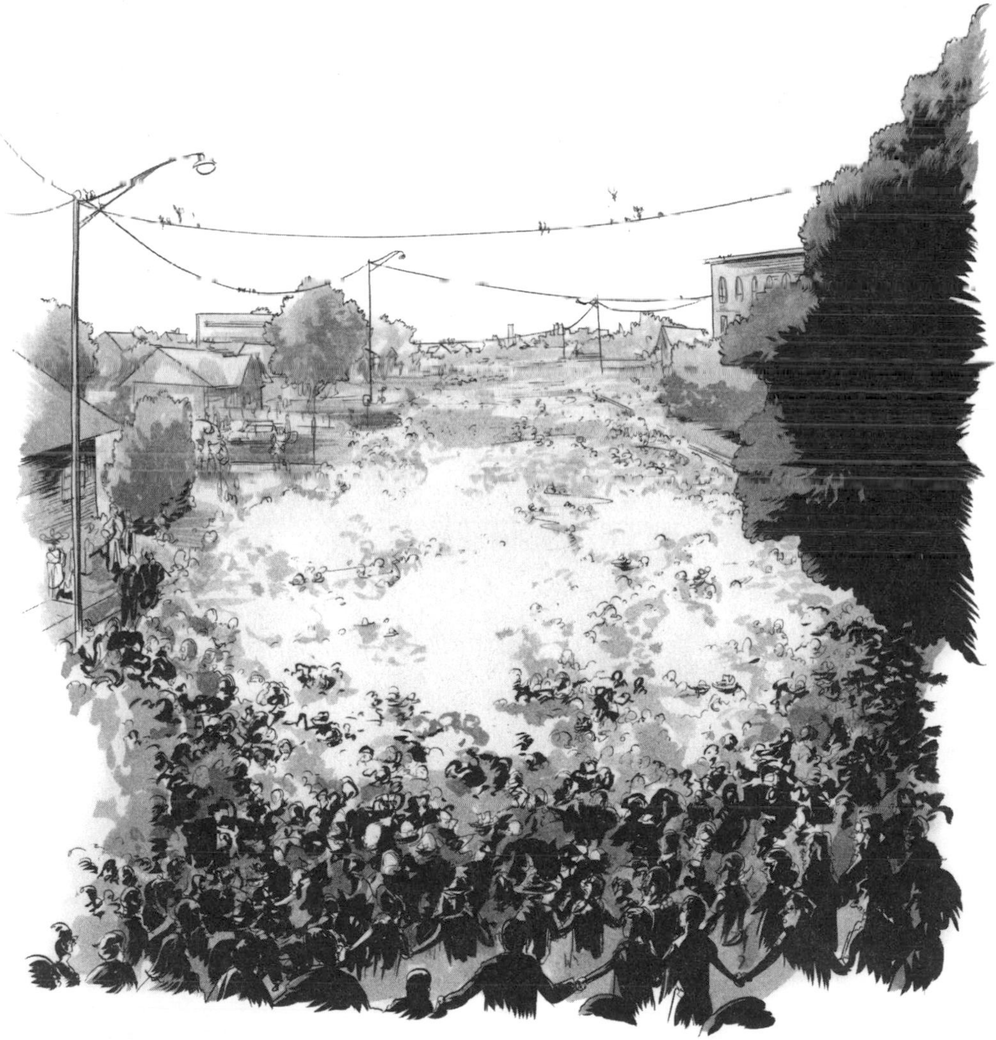

AUTHOR'S NOTE

The past is a foreign country. They do things differently there.

—L.P. Hartley

In 1966 my father moved our family from San Antonio to Houston to take a job there as a local television reporter. Television reporting back then was more like newspaper reporting—hard work, long hours, and decidedly little glamour. In the years before live broadcasts or even videotape, TV reporters were one-man bands, investigating, filming, interviewing, and then racing back to the station to develop and edit their film while writing and recording the voice-over. The film was often still wet from the lab as it was thrown up on the reel minutes before broadcast.

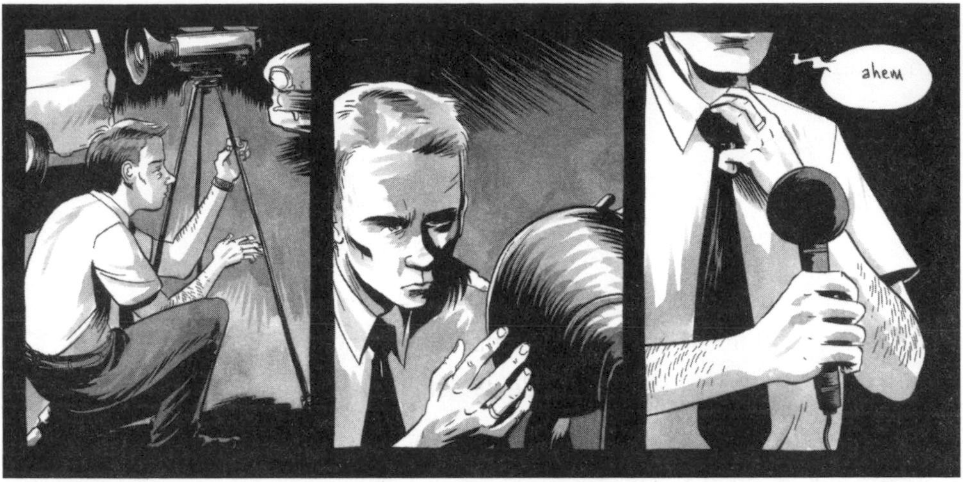
ahem

For a reporter, race was *the* issue in the late sixties. It was exciting, dangerous, and the local news outlets competed with each other to cover it. My father had covered the barrio in San Antonio and joined KPRC to cover Houston's equivalent in the Third and Fifth Wards, but things were different in Houston. Civil rights protests were moving on to university campuses, and the clashes were becoming violent. And in 1967 the crucible of racial tension in Houston was Wheeler Avenue.

Wheeler was a downtown street that ran through the heart of Texas Southern University, a historically African American college. Today the TSU section of the street is a beautiful red brick pedestrian way shaded by live oaks. But in the late 1960s, at the height of the civil rights struggle in Houston, racist whites would cruise down Wheeler in cars, hurling obscenities at students, and often doing violence. TSU was at one end of the street. At the other was Wheeler Avenue Baptist Church, Houston's "Ebenezer" and the spiritual seat of Houston's Third Ward. It was said you could go from terror to joy in a city block on Wheeler. It was on Wheeler that my father met Larry Thomas.

Larry was the editor of *The Voice of Hope*, an antipoverty weekly put out by the Human Organizational Political and Economic (HOPE) Development—the most grass roots level group of the Fifth Ward. Larry was also an activist, organizing for the right of the Student Nonviolent Coordinating Committee (SNCC) to meet on the TSU campus. After the riots at Fisk University in April of 1967, the SNCC and in particular its chairman, Stokely Carmichael, were increasingly portrayed in the media as outside agitators bringing violence to any school that allowed them on campus. On Wheeler, Larry protected my father from an angry crowd of students who had just been denied the right to meet as SNCC on the TSU campus, and the two struck up a friendship that soon included their families.

Crossing the color line in Houston was literally an act of courage in 1967. There was the real possibility of violence, especially in our neighborhood, Sharpstown, where the Ku Klux Klan left fliers advertising rallies rubber-banded to our front doorknob. When the Thomas family first visited our home, it was as if aliens had landed in our front yard. The entire block came out to gawk, and we weren't much better ourselves. I had never met a black person before. And I don't think they had ever played with white kids. I recall our fascination simply with the texture of each other's hair.

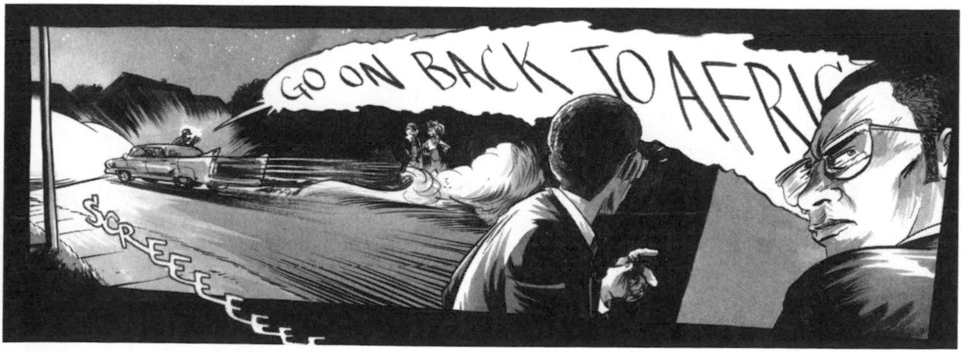
GO ON BACK TO AFRIC
SCREEEEEEEE

After SNCC was banned on campus, TSU students began a boycott of classes, and on May 17 staged a sit-down protest on Wheeler over conditions at the nearby city garbage dump. The protest evolved into an infamous police riot that night. An undercover officer was shot and over 200 officers responded by pouring rifle and machine-gun fire indiscriminately into the men's dormitory. The police later stormed the dormitory and arrested 489 students after a policeman was shot and killed. All but five of the students were released the next day. They came to be called the "TSU Five" and were charged with the murder of the slain officer. Only one of the students stood trial—in Victoria, Texas, due to publicity in Houston. His trial ended with the dismissal of all charges against the five when it was discovered that the officer was shot accidentally by another officer.

Some details from these events—as well as names and details about my family and Larry's—have been changed for storytelling purposes in *The Silence of Our Friends*. Creating a book like this one requires finding a balance between factual accuracy and emotional authenticity. What we have striven to create is a story that offers access to a particular moment in time, both for those who lived it and those who are just discovering it.

Dr. King said, "One day the history of this great period of social change will be written in all of its completeness. On that bright day our nation will recognize its real heroes. They will be thousands of dedicated men and women with a noble sense of purpose that enables them to face fury and hostile mobs with the agonizing loneliness that characterizes the life of the pioneers." We've used King's words elsewhere in this book, and those of his nemesis—George Wallace—to illustrate how even this little-remembered event reverberated through "Dixie." And how it echoes there still.

—Mark Long

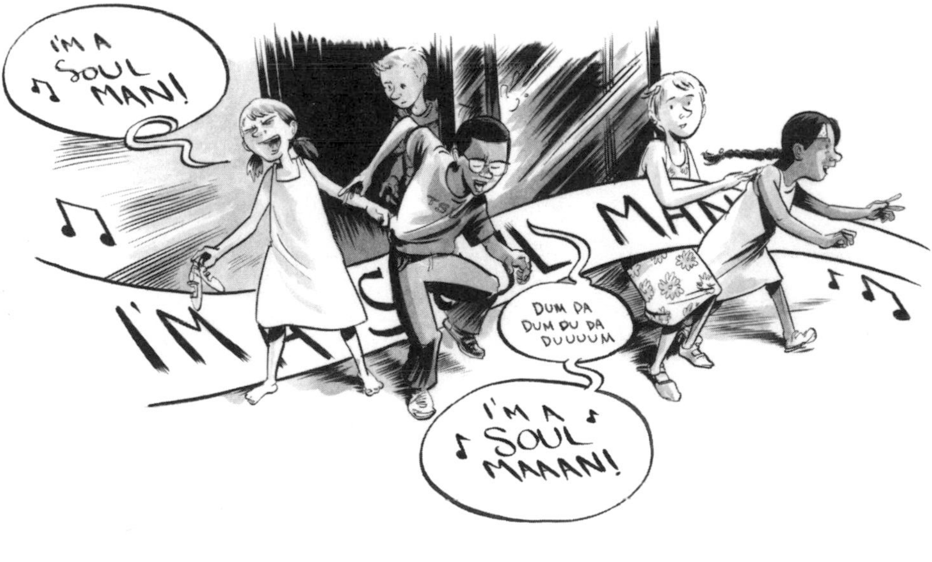
I'M A SOUL MAN!
I'M A SOUL MAN
DUM DA DUM DU DA DUUUUM
I'M A SOUL MAAAN!

To Mom and Dad.
      —JIM DEMONAKOS

I'm grateful for the help and support of Paula Cuneo, Joanna Alexander, Caroline Alexander, Nick Sagan, Judith Hansen, Calista Brill, Patricia Long, Michelle Bennack, Julia Long, Jared Gerritzen, and Jason Dean Hall.
      MARK LONG

Thanks to Mark and Jim for the trust, openness, and collaborative spirit; everyone at First Second; the spectacular Rachel Bormann for sharing our lives together; and Erin Tobey for crucial artwork production assistance.
      —NATE POWELL